SOE
HEROINES

SOE
HEROINES

THE SPECIAL OPERATIONS EXECUTIVE'S FRENCH SECTION & FREE FRENCH WOMEN AGENTS

BERNARD O'CONNOR

AMBERLEY

First published 2018

Amberley Publishing
The Hill, Stroud
Gloucestershire, GL5 4EP

www.amberley-books.com

British Library Cataloguing in Publication Data.
A catalogue record for this book is available from the British Library.

ISBN 978 1 4456 7360 8 (hardback)
ISBN 978 1 4456 7361 5 (ebook)

Typesetting and Origination by Amberley Publishing.
Printed in the UK.

Contents

Foreword & Acknowledgements

It was not until the last few decades of the twentieth century that history books and media coverage of the Second World War began to change their focus from men's roles to include the experiences of women and girls. It was the rise of feminism in the 1960s and 1970s, the introduction of women's studies in universities and changes in examination syllabi that ensured young people began to get a more balanced view of history.

Researchers began to investigate what life was like for women and girls during the war years. Instead of their traditional portrayal in wartime films and books in secondary, subservient roles or included only for a love interest, the importance of many women's roles in the Second World War, including in the secretive world of the Intelligence Services, has begun to be told.

Academics and authors like Juliette Pattinson, Kate Vigurs, Penny Starns, Margaret Collins-Weitz, Clare Mulley and Susan Heim, among others, have brought their stories into the public eye. While Gillian Armstrong's 2001 film *Charlotte Gray* portrayed the life of a woman secret agent in France, a more realistic portrayal was Jean-Paul Salomé's 2008 film *Les Femmes de l'Ombre* (The Women of the Shadows).

Living near RAF Tempsford, a Second World War airfield about 80 km north of London and about half way between Cambridge and Bedford, I have spent several decades researching and writing about its role in supplying the Resistance movements across Western Europe. It was from there that agents of the British, American, Soviet, Polish, Czechoslovakian, Norwegian, Danish, Dutch, Belgian and French intelligence services were infiltrated into occupied Europe as organisers, couriers, wireless operators, weapons instructors, saboteurs and assassins. It was also involved in exfiltrating downed pilots and aircrew, escaped prisoners of war, politicians, diplomats, military personnel, Resistance leaders and others who were evading capture by the authorities.

I found that most of the 2,000-plus personnel, both men and women, based on the airfield had signed the Official Secrets Act and were unprepared to talk or write about their experiences. Some who had been awarded medals after the war, under pressure from reporters keen to tell the stories, had their experiences printed in newspapers. However, the British, and I imagine the French government, vetted such articles to ensure no sensitive information was revealed like the names of members of the intelligence services or of people who were still alive.

The biographies of pilots and secret agents, however, were published after the war; films and TV documentaries were produced and eventually autobiographies appeared. While most books have been about the men, there is an increasing number appearing about the women.

The government restriction on the release of sensitive documents to The National Archives, formerly the Public Record Office in Kew, has meant that formerly top secret documents are only gradually becoming available. The introduction of the British Freedom of Information Act in 2000 has released thousands of files into the public domain. The National Archives' online discovery catalogue allows anyone to locate and occasionally download personnel files, mission reports and other secret government documents related to RAF Tempsford and the wartime intelligence services, and has encouraged an increasing number of people to publish their memoirs and historians to reveal their secrets. The Imperial War Museum also has taped interviews with individuals who had a connection with Tempsford and the intelligence services.

While giving talks to local history societies, the Women's Institute, townswomen's guilds, churches and other groups, numerous members of the audience would ask for details of what their father, grandfather, husband, uncle, brother or cousin was doing during the war, as they had never talked about it. They had kept their promise, having signed the Official Secrets Act. Based on my research, I was able to tell them as much as I had learned.

Focussing on the women's stories, I published *Women of RAF Tempsford: Churchill's Agents of Wartime Resistance* (Amberley) in 2011, which covered not just accounts of the women agents but also the Women's Auxiliary Air Force, the First Aid Nursing Yeomanry and the catering staff. *Return to Holland* and *Return to Belgium*, also published in 2011, tells the stories of the women agents infiltrated into the Low Countries. *Churchill's Angels*, a revised and updated account of the British women agents, was published in 2012; *Agent Rose: The True Spy Story of Eileen Nearne, Britain's Forgotten Wartime Heroine*; *Designer: The true Spy Story of Jacqueline Nearne, a courier sent on a top secret mission to France during World War Two* in 2014 and *Agent Fifi and the Wartime Honeytrap Spies* (Amberley) in 2015.

Having been a Trustee of the Tempsford Memorial, which commemorates the women agents infiltrated behind enemy lines, mostly from RAF Tempsford, I had a tentative list of over eighty women, some of whose stories had yet to be told. I decided to focus on the many French women who parachuted or were landed by plane or boat into remote parts of France on moonlit nights between 1942 and 1944.

I apologise in advance for any misspellings or missing accents. While some may be my typographical errors, I have often used the spellings found in the primary sources. So for example, one might find Marseille and Marseilles, Lyon and Lyons. I do not speak or write fluent French, and my translations of French documents may have missed certain nuances. There may be some repetition as some of the women shared similar experiences. There may be chronological errors, as bringing together a wide range of primary and secondary sources is rather like doing a jigsaw puzzle, piecing together snippets of information and trying to build up a picture without having the box lid to help. Sometimes I feel like an archaeologist searching for artefacts scattered over a wide area.

Trying to complete the story of the thirty-six documented cases of French women infiltrated into France has been nigh on impossible. There are obvious gaps and while some historians may complain that my reconstructions do not hold water, my aim has been to provide insight into their wartime experiences and the contribution they made to the eventual liberation of France. I have been accused of 'quotitis', the extensive use of quotations. If you do not want to read what people seventy or so years ago were thinking about, then do not read this book.

I have included predominantly primary sources to give insight into the mindset of those involved in secret operations during the war, the political and diplomatic tensions as well as the human stories of the women's successes and failures.

I must also confess that I started this research too late. As far as I knew, none of the French women agents were still alive and I apologise for not contacting their families, a task too daunting with only my schoolboy French. Marie-Madeleine Fourcade's *Noah's Ark* and Jean Bohec's *La Plastiqueuse à Bicyclette* tells their wartime stories but there may have been other women who managed to tell their families and friends about their wartime experiences, had their memories written down for them or recorded in other ways. If these are available, and other photographs can be found, I can include them in a subsequent edition. For the majority of the French women agents, this book tells their story for the first time.

There are still women alive today, now in their 80s, 90s and some in their 100s, who have memories of the war years. Talk to them; encourage them to tell you about their history. Document their stories for your children and your children's children and annotate their photographs, before their stories are lost forever.

I would like to thank Françoise Swan and Jane Moore in particular for editing my initial drafts and making valuable suggestions to tie up loose ends. Any typographical errors are mine. I would also like to acknowledge the following people for their research, publications and reminiscences on Britain's Intelligence Services and the Second World War: Pat Bassett, Bob Body, Bill Bright, Reginald Bryon, Martyn Cox, Justin Davis, Thomas Ensminger, Beryl Escott, Nick Fox, Frank Griffiths, Steve Harris, David Harrison, Chrystel Huq, Keith Janes, Alan Judge, Anne Keleny, Steven Kippax, Bob Large, Emeline Lebrun, Paul McCue, Denis O'Connor, Juliette Pattinson, Jim Peake, Jack and Dorothy Ringlesbach, Penny Starns, Martin Sugarman, Francis Suttill, Pierre Tillet, Roger Tobbell, Steve Tomlinson, Jean-Marc Valentine and James Wagland.

The following organisations have also been invaluable sources of background information for which due credit is noted: The National Archives Kew, Imperial War Museum, King's College London Library Service, Harrington Aviation Museum, RAF Museum Hendon, RAF Tangmere Museum, and the Jewish Virtual Library. Full details are provided in the bibliography.

Bernard O'Connor
2018

Background to the Second World War and the British Intelligence Services

The economic depression and political uncertainties in Western Europe during the 1930s and the rise of Adolf Hitler's Nazi Party led some to believe that there might be another global conflict. Research by Tom Keene and Malcolm Atkin into the origins of the Special Operations Executive, one of the secret organisations responsible for supporting Resistance movements in occupied Europe and Asia, revealed that as early as 1935 a sub-committee of the Committee of Imperial Defence investigated the use of sabotage attacks against enemy states. No recommendations were made as sabotage was not one of the British military's fields of expertise.

In 1938 Hitler's *Anschluss* (the annexation of Austria) identified Germany as the greatest threat to Britain's allies and its global empire. In response, Sir Hugh Sinclair, head of the Secret Intelligence Service (SIS) (the Foreign Office's undercover intelligence-gathering section), instructed Section III (Naval) and Section VI (Industrial) to re-examine the use of sabotage. He appointed Major Lawrence Grand of the Royal Engineers 'to investigate every possibility of attacking potential enemies by means other than the operations of military forces.'[1]

On 31 May 1938, Grand's directive for what became known as Section D was a list of German targets which could be demolished by sabotage. 'D' was said to stand for destruction. or the 'dirty tricks' organisation. However, without funding or staff, Grand's proposal that £20,000 be provided to identify further targets, research sabotage devices, produce stocks, create sabotage depots and develop contacts with potential saboteurs in neutral countries was met with 'a combination of alarm and fascination' by Sinclair and his top executives.[2]

Various plans for halting Germany's supply of oil by blowing up the Danube Gorge, stopping the export of ball bearings from Sweden and iron ore from Norway and creating secret dumps of explosives in England and Scotland for stay-behind auxiliary forces in case Britain was invaded, were largely unsuccessful and added little to Grand's reputation. There were worries that should Britain's involvement in such action be identified, it would threaten its diplomatic position in the international community.

In March 1938, the Foreign Office established the Enemy Publicity Section, a new and secret organisation to investigate the ways in which British propaganda might influence public opinion in Europe. Known as EH after Electra House, where it was located, it examined how black or unattributable propaganda could be transmitted into Europe.

By December 1938, the War Office had appointed Lt-Col. J. C. T. 'Jo' Holland of the Royal Engineers to investigate the possibility of using irregular warfare in any future foreign conflict. Holland had served in the Balkans during the First World War and had experience of anti-British guerrilla warfare, including sabotage and assassination in India and Ireland.

In January 1939 the War Office created a working group named General Staff (Research), known as GS(R), headed by Holland and assisted by Major Mills Jeffries, Lt-Col. Colin Gubbins and one secretary, to study the practice and lessons of actual warfare. In particular they studied the methods and tactics employed by IRA activists in Ireland and communist cells fighting in China and in the Spanish Civil War. They looked in general at the use of sabotage and subversion overseas in the event of war, the setting up of networks of British and foreign agents, and the acquisition and hiding of weapons, ammunition and explosives in Britain and abroad.

With Holland and Grand working together from offices in Caxton Street, London, they decided which action the government should admit was the responsibility of GS(R) while D Section's work was to be unattributable.

As SIS had a fondness for symbols, it became known as 'C'. With GS(R)'s funding coming from D Section, it was referred to subsequently as D/M, then MI1(R), D/MIR and finally MIR under the Directorate of Military Intelligence (DMI).[3]

On 12 March 1938, German troops invaded Austria. A year later, Hitler's armed forces marched into Czechoslovakia and on 1 September they invaded Poland. Britain declared war on Germany on 3 September 1939 and assembled the British Expeditionary Force (BEF) along France's border with Belgium.

The British government was keen to keep abreast of the changing political, economic and military situation in German-occupied countries once its embassy and consulate staff had been evacuated. This was the task of the SIS and D Section. Their agents, using cover as Passport officers, having lost their contacts, needed to re-establish links, identify others who might be sympathetic to the Allied cause, and provide wireless sets to allow them to communicate with London.

To this end, agents needed to be selected and trained. Guy Burgess, a D Section officer who was later discovered to have been a Soviet agent, suggested that a training school was needed. Bletchley Park, near Newport Pagnell, Buckinghamshire, had been acquired by MI6 in 1938. MI6 was responsible for Britain's overseas security. The property may well have been used initially for training agents until the decision was taken to use it instead as the Government Code and Cypher School (GC&CS).

MI6's alternative choice was Brickendonbury Manor, near Hertford, about 32 km north-east of London. The house and several hundred hectares of parkland were requisitioned in late 1939. Burgess's idea that it should be called the 'Guy Fawkes School' was rejected. Officially it was known as the 'The Inter-Services Experimental Department', unofficially as 'D School'.

Its commanding officer was Frederic Peters, RN, with Burgess as second-in-command. The first students, Norwegian, Belgian and French, followed a curriculum designed by Kim Philby, another SIS officer and Soviet agent.

After the German armed forces were successful in taking over Czechoslovakia and Poland in 1939 and invading Denmark and Norway in April 1940, on 10 May, Hitler ordered the *Sichelschnitt*, an armed offensive on the Netherlands, Belgium, Luxembourg and France. It was the Whitsun weekend, when almost everyone was on holiday.

Due to the extensive preparations that France had made in the 1930s by building the Maginot Line to prevent another German invasion across its mutual border, it was considered able to defend itself against Hitler's armed forces at the start of the Second World War. However, the speed and ferocity of German Panzer divisions in their push through the Ardennes, crossing the Meuse and onwards towards the Channel ports, caught the French and Belgian armed forces off guard. German paratroopers rained down onto Belgian soil and Stuka planes dive-bombed important transport links. By 20 May 1940, German tanks had reached Amiens and the Allied forces in the country ordered a retreat, blowing up bridges as they left.

While many French government officials, military personnel, foreign diplomats and others managed to escape to England, some with their families, on 22 June an armistice was signed between France and Germany. This resulted in a division of France whereby Germany would occupy the north and west, with the newly formed Vichy government led by Marshal Philippe Pétain governing the unoccupied zone. Italy was given control of a 50 km 'demilitarised zone' alongside their north-western border before claiming the Haute-Savoie and Cote d'Azur.

All refugees arriving in Britain were sent to the requisitioned Royal Victoria Patriotic School on Trinity Road, Wandsworth, South London. Given the numbers, another property, 101 Nightingale Lane, was used to interrogate the women and both became known as the 'London Reception Centre'. Over several days officers from MI5, the British intelligence service responsible for domestic security, interrogated them to identify whether they might be double agents acting for the German, Italian or Japanese intelligence services. They were questioned about their family background, employment, religious and political views. Enquiries were made about conditions in occupied Europe and how they had reached Britain. While their intelligence could have been useful for the Army, Royal Navy, Royal Air Force, SIS, Special Operations Executive (SOE) and MI9 (the agency responsible for helping people escape occupied Europe), the interviews also identified potential recruits for SIS and SOE's Country Sections. Others were recruited into their countries' armed forces or found work and accommodation in and around London. According to the London Reception Centre's web page, Colonel Oreste Pinto interviewed over 30,000 immigrants.

The British intelligence community had to come to terms with their officers returning home after being forced to leave embassies and consulates in Norway, Denmark, Holland, Belgium, Italy and France, as well as losing touch with all their contacts. The British government found itself in a quandary.

To assist the French and other people in other German-occupied countries, Dalton, with the agreement of Sir Stewart Menzies (the new head of SIS), Sir Alexander Cadogan, the Head of the Foreign Office, and the Heads of the Armed Forces established another secret intelligence organisation. It was one with more ability to undertake violent direct action. The Special Operations Executive (SOE) was formed on 22 July 1940. Winston Churchill, the British Prime Minister, officially ordered it 'to set Europe ablaze'. Unofficially he ordered it 'to rot the buggers from within'.

Headed by Sir Frank Nelson with Major David Keswick, its Regional Controller of Western Europe, SOE was divided into three branches: SO1 for underground propaganda, SO2 for unacknowledgeable operations, sabotage and supporting the Resistance groups in enemy-occupied countries, and SO3 for planning. D Section became part of SO2.

SOE staff were mostly recruited from men working in the City of London who had lived and worked overseas and were fluent in languages. Its headquarters were offices at 64 Baker Street in the Marylebone district of Westminster. A Requisitioning Section then set about acquiring properties for SOE use. The Luftwaffe were reported to have been given orders not to bomb these larger properties as the Nazis wanted them for their accommodation having defeated the British.

The SOE created Country Sections for Scandinavia, Poland, Czechoslovakia, Denmark, Holland, Belgium, France, Iberia, Italy, the Balkans and the Middle East. Administrative staff was taken on and, generally speaking, all their communications used a system of code numbers and letters for each employee. Given the secret nature of their work, all SOE staff and students had to sign the Official Secrets Act.

France was known as '27 land' and its agents' numbers were preceded with 27. It had two sections, not because of its size as the largest country in Europe but because of its politics. On 17 March 1941, Colonel Maurice Buckmaster was appointed the head of F Section, responsible for pro-British agents who had chosen not to ally themselves with General de Gaulle. It supported the strictly non-political Resistance groups under British control and at its height had ninety-five organisers in the field.

Buckmaster was assisted by Squadron Leader Vera Atkins, also fluent in French, and his offices were on two floors of Norgeby House, 83 Baker Street, Marylebone, London, opposite number 64 where SOE had its headquarters.

2

The Special Operation Executive's RF Section

When de Gaulle learned that the British were sending agents, including Communists, into France without his knowledge, he accused SOE of infringing French sovereignty. In response, SOE set up the République Française (RF) Section to liaise with his staff at Duke Street, although this was reported as doing little to prevent the mutual distrust between them.

In April 1941, Colonel Harry Sporborg, deputy head of SOE, appointed Captain, later Major Eric Piquet-Wicks as head of RF Section. He was given the task of liaising with General de Gaulle's Free French staff at 4 Carlton Gardens, the Sûreté de l'Etat, their security service, the Deuxième Bureau, their intelligence branch, the Bureau Central de Renseignements et d'Action (BCRA), the Central Bureau of Intelligence and Operations at 3 St James' Square, and later its counter-espionage unit at 10 Duke Street. There was also liaison with the War Office (WO), the Royal Navy (RN) and the Royal Air Force (RAF).

RF Section had offices in Berkeley Court, Glentworth Street, a few minutes' walk from 64 Baker Street. Piquet-Wicks, code named DRF, was assisted by Lt Herbert O'Bryan Tear, known as OBT, and Lt Seeds, whose jobs entailed liaising with the RAF and the Royal Navy to infiltrate their agents into France. They were joined in February 1942 by Flight Officer Forrest Yeo-Thomas, code named DRF.1 and RFP. Their secretary was Pauline May.

Part of Piquet-Wicks' job included selecting potential recruits from among the French refugees coming from the London Reception Centre, arranging their training and accommodation while on leave, their briefing for their missions, and negotiating with the RAF or Royal Navy for their infiltration and exfiltration.

As RF Section expanded, in August 1941 it was transferred to 1 Dorset Square, Marylebone, close to Baker Street underground station. Outside there was no Tricolore, no sign on the wall, only piles of sandbags to protect the doorway from any bomb blast in the street and an armed guard.[1]

Piquet-Wicks retired due to ill-health in August 1942 and was replaced by Lt-Col James Hutchinson, known as 'Hutch'. Before the war, he had shipping and business interests in France, acted as an interpreter with the British Expeditionary Forces in 1939, and offered his services to de Gaulle following the evacuation. His initial role was interviewing French and French-speaking refugees at Olympia with MI5's Security Section officers. Questions about their motives for coming to Britain, their family, friends, personal history and political views were recorded and used for double-checking in subsequent interviews. Once cleared by MI5, there was competition between SIS, F Section and RF Section for potential recruits.[2]

As more staff were needed, Hutchinson appointed Major 'Johnny' Johnson, Bruce Marshall and Peter Storrs, assisted by secretaries 'Fin' Finister, Alicia Grace, Kay Hammond, Miss Block and Kay Moore (later Kay Gimpel).[3]

When Hutchinson volunteered to be sent into France on a secret mission under the new name of James L. Hastings, he underwent plastic surgery to disguise his facial features and was given special tuition in changing his speech and walking style. Some of the French women had similar training. Consequently, in autumn 1943, his position as head of RF was taken by Bickham Sweet-Escott. He only stayed until December when, following the Italian surrender, he was transferred to Cairo as SOE's advisor to Force 133, a subsidiary organisation of SOE to control operations in the Balkans, Northern Italy, and Asia. His role was taken by Lt-Col. Leonard Dismore, who had previously worked for the *Paris Daily Mail*.[4]

Bertram Mills was a well-known British circus manager and, according to Hutchinson, some SOE humourists used to say that his building at 1 Dorset Square, requisitioned by SOE for the French, still housed a circus. They had a depository of male and female French clothes, hats, shoes, coats, toiletries and valises, and a French tailor to ensure everything fitted.[5]

Although there were officers who liaised between F and RF Sections, tensions between them lasted throughout the war. For example, de Gaulle was not informed when F Section started infiltrating Communist agents as part of the secret agreement between Churchill and Stalin. While F Section liaised with SIS, the War Office, the Political Warfare Executive, the RAF, the Royal Navy, the Army, the Special Armed Services, the American Office of Strategic Security and the NKVD, the Soviet Intelligence agency; RF Section and the BCRA were entirely dependent on SOE and SIS for the infiltration of their agents.

3

The BCRA and the Corps Féminin, Corps de Volontaires Françaises and the Corps des Auxiliares Féminins de L'armée de Terre

The 'Exode', the migration of around eight million civilians from Belgium and Northern France carrying their belongings in cars, bicycles, prams, horse and carts and wheelbarrows, made their way south and west to escape the German advance. Forrest Yeo-Thomas, who joined SOE's RF Section, observed in his memoirs:

> In Paris crowds were besieging the stations laden with luggage and parcels, clutching children of all ages; queues were terrific and panic striken. Cars were streaming out of the fore-doomed capital piled high with the most miscellaneous collections of goods. Mattresses, beds, pillows, baby carriages, even stoves were tied with ropes and straps on the top of cars. The roads, already cluttered up with refugees from the north and east, now became completely blocked The whole picture was one of fear, panic, demoralisation and defeat. France was rapidly crumbling up. [His unit headed for Tours.] It was a nightmarish trip, the roads were cluttered up with refugees, cars, carts, wagons, lorries, buses, cyclists, pedestrians, women, children, pushing prams, barrows, anything that had wheels and could carry something. Old people stumble along, drawn faces, eyes that brimmed with tears, sad eyes, hard eyes, haunted eyes, eyes full of despair, fury.[1]

A fifth of the French population was reported to have fled the German Blitzkrieg. Exactly how many civilians managed to catch ships to Britain before the Germans arrived is unknown, but I have found evidence of eight women who volunteered to be trained and sent back as secret agents.

Once the Germans established their power base in Paris, they divided France into the Occupied Zone in the north and along the Channel and Atlantic coast and the Unoccupied or Free Zone in the south, where the Vichy government had control. The Occupied Zone included the greatest percentage of the French population, its principal coal, iron and steel industries and most of its fertile land. The Germans also retook Alsace and Lorraine sending 400,000 residents into the Unoccupied Zone. This area, apart from some industrial cities, was dominated by the wooded Central Massif, the French Alps, and the Pyrénées.

The leader of the French government-in-exile was General Charles de Gaulle. In June 1940, Churchill asked him to establish his own Intelligence Service in England which could inform SIS on the evolving situation in occupied France. In particular, intelligence was needed on Germany's military potential, the strength of the Wehrmacht, the Luftwaffe and the Kriegsmarine, their communication networks and the rivalry between the Giraudists. This latter group was those in France who supported General Henri Giraud, the leader of the defeated French army, whereas the Gaullists, obviously, supported de Gaulle.

Since 1871, France had the Deuxième Bureau, its external military intelligence agency, but on 1 July 1940, de Gaulle established his own, the Service de Renseignements (SR). It was based in offices on the 3rd floor of St Stephen's House, 4 Carlton Gardens, near St James's Park, London, which became the headquarters of the Free French.

Captain (later Major) André Dewavrin, code named Colonel Passy, headed the organisation and he was assisted by André Manuel, code named Pallas. Captain Raymond Lagier, code named Bienvenue, was responsible for Action Militaire and was also the primary liaison with the SOE, assisted by Fred Scamaroni. Other BCRA staff included Maurice Duclos, code named Captain St Jacques, and Alexandre Beresnikoff, code named Captain Corvisart.[2]

On 7 August 1940, Churchill signed an agreement allowing SR to receive financial aid and support from the British Armed Services in their missions to identify German capabilities for invading Britain. On 19 March 1941, financial credit facilities were opened to allow the Free French to cover their military and civil expenditure.

SR, whose motto was 'To serve and be silent', changed its name several times. On 15 April 1941, when sabotage was added to its responsibilities, it became known as Bureau Central de Renseignements et d'Action Militaire (BCRAM) and on 17 January 1942, it changed to Bureau Central de Renseignements et d'Action (BCRA). In June 1942, needing more office space, it moved to 3 St James's Street.

BCRA was the central office for intelligence gathering. Its S2 section collected information on military, political, economic and social groups and individuals in France and its S3 section, headed by Captain Pierre de Hautecloque, was responsible for operational planning and preparations based on intelligence received from S2 and for organising and supporting pro-de Gaulle resistance in occupied France.

With the Allied success in North Africa and the German takeover of the unoccupied zone in November 1942, another section, BCRAL was established in Algeria. Women from the Corps were sent over to help in the planning, supplying and communications needed for infiltrating French agents into Corsica, Sardinia, Italy and southern France, as well as preparing a new administration for post-liberation France.

Another women's organisation started at this time in North Africa was the Corps Féminin des Transmissions (Female Signals Corps), also known as 'The Merlinettes'. Their work included telephone operators, signals analysts, teletype and radio operators. It was established on 22 November 1942, six months after the creation of the military 'Signals' arm under General Lucien Merlin as part of Admiral Giraud's forces in Algiers. It was attached to the Service Renseignments et Operations/Intelligence and the Operations Service (SRO), part of the 'special services' set up within General de Lattre's 1st French Army and trained by the Direction Générale des Services Spéciaux (DGSS).

Although I have found evidence of seven French women members who volunteered to be trained and infiltrated into France, a blog on 'Le Signaleur' website claims that of the 2,000 recruited, almost fifty were trained to be parachuted into France.

On 26 April 1944, the women of the Corps de Volontaires Françaises (CVF), the Forces Françaises Libres (FFL), and the Forces Françaises de L'intérieur (FFI) were combined into the Corps des Auxiliaires Féminines de l'Armée de Terre (AFAT) under the command of Hélène Terré.[3]

Before D-Day, BCRA was tasked with helping to amass intelligence on the German order of battle and their defences against an Allied invasion as well as being involved in the planning and implementation of Operation *Jedburgh* and Plan *Sussex*, the latter of which included two French women.

Research on the de Gaulle Foundation website shows that having arrived in London, de Gaulle was based initially

...on the first floor of a comfortable house at 7-8 Seamore Grove, now 7 Curzon Place, off Hyde Park, in a small flat loaned to him by Jean Laurent, his former civilian private secretary in Paris [...] Not long afterwards, on 23 June, buoyed by the official recognition of the British Government, the provisional French National Committee moved to slightly larger premises [...] at St. Stephen's House on Victoria Embankment, where Sir Edward Spears, who had flown with De Gaulle from Bordeaux, had his offices. Free France stayed here for only one month [...], before moving into [...] 3 Carlton Gardens, a leafy square off the Mall near St. James' Park. [...] Up to 1943, Carlton Gardens housed the political nucleus of Free France and produced offshoots that gradually spread into the surrounding streets and neighbourhoods, particularly Mayfair and Victoria Station. Then it became the headquarters of the CFLN (French Committee of National Liberation) in London before the Liberation made it possible to reclaim possession of the former French embassy in Knightsbridge. The Naval administration was housed first in the Institut Français, then in Stafford Mansions. Interior Affairs, in particular, the propaganda services, was based at 17–19 Hill Street. The BCRA [Bureau Central de Renseignements et d'Action, de Gaulle's intelligence service] was at 10 Duke Street, Oxford Street [...] Although the political leadership of Fighting France moved to Algiers in June 1943, most of the administrative services continued to operate with greater efficiency in London, thanks to its proximity to the continent. [...]

French volunteers were recruited primarily from units arriving from Norway or Dunkirk: in June 1940, these units were quartered in camps around the ports, particularly on the Channel and North Sea coasts and around Liverpool. Infantry units were quartered in camps at Trentham Park near Stoke on Trent and at Arrowe Park near Liverpool, airmen at the Saint Athan base and sailors at the Haydock and Aintree racecourses [...]. The small number who opted not to be repatriated to France but to stay and continue the fight with De Gaulle were gathered together from the various camps. They then joined up with the volunteers arriving individually from France or the colonies and all underwent several days of preliminary investigation by the '[Royal Victoria] Patriotic School', where British police officers painstakingly but courteously checked their identity and motivation to minimise the risk of espionage.

The Free French reception and recruitment centre was in London, at Olympia Hall [...] As soon as possible, thanks to the material resources provided by the British government, military camps were organised and set up, mainly at Aldershot south-west of London, with Delville Camp and Morval camp, named after battlefields on the Somme in 1916. Later, the main base of the Free French forces would be the camp at Camberley, close to both Aldershot and Sandhurst. Airmen remained at the Saint Athan base, while sailors embarked on naval vessels that had rallied to Free France, at Portsmouth and Plymouth in particular. Future officers, or Free French Cadets, were trained at the 'Free French

Saint-Cyr' in Malvern, then at Ribbesford (a former public school in Worcestershire). The youngest, after joining a sort of scout camp at Brynbach in Wales, went on to study at Rake Manor near Milford (Surrey), laying the groundwork for a Free French military school.[4]

De Gaulle's speech on 18 June 1940, while acknowledging Germany's victory in the battle for France, he questioned whether the last word had been said: 'Is all hope lost? Is the defeat absolute? No. France is not alone. She has a vast empire behind her. She can unite with the British Empire, which holds the seas, and is continuing the struggle. She can utilise to the full, as England is doing, the vast industrial resources of the United States.' He invited the French armed forces who had arrived in Britain to join him in continuing the fight. 'Whatever happens, the flame of French Resistance must not and will not be extinguished.'[5]

While there was sympathy for the French from many in British society, there was criticism that the Britain's only ally had failed them, that France's armed forces had failed to repel the German military and that General Pétain had surrendered so quickly.

British women were encouraged to join the war effort. Many took the jobs of the men who had joined up or were later conscripted into the Armed Forces. Those considered having language skills were recruited from the War Office, the Admiralty, Air Ministry, Central Registry and Telegraph Office. Others were 'introduced' as having lived overseas and joined the Auxiliary Transport Service (ATS) of the British Army, the Women's Royal Naval Service, the Women's Auxiliary Air Force (WAAF) and the First Aid Nursing Yeomanry (FANY). Some French women responded to de Gaulle's request for volunteers and on 7 November 1940 he set up what he called the Corps Féminin, an auxiliary force modelled on the ATS.

In *Women in Fighting France during the Second World War: The French Corps Volunteers and Rochambeau Group*, Elodie Jauneau stated that its purpose was, 'to replace all able-bodied men by women in jobs they can perform without ... "denaturing" the female sex. The woman fighter does not exist ... If Paul Boncour's law [of 1938, allowing women to join the French military] opened the doors of the army to women, it does not give them access provided to the sphere of combat and the use of weapons that remain the preserve of men.' The Rochambeau Group was created in New York in 1943 and attached to the American Second Armoured Division.

Unlike the FANY, which was the only British service which allowed women to carry arms, it was the first time in French history that women had been allowed to join the Armed Forces, and they were led by Lieutenants Simone Matthieu and Hélène Terré and sub-lieutenants Burdet and Hackin.

The women of Corps Féminin were accommodated first at 40 Hill Street, Mayfair, and then at Moncorvo House. As the double entendre of their name provoked unwanted smirks, in November 1942 it was changed to the Corps de Volontaires Françaises, the French women's Volunteers Corps.

Research by Gerard J. De Groot and Corinna Peniston-Bird revealed that the women's ages ranged from 17 to 50 and included teachers, students, secretaries, nurses, cooks, conductors, telephone operators, photographers and maids, not just from France but also from her overseas colonies. Jean Bohec, one of the first five recruits who was later infiltrated into France, was uncertain that her colleagues fully accepted the Corps' discipline:

Several young women provoked gossip because they appeared overly interested in men. In addition, FFL women replaced the gas masks they were issued with personal effects – the canvas carrying bag became, in effect, a handbag. Some insisted on wearing silk rather than regulation wool stockings and had their uniforms tailored to fit better. Upon completion of basic training, the women were assimilated into the French forces and assigned to secretarial duties or nursing.[6]

The france-libre website includes the daily routine of one of the Corps' women:

We led a very active life. Woke up at 7:00, breakfast at 7.40, exercise, starting for the office, working 9:00 to 6:00 with 1:30 pm for lunch, dinner at 7.30 pm. Free time or going out, curfew 10.30. During the 1941 bombing, our barracks was demolished by a bomb that exploded at the door, injuring and killing three volunteers. Among our volunteers were a few who had escaped from France, some had to accomplish real feats to reach London. For example, Camille who escaped by bicycle through one door, while the Germans went in another, and was able to reach the port where she embarked with the complicity of a sailor. There was Jeanne who crossed that part of France on foot rather than serve the enemy. Yvonne who escaped from Brest with her husband, and Lucy, who had embarked on small overcrowded boats, thanks to providence, and many others. [...]

After a severe examination of physical fitness volunteers are incorporated; they have committed themselves to follow the armies of Fighting France on all fronts wherever the command will decide to send them. Military life begins with a four-week internship in a British female army training camp. Right out of the camp, they are directed to a school where they learn the specialties that allow them to replace men in positions that are not in combat positions. They are introduced with an ease and rapidity with wonderful secrets of the most modern techniques, mechanical, electrical, wireless, mapping, etc. Every day the work of the volunteers is affirmed more useful. The staff recognizes this by always asking them to do more.[7]

When de Gaulle came to inspect the Corps on 22 November 1942, Bohec reported how the women went to extreme lengths to look presentable but all he noticed was the absence of bidets in their bathrooms. Having completed their six weeks' training, they were assigned work as office staff, telephone operators, drivers, tailors, messenger, translators, interpreters, cooks and nurses.[8]

Following the Allies setting up a forward base in Algiers in late 1942, some of the Corps de Volontaires Françaises were transferred to help with the operations in Southern Europe.

4

Training the Women Agents

When the SOE was established, this top secret organisation, known to the general public as the Inter Service Research Bureau, was given responsibility for getting information out of occupied Europe; finding out where the Germans were garrisoned; how many there were; what their vulnerable points were and who the people were who could be counted upon to engage actively in helping to liberate their country. It was also tasked with sending in wireless sets and wireless operators to enable communication between London and the Resistance movements as well as taking over from SIS the task of selecting, training and infiltrating agents and co-ordinating attacks on identified targets in accordance with the Allied High Command's plans.

They also needed to find out what weapons, ammunition, food, clothing, medicines, money and other supplies were needed; what training was necessary. The needed to locate safe dropping grounds for supplies and agents and identify trusted people in France who would be willing to help receive specially trained agents, provide them with safe houses as well as to receive, store and distribute parachuted containers and packages of weapons, ammunition, explosives, money and other supplies.

As well as taking over SIS's propaganda section, SIS staff at Brickendonbury were offered similar jobs in SOE's Training Section, and the house and grounds were used instead as a specialist industrial sabotage training school.[1] SOE needed to recruit foreign language speakers from the academic and business community, but also drew them from government organisations, the Armed Forces – not only those French-speakers from the ranks of the military who had escaped from Dunkirk but also those who had previously lived or worked in France. They were also able to draw on those French men and women who, with the help of SIS-controlled escape lines, crossed the Channel, made their way into Switzerland or got a guide to take them over the Pyrénées and reached Britain via Lisbon or Gibraltar, or who had come from French-controlled North Africa or its other colonies.

By early 1942, the SIS and SOE's attitude to women being sent as secret agents changed as they had distinct advantages over male agents. Writing about the Soviet women infiltrated into Western Europe, Joseph Persico commented that,

> A woman did not have to explain why she was not in military service. She did not need the sheaf of passes that a working male or soldier had to carry. That a woman might be involved in secret military intelligence simply seemed less likely on the face of it. There were always risks, but the odds of exposure were sharply reduced.[2]

Among the many and varied reasons why both men and women volunteered to be trained as agents was what Hutchinson called 'that drug danger.' One example he mentioned was,

> [An] attractive young French countess implored me to let her go on a mission. She had already worked with the underground in France. We were planning a particularly dangerous mission and had decided to send no women. She kept coming to me and urging me to send her. There was a look of desperation in her eyes. Her nerves were strung up and taut, and she was near to breaking down when I had to gently refuse her. Eventually, she persuaded the French to send her to the Far East where she was used as a parachutist and was killed. The drug had hooked her deeply and she followed it to her end.[3]

Those men and women considered potential agents by F Section received a letter inviting them for an interview at the former Victoria Hotel, 8 Northumberland Avenue, or at Sanctuary Buildings, Westminster. Captain Selwyn Jepson, one of the Directorate of Military Intelligence and SOE's head of recruitment, told them they had been identified as potentially helpful in the war effort. He questioned them in French about their life and experiences to assess their fluency and then asked them if they would be prepared to undertake dangerous work. If they were not enthusiastic, they would return to their unit or former occupation. If they expressed willingness, they were told that they would receive another letter. This gave MI5 time to do background security vetting. If this was positive, on their second interview Jepson would question their motives for wanting to help and told them they would be trained for a mission in France, and they might have to parachute in. For those identified as too old or frail to jump, alternative arrangements would be made. If they accepted his offer they were told to wait for another letter providing travel arrangements for the assessment course.

Michael Foot, the SOE historian, remarks in his book *SOE in France* that there were,

> ...plenty of women with marked talents for organisation and operational command, for whom a distinguished future on the staff could be predicted if only the staff could be found broad-minded enough to let them join it. The SOE was such a broad-minded staff.[4]

He quoted Jepson as telling potential recruits; 'I have to decide whether I can risk your life and you have to decide whether you're willing to risk it.' In a post-war interview, Jepson commented that,

> I was responsible for recruiting women for the work in the face of a good deal of opposition from the powers that be who said that women, under the Geneva Convention, were not allowed to take combatant duties which they regarded resistance work in France as being... There was a good deal of opposition from various quarters until it went to Churchill, whom I had met before the war. He growled at me, 'What are you doing?' I told him and he said, 'I see you are using women to do this,' and I said, 'Yes, don't you think it is a very sensible thing to do?' and he said, 'Yes, good luck to you.' That was my authority![5]

Those considered by RF Section were interviewed by Piquet-Wicks at Olympia Hall, West Kensington. In his wartime memoirs, he commented that those he recruited,

> ...were of every class, category, and size, and common to them all was an unflinching determination to regain their country. Few were regular soldiers, or sailors or airmen; frequently they were non-commissioned officers who had been clerks or garage hands – the little people of France. Less frequently was the élite – by birth – to be found, although when such elements did materialise, their heroism was of the highest. From this heterogeneous mass of volunteers, we endeavoured to find those most suitable for the perilous missions that awaited them; works of sabotage, of direct attack – for organised acts of destruction of vital points: railway communications, electric power stations, factories manufacturing strategic material, or material helpful to the enemy.[6]

Given the scale of the SOE's training programme, its Requisitioning Section had to acquire large country properties outside London and some in the north-west of Scotland, far from the inquisitive eyes of the local people. Potential agents for RF or F Section, having signed the Official Secrets Act, were given a cover name and instructed never to tell anyone on their courses their real name. In the early part of the war, they were sent on a three- or four-week assessment course at Wanborough Manor (Special Training School (STS) 5), near Guildford in Surrey, where they were only allowed to speak the language of the country they were being sent to. Their cover story was that it was a training school for Allied commandos. The French women often went with a group of French men and had French-speaking conducting officers who interpreted for them if their instructors could not speak French. On occasions there was only one woman in the group. In the early years of the war, group sizes were about a dozen. Later there were up to twenty-eight.

After June 1943, agents were given a much shorter five-day assessment at Winterfold Manor (STS 7), near Cranleigh in Surrey, which had previously been used for training Danish and Dutch agents as STS 4. Its cover was a Military Training School for Allied Personnel – Commandos. Instructors observed them doing basic military and physical training, learning how to live in an occupied country, Morse code and message sending, elementary map reading, and weapons and explosives training. Nancy Wake, an Australian agent, reported being bewildered by the array of psychometric and practical tests given her by a small team of psychologists, psychiatrists and military staff.

Their conducting officer, instructors and commandant sent their reports to the head of the Country Sections, who assessed their suitability for one of the Group A Schools. Four- or five-week paramilitary training took place in one of ten shooting lodges near Arisaig, a remote area of Inverness-shire, north-west Scotland.

The training, which was the same for both men and women, included physical exercises to build up strength and stamina. This included rock climbing, mountaineering and forced marches over the difficult Scottish countryside in rain, hail, snow or sunshine, including overnight. Students reported having to carry logs or heavy stones to build up their muscles. They learned how to avoid detection, including avoiding ridges and hill tops and using rivers and streams to put dogs off their trail.

There were lessons in field craft, outdoor survival, how to sleep rough, learning what plants and roots were edible (including the different seaweeds), how to catch and kill fish, birds and other animals, including shellfish, and how to cook them without producing a lot of smoke. This was designed to get them used to living outdoors should they have to live with the Maquis or if they had to make their escape across the French Alps to Switzerland or the Pyrénées into Spain.

They practiced using dummy and then real explosives to blow up bridges, railway lines, locomotives and boats. They practiced using British and German weapons and how to throw grenades. They practised advanced map reading, orienteering, and knife work, rope work and boat work, as well as unarmed combat and silent killing. What was called 'the art of ungentlemanly warfare' was taught by 'Bill' Sykes and his ex-Shanghai police partner, William Fairburn, both in their 50s and known as 'The Heavenly Twins'.

They were well fed throughout the course, and entertainment was provided at the local hostelry with live music and dancing. Although female agents attended these courses, they were small in number compared to the men so local girls were trucked in as 'dance partners' for the Scottish jigs and reels.

If they were successful after this course they then underwent, depending on the weather, a three- to five-day parachute training course at the British Army's Central Landing School at Ringway aerodrome (STS 51), now Manchester Airport. They were accommodated at Dunham House (STS 51a), Altrincham, or Fulshaw Hall (STS 51b), Wilmslow. They learned how to jump and land properly from increasing heights. Most were given three jumps from a basket attached to an air balloon and then two drops from a Whitley bomber, one of them at night into the grounds of nearby Tatton Park. Some students died when their parachutes failed to open, and others suffered minor injuries when they did not land correctly. It needs to be stated that the French women did not excel at parachuting, some of them only being awarded 'Third Class'. On occasions when the trainee agents had completed their day jumps, and the weather was too bad for the final night jump, this would be simulated the next day by having a balloon jump carried out while the agent wore welding goggles. Beryl Escott described how,

They usually did four or five practice jumps, the last one at night and in later years with a leg bag for carrying equipment. Of course, the station had its usual complement of airwomen. Having spent about two years at Ringway working on parachutes, 'where most of the time 1,000 troops were dropped day and night', Winifred Smith has clear memories of 'cycling across the tarmac to our section, seeing girls preparing to parachute, complete with lipstick and make-up – otherwise it was hard to tell that they really were girls, what with their parachute suits, crash helmets, and so on. We often watched them waiting to board the plane. It was like follow-my-leader. The girls were towards the back but they were always laughing and we would wave and call good luck. I don't remember more than about three or four together boarding the same plane, in fact often I could only see one.' Trainees sometimes said that they put the girls to jump first out of the aircraft into the grounds of Tatton Park since they reckoned that the men would not hold back if a woman led the way. As part of her work on modifications to 'chutes and packs, Winifred also went into the training hangar' and saw them training on what we called the Fan. They were completely fearless. They were also quick off the mark in getting away afterwards. One had the feeling they didn't expect to come back, so they were living for the moment. When VE Day was over and we could talk more freely, it was agreed by all who had contact with these WAAF that they had an inner strength and sheer determination which allowed them to do what was asked of them. They were inspired by something greater than the ordinary person.[7]

Having completed this course, they were sent for a month to what was called the 'Group B Finishing School'. This was based in one of eleven secluded country houses in New Forest, near Southampton, in the grounds of Lord Montagu's Beaulieu Estate.

There were five sections: agent techniques, exercises, enemy organisations and order of battle, propaganda, and codes and ciphers. Depending on what role SOE had chosen for the agent, they were more lessons in coding and ciphers; further map reading; microphotography; disguises; how to use and arrange messages on the BBC; ways of recognising and making forgeries; the use of new weapons; more handling of explosives; demolitions; how to burgle buildings, including climbing up and down drainpipes; key-cutting and forgery; safe- and lock-breaking; withstanding interrogation and torture; choosing and marking out landing grounds for landing and parachute drops; and spy-craft. This included observation and memory exercises, lessons in constant vigilance, organising safe letter boxes (*boites aux lettres*), rendezvous and clandestine meetings, message passing in a town, choosing safe houses, using a cut-out, leaving signals to let visitors know the situation was safe like moving a flowerpot on one side of a windowsill, recognising enemy counter-intelligence uniforms and how to deal with them. They were warned against using the phone for clandestine work as the operator might report the conversation to the Gestapo. While the women underwent the same rigorous training as the men, they proved themselves quite capable at subterfuge.

In her PhD thesis on SOE's women agents, Kate Vigurs pointed out that,

This course was aimed at drilling the hard facts of life in France into the trainees; it also aimed to highlight the implications that simple mistakes could carry. It was on this course that agents were trained to think and behave as if they were actually French. Many changes had occurred in France during the Occupation, for example, women were not given a cigarette ration, coffee was only available without milk (so asking for a café noir would raise a few eyebrows) and certain foods were only available on set days of the week. Agents had to be aware of these changes which would be second nature to a French person, otherwise a small error could mark them out as different and potentially cost them their lives. Other mistakes that could be ironed out at Beaulieu included teaching an agent not to put milk in her teacup first as this automatically gave her away as English and to look right and not left before crossing the road and not to cycle on the wrong side of the road.

Agents were taught about the two different zones and the demarcation lines, the importance of false documents, papers and cover stories. Agents also learnt to recognise military uniforms, ranging from the Abwehr (Nazi Military Intelligence) the Milice (Vichy paramilitary force) and the Gendarmerie. During the Nazi Occupation France was teeming with collaborators, and agents were taught that no one could be trusted.

Another vital element of training at Beaulieu was the art of clandestinity. Agents were taught various methods of contacting one another through the use of letter boxes, cut outs or dead drops. These were hidden places where messages could be left such as in church bibles, underneath a preordained stone or in between bricks of a wall. It became second nature to them to use passwords when meeting with strangers and if they believed that something was wrong at a rendezvous they were to leave as there could be a trap.

They were taught to write messages on cigarette papers and onion skins and the methods of passing these messages included hollowed out corks, inside cigarettes or hidden inside newspapers. Some of these methods may seem somewhat far-fetched and fantastical, but this is the world in which these agents existed and had to become comfortable with, to ensure their success in the field.[8]

There were also lessons in choosing and describing dropping zones; setting up and training reception committees; learning correct procedures for parachute drops and landings, and disposing of containers and parachutes. Although the latter were supposed to be put into the container and hidden, silk cords and silk material was considered an invaluable luxury for dresses and pyjamas that some French resisters could not resist keeping it, despite the possibility of being arrested for being complicit with 'enemy' agents. Their instructors had guidelines to follow, based on the experiences of organiser's reports and debriefs of returned agents.

Look for a space not less than six hundred yards, unless it is anticipated that several containers and/or men will be dropped, in which case it should be eight hundred yards square. By taking this area the ground would be suitable for any wind direction.

Avoid agricultural land because of the risk of injury, especially to ankles. Evidence will also be left in the form of tracks and damaged crops. Avoid swamps. Grass parkland is ideal for personnel, but for containers, most types of ground will be found suitable.

There should be no high tension wires or telegraph poles in the vicinity. There should be no clumps of trees in the middle of the dropping point. Further, for an aircraft to see the light from five hundred feet the latter should be at least five hundred yards from one hundred foot trees.

If possible there should be at least one 'safe house' within a mile, but not nearer than a mile for security reasons.

Allowance must be made for 'wind drift'. It is estimated that there is a sixty yard drift for every five miles per hour increase in the velocity of the wind. This is estimated for a plane flying at the height and speed previously mentioned. No dropping operation should take place if the wind speed is over 20 miles per hour. [...]

Six men may conveniently handle a container, but it is not necessary to provide that number per container if the men understand their job. Each member of the party should be equipped with gloves as carrying becomes painful owing to the thinness of the handles.

If there is a deep lake or river near the dropping point, the container may be conveniently disposed of there. If it is to be buried a suitable burying point should have been chosen beforehand, and if possible holes dug.

Always remember disposal of the outer container must be permanent.

To ease carrying of cells, a strap or rope may be used to string them on a man's back. In this way one man can carry one cell without much difficulty or fatigue.[9]

Beaulieu's instructors were provided with guidance materials which they had to use with their students to ensure they could develop an information service in the field. The advice was based on organisers' reports from the field and their mission reports on return.

Without good information, it is impossible to protect oneself from the enemy or to plan and time operations. You need to know local conditions e.g. the danger of ordering wrong drinks or cigarettes. Transport services and restrictions. You need to provide a good reason for travelling. Avoid market days when there is a search for 'black market' goods. Understand new slang or colloquialisms brought about by war, and the general temper of the local population. Check that your identity papers are in order. Find out how to procure ration cards. Discover what passes are necessary to overcome movement restrictions. Are there control posts manned by enemy troops or local police? Clarify evacuation procedures from forbidden zones and observe curfew hours and blackout regulations. Check licenses and travel restrictions.

Observe the enemy methods and their personnel. Locate their troop positions and that of the Gestapo. Find out the attitude of the local police. Are there any civilian police spies or agents provocateurs? If so, find out their names.

Decide on possible targets: enemy communications, Headquarters, supply dumps and factories. Are there any bottlenecks in enemy production? What are the internal workings of factories, power stations, railway and communication networks? Get to know the personnel employed in these areas, the means of entry, layout of machines, number of guards and control systems. Find out what documents or workers passes are needed to gain access to these targets.

This information is obtained by direct interrogation, constant personal observation, reading newspapers and listening to radio and by cultivating an informant service.

The Informant Service: Very few should know that they are informants. The great bulk will be quite unconscious of it. Select people from as many strata of society, trades and professions as possible. Best people are those who constantly mix with all sorts. These include priests, innkeepers, waitresses and barmaids, doctors, dentists and hospital staffs, postmen, telephone and telegraph operators, bankers, shopkeepers, railway officials and workers, servants and all grumblers and malcontents. In due course you may decide to approach a few of the more trustworthy informants with a view to recruiting them.

You need to be able to develop a technique of eavesdropping on the masses. An ability to hear and separate two simultaneous conversations while ostensibly listening to a third. Take advantage of other people's bad security, for example – careless talk, disgruntled enemy personnel, affecting ignorance and thus encouraging others to air their knowledge and making false statements to elicit a correct reply. Do not discourage informants, however trivial their information.[10]

In an SOE file was a memorandum dated 27 November 1941 which stated that,

Each organiser is instructed, unless he has some special mission, to form (a) a network of cells for rumour spreading, passive resistance and recruiting, (b) to organise the training of saboteurs, (c) to organise cachettes for agents and armies, (d) to organise secret printing presses and disseminate propaganda. The propaganda is carried out on instructions in collaboration with P.W.E. [Political Warfare Executive].[11]

Agents' security was paramount. SOE was concerned that early agents were caught because their security awareness was poor. Hence, F Section employed Christine Chilver, an attractive, well-educated and French-speaking British-Lithuanian as an agent provocatrice, a honey trap, to test how much agents were prepared to talk while they were on the 'scheme'. Men had a 96-hour scheme and women 48 hours.

Having learned the theory, the scheme was to visit one of the British provincial towns or cities where agents had to complete a number of tasks as if they were in the field. It might include finding details of suitable accommodation for other agents, reconnaissance of a target, breaking into a building, smuggling and planting dummy explosives, stealing documents, rendezvousing with a contact and returning to Beaulieu without being arrested. They had to ensure they were not followed and if they spotted a 'tail' they had to shake it off. For the women, this often involved going into a department store, finding the underwear department where a male follower would be more conspicuous and then escaping down the back stairs, or going into a hotel and out of a side entrance.

Agent Fifi, as Christine was known, was reported by Michael Foot to have been used to find out whether the agents spoke in English when they woke up, a definite lapse in security. What the agent did not know was that other agents were sent to follow them and the local police were informed should they run into trouble. Christine was provided with a detailed description of the agent, their accommodation and the name of their contact, the time and place of their rendezvous, and £10 for the weekend. Any change had to be returned to the Finance Section and receipts provided as evidence.

Using a variety of strategies, she had to make contact with the agent and inform them that the contact they were supposed to meet was unavailable, apologise for their absence and claim he had sent her instead. If they believed her, over drinks and a meal, she would then chat up the unsuspecting agent and find out how willing they were to talk about their family, their background, their training, their instructors, even their mission.

Her detailed reports were then sent to the Training Section in Beaulieu and compared with the agents' own reports about their scheme. On occasions, she was brought into the room to challenge the veracity of their statements. One man claimed she had a mole on her inside thigh, and she challenged him to find it.

Mostly male but some female agents were tested in this way; some failing the course because they talked too much. None of the French women's personnel files indicated that they had been subjected to a honey trap. It tended to be used on those SOE agents already deemed a potential security risk. For those who succumbed, there was only one mentioned in her file as having completely failed. For the others it was a salutary lesson. Lax security in the field would jeopardise not just their own lives but those of fellow agents and Resistance members.[12]

F Section employed a number of other agents provocatrices, including Noreen Riols.

In an article for *The Telegraph* on Britain's forgotten female spies, Clare Mulley stated that the honey trap had often been parodied in James Bond films, with the beautiful women who set out to entrap their male target quickly finding themselves seduced. 'But women like Chilver and Riols were made of sterner stuff.'[13]

Before they left Beaulieu, the agents would have been given a translation of Gubbins' pamphlet, *The Partisan Leader's Handbook, a Tactical Guide* to read. It contained the principles of guerrilla warfare and sabotage; road ambush; rail ambush; the destruction of an enemy post, detachment or guard; concealment and care of arms and explosives; the enemy's information system and how to counter it; how to counter enemy action; guerrilla information service and sabotage methods.

In Marcus Binney's *The Women who Lived for Danger*, he quotes Leslie Fernandez, one of the women's trainers:

> During training we attempted to prepare them physically, building up their stamina by hikes through rough countryside. All were taught close combat, which gave them confidence even if most were not very good at it. These girls weren't commando material. They didn't have the physique though some had tremendous mental stamina. You would not expect well brought up girls to go up behind someone and slit their throats, though if they were grappled, there were several particularly nasty little tricks that we handed on, given us by the Shanghai police.[14]

For many of the women agents, and men for that matter, they had to overcome an instinct instilled in them since birth: that of looking someone important in the face and telling them the truth. Lying was an essential skill while in the field. They had to take on the role of an actor in which, as in life, some took to the stage much better than others. Escott provides a fitting tribute to them:

> To know what they did and what happened to them can, therefore, act as a memorial to those who died, and a reminder of the great courage shown by all these remarkable individuals who, in abnormal times, when their world was turned upside down, displayed extraordinary qualities to match their unusual and perilous role.[15]

She goes on to say that it was in the spirit of self-sacrifice that most agents undertook this work:

> When deaths occurred it was only for the greater good. On the way, of course, there was excitement, friendship and a gruelling test of the human spirit, but there was also fear, loneliness, hard work and sometimes torture and death.[16]

Those that failed the training course, mostly for serious breaches of security, were not allowed to return to their previous unit or employment as they had detailed knowledge of top secret organisations. They were sent to what was called 'The Cooler'. There were two in Scotland: the Craigerne Hotel for officers and Inverlair for the others. There was also Tyting House, St Martha, near Guildford. Although residents were 'fed and watered and provided with work and entertainment, they were not allowed to leave for the duration of the war. There is no evidence that any of the French women had lax security and were sent to 'The Cooler'.

Other specialist courses were provided, including industrial sabotage training at Brickendonbury Manor (STS 17), near Hertford. Jean Bohec was the only French woman documented as attending a course there.

Other training at specialist schools included propaganda, raids using mini-submarines and micro-photography. Those whose Morse skills had identified them as potential wireless operators were sent on a coding course at Grendon Hall (STS 53a), near Aylesbury or Fawley Court (STS 41 from 1940–1942 then renamed STS 54a), near Henley-on-Thames, Oxfordshire. They then went to Thame Park (STS 52), also near Oxford, which was the main training station. As well as keep-fit exercises, potential wireless operators were given a sixteen-week specialised radio, cypher and security training course. They had to learn how to use and repair sets, tap out messages in Morse at 18–22 words per minute (wpm), and use codes and checks to verify their transmission. For some it took nine months and included a two-week practice exercise in Belhaven, near Dunbar in southern Scotland. Closer to D-Day, some wireless operators were sent before having completed their training as there was an urgent need to replace those caught and arrested.

Hutchinson comments on how invaluable wireless operators (sometimes referred to as wireless telegraphists or radio operators) were to SOE's missions:

> Without communication both ways the whole organisation could become valueless and there were many occasions where a radio operator got into danger and all messages died away until a new sender was contacted in the field or sent out from home. The enemy had developed special radio-direction finding vehicles and, if an operator worked too long from the same hide-out, he ran grave risks of being located and caught.
>
> In message sending by morse, each wireless operator had their own individual style or 'fist' that an experienced wireless listener could recognise, rather the same as one's own handwriting. They might always hurry or hesitate or hurry over the dots and dashes for the same letter allowing their identity to be immediately recognised. All wireless operators were given a security code to include in each message. If it was missing it indicated that they were operating under duress. The theory was that, if their security code had been bribed or tortured out of the operator, those at the listening station in Britain would have known whether it was they who was sending the message or not.
>
> This did not happen in the early years of the war. Following the eventual realisation that many wireless operators had been captured in Holland and France and their sets played back to London by the Germans with the resulting loss of numerous agents, containers, weapons, ammunition, up-to-date wireless sets, money, etc., Leo Marks, the head of SOE's codes, developed a library of operators' 'fists' allowing every message to be compared with those recorded during their training. He also developed a security question which only the operators would know the answer to, so, even if their code became known to the enemy, only the operator would know the right answer to the security question. Added security was Marks' 'one-time pad,' a list of codes specially printed on silk which, once used, could be cut off and burnt or, if circumstances demanded, swallowed.[17]

Wireless operators were expected to lead a solitary existence, able to stay awake until the transmission time was due and to minimise their use of the equipment to less than twenty minutes. They were made familiar with various codes and ciphers that were in use at the time for communication with agents in the field and with main stations of the Mediterranean Allied Air Force at Cairo in Egypt and, following the Allied landings in North Africa, at Massingham in Algiers. Pawley details some of those taught.

In the early days, a code called Playfair was taught. It involved putting messages into rectangular 'boxes' on squared paper according to a numbered order of letters determined by the line of a poem (of which some were original and some borrowed) or sentence from a book. The message was encoded by selecting letters from the opposite corners of the rectangle. The code was superseded by a more secure one, named double transposition. Again, it was worked in 'boxes' on squared paper; it placed the letters of a message horizontally under a 'key' word or words which were put in numerical sequence; a fresh selection was made by transposing them vertically, again in numerical order; the final version was read horizontally. The field operator and base coder would be in possession of the identical poem or novel from which the 'key' word or words would be drawn; the page and line would be indicated in figures at the beginning of the message.[18]

Leo Marks, the above-mentioned head of codes at SOE, reported that,

> Great care needed to be taken to include two types of 'checks' in every message, a 'bluff' check, to confuse the enemy, and one 'true' check which it was hoped would not be discovered. Many field operators in the heat of the moment left out their checks when encoding messages. At the base, two possibilities occurred to the coder; was this a genuine lapse or had the set been seized by the enemy and was being worked back by them, as happened on several occasions.[19]

Wireless operators were vital to the success of all these secret missions. They had a dangerous job, and it was said that at the beginning of these secret operations the average life expectancy of a radio operator in the field was only six weeks. Francis Cammaerts, a French Resistance leader, reported that, 'Without your radio operator, you were a pigeon without wings.' It is worth including a few paragraphs from Pawley's *In Obedience to Instructions* as she provides fascinating detail of what exactly their work entailed:

> This knowledge needed to be transferred to operating a special key which represented the dots and dashes in terms of short and long sounds. When proficiency was attained, the mock practice key became part of a B2 radio set which relayed the sounds into the atmosphere and could be captured at a distance on a specified wavelength, previously determined.
> ...at Fawley Court ... a group of twelve girls ... sat at a series of wooden tables, practicing their morse on a dummy key day after day. As it became possible to speed up, one moved to the next table, with

an instructor sitting at the end. Most trainees would stick at one letter and not be able to overcome the resultant pause for a short period. There was a test once a week when the atmosphere was really tense. Ann Bonsor recalls going to the cinema and quite involuntarily turning the sign EXIT beside the screen into morse. Probably on this account, radio operators, like coders, became obsessional; many FANYs have never lost the skill, only some of the speed, fifty years later.

For the last part of their training radio operators were often posted to Scotland to take part in a scheme called SPARTAN, at Dunbar. FANYs would be based in a mobile signal station, to which agents in training, dispersed throughout the countryside, would work back their sets. Before proceeding overseas, most coders and radio operators received some experience on an operational station, dealing with live traffic from the field. This would be at Station 53A, Grendon Underwood, or Station 53B, at Poundon, Messages came in from Holland, France, Denmark, Norway and so on. During their earlier training radio operators would have become familiar with the Q code and the sending and receiving procedures based on this international method of communication; no other means were allowed, never plain language, though some agents in distress, anger or jubilation, might sometimes resort to it.

A FANY operator on duty at her set would be allocated to what was known as a 'sked' (terminology for a scheduled, expected message at a previously defined time from an agent), with the appropriate frequency, code name and call sign, by the signal master, or other authorised person. She would listen for the three-letter particular call sign of the out-station which should be calling at intervals of one minute, and then listening for one minute. If contact were established, the home operator would send the call sign, followed by QRK How are you receiving me, plus IMI Question mark. The field would answer QSA Your signal readability is, followed by a number from one to five. If it were over three, and therefore fairly audible, the home operator would wait for the field to send QTC I have a message for you. Field messages were always sent first. With numbers less than three, each group of five letters (the invariable number in which signals were sent) would be repeated. The base operator then took down the message in pencil in block capitals on special forms and then wait until QRU appeared I have nothing more. If the base operator had messages, the procedure would be reversed. To ask for repeated groups, or QRS send slower, was not well regarded, unless interference was particularly bad, since it would expose the field operator to danger. At the end of a transmission, the base would send VA close down. In the event of sudden enemy attack, the field could send QUG I am forced to stop transmitting owing to immediate danger, whereupon a FANY operator would report this at once to her senior officer. In the event of gross inaudibility, it was possible to ask for help from a second base operator, but this was an exceptional measure in particular circumstances. 'Listening watches' were set up when a field mission failed to respond at its allotted time according to its signal plan.

A specialised training was given to become a signal planner. A small group of FANYs learnt to provide a signal plan for every mission which went into the field. It included a call sign by which to be recognised by the base station, an allocated frequency, obtained by the supply of the appropriate crystals (two slices of quartz cut to a precise wavelength which determined frequency, about the size of a postage stamp) and specific times on a regular basis at which attempts to transmit to the base station were to be made. Trained signal planners who undertook this skilled technical work were given the rank of Lieutenant.

Another technique in which the FANYS were instructed later in the war was that of 'finger printing', i.e. the recognition of morse-sending methods. All who learnt to send morse developed their own individual style. If an agent in occupied territory were captured, attempts would be made to work the radio back to base in England. A FANY operator who could detect a change in field operator would prevent unwise future communications, drops, or reinforcements to that mission.[20]

Not everyone passed the four-month wireless course. They had to reach at least 20 wpm, much higher than the peacetime requirements of the services or Post Office. Those who failed, and there were many, were transferred to become coders, registry clerks, copy clerks, signal distributors, teleprinter or switchboard operators. Ryder mentioned that the men and women who were successful in their training as radio operators included the bravest,

> ...for if they were caught with a set they knew they faced death. To escape detection, they frequently had to change the place from which they transmitted messages and, to avoid capture, they often had to disguise themselves – sometimes at barely a moment's notice. German radio-telegraphists were on duty at their listening posts twenty-four hours a day. The Gestapo always had a flying squad ready to go into action immediately to hunt and seize these Bods.[21]

An indication of their work in the field was provided in Frank Griffiths' memoirs of his years as a pilot in 138 Squadron:

> The resistance units in the occupied countries grew and grew until finally some 1,400 independent units were on the books. Initially, an agent

and his pianist (radio operator) would be dropped and, in its simplest form, the agent would recruit patriots in small units in various towns and villages. They, in turn, would select suitable fields for the reception of the drop materials such as guns, ammunition, clothing, money etc. The agent would, through his pianist, inform London of the place of the reception, give it a code name, a recognition letter and a message which the BBC could broadcast on the day an aircraft was being sent with his supplies. This message would be something in the nature of 'Tartes aux pommes de la tante Helene' repeated twice each time it was broadcast on the BBC transmission. The first time at 1300 hours. The broadcast of the message would indicate merely that the flight was being planned. The 1800-hour transmission confirmed that the flight really would take place – that is, if the aircraft remained serviceable, the weather didn't deteriorate and if the aircraft didn't get lost or shot down on the way. There were lots of 'ifs' even after all the planning was done.[22]

These times may have been for another Country Section as another source gave different times. F Section broadcast their messages personnels after the BBC World Service's Radio Londres' news at 1730 and 1915 and the RF's went out at 0615, 1315 and 2115. The first time indicated the mission was planned for that night, the second to confirm it was on and for RF Section the third indicated the aerplane took off. Although having a wireless set was illegal in France, many French families had them and the Resistance listened to them to keep up to date with the progress of the war as well as to listen to the messages personnels.

The Security Section's interrogation of refugees and returned agents' debriefing sessions and mission reports eventually led SOE to learn that the Gestapo were using a variety of torture techniques on captured wireless operators during their interrogations. Being stripped naked, being hung up by the wrists or skewered on meat hooks, having your teeth and nails pulled out with pliers, having cigarettes stubbed out on your skin, being given electric shocks all over your body or being given the 'baignoire' (nearly drowned) were reported. Most forms of torture left one semi-conscious after a time. It was said that if you could withstand the first quarter of an hour without 'talking', you probably would not talk at all. It was recommended that a mind-numbing exercise to help withstand torture was counting – if necessary into the thousands.

To help agents resist the interrogation techniques, SOE provided special exercises at Beaulieu. All female agents underwent at least two mock interrogations. Several described being woken up by loud banging on the door at some ungodly hour in the morning. An officer would storm in shouting at them to get up and, without dressing, they were ordered downstairs for questioning. Two men dressed as Gestapo officers in long black leather coats and wide-brimmed black hats shouted and screamed at them, asking them questions about their identity and demanding they answer. They had to make sure their cover story was kept exactly to the letter.

As their interrogators were also their examiners, there was double the anguish as they wrote thorough comments on their performance, which were read out during their debriefs at the end of each course. As the interrogation intensified, it became more and more realistic. Bright spotlights were shone in their face. Sometimes they were tied to a chair, handcuffed so they could do nothing as they were hit about the head and had their legs kicked. Some reported being forced to strip naked and stand there while they searched her mouth, vagina, and rectum.

The tension must have been extreme. There would have been the smell, not just of the human bodily odours, but of fear. 'What were you doing at five o'clock? Why did you go out? Why were you at the railway station? Were you meeting a friend? What was his name? What were you wearing? Your accomplices have confessed. We know everything. You're lying. You're lying.' They were very realistic. Far too good perhaps, but the women knew that this was probably one of the best exercises they could get.

Officers in their Country Section had to create a convincing cover story for every agent. Based on their interviews with the Security Section, a detailed biography was typed up including birthday and feast day of their patron saint, parental details, early life, holidays, education and employment history. While most of their cover story was true, alterations were made to protect any family members still living in France.

There was almost a husband and wife team in SOE. While Marjorie March-Phillips's husband was conducting his 'Small-Scale Raiding Force' on various missions overseas, SOE recruited her for operational duties. After working as a conducting officer attached to F Section, she underwent parachute training with a view to being sent into France. However, the situation changed when she discovered that she was SOE's first pregnant parachutist.[23]

SOE had a Forgery Section at Briggens (Station XIV), near Royden in Essex. Using samples of identity cards, ration cards, travel passes, employment certificates and currency brought back from the field, highly skilled forgers seconded from London printing companies produced replicas. All the French women were supplied with appropriate documentation which corresponded with their cover story. The conducting officer would spend several days ensuring the agent knew every detail off by heart, the names of all their family members, where they stayed on holidays, what schools they had attended, the names of the streets in their town or village as well as workplace regulations, what was rationed, travel routines, times of curfews, etc.

Miller reported an interview he had with Viennese Claudia Pulver, one of the seamstresses at SOE's clothes section at the Thatched Barn. Here and under the police station in Savile Row, London, a staff of Jewish tailors and seamstresses produced first-rate copies of French suits, shirts, dresses, blouses, bodices, knickers, and handkerchiefs. Those for the agents going to France were dubbed with the laundry marks of establishments in Paris, Arles or Lille – wherever the agent would be operating.

Claudia mentioned providing dresses for a pregnant French countess who came to England in a rowing boat and another girl who had to have the most unusual and very elegant clothes, a riding outfit and an evening dress. Who these women were remains a mystery.

When it was mentioned earlier that there were thirty-four documented French women infiltrated into France, she provided evidence that a number of other women, presumably French, were secretly brought out of France, debriefed, prepared for another undercover mission and sent back. This has to have been organised by the SIS, who neither accept nor deny such an operation. Claudia claimed that,

We also had quite a lot of prostitutes from the brothels of Paris coming in. We made appropriate underwear, very provocative, whatever they needed. They were very important to whoever was in control of them because their clients were a lot of German officers and they got quite a lot of information out of them. They were the ones that came backwards and forwards more often than others, because I think possibly they had to bring their information back personally. We had one who came backwards and forwards ten or twelve times and survived, only to die of a botched abortion after the war, which was quite sad.[24]

In *Secret Agent*, David Stafford includes Claudia's reminiscences of her time working for SOE. Her attention to detail must have saved hundreds of lives:

'We started with shirts; I would imagine we made a hundred or two hundred shirts a week, all by hand and individually. We had all these lovely young men coming. I quite enjoyed all these handsome, dashing officers from France, French Canada, England, from all over the place. They wouldn't say very much; we had to guess a great deal. They came into the showroom which was actually in Margaret Street, around the corner from the workroom in Great Titchfield Street. We had to take their measurements. We started making shirts for them in the Continental fashion, which is quite different to anything in England. We got old shirts from the refugees again. We took them apart, we looked at the various collar shapes, looked at the way they were manufactured. We looked at the seams, and there certainly was an enormous difference between the side seams. The shape of the cuffs was different, the position of the buttonhole on the under collar was entirely different, and sometimes the plackets of a shirt were different. The width of the stand underneath the collar was different. I think the Continental were a little lower than the English ones, they were quite high, probably because Continental people have shorter necks than the British. They have their own type of collar, because every man likes a different shape of a collar, but they were allowed to choose from the Continental versions. So we made a lot of cardboard patterns of European shapes so that we would have a library for people to choose from.

'Labels were taboo.... I remember a pair of gloves went across and the agent came back saying you made a mistake. I turned them inside out and there was a "Made in England" label in one of the fingers. That's really the only mistake we ever made, because we were terribly careful about the labels.'[25]

As the only people in France who wore new suits were Germans, costume people from the film and theatre world were employed to make the clothes look old in a technique known as 'distressing'. It involved wearing them every day for a week, even sleeping in them, so they stank to high heaven. Then the 'rotten stone', Vaseline and sandpaper technique was used. It is said that Station XV could supply sixteen agents a day, with meticulous attention to detail, even ensuring that the word 'Lightning' on zip fasteners was removed with a dentist's drill and 'size seven' converted to a label with the continental measurement (there was no size seven on the Continent). Although some of these clothes were sent in the containers, most went on the agents.

Suits, cap comforters, pullovers, trousers, underpants, knickers, vests, boots, dubbin, laces, insoles, soles, leather, heels, nails, socks and a 'housewife' (a small portable sewing kit) were carefully packed into the containers. Special requests for German, Spanish and other national uniforms were also catered for. One unusual request was for a new battle dress to be dropped behind the lines for those agents who wanted to be in full uniform on the day of liberation.

In Hutchinson's opinion, nothing was spared for the agents' safety. The female French agents' false papers were perfect, printed on French type paper in Britain, filled in by a French handwriting expert with a photograph where necessary taken by a Frenchman in this country. Her clothing was prepared by a French tailor in London. She was not allowed to take anything from Britain with her, and he had never heard of any agent infiltrated from Britain being caught as a result of faulty papers or clothing.[26]

Having been provided with appropriate clothing, perhaps having their hair done and visited the dentist, the women were expected to write a will. F Section women left them with Vera Atkins. No doubt RF Section women left them with one of their secretaries. They were also given a collection of anniversary cards which they had to write a brief greeting on and provide names and addresses of people, in Britain, they wanted them sent to and dates so that birthdays, other anniversaries and Christmas cards could be sent to their nearest and dearest, letting them know that all was well. Obviously there was no mention of their secret mission in France.

F Section women would have briefed for their mission at Orchard Court, Westminster, or one of SOE's flats in London.

Orchard Court was an imposing seven-storey apartment building behind Selfridges, near Portman Square, just around the corner from Baker Street tube station. Agents reported being met by Mr Park, who escorted them to the green door of No. 6. A brass pot by the door held umbrellas. Many recall being shocked by the extravagance of the bathroom, with its plush pink carpet, jet-black bath and sink, an onyx bidet surrounded by peach-pink mirrors and black glass tiles. The rest had rather expensive 1930s-style Art Deco apple-green wallpaper and lime-green woodwork. The net-curtained sash windows had heavy brocade curtains tied back with plaited ropes. Statues of stretching nudes draped with silk stood in the alcoves backlit in pink. Green round-armed settees and armchairs were arranged on a deep pile cream carpet.

Exactly where RF Section women and those from the Corps de Volontaires Françaises, were briefed was not revealed in their personnel files. Those recruited in North Africa would have been briefed in Algiers.

Once agents were fully prepared for their mission, their infiltration into France had to be arranged. A FANY officer would drive them and their conducting officer to the port if they were deemed unfit for flying, or to Tempsford, Tangmere or Harrington, where, after dusk on one of the nights on either side of the full moon, a plane would fly them out. Most were driven in a Wolsey or a Rolls-Royce donated to the war effort by owners unable to get petrol rations. Given its importance, SOE had no problems acquiring petrol. Closed curtains over the car windows and being taken on a tortuous route around country lanes ensured the agents would not be able to reveal the location of the airfield if they were captured and interrogated.

Should there be a delay, like fog, heavy snow or strong wind, they would have been driven to one of SOE's 'Holding Schools', other requisitioned country houses in the English countryside. Bignor Manor, near Chichester,

West Sussex, about 15 km from RAF Tangmere, provided accommodation for around 200 French agents before their flight. Although it was used for SIS operations into France, whether any of the French women stayed there is unknown.[27]

Those whose flight from Tempsford was delayed would normally have been accommodated at Gaynes Hall (STS 612), near Perry, Cambridgeshire, about 8 km north-west of St Neots and about half an hour's drive from the airfield. It was a three-storey, yellow brick Georgian mansion set in 23 acres of parkland, with thirteen bedrooms, nine bathrooms, a ballroom, sitting room and lounge, dining room and library.

When it was first requisitioned, it was used as a packing station. Huts were rapidly erected in the grounds for packing the containers and panniers before they were trucked to Tempsford. The operation was transferred to Holme Hall, near Peterborough, when the Americans took over the operation and the hall was used initially by the Norwegian section under Major C. S. Hampton. Later, agents of other nationalities were accommodated there. Some described it as a 'hotel' providing a place for liaison and up-market rest and recreation for agents before the half-hour drive to Tempsford.

According to Michael Foot, the agents' stay there was made 'as delectable as possible. A large number of FANYs, girls in their late teens when recruited, with quick brains and quiet tongues, performed an essential service for SOE.'[28]

Oluf Olsen, a Norwegian agent, stayed there before being flown out from Tempsford in early 1943 to attack the heavy water plant at Vermork in Norway. In his wartime autobiography, *Two Eggs on My Plate,* he wrote that,

Late in the afternoon of April 17 we drove into the grounds of an old English country house surrounded by high walls, 'somewhere in England.' Everyone here was sworn to secrecy; every man or woman, from the C.O. down to the washerwoman, was chosen with special care. The same rules applied to all personnel, both ground and flying, at the great airfield half an hour away...

The house contained an extremely cosmopolitan collection of persons who were 'guests of honour' in the place; agents from various European countries. We talked together, ate together, did physical exercises together, but no one knew who any individual was or where he was going. One could only guess from the accent with which he spoke English. No one asked questions; nor did anyone talk about himself.

The thing which perhaps we all remember best about the place, apart from our marvellous entertainment by its young ladies, was the so-called 'Operational Egg.' Fresh eggs were at that time largely unobtainable by the English public. Only dried eggs from Canada or America were used. At supper-time it might happen that two fine fresh eggs were carefully laid on a plate before a particular person. The person in question, even if he liked eggs better than anything, seemed suddenly to have lost taste for this previously so tempting delicacy which now actually lay before him. His turn had appeared on the programme for the night's operations; a reminder of this, and a last special piece of hospitality, was the 'Operational Egg.'

That evening I was to sit down in a few seconds and look at the two fried eggs on my plate. My appetite was nothing out of the ordinary. There was too much to think about, too many still unanswered questions connected with the coming hours and days.[29]

Knut Haukelid, another Norwegian agent involved in the attack on the heavy water plant, had a vivid memory of Gaynes Hall:

The place was very closely guarded. A number of servicewomen kept the place in order, cooked the meals, and gave the men some social life. They belonged to the special section called 'Fannies' [*sic*]. These girls did an uncommonly good job, seeing that everything went as it should and doing their best to prevent the delays from getting on our nerves. And, when the commandant suggested it, they were always willing to come to Cambridge in the evening for a little party... The fannies had their own cars, and very fine ones. When we drove into Cambridge for an evening it was usually to the best restaurant in the city where we would eat and drink at the expense of the War Office; the main thing being to enjoy ourselves as much as possible.[30]

FANY officer, Mrs Park of Bournemouth, submitted her reminiscences of her time at Gaynes Hall to the BBC's WW2 People's War website:

I hadn't realised that it was only a section of the FANY that had been drafted into SOE. I went to get my beret and said I was in SC61 and they hadn't heard of them. We were stationed in Gaynes Hall, Buckton [*sic*] near St Neots and Cambridge. An old hall deep in the heart of the country. This lady who owned it was Mrs Jubilee [*sic*]; she was an elderly lady who had her house requisitioned. We did orderly work, we had a small switchboard, there were two or three cooks there and the food was lovely, because we looked after these 'BODS' (Secret Agents) very well. We housed and looked after the BODS. They had their training and came to us to wait for the RAF to take them in Lysanders on their missions. Sometimes they were brought back if the conditions were not right or if they had received a signal from the ground to abort the mission. We had many different nationalities come through there. Odette [Sansom, one of the female agents] went through Gaynes Hall. You weren't taught to drive, and I was unable to drive although I would have liked to. The men would be dropped by parachute, and then a canister would be dropped with a parachute also. These canisters would contain all sorts, folding bicycles, dead rats or dung filled with explosives. The RAF would stay at Gaynes Hall also. We used to go out with some of the BODS, but we had to go right away from where we were stationed so that we did not draw attention to it. I am sure that some people must have known that something was going on. We were not supposed to get attached to them, but we did, and when they went on a mission you never saw them again.[31]

The secrecy was said to be under penalty of death! Along with all the other 'country houses', Gaynes Hall was a vital centre of the operation. Writing in an article in the *Hunts Post* about Huntingdonshire being a nerve centre of Allied espionage, Gordon Thomas added:

...the charwomen were hand-picked. Life at wartime Gaynes Hall was fantastic. It was run on the lines of a luxury holiday camp. There was no shortage of food, drink or entertainment. From the very beginning, the Government had realised that nothing could be too good for the men and women who gambled their lives in the grim game of spying on the Continent.[32]

Gaynes Hall is reported to have also been used for briefing the Joes flying into France as well as debriefing the 'passengers' lifted out and flown back to Tempsford. When flights were postponed or cancelled due to bad weather, the FANY drove them back in the early hours of the morning. As the weather conditions normally took about six days to improve, it gave a rest to aircrew and agents and a breathing space for the maintenance crew.

As they waited, the agents went over and over the details of the life of the person they had become. To distract them, a group of 'very glamorous' young FANYs were on hand as 'entertainers'. Local delivery men were said to have been more than willing to drive into the grounds to catch a glimpse. Local teenage boys used to toboggan on a snow-covered hill in the grounds and loved having these 'dream' girls sledding with them. One lady told me that when she was stationed at Gaynes Hall, it was to 'entertain' the agents – not in the modern sense she stressed – but playing ping-pong, cards, and dancing. One afternoon after a good lunch, two parachutists attempted to take her around the whole of the ground floor without touching the floorboards. They could use the skirting boards, the picture rails, and any available furniture – much to the entertainment of the onlookers. When all three of them were standing on top of one of the old oak mantelpieces, it came away from the wall in one piece, crashed to the floor around them and 'brought the house down'!

Should Gaynes Hall be fully occupied, agents could be accommodated in Hasell's Hall, the Officers' Mess. Another requisitioned mansion, it stood on top of the Greensand Ridge, about ten minutes' drive from the airfield. Another of the 'stately 'omes' where FANYs looked after SIS agents was Tempsford Hall, a few kilometres from the airfield on the western side of the railway line. At the time of writing, it is the headquarters of Kier Construction company. When Mr Kier, the founder, moved his offices to Tempsford after the war, he was surprised to find that behind the property was the airfield which supplied him and his wife when they were in the Danish Resistance.

For those leaving from Harrington, they stayed at Brock Hall (STS 1), near Flore, Northamptonshire, about 13 km from the airfield. The house and the grounds were also used for training French, Norwegian, Danish, Czech and later OSS agents, but no accounts of agents' stays there have come to light.[33]

5

The Special Duties or
'Moon Squadrons'

Although infiltration into France by an 'illegal' fishing boat to a secluded beach on the Normandy or Brittany coast was possible, it was considered dangerous. By 1942 the Germans had largely completed the '*Atlantikwall*', an extensive defence network along the North Sea coast, the Channel, and along the Atlantic coast down to Spain. Some agents were infiltrated by motor gunboat and others by felucca onto the Mediterranean coast. As virtually all French airports and airfields were occupied by the Germans, by far the safest way was to be parachuted or landed in a flat, secluded field. France, being a largely agricultural country, had many remote rural areas where isolated drop zones were found.

In the first months of the war, when the Brickendonbury agents' training was complete and a flight was arranged, they were driven to North Weald Airfield, about 15 km away in Epping Forest. On 21 August 1940, the RAF's newly formed 419 Flight, using a hut as a base, began operations using two small, short take-off and landing Westland Lysanders. A further two arrived later with two brand new Whitley bombers, but they had no radio and no guns. For the Lysander flights to France, the planes were flown down to RAF Tangmere, near Bournemouth, where they were topped up with fuel and picked up passengers.

After three Luftwaffe attacks, on 3 September 419 Flight moved to Stapleford Tawney, 8 km to the south, where pilots and crew flew from two grass runways and slept in bell tents. When this was attacked, on 9 October, they moved to RAF Stradishall, about 15 km south-west of Bury St Edmunds in Suffolk. Operations continued from there until March 1941, when they were renamed 1419 Flight.

For the Lysander flights to France, 161 Squadron transferred to RAF Tangmere for the moon period. This forward base close to the south coast, about 7 km east of Chichester, West Sussex, was closer, which meant their range of about 1,200 km would take them much deeper into southern France than starting from Tempsford. They were also able to land their passengers there on their return. Their first flight to France was on the night of 19/20 October 1940. Later in the war an auxiliary fuel tank was added between the wheels, allowing pilots to reach the foothills of the Pyrénées.

On 22 May, 1419 Flight was transferred to Newmarket Racecourse, about 75 km north of Brickendonbury, just over an hour's drive through country lanes. It had the longest grass runway in the country of almost 3,000 metres and ideally suited for the Whitleys. Initially, the men camped outside but later their offices were underneath the grandstand.

As the need for more supplies to be dropped to the Resistance movements across Europe increased, six more planes were allocated to 1419 Flight and on 25 August it was renamed 138 Squadron, by which time it had four Lysanders and six Whitleys.

Two Handley Page Halifaxes with one in reserve were added in November 1941, which had to be modified for 138 Squadron's clandestine night-flying operations. To reduce weight, only essential guns and cladding were kept and special shrouds were placed over the engine exhaust pipes to avoid the flames being seen from the ground. In March 1942, as demand for more planes to drop supplies, infiltrate agents and pick up personnel increased, the King's Flight, captained by Edward Fielden, was added to 138 Squadron.

With Bomber Command taking over Newmarket Racecourse for its long runway, in March 1942, 138 Squadron was transferred to the newly built RAF Tempsford. Bomber Command had refused it as it was described as the foggiest and boggiest airfield in Britain. A new Squadron, numbered 161, was formed, headed by Squadron Leader Fielden. King George allowed him to use the Royal Hudson aeroplane, which could seat twelve passengers comfortably, ideal for larger scale landing and pick-up operations. This was the common method of infiltrating older passengers considered too unfit for a parachute drop, as well as for bringing back larger groups.

What has subsequently been termed 'Churchill's most secret airfield' was where most of the flights to France took off from. Its location was about an hour and half's drive from London. Both Squadrons parachuted agents and supplies but 161 Squadron also landed on remote fields behind enemy lines to land agents and pick up passengers that the SOE deemed necessary to be brought back to England.[1]

The whole operation was top secret. Tempsford was said to have been designed by an illusionist to give overflying enemy pilots the impression that it was disused. The original farm buildings were either demolished or made to look dilapidated and some wooden barns reinforced with bricks. The roofs of newly constructed offices, storerooms and hangars were camouflaged, the runways had green and brown patches painted on them to look like grass. A black line was painted across the runway to look like the continuation of a hedge. Cows grazed on the fields during the day, and there were ducks on the pond outside Gibraltar Farm. This building, the nerve centre of the secret operations, was out of bounds to the more than 2,000 personnel based on the airfield, which included over 200 WAAFS. A special pass was needed. Although there were defensive anti-aircraft guns, they were never used. It was never attacked throughout the war. Planes only took off after dusk on the nights on either side of the full moon.

With the addition of modified Halifax and Wellington bombers, pilots flew without lights and, until sophisticated ground-to-air communications were introduced later in the war, the navigator had to use the reflection of the moon on rivers, canals, lakes, roads and railway lines to direct the pilot to the drop zone. This was termed DZ by those 'in the know'. Lysander pilots had to study Michelin maps and plot a zig-zag route avoiding dangerous areas as they did not have a navigator. Given the nature of their work, the Special Duties Squadrons were sometimes called the 'Moon Squadron' and its pilots and crews the 'Moon Men'.[2]

Top secret SOE and SIS missions were sent to drop supplies to the Resistance in France, Belgium, Holland, Denmark, Norway, Germany, Austria, Czechoslovakia and Poland, as well as nearly 1,400 'Joes' or 'Bods', the USAAF and RAF slang for secret agents. Sometimes these agents needed bringing back to England. So too did stranded aircrew, Resistance leaders, and VIPs. Many were lifted out from behind enemy lines by Tempsford crews or helped to return to Britain with the assistance of dedicated escape networks.

When the Americans joined the war after the Japanese attack on Pearl Harbor, the USAAF 801st/492nd Bomb Group was sent to Tempsford to learn from the RAF the requirements of night flying and clandestine dropping of supplies and agents behind enemy lines. Having completed two 'Buddy missions', they used their Liberators and Dakotas on similar missions from RAF Harrington, near Kettering, Northamptonshire.

Nicknamed the 'Carpetbaggers', starting in January 1944 they flew 2,555 missions to France, 1,909 of which were successful, dropping 284 agents, landing 74, including 13 SIS agents, and picking up 189 personnel.[3]

RAF Tempsford, perhaps a lot more than other Second World War airfields, was very cosmopolitan. Americans, French, Belgians, Dutch, Czechoslovakians, Norwegians and Poles were all stationed there.

However, Britain's links with the Commonwealth meant that there were also pilots and crews from further afield. Many did not return.

French agents took part in vital operations such as the destruction of hydro-electric power stations, aircraft, car and tyre factories, port facilities, trains, track, tunnels and bridges, the latter being attempts to delay German support reaching Normandy after the D-Day (Decision Day) landings.[4]

Analysis of the Squadrons' record books shows that between 1942 and 1945 there were 5,634 sorties from Tempsford to France. 138 Squadron took 995 agents and dropped an estimated 29,000 containers and 10,000 packages. Seventy of their planes failed to return but these were not only on missions to France. 161 Squadron parachuted 584 agents and an unspecified number of SIS agents into France, landed 422, including 190 SIS agents, and picked up 577, including 194 SIS personnel, at the loss of forty-nine aircraft.[5]

Exactly how many of the thirty-four documented French women agents were flown out from Tempsford or Tangmere is uncertain, but it is estimated that there were at least twenty. Of the estimated 1,500 agents, six were killed either by being dropped too low or by jumping without static lines attached to their parachutes. None of the women featured in this book suffered in this way. Across occupied Western Europe, there were around 5,500 dropping grounds.

Before D-Day, the Tempsford planes had dropped an estimated 2,151 million propaganda leaflets over the continent. Few, if any of the pilots and crew, recognised the role they played in the Allies' psychological warfare of disinformation and propaganda! Other missions flown from Tempsford included dropping pigeons.

People finding the pigeon container could open the canister attached to their leg, fill in the questionnaire with details about German gun emplacements, troop movements, etc. and then release the bird to fly back to its loft. Bletchley Park had a pigeon loft above the Station Commander's garage where agents' messages could be collected. Most messages were sent to Wing House, Piccadilly to be translated, transcribed and copies disseminated to the relevant section – Army, Navy, Air Force, MI6, MI9, etc. The information was then added to that already obtained by the decoders using the Enigma machine. This provided vital intelligence of the German, Italian and Japanese communications. Agents were sometimes given a pigeon to take in their jumpsuit so that they could release on landing to let London know they had arrived safely.

To give the pigeons a better chance of returning to the loft safely, a cull of peregrine falcons, the pigeon's major predator, was undertaken along the south coast of England. When the Germans realised what was happening, they introduced peregrine falcons along the Channel coast and ordered personnel along the Atlantic Wall to shoot down any overflying pigeons. Of the 16,554 birds dropped by the Tempsford squadrons, only 1,842 returned; an 11 per cent success rate. One message was reported to have said that its sister tasted really nice with peas![6]

Foot identified a number of problems that the SOE experienced in the first few years of the war. The Special Duties Squadrons experienced a shortage of available aircraft. The RAF was unwilling to allocate large numbers of planes to secret operations while there was a threat of German invasion. They wanted planes for bombing missions.

Not all the flights were successful. Bad weather, like fog, snow or strong winds at the airfield or reports of bad weather at the drop zone caused the RAF meteorologists to cancel the flight. The threat of being shot down by German night-flying aircraft, being caught in a searchlight, flying too close to an urban area, and being hit by 'ack-ack' (anti-aircraft fire), were all problems pilots had to try to avoid. Not being able to locate the flashing recognition torches of the reception committee or being flashed the wrong Morse code signal meant pilots aborted their mission and returned to base with their containers and agents. Some French women had several flights cancelled or aborted in this way, but there is no evidence any were in planes shot down.

6

Supplies for the Resistance Movements

One of the purposes of the Special Duties Squadrons was to provide supplies for the Resistance units across Europe. Given its size and population, most were sent into France. While you might be able to guess the most common items that were sent, the range was surprising. It is worth detailing everything: Sten guns, Bren guns, bazookas and PIATs (Projector Infantry Anti-Tank Guns), .33 Lee Enfield rifles, British Enfield, Webley, Smith & Wesson, and captured enemy revolvers and Parabellum (automatic pistols). They were also sent holsters, belts, ammunition, spares, hand grenades, mortar bombs, paraffin incendiaries, eye-shields, plastic and ordinary explosives, limpet bombs, petrol, oil, fire-pots, fog signals, flares, tyre bursters, tyre tearers, instantaneous detonator fuses, safety fuses, wires, trip wires, string, crimpers, detonators, percussion caps, magnets, matches, striker boards and timing devices.

Because of the nature of these items, these were dropped separately from the containers carrying printing presses, typewriters, printing ink, pencils, glue, adhesive tape, ordinary and miniature Kodak and Bantam cameras and film. Top quality Swiss watches were supplied to pilots, agents, the Maquis and Resistance networks, sometimes called circuits by F Section and réseaux by RF Section. Accuracy and precision were vital in secret operations.

Folding bicycles, bicycle pumps, bicycle repair kits, flashlights, torches, batteries, bulbs, spare tyres for lorries and bikes, oil and petrol were sent, all with foreign manufacturers' names stamped on them to avoid suspicion. Small bandage kits, surgical gloves and a compact medical and first-aid kit, suitable for units of ten men and upwards, were sent as well as air and seasickness pills and water purifying tablets. Underwater equipment including amphibian breathing apparatus, 'deep-water, quick-opening' steel containers, buoys, grapnels and several kinds of fishing tackle were packed in separate containers. Sunglasses, goggles, sleighs, skis, ski sticks, snowshoes, ice axes, rope, tents, Coleman stoves and hand grenades were needed in Norway. Even the parts of a Jeep were said to have been parachuted in.

Paper and stationery, balloons, newspapers, money, forged documents, soap, needles, first-aid kits, field dressings, Vaseline, medicines, haversacks, regimental panniers, blankets, sleeping bags and toilet paper were carefully packed in bucket bags and placed in 8 ft- (2.43 m) long aluminium containers. Splinter-proof windows were supplied so that the agents could build them into their observation posts. Rope ladders, jemmies (crowbars), wire cutters, wood saws, metal saws and 'Giglis' were sent. The Gigli was a flexible surgical saw of interlaced cutting wire, which could be concealed in a cap badge, an ordinary boot or shoelace. They were vital for evasion, being able to cut through wood and metal bars. Some bicycle pumps had torches specially built into the handle end. Compasses were hidden in specially made fountain pens, shaving brushes, hairbrushes, pipes, golf balls and dominoes. Miniature batteries and miniature cameras were sent. Tiny telescopes, 1½ inches long by ½ inch wide (39 x 13 mm), were made to look like cigarette lighters! These were some of what were called 'Q gadgets' provided by what the Ministry of Supply, euphemistically called the 'Clothing Department'. Charles Fraser-Smith, its head, noted in his wartime biography that,

Food supplies included concentrated blocks of sugar, tea, coffee and dried milk, tins of condensed milk, margarine, sardines, nut oil, biscuits, dried beef, sage and mutton, dried fruit, raisins, boiled sweets, tins of baked beans, bully beef, dried soup, powdered egg, powdered potato, jam, porridge oats and cigarettes. Half a million cigarettes were dropped in Holland for the Dutch resistance to sell on the black market to purchase information and to convert into currency.

Genuine French tobacco had to go into the making of the black cigarettes customarily smoked. Even matches had to be minutely copied in order to perfect the exact type of striking material used on their small boxes. It was entirely different to anything used in this country.

In a storeroom in London's Saville Row (actually under the famous police station there) we kept a mass of equipment of all sorts, besides clothing. Our foreign cigarettes were made for us by the British American Tobacco Company, with no detectable difference from the real thing. They only had one snag. When kept for any length of time, the tobacco used to dry and fall out. We then had to waste time replacing the stock with fresh supplies.[1]

Supplying British chocolates to France was a dead giveaway. French Menier chocolates and Swiss Nestlé chocolates were specially made in Britain to supply agents and the Resistance. Prisoners of war were sent special chocolate. Those who ate the blocks containing up to 45 per cent fat felt it was worth its weight in gold. Some were in the shape of a 'V' for Victory. However, the 'back-room boys', the technicians in the Clothing Department, had to be clever. The Germans were using ingenious chemicals to produce *ersatz* confections of all sorts. So, poorer quality sweets had to be supplied to the agents to avoid the prospect of them being found out.

Because of their delicate nature, portable wireless receivers and transmitters, hand generators, trickle chargers, spare dry batteries, voltmeters, hydrometers, medical supplies, blood plasma and other specialised tools were sent in panniers. These were wire and sacking cages, about 3 ft by 2 ft by 2 ft (1.05 m x 0.74 m x 0.74 m) and reinforced with horse hair, latex, and corrugated paper to absorb the impact.

Continental overcoats, hats, ties, shirts, perfumes and aftershave were sorted by country and stored ready to be distributed to the agents. There was clothing for professional, business and working-class men and women, large, old, leather suitcases for the professionals and small fibre suitcases for the others. Most people are not aware that when refugees arrived in this country from France, Germany, Netherlands, Belgium, Russia, Norway and Austria they were given British clothes. Their old clothes were collected and sent to the Thatched Barn (Station XV), SOE's camouflage research outfit, now a Holiday Inn, on the A1 in Borehamwood, north London. Painted in large letters on the wall of one of the workshops was the message, 'Silence is of the Gods ... only monkeys chatter.' It was top secret work. Leather briefcases, suitcases, shoes and gloves were treated to make them look old.

By 1944, supplying the Resistance was a vast operation. Steve Kippax's research into the history of the Air Liaison Movements (ALM) of the SOE revealed a great deal about the cylindrical steel containers. They resembled the water cylinder you might expect to see in your airing cupboard with special padding on the inside, 8 ft long by 18 in wide (2.96 x 0.55 m). There was a small recess at one end for a folded parachute. A shock-absorbing buffer was attached to the other. Weighing about 300 lb (136 kg) when loaded and planes taking between thirteen and eighteen containers, up to six tons of supplies could be taken per mission.

The Special Parachute Equipment Section was formed with a staff of thirty, mostly members of the WAAF. According to Rigden's *SOE Syllabus*,

From May 1942 to January 1945 this section, working in isolation, handled 19,863 packages, made 10,900 parachute harnesses and packed 27,980 parachutes, as well as doing much repair work. The section also became a centre of research into the use of parachutes in special operations.[2]

The record pack for one day, 6 July 1944, was 1,160 containers by a staff of 150, though ninety-six soldiers from the Pioneer Corps and 100 RAF men were drafted in occasionally to augment the workforce. German prisoners of war were also said to have been drafted in and some reports suggest that they may have sabotaged some containers.

When the Americans joined in these secret operations they had their own packing base at Area H, Holme Hall, close to the main London–Edinburgh railway line near Peterborough and about 28 miles (45 km) east of RAF Harrington. They employed more than 250 workers. Once the containers were ready, they were loaded into lorries and driven down to RAF Tempsford. They were offloaded and stored in corrugated-roofed Nissen huts on the northern outskirts of the airfield.

One container carrying agents' 'pay' fell off the bomb rack when it was being loaded, and its contents were spilt over the tarmac beneath the plane. A guard was immediately set up around it and each gold sovereign was retrieved and sent in a repaired container. There are claims that many groups in the French Resistance demanded gold as it was invaluable for getting supplies on the black market, bribing French and German prison guards, policemen, government officials, and even paying boat owners and guides to help take people out of the country.

Gold was in the form of British Sovereigns, US Gold Eagles, and Louis d'Or, but other funds were sent in a variety of negotiable manners – local currency, US Dollars, precious stones and valuable postage stamps.

There was an active trade in used banknotes in Lisbon, and at least one of the Geneva private banks had an arrangement with the British Treasury to provide large denomination French Franc banknotes against reimbursement after the war. The Banque Industrielle et Mobilière Privée in Paris ran some safe deposit boxes for Resistance networks.

Many millions of pounds were sent to the various Resistance groups, most raised by SOE's DF Section which smuggled money out of Europe as well as financing the escape lines. French businesses also loaned money to the Resistance. When taking local loans, a BBC 'message personal' would indicate to the lender that the loan terms had been agreed by London.

7

German Intelligence Services in France and Hitler's 'Commando Order'

Agents infiltrated into France faced numerous challenges, not just from the Germans but also from disagreements within the French Resistance groups. The Vichy intelligence service helped F Section but not RF Section as they did not support de Gaulle. The Communists distrusted right-wing groups, and there was little cooperation between the SOE and SIS.

The challenges they had to face from the Germans were Geheime Feldpolizei (GFP), the secret military police, the Abwehr, the German military intelligence service, the Sicherheitsdienst (SD), the security police, and Geheime Staatspolizei, Gestapo, their Security Service. There were also the Radio Defense departments of the Armed Forces and the police.

The greatest threat to the agents was the Gestapo. Their headquarters were at 72 Avenue Foch in Paris but they had numerous offices in adjoinging properties. Nos 82–24 Avenue Foch was where captured agents and members of the Resistance were taken for interrogation and sophisticated torture techniques.

The headquarters of the SD at 11 Rue de Saussaies, Paris was also used for interrogation. Fresnes Prison, in the suburb of Val-des-Marnes, was where both agents and Resistance members were incarcerated. Depending on their 'crimes', they were executed or transported to concentration/ extermination camps.

The Geheime Feldpolizei operated in fifty-man units in plain clothes on counter-espionage activities, counter-sabotage, detection of treasonable activities, counter-propaganda and the provision of assistance to the German Army in court-martial investigations. Their headquarters were at 128 Avenue de Wagram, Paris but they also requisitioned six hotels.

It ran the infamous Balard shooting range at Issy-les-Moulineaux, which was used to torture and execute 143 prisoners and oversaw the Brigades Spéciales, part of the Renseignements généraux. These units, which were part of the French police's intelligence service, specialised in tracing 'internal enemies', particularly Resistance groups, the Comet escape line, Jews and those evading forced labour.

Of all the German intelligence services, the most similar to the SOE was the Abwehr – German military intelligence which included officers in the Luftwaffe and Kriegsmarine. Their headquarters was at Hotel Lutetia, 43 Boulevard Raspard in Paris but they also had six offices across the city. Having acquired the French Sûreté de l'Etat files, they went on to amass intelligence on French citizens, including the various Resistance groups, as well as recruiting and training agents to be infiltrated into Britain. The Abwehr also had had dienstelle, offices, at Le Havre, Nantes, Angers, Lyons, Bordeaux, Marseilles, and Arras.

Following the Abwehr's successful infiltration of Dutch Resistance networks and the turning of captured wireless operators in what became known as 'Operation North Pole' or the 'Englandspiel'. some of their experts were sent to the Gestapo's Radio and Telegraph office at 78 Avenue Foch. There were staff on shifts keeping a continuous lookout for 'enemy' wireless operator signals.

Wireless operators were told by their SOE trainers that transmitting for more than thirty minutes was suicidal. Fifteen minutes was the maximum as that was the amount of time the direction finders needed to triangulate their position. Changing locations regularly was essential, as was having a minder, someone to warn them when the police or Gestapo was nearby.

The SOE called the direction finders 'D-Fers' while the French called them goniometrists or more commonly 'gonios'. They hid their detection equipment in bakers' vans or ambulances and drove around trying to pick up a transmission signal. A bearing from north was taken and plotted on a map. They then drove away, picked up the signal and plotted its bearing on the map. Taking a third and plotting it on the map ought to identify where the lines crossed the area where the wireless operator was transmitting. In rural areas, it was easier to locate the building. In urban areas, once a location was identified, a man with a receiver hidden under his coat and headphones under his hat would then attempt to locate the apartment, removing fuses one by one from the outside fuse box until the transmission stopped. The Gestapo, armed with revolvers and accompanied by Alsatian dogs, would then attempt to arrest the operator before they had a chance to hide the set, codes, incriminating papers, etc. or take their suicide pill.

It was common for the Abwehr to 'encourage' them, either by torture, financial bribes or threats to family and friends, to reveal their codes and transmit German-inspired messages to London. Sometimes a tape recording of their transmission was taken and a German wireless expert would learn from their 'fist', their style of transmitting, how to copy it and transmit themselves.

Many wireless operators were caught and turned in this way which was why SOE added to their agents' training the requirement to include a security check in their message. This could be a deliberate misspelling of the sixteenth word, for example. If it was not included, SOE would know the agent was compromised.

Unfortunately, on several occasions, captured agents omitted this check and then got the message back from the wireless operator at Grendon Hall, where SOE and SIS transmissions were picked up and decoded, that they had omitted to include it and not to forget the next time. The Germans were able to decode this reply and the agent, irritated that he or she had been caught out, agreed to work for the Germans. As a consequence, the Germans were able to request the most modern wireless equipment, more quartz crystals, which provided the right frequency for the transmission, modern weapons, ammunition, money as well as more agents. As the Germans then controlled some of these sets, they could arrest agents on landing or follow them to identify safe houses and other members of the Resistance. A number of women were captured in this way.

The Sicherheitsdienst in France oversaw security in the occupied zone and Belgium. Its officers were involved in the deportation of the Jews and the execution of thousands of French citizens, as well as locating and arresting the agents sent into France, infiltrating double agents and amassing intelligence on the British intelligence services.[1]

Other threats included the milice, a French paramilitary organisation set up by the Vichy government who liaised with the Germans in anti-Resistance activities. Most railway stations had controls, checkpoints, where tickets, travel passes and identity papers were checked. Having up-to-date knowledge of what regulations were in place was a top priority for F and RF Sections. Acquiring copies which could be forged, helped provide greater security for their agents.

The Gestapo in Paris utilised the 'Carlingue', a gang of up to 30,000 paid French collaborators under the command of Pierre Bonny, a corrupt ex-policeman. They also recruited Henri Lafont's criminal gang to arrest, torture and extract money and jewels from anti-German residents as well as to infiltrate escape lines, réseaux, and deport Jews.

Following the German takeover of the Unoccupied Zone, SS-Hauptsturmführer Klaus Barbie was transferred from Amsterdam to head the Gestapo in Lyon. Barbie is reported to have been personally involved in the torture and interrogation of about 10,000 Resistance members and there are claims that the Gestapo in France were responsible for the deaths of around 75,000 Jews and 60,000 Resistance members.[2]

There was competition between many of these agencies, particularly for funding but also for the prestige they were given by Hitler for successful operations. There were also political differences, the Abwehr being seen as anti-Nazi. The Abwehr had its own wireless listening stations and were keen to turn captured wireless operators, whereas the Gestapo were more keen on getting whatever intelligence they could about the Allies' intelligence services' planning and operations – even using torture.

On 7 October 1942, three days after the Allied Commando raid on Dieppe, the daily Wehrmacht communiqué stated that, 'all terrorist and sabotage troops of the British and their accomplices who do not act like soldiers but rather like bandits will be treated as such by the German troops and will be ruthlessly eliminated in battle whenever they appear.' On 18 October, Hitler issued his top secret *Führerbefehl*, or Commando Order, which stated that,

I therefore order that from now on, all opponents engaged in so-called commando operations in Europe or Africa, even when it is outwardly a matter of soldiers in uniform or demolition parties with or without weapons, are to be exterminated to the last man in battle or in fight. In these cases, it is immaterial whether they are landed for their operations by ship, or aeroplane, or descent by parachute. Even should these individuals, on being discovered, make as if to surrender, 1 quarter is to be denied on principle. [He later added that] I have been compelled to issue strict orders for the destruction of enemy sabotage troops and declare non-compliance severely punishable ... It must be made clear to the enemy that all sabotage troops will be exterminated, without exception, to the last man. That means that their chances of escaping with their lives in nil. Under no circumstances can they be expected to be treated according to the rules of the Geneva Convention. If it should become necessary for reasons of interrogation to initially spare one man or two, then they are to be shot immediately after interrogation. This order is intended for commanders only and must not under any circumstances fall into enemy hands.[3]

While some of the French women agents were involved in sabotage operations, most of those arrested and executed were couriers or wireless operators. It needs to be stressed that, as Hitler's Commando Order was top secret, it was only later in the war when SOE learned that captured SOE agents were being tortured and executed. SOE instructors told the women students that, as they had been given a military rank in the FANY or WAAF, all they needed to divulge if caught and questioned and their cover story was not believed was their name, rank and serial number. However, from the evidence, it appears that most kept to their cover stories, even under torture

Sending Women into Occupied Europe

Secrecy was vital. All agents and staff had to sign the Official Secrets Act, what some called 'The Poison Book', and the women were forbidden to talk to anyone about their work – boyfriends, husbands, fathers, mothers, brothers, sisters or friends. 'Anybody who comes here is not expected to ask questions. You will find out what you need to know, but always keep your own mouth shut.' The Military Police were very active, keeping their eyes and ears open. Anyone suspected of leaking secrets was temporarily removed from circulation. Their bed would be empty, and blankets folded ready for the next recruit. As has been mentioned, the only address the women could give family and friends was 'Room 98, Horseguards, London SW1'. Their mail was collected and then brought to the stations by despatch riders.

Known as 'The Organisation', 'The Org' or 'The Racket', 'The Outfit', or 'The Firm' by those 'in the know', the SOE appointed numerous women to its administrative staff. Squadron Leader Beryl Escott, the WAAF historian, approximated about 3,200 out of a total staff of 13,200, whereas the Air Ministry only had 300.

The taboo of women using arms was abandoned by the SOE when they recognised them as being badly needed in occupied Europe, and they needed to be able to defend themselves like any man. Jepson argued that the Geneva Convention did not relate to modern war which involved wholesale involvement of civilian populations. As he put it, 'Air-raid bombs that demolish homes and kill children bring to every woman by every natural law the right to protect, to seek out and destroy the evil behind these bombs by all means possible to her – including the physical and militant.'[1]

Many in government and the military establishment, both French and British, did not consider sending women into action the right thing to do.

Rules had to be broken therefore to send them out. As women in the armed forces were not allowed to carry weapons and engage in combat, the SOE gave female agents commissions in the FANY as it was a civilian organisation with no such restrictions. Others were given commissions in the WAAF, Corps de Volontaires Françaises or the Corps des Auxiliares Féminins de l'Armée de Terre.

Some considered FANY agents as 'cap badge FANYs', commissioned into the service as a cover while they were on operations. Should they be captured they could claim to be an officer in the FANY in an attempt to ensure that they would be treated as prisoners of war according to the Geneva Convention and not be sentenced to death without trial. According to Sue Ryder, a FANY officer who drove Polish agents to Tempsford,

> FANYs too were dropped behind enemy lines by parachute or landed by Lysander aircraft. They took part in armed resistance and sabotage and, in the course of their everyday duties, travelled many miles carrying information, arms, and often wireless parts, bluffing their way through enemy posts. The necessity for being constantly on the alert in enemy-occupied territory was an appalling strain. During the war a number of FANYs were captured, tortured and executed; a few died in concentration camps, others were killed in action, some survived.[2]

Becoming a FANY member provided a plausible reason for their family and friends to explain why they were away from home and allowed them to undergo the specialist training without any awkward questions. Eleven French women were given commissions in the FANY and one in the WAAF.

Their uniform was khaki drill, KD as it was known, a lightweight four-pocket jacket and divided skirt, battledress and tin hat. They had two hats, a peaked, khaki service cap with leather strap over the crown and the FANY 'bonnet', a khaki beret with maroon flash and the Corps badge on it – a Maltese Cross in a circle. Ryder explained that it meant self-sacrifice to achieve unity and service. Jane Buckland, an 18-year-old FANY and trainee radio operator, said that 'the nicest part of her uniform was the most beautiful Sam Brownes, lovely wide belts which we had to polish all the time. It was just like the army — we were in the army, but special.'[3] The uniform of the Corps de Volontaires Françaises or the Corps des Auxiliares Féminins de l'Armée de Terre was virtually the same.

After a certain date in spring, KD had to be worn with the sleeves rolled up above the elbow. Those who were posted overseas stocked up with boot polish and soap and were given an extra allowance of coupons to buy items of uniform. Those in charge wore the round, cherry-coloured insignia of a commander on their epaulettes, which signified that they had served during the First World War. They were nicknamed 'raspberry tarts' by the younger members but greatly revered. There were few written rules but there was a strong *esprit de corps* and discipline among them.

The reality for the agents was that, if they were caught in civilian clothes and found to have been sent by the British, they would in all likelihood be interrogated and tortured to get any useful information out of them, and then executed. What they did not know was the types of torture they might experience if caught.

As a lecturer in Modern British History at Strathclyde University, Juliette Pattinson specialised in gender and examined the testimonies from those who survived imprisonment. She reported women being beaten with implements, kicked about the body, had toenails extracted, toes trampled upon by boots, chained to furniture, deprived of sleep, forced to stay awake during many hours of interrogation, deprived of light, food and medical treatment for wounds, threatened with mock executions, had their fingers crushed, immersed in water to the point of drowning, burned with hot pokers, hearing others being tortured or shot, subjected to electric currents passing through their bodies, and kept in solitary confinement. Agents reported numerous injuries including broken ribs, fractured fingers, teeth being knocked out as well as suffering bruises and cuts. Pattinson's interviews with three of the women who were repatriated found that they were all beaten and badly mistreated with distinct sexist and sexual overtones.[4]

Sue Ryder commented that, 'All the men and women who trained as agents had to be in top mental and physical condition and possess initiative; they were self-reliant and discreet and capable of standing up to rough and arduous training and work.'[5] The female agents were generally much younger than their male counterparts.

It was thought early in the war that French women were rarely stopped, but, as it progressed, most women were subject to 'controls', stopped and searched as well. What was true was that they made excellent cover while travelling around the country on bicycles taking messages, papers, money, weapons, sabotage and wireless equipment while pretending to be going shopping, collecting milk and eggs from a farm, foraging for nuts, mushrooms, fruit and berries in the countryside, or visiting friends. It was thought that the Germans would not expect women to be involved in Resistance activities. They were expected to be fulfilling the traditional roles of 'Kinder, Kirche und Küche' (Children, Church and Kitchen). They were slow to realise that young, attractive women could be politicised and intent of carrying out deadly work. While there were circumstances when a bike was vital for getting around, for long journeys it was recommended that the women travelled first class on the trains as the Germans were less likely to thoroughly search wealthy middle-class passengers than those in third-class compartments. Businessmen and Germans who travelled in first class did not want the police to annoy them. The women were taught to hide incriminating items where they would least likely to be found. Objects in false-bottomed bags, inside bicycle frames or bicycle tyres, nder dress belts, under the soles of stockings, inside powder compacts or even inside long hair had less chance of detection during perfunctory searches. Should their cover story be doubted, they had to expect a full body search.

Women were also thought to be more resourceful and composed than men and could better talk themselves out of tight spots at checkpoints using their feminine charms. They were also more inventive, conjuring ingenious cover stories. Questions they had to be able to answer were, 'Where did you get your laundry cleaned?' or 'Where did you get your hair done?'

Although there was concern expressed about sending women into occupied Europe on dangerous missions, Colonel Gubbins, the then head of SOE, argued that they would be less conspicuous and find it much easier to get accommodation than men. In Foot's *SOE in France* he expressed the opinion:

> By no means all of F Section's women agents had that ordinary, unassuming air which is so precious an asset for a clandestine; several had the stunning good looks and vibrant personality that turn men's heads in the street. This helped to make them noticed; it was counterbalanced, in the sections' view, by making it more easy for them to appear to belong to that leisured class, the comings and goings of which only the surliest policeman is ever going to disturb. It was a mistake to forget how surly some of Hitler's or even Pétain's [Prime Minister of Vichy government] policemen could be.[6]

Flight Officer Yeo-Thomas, while in France, had assisted Jean Moulin, who had been sent to unite the left and right-wing Resistance groups into a Secret Army, which was commanded by General Charles Delestraint but under Allied direction. On returning from his first mission in mid-April 1943, he got the chance to speak with Churchill about the difficulties that many French Resistance groups were experiencing, particularly with lack of arms, ammunition, and explosives but also due to the lack of wireless sets. Churchill's response was to order an additional 100 planes for the Special Duties Squadrons. Although the order was given, that number was never realised, but it helped increase significantly the number of operations possible throughout the rest of 1943 and leading up to D-Day.

Returning from his second trip, he warned SOE that the German proposal to raise the age limit for compulsory work service, first to 42 and then to the middle-50s, would reduce the strength of the Secret Army in France. He suggested that the BBC and SOE use whatever means they could to encourage Frenchmen to avoid conscription by leaving the country or living clandestinely as members of the Resistance in the countryside. Money needed to be sent, as well as weapons, ammunition, food and forged identity and ration cards, so they could survive and defend themselves. He was convinced that these deserters, financed by Britain, armed and trained by SOE agents, would form the nucleus of a Secret Army. The concept of the Maquis was born. The result was that women would be much more visible on the streets than men. It was the ideal opportunity for F and RF Section to increase the numbers of women agents. They could invent a hundred cover stories as they could travel extensively and arouse little suspicion.[7] Escott commented that women

> ...often substituted for a missing husband or brother, as the wage earner of the family. They searched for missing relatives or children. They covered incredible distances hunting for scarce items of fuel or clothing and particularly on a regular search for food to feed their families, with the fierce and protective care that distinguishes a mother for her children. They were to be found on all the roads—in their locality and out of it—most going about their lawful and innocent duties equipped with the legal and correct passes and papers required of every French citizen. A girl on a bike with a carrier was therefore, a common sight everywhere, and the Germans had such a stereotyped idea of the role of women that it could take a long time before they would suspect one of being an agent. She was therefore more unobtrusive and less liable to be caught. She might also to be able to use more charm and devious wiles that might hoodwink a questioner. Many trainers objected, but they soon discovered that women could be just as skilful and brave as men, and this was soon proved in the field, where they had to overcome the extra obstacle of the ingrained prejudice to women of the people in the countries where they worked, no small task in itself. Thus the most unlikely of agents became assets.[8]

Exactly how many women were sent into occupied Europe is uncertain. The number of women SOE took on as agents is thought to have been over eighty but not all passed the training. F Section sent thirty-nine women into France and RF Section 11 but there were others belonging to SIS and the French, American and even the Soviet intelligence services. There are documented cases of over eighty, at least thirty-four of whom were French. Unofficially, there were more as the SIS sent in women as prostitutes but their records, if they still exist, have yet to be released from MI6's archive into the public domain. Hugh Verity, one of the 161 Squadron Lysander pilots, commented in his autobiography that 'There were a number of different clients, none of whom wanted any of the others to know about their operations. In fact, SIS forbade any written matter. Their operations were "officially inadmissible."'[9]

While the majority were flown out from Tempsford, others were sent from Tangmere, Harrington and in one case, Waterbeach, near Cambridge. A few were sent by motor gunboats in the middle of the night to remote beaches in Normandy or Brittany and some by boat to Gibraltar from where a felucca, a 40-foot-long, narrow beamed, 20-ton wooden sardine trawler, commonly used along the North African coast, would take them to the Mediterranean coast of France. Three women were sent to Belgium, three to Holland, three to Germany, but the rest were sent into France. There are also records of French women being infiltrated by plane from Algeria later in the war.

While most of the French female agents were unmarried, a few were divorced or in failed relationships. A number were married, several had children and one was a grandmother. There was also one mother-and-daughter team. Before joining, the women had been told that their chances of survival were about evens, but in fact something like three agents in four survived. Of those sent to France, thirteen made the ultimate sacrifice.

The first hint in the British media of these women's roles during the war was not until 11 March 1945. The *Sunday Express* included an article on them by Squadron Leader William Simpson, DFC (Distinguished Flying Cross). As there was no mention of the FANY officers infiltrated, it suggests the secret had been kept.

WAAF girls parachuted into France

Who are the Waaf officers who parachuted into France to join the Maquis months before D-Day?

This question has plagued Air Ministry officials ever since Sir Archibald Sinclair [Leader of Liberal Party] praised Waaf parachutists in the House of Commons last week.

Officially it remains unanswered – for reasons of security. Two only have been named in the press. One Sonia d'Artois (née Butt), is the young daughter of a group captain. She married the French-Canadian officer who jumped with her.

The other, Maureen O'Sullivan, is also young and pretty. She comes from Dublin.

Demure girls

The interesting thing about these girls is they are not hearty and horsey young women with masculine chins. They are pretty young girls who would look demure and sweet in crinolines. Most of them are English girls who speak perfect French. Some were educated in French convents; others attended Swiss finishing schools. A few are French girls who escaped from France and agitated for a chance to go back and work underground. Cool courage, intelligence, and adaptability are their most important attributes. They have to be able to pass themselves off as tough country wenches, and smart Parisiennes.

They were taught parachute jumping in the North of England. They trained with male agents and paratroopers of all nationalities, and leapt with them from fixed balloons and moving aircraft.

But parachuting was a secondary part of their training. They also had to absorb complicated secret details of underground organisation and train the Maquis in radio operating.

After months of intensive training, there often followed weeks of anxious waiting. Then, dressed in the appropriate French civilian clothes of their first role, they were flown by night bomber into moonlit France.

Sometime they dropped 'free' at a pre-determined point. On landing, they tended for themselves; reported to a friendly farmer, then set off at dawn to contact the leader of their resistance group.

Usually, however, they landed with arms and food, floating down with the packages and containers. As a courier, she went from group to group of the Maquis. It was easier for a girl to pass unnoticed in a France stripped of men by the Germans.

Great courage

Often she was on the spot when supplies were dropped, and helped to unload and hide the containers.

It sounds easy enough. In fact, it is about the most cold-blooded and creepy task that any young woman could choose.

Death and torture are present realities. Atrocity details are well known. There were traitors in the Maquis itself working to betray. Sometimes they succeeded.

But so great was the courage and spirit of these girls that they could afford to send back humorous messages.

One – behind with routine signals – complained that what with washing and darning, and running around with messages, she had little time for routine work!

Another, who had walked for weeks to return to France, had to jump over Kent – due to engine trouble in the bomber which carried her. As soon as she had collected herself, she asked to be allowed to go on with the job the same night.

Behind the veil of secrecy, not yet raised by the Air Ministry, there are great stories of courage and endurance.

For the agent has no status; no friendly uniform or consul to rely on. With her friends she is outside the law – until it catches up with her.

Her first aim

There was one girl I met in Vichy France four years ago. Since then, although not in the Waaf, she has been back and forth many times. Acting as courier and radio operator, she has also organised Maquis bands. No doubt she has fought with arms, for her first aim is to kill Germans.

Amongst her perilous adventures are included escapes over the Pyrénées into Spain. And she knows the filth, discomfort and despair of Spanish prison camps. But nothing could dismay her. She went on.

All these unknown young girls of the Waaf have proved one thing for ever. The toughest tests of courage and endurance faced by men can be passed with honour by women.[10]

9

Preparing for the Drop

Once the agents arrived at Tempsford, they were driven around the eastern perimeter track to Gibraltar Farm. Inside they were given a final chance to look at the aerial photographs and Michelin maps of their drop zone or landing strip, the location of a safe house and the nearest bus or train station. Their conducting officer then escorted them into the barn.

Checks were made on their clothes, shoes, and other belongings. No British tags were to be on them, no used bus or train tickets, cigarette packets or matchboxes, no initialled handkerchief. Shoes had not to be new so as to arouse suspicion. Their hair had previously been cut in the appropriate style of the country they were going to, and even teeth were checked to ensure that the SOE dentist had replaced fillings with the appropriate gold.

If they were to be parachuted in, their ankles were strapped with bandages to give better support, and they were given stout boots with rubber cushions under their heels to further reduce the chances of injury on landing. There were also knee pads, spine pads, elbow pads, shoulder pads and a 'Sorbo' helmet to give them added protection. Just the same as the men, the women were dressed in a 'striptease' outfit, a heavy canvas jumpsuit, suitably camouflaged with patches of green and mustard brown. They had extra wide legs and arms to fit over the agents' ordinary clothes. They had two zips down the front to help them get out of it quickly when they landed and spacious pockets into which went a dagger, hard rations, a flashlight, first-aid equipment, wireless parts, secret maps, and papers. The RAF Air Liaison Officer in charge would refer to them only by their code name. Their passwords, messages, and other information were checked to see that they had learnt them off by heart.

The cashier would issue them with foreign documents, enough forged foreign currency to run a Resistance operation and a collection of loose change for use on arrival. The serial numbers were never consecutive, and notes were often trampled on to give them a slightly tattered look. A harness was fastened over the 'jump suit' and a parachute attached. Many were given a Colt revolver and bullets. Other useful items included a jack knife to cut through the parachute rigging should it be snagged, a folding shovel to bury the parachute and be used as a splint if bones were broken, a hip flask full of rum, brandy or whisky, a tin of sandwiches for the flight, French cigarettes and their choice of drugs. In his book *SOE AGENT: Churchill's Secret Warriors* Terry Crowdy mentions them:

> 'A' tablets for airsickness; (blue) 'B' pills containing Benzedrine (sulphate) for use as a stimulant (the amphetamine Mecrodrin was also issued); the 'E' pill: a quick-working anaesthetic that would knock a person out in 30 seconds; 'K' pills for inducing sleep and 'L' pills.[1]

'L' pills, should they decide to take them, were lethal potassium cyanide crystals in a biteable-through thin rubber coating and hidden in the top inside part of their jacket, in hollowed-out wine bottle corks or tubes of lipstick. You would be dead in fifteen seconds. Agents were told that the Catholic Church had given them a special dispensation to use the pill 'in extremis'. The final thing to be given was a good luck gift. This might be cufflinks, a cigarette case, powder compact or a piece of jewellery – a reminder that SOE was thinking of them. When they ran out of money, they were told it could be pawned or sold on the black market.

Some of these smaller items were used to conceal codes, messages, and microscopic photographs. Hiding places included fountain pens, pencils, wallets, bath salts, shaving sticks, toothpaste, talcum powder, lipsticks, manicure sets, sponges, penknives, shoe heels and soles, shoulder padding, collar studs, coat buttons, and cigarette lighters. SOE boffins at Aston House, near Stevenage, developed a 2⅝ by ⅝ inch aluminium cylinder as a rectal/vaginal container. It could be unscrewed in the middle and the message inserted. Understandably, no mention of their use appeared in any of the women's stories.

Sue Ryder, one of the FANYs who accompanied Polish agents to Tempsford, commented that,

> Though the pre-mission hours were naturally very tense, there was also a wonderful sense of humour and cheerfulness among the Bods. I can't remember any false bravado; on the contrary, it was real wit that came through. No written word can recapture the warmth of the atmosphere throughout the station. Whenever the atmosphere was especially tense or a feeling of dread prevailed, someone in the small group would

rally the spirits of the others. They had, too, an extraordinary humility and a religious faith which was exemplified in the way they prepared themselves for their missions, such as making their confessions to a priest who would come to the ops station especially for this purpose.[2]

Once they were ready, their accompanying officer would take them outside to the perimeter track where the aircraft was waiting. Atkins was reported to have attended the departure of F Section women to give them moral support. On occasions, Buckmaster was there to see them off.

Usually waiting by the plane was the station's Padre in his black cloak, cassock and surplice, offering departing agents God's blessing. Maybe he had become immune to the commonly used farewell phrase of departing 'Joes' – '*Merde*'. He was also reported to be waiting for the pilots and aircrews on their return.

If they were flown by Lysander, they climbed the ladder and into the space behind the pilot where there were two wooden seats facing each other. The luggage, a valise and perhaps a wireless set were passed up and stored beneath the seats. The pilot set up a link so he could communicate with them. The Perspex cover was slid closed, and the plane would taxi to the runway and take off.

Once on board the Whitley, Halifax, Stirling or Liberator, it was the job of the despatcher to make the agents comfortable. Wing Commander Percy Pickard of 161 Squadron was particularly kind to what he called his 'female passengers'. He used to hand over the controls to his co-pilot and go to the back of the plane to sit with them to put them at their ease by chatting. It was often too noisy for lengthy conversations but appreciated nonetheless.

Once the planes had left, there was an opportunity for the staff and ground crew to get some rest. However, they had to be ready to welcome planes returning from their mission when the pilot reported 'duties carried out' or 'duties not carried out'. As mentioned earlier, should the flight have been aborted, arrangements had to be made to accommodate the agents until a replacement was available. This could have meant a wait of several weeks until the next moon period.

The same procedures would have been carried out at Tangmere Cottage, near RAF Tangmere, where the Lysander Flight was based during the moon period. Yvonne George, another WAAF mentioned in Escott's book, said that she liaised between SOE and SIS headquarters, phoning the Intelligence Officer at Tempsford, who, depending on the availability of aircraft and the meteorological report, would decide whether a flight was possible:

On one occasion I was at Tangmere to see the take-off of an aircraft with three agents on board and waited until about 3 am., early morning, for its return. As one of them alighted, I caught a strong smell of Guerlain perfume—something we in England had not known for some years![3]

The Special Duties Squadrons and the Carpetbagger crews were completely ignorant of the women's missions. They were not supposed to know. They undoubtedly heard on the grapevine, or sometimes first-hand, what happened to their colleagues if they crash-landed behind the lines and survived. If they were very lucky, they themselves might be rescued by the Resistance and sent down one of the escape lines back to Britain. However, there was always the chance of being captured and imprisoned. As prisoners of war, they knew they would be reasonably well-treated until the end of the war. However, they probably guessed what happened to captured agents, especially women. The details of what happened to the French women only came to light after the war ended.

10

French Women Infiltrated in 1942

Contrary to most of the accepted literature dealing with the British Intelligence Services' infiltration of agents into France during the Second World War, the first woman was 31-year-old Chilean-born Giliana Gerson (*née* Balmaceda). A beautiful young actress, she was working in theatres in Paris in the 1930s and married Victor Gerson, a British rug and carpet dealer, who had settled in the capital after fighting in the First World War. His first wife had died, and his son was killed in a road accident. They fled to England in June 1940, where both were recruited into the SOE.[1]

In Edward Cookridge's *Inside SOE*, he mentions Victor Gerson suggesting to Leslie Humphries, the Head of SOE's clandestine communications and escape routes, that he and his wife could help set up an escape line to get people across the Pyrénées into neutral Spain. From there, British embassy and consulate staff could arrange their return to Britian via Gibraltar or Lisbon. Giliana volunteered to use her Chilean passport to return to France, crossing the frontier legally from Spain, contact people she thought might help and collect intelligence and documents useful for the SOE. Her idea was agreed and arrangements were made to send her.

In May 1941, she made her way north to Lyon, where, as well as amassing intelligence on Pétain's government, she met several Spanish ex-Republicans who were prepared to help with the planned escape route and collected documents that could be reproduced by the SOE for its undercover agents in France.

According to Escott, acting as if she was a tourist, she pretended to be lost, asked lots of innocent questions and people trusted her with her brilliant smile.

With her sharp eyes and the retentive memory of an actress, she wandered unrebuked into forbidden areas. She learned about the passes and papers people had to keep on their persons at all times. She watched for the extent of railway and bus controls and collected timetables and information on all kinds of transport. She discovered the legal and illegal ways of crossing between the occupied and unoccupied zones, the checks on hotels and lodging houses, the times of curfew and penalties for breaking it. She copied ration cards and noted prices of foods and shortages of all kinds. In the cafés, she tested the reactions of the French to the German occupation and cultivated useful contacts for the future.[2]

In mid-June she left the country and went first to Madrid, visiting a contact in the British Embassy, and then to Gibraltar, from where she was returned to London, bringing back valuable information.

A few months after her return, on 6 September 1941, Victor was dropped by parachute near Chateauroux, and he went on to set up groups of resisters in the Lyon area, what became known as the 'Vic' escape line.

The next woman infiltrated into France was Virginia Hall, a 35-year-old American agent who had travelled around Europe with her parents and studied in France, Germany and Austria. After working in the American Consulate in Warsaw, her chance of a future in the diplomatic service was thwarted by a hunting accident in Turkey which led to her having the lower part of her left leg amputated and replaced with a wooden stump which she called 'Cuthbert'. Events in Europe led her to resign in 1939 to take up graduate studies in Washington, United States.[3]

When the war started, she was in Paris where she volunteered for the French Ambulance Service, but, as her wooden leg proved a difficulty, she moved to Vichy following the armistice and managed to escape to England via Spain.

After working for a few months at the American Embassy in London, she was recruited by SOE who recognised her language and diplomatic skills as being valuable in the field. As the United States had not declared war on Germany at that time, she was free to visit France. Having an American passport made her travel arrangements simpler. On 23 August 1941, after eight months' training, she was flown to Lisbon where she caught a Lufthansa flight to Barcelona and a train to Vichy.[4]

Using her cover as the foreign correspondent of the *New York Post*, she acquired a safe house in Lyon and created her own HECKLER network helping newly arrived SOE agents, collecting intelligence and arranging its transfer back to London. The rest of her story can be read in Escott's *The Heroines of SOE*.

On 10 January 1942, SOE arranged for a motor gunboat to land 26-year-old Jeannette Dupont in Lannion Bay on the northwest Normandy coast. Her poor health meant she could not be dropped by parachute. It was not her real name, and she was not French. She was Szyfra Lipszyc, also known as Anna Ouspenskaya, code named Hannah, from Warsaw, Poland, who was one of more than thirty Soviet agents sent to Britain as part of Operation *Pickaxe*, a secret agreement between Churchill and Joseph Stalin, to be infiltrated by the SOE into Western Europe.

Research by Guillaume Bourgeois and Donal O'Sullivan revealed that, after studying medicine in Caen, she worked as a waitress in a bar in Toulouse and was thought to have joined the Comintern, Communist International. During the Spanish Civil War, she fought with the International Brigade, and, trained in sabotage, was thought to have worked with the Pozo Rubio detachment before being captured.

After her release from a Spanish prison, she returned to Poland via Sweden and Latvia before going to Russia where she was selected to train as an agent to be infiltrated back into France. Her mission was to contact the Soviet network at 118 Boulevard Raspail in Paris, whose people, known as the Red Orchestra, had been cut off from Moscow following the German invasion. She had to deliver instructions and provide them with funds and new codes for their wireless sets.

In Paris, she rendezvoused with Robert Beck, known as Roma, the head of the Communist Action Network and someone called Gustav. Until her arrest in Pithiviers with Gilbert Bacot, on 1 July 1942, she admitted following instructions and burning grain crops and reserves of straw destined for the Wehrmacht. It is thought she betrayed Beck, probably under torture, as he was arrested shortly after her. He was executed and although she too was sentenced to death, no evidence has come to light confirming the order was carried out.[5]

THE AGENTS

Of the thirty-six documented cases of French women infiltrated into France, six escaped during and immediately after the German invasion, thirteen were subsequently brought back by plane or escaped to Britain over the Pyrénées, seven were living in North Africa and were infiltrated from Algiers, and the rest were already living in Britain.

Eleven were given a commission in the FANY and one in the WAAF. Six joined the Corps Auxiliaire Féminin in London, two joined the SUSSEX Plan, an SIS/BCRA operation; seven joined the Corps Féminin des Transmissions in Algiers, and there was no evidence that the others were given any commission.

Of those infiltrated from Britain, one went by motor gunboat, one by a Liberator, two by felucca, two by a Whitley, three by a Hudson, four by Lysander and thirteen by a Halifax. Those infiltrated from Algiers were parachuted from American Liberators.

They were very brave women to do what they did, knowing that the consequences of capture included interrogation, torture, imprisonment and deportation. What follows are accounts of their lives, particularly their wartime experiences, based on SOE's personnel records, mission papers, intelligence reports, pilots' reports as well as articles in newspapers and academic journals and accounts found in history books and on websites.

'ANATOLE'
Landed by Lysander near St Saëns between Dieppe and Rouen (Seine-Maritime) on 28 February 1942.

The real identity of the fourth woman infiltrated into France is unknown. She appears to have been French but not enough evidence has come to light to confirm it. In Hugh Verity's *We Landed by Moonlight*, he mentions her being landed by Lysander in late February 1942.

> For Operation 'Baccarat' Murphy took off [from RAF Tangmere] at 2145 on 27 February. He found solid cloud cover over the French coast at 1,000 ft and only 3,000 yards visibility below. Failing to fix his position near Abbeville, he flew north-west until he could get a radio fix from base. Then he found Abbeville and set course for St Saëns where, at midnight, he landed one passenger and picked up two, including Rémy.
>
> The new arrival in France was an unknown young woman called 'Anatole'. Rémy reported: 'She laughs, very happy to be back in France. I understand that she totally vanished.'[6]

Le Service Historique de la Défense (SHD) catalogue of Resistance personnel at Vincennes holds about 607,000 personnel records, of which about 31,000 are women. Of these, none has an alias or a forename resembling 'Anatole'. Clearly Verity used this name to disguise her real identity. She was probably one of SIS's women agents.

Freddie Clark did not mention 'Anatole' but confirmed that Murphy's mission was 161 Squadron's first Lysander operation for SIS. In Pierre Tillet's list of infiltrations into France, he identifies Remy as the code name of Gilbert Renault, the other passenger being Pierre Julitte. Renault, code named Colonel Remy, was a Breton insurance executive who had set up an important Resistance network in the Normandy area.

With the assistance of Louis de la Bardonnie, he created the Confrérie Notre Dame and Centurie intelligence-gathering networks.

FRANÇINE FROMONT
Aged 25. Parachuted from a Whitley near Montpellier (Languedoc-Roussillon) on the night of 3/4 March 1942. Executed at Fresnes Prison, Paris.

The first acknowledged Frenchwoman to be parachuted into France was Françine Fromont, another Soviet agent. Her Russian name was Anna Frolova, but she used the aliases Annette Fauberge, Jeanne-Claude Garnier, Marie-Claude Valant, Fernande Guyot and the code name Coutourier.

In Freddie Clark's *Agents by Moonlight*, he used the Operations Record Books of 138 and 161 Special Duties Squadrons to provide a detailed chronological account of their top-secret flights between 1941 and 1945 to help the Resistance groups in occupied Europe. He mentioned that on 12 February 1942, the Soviet ship SS *Arcos* docked in a Scottish port and five passengers disembarked. Which port it was, who the passengers were, who they were met by, where they were taken and what they did over the following few weeks was not stated but, on 4 March, he wrote that three of them arrived at Tempsford, were flown out and parachuted into the Mediterranean area of France.

He added that they were NKVD agents, one of them a woman, and that their mission was to set up a radio link between Lyon and Moscow. The NKVD (*Norodny Kommissariat Vnutrennich Dyel*) was the Soviet People's Commissariat for Internal Affairs – the forerunner of the KGB (*Komitet Gosudarstvennoi Besopastnosti*).

In the research for my book on Operation *Pickaxe*, the British infiltration of Soviet agents behind enemy lines, I found that following Operation Barbarossa, the German invasion of Russia, Winston Churchill and Joseph Stalin made a secret agreement. In September 1941, His Majesty's Government, represented by the SOE, agreed to assist the NKVD by supplying intelligence, training facilities, documents and logistics for infiltrating Soviet agents into Nazi-occupied Europe. In return, the Soviet government agreed, among other things, to assist the Allies by mobilising longshoremen around the world to help sabotage German shipping.

It was further agreed that, following general military strategy, they would conduct subversive activities together but would not operate in each other's 'sphere of responsibility'. Workers in occupied countries were to be provided with propaganda aimed at hampering German trade. This was particularly appreciated by the British as they recognised that many shipyard and railway workers were communist members or sympathisers. Britain's 'sphere of responsibility' was from Norway to Spain, Yugoslavia and Greece. The Soviet's included Finland, Bulgaria, and Romania. Germany, Austria, Poland and Hungary were not mentioned.

At the time, the Soviets were desperately short of transport planes of any sort, even to support their front-line forces. As the Nazis controlled virtually all the territory between Moscow and the English Channel, the prospect of Soviet planes parachuting their agents with their wireless transmitters was considered unrealistic. It was about a 2,200 mile (3,540 km) return flight from Moscow to Berlin but only about a 1,200 mile (1,931 km) return flight from RAF Tempsford.

Hence, a formal arrangement called the 'Preliminary Survey' was signed whereby SOE would arrange their infiltration. According to Donal O'Sullivan, their general targets were believed to include oil fields, electricity generating stations, chemical industries, armament factories as well as the transport infrastructure, rail, road, canal and shipping.[7]

> The British and Soviet organisations will give each other every possible assistance in making contact with their respective agents, especially when one party has no means of communication. One of the methods by which such communications could be arranged is through accommodation addresses. The agents of the party which has no communication could then pass messages, already enciphered in their own code through these addresses. The other party would then send these messages which would be passed on to the liaison sections concerned.[8]

It was not until after the publication of my book that I found details of Françine's early life. The Maître online website reported that she was born in Paris on 2 October 1917, the daughter of a fitter-mechanic who was killed in a demonstration of the unemployed when she was fifteen. As her mother worked as a seamstress at the family home in Lilas, an eastern suburb of Paris, she could not afford to continue her studies after graduating and found work as a saleswoman and shorthand typist.

Influenced by her brother, Marcel, the secretary of the Communist Youth in Lilas, she joined the Communist Party in September 1933 and quickly became their treasurer. The economic depression and her political views encouraged her to accept an invitation in June 1935 to visit Moscow, and she became a typist at the Executive Committee of the translations department of the Communist International (Comintern). From November 1935, she studied the International Leninist School using the name Madeleine Dupuy and received a thorough technical training, specialising in the field of wireless communication.

Returning to France, between 1936 and 1939 she was secretary of Giulio Cerreti, the manager of the France-Navigation Company. Code named Pierre, he and Françine clandestinely supported the Spanish Republicans in their fight against General Franco's Nationalists. She also continued her work in the Union of Young French Girls, becoming secretary of the Paris-Est group in 1938. That year, her brother was killed fighting with the communists in Spain.

In September 1939, she travelled to Belgium for a few months' work with Eugen Fried, the French delegate at the Third Communist International. Secretary of the journal Cercle d'Art, his publishing work was a cover for his clandestine activities. At the end of the year, she went to Denmark and in May 1940, she was arrested by the Germans but, through the intervention of the Soviet ambassador, she was released on 6 June and returned to the USSR. While working with the leadership of the Comintern, she perfected her wireless skills until Georgi Dimitrov, the Secretary General of the Comintern, selected her for a top secret mission to France. She was accompanied by Raymond Guyot, the head of the French Communist Youth who had fled to Russia and in 1940 was Secretary of the Communist Youth International, and Daniel Georges, another French communist who had fought in the Spanish Civil War and was in Russia recovering from a torn ear drum.

Between the 12th and 16th of February 1942, the three Soviet agents were accommodated at the Rhodesia Court Hotel, 29 Harrington Gardens, in London, where they would have been briefed by 46-year-old Colonel Ivan Chichaev (sometimes written Tchitchaeff), the head of NKVD mission in Britain. Opposition was expressed to this venue as it was too open to the public. Accordingly, SOE arranged that between 16th and 22nd they stayed at The Drokes (STS 34), one of a number of requisitioned country houses in the grounds of Lord Montagu's estate in Beaulieu in the New Forest. While there, SOE was informed that their operation's name had been changed to RUM as there already was an agent in Holland called BRANDY.

From the New Forest, 2nd Lieutenant Walsh, their Conducting Officer, and Mr. Toropchenko, their Accompanying Officer, escorted them by train for their parachute training. Major Edwards' report summed them up as 'a very mixed party, whose chief faults were indecision and unpunctuality. They got through their program of drops with fair success.' Toropchenko did not jump, but was 'very determined and forceful. Very stern over his party's jumping.' Dandin was described as 'rather a nervous type. Very poor on ground training. He made a poor descent from the balloon, but improved greatly, and made a good aircraft drop.'[9]

Fauberge [Fromont's cover name in England] showed good spirit throughout. Could not master the technique of dropping cleanly through the aperture, and would always slide through in a dangerous manner. Continuous practice made her very nervous, and this, combined with her lack of skill made it inadvisable for her to make the first balloon drop with Robigot [Guyot] and Dandin [Georges]. Nevertheless, she was still anxious to drop, and showed great determination, concentrating on her training, and improving greatly. She was quite calm and collected when taken up for a balloon drop, and showed no hesitation. Her egress was rather bad and might have been dangerous from an aircraft, but her descent and landing were good. Made only one drop.

Commandant's remarks.

This Pickaxe party certainly contained better material, and there was no doubt about their desire to jump. Fauberge soon became proficient on the trapeze, but could not bring herself to go through the 'mock-up' aperture without a good deal of persuasion. She was so incapable of pushing off, that I could not accept the responsibility of her jumping, and informed H.O. [Head Office in Baker Street] This seemed to give her fresh determination, and she improved considerably next morning, and so I arranged for the balloon to be flown especially for her. This was done, and she jumped between two of my instructors.

Possibly Lieut. Walsh has a difficult task, and Toropchenko takes all responsibility for his men, but I feel that a more forceful personality might make these Pickaxe parties a little more normal.

They were treated as Officer students but messed separately from the other students in the house.[10]

A separate mess was provided to prevent the other students discovering that Britain was training Soviet agents. They returned to London on 26 February and stayed at 40 Porchester Court. This had been rented to house Pickaxes and to be a meeting place for SOE's Russian section and the NKVD. During this time, they were provided with cover stories which were not included in their files, forged identity cards, demobilisation forms and personal letters. Exact copies of '*le commissaire de police's*' signature and accurate official stamps had to be added to ensure that they looked authentic. The 500 US dollars and 85 Swedish Crowns the three of them had been given in Moscow were converted to francs and they were all supplied with appropriate clothing for France. Anna Frolova was given a new identity as 'Jeanne-Claude Garnier', her report describing her as,

A good-looking Frenchwoman; extremely hard, and it was impossible to find out from her any facts about her former history. Her luggage was carefully examined and from the enclosed photograph, we deduced that she had been 'married' and had produced a small son during the autumn of 1939.

She was a stenographer by trade and had lived in Paris. For some reason which we do not know she left France for Copenhagen in 1940, whence she proceeded to Russia. From her clothes, it would appear that she had been well-off and belonged to the bourgeois class.

She would make a good agent and should successfully pass any normal police examination.[11]

Ivan Danilov's new identity was 'Louis Pierre Dupré and Grigory Rodionov's was 'Marcel Jacques Ménard'.

The original plan was for three accompanying officers and Miss Jackson, a FANY officer, to take them to Gaynes Hall (STS 61), another requisitioned country house, to wait for their flight from Tempsford. Because of the political sensitivity of Britain infiltrating Soviet agents, the instructions were for them to be,

...kept most strictly apart from any others. Those directly concerned should be told that there is a girl in the party; those not directly concerned should be given to understand that the girl is a secretary from H.Q. with Miss Jackson, who will, as far as possible, avoid speaking French to her in the presence of those who are not aware of the fact that she is a passenger.[12]

Circumstances must have changed as, on 3 March 1942, the three of them, accompanied by Toropchenko, Douglas Dodds-Parker (MO/B) and Milnes Gaskell, two SOE officers, left London at 1530 hours and proceeded to Tangmere Airfield. The original time of departure was scheduled for 1930 but at 1900 hours it was cancelled. Later at 1945 hours this decision was reversed and the agents' dressing was completed by 2015 hours. Having been given their farewell drinks, their general morale was described as 'excellent.' SOE had provided them with a wireless set camouflaged as a suitcase, thought to be tactful as a Soviet wireless set had been destroyed when Pickaxe II crashed.[13]

Although the pilot reported dropping three agents, Clark referred to a letter from Lt-Col. R. M. Barry to Captain Wooler of 138 Squadron, in which he said that,

Her name was Anna Frolova, aged 25, her pseudonym was 'Annette Fauberge' and she was the first woman agent to be dropped by parachute into France. The other two agents were Grigory Rodionov, aged 40, who went under the name of 'Georges Robigot', and Ivan Danilov, aged 31, using 'Pierre Daudin'.[14]

The NKVD did not keep SOE informed of the success of the RUM party. The Maître online website revealed that Françine met her mother and moved with her to Saint-Vérand, Saône-et-Loire, where on 30 July 1943, denounced by French collaborators, they were arrested by the Militia.

The Germans had stuck notices on walls warning people that,

It is forbidden to conceal, befriend or aid in any way persons who are part of the Army of the enemy (particularly members of air crews, enemy parachutists and enemy agents).

Whoever contravenes the above order exposes themselves to being brought before a military tribunal, and they will be punished with the utmost severity, in some cases the pain of death.

Whoever declares openly the discovery of an airman who has made a forced landing and cites the day, time and exact location of the landing, or presents irrefutable evidence of an airman's body or parachute will be rewarded. Reward will be on the assurance of military personnel or where any enemy agent's admission has aided his capture.[15]

Délation, denunciation by colleagues, friends or acquaintances hoping for at least a 10,000-franc reward, led to the arrest of many agents and members of the Resistance. Handed over to the Gestapo, they were interrogated and tortured. Some were unable to withstand the pressure and talked, leading to further arrests. Others refused.

Transferred to Fresnes Prison in August, Françine's mother died from her beatings soon after their arrival. At the beginning of 1944, Françine was brought before a war tribunal and sentenced to death for espionage. When the verdict was read out to her, she stood up and made a little speech to the presiding judge. She told him it was an honour for a Frenchwoman to be sentenced by a French court rather than a German court and thanked him. He was furious. She was shot on 5 August 1944 at the age of 26 years.

A plaque was erected on the wall of the family home in Lilas, a tribute to Françine, her mother, and her brother. A street also bears her name there. Lyon city council honoured her by naming streets and schools after her in Vaulx-en-Velin. Several kindergartens in Bagnolet, Aubervilliers, and Drancy, and a college in Fresnes are named after Françine Fromont.

YVONNE RUDELLAT

Aged 45. Landed by felucca on 30 July 1942 at Cap Antibes (Alpes-Maritimes). Awarded the Croix de Guerre.

SOE records show that the first woman agent they sent into France was 45-year-old grandmother Yvonne Rudellat, described by Escott as 'a vivacious, dainty charmer with dark hair and hazel eyes, whose art of fragility was deceptive'.[16]

Her personnel file and research by Stella King and Beryl Escott revealed that she was born Yvonne Cerneau at Maisons-Lafitte, near Paris on 11 January 1897, the eighth of ten children. Her older brothers and sisters had all died in infancy. Her father sold horses to the French army, and when she grew up, she accompanied him when he travelled around the country buying horses. When he died, she found living with her mother difficult so moved to London where she worked in the Galeries Lafayette on Regent Street.

Her mother also moved to London, and they lived in Pimlico until October 1920 when she married Italian Alex Rudellat, a spy for the Italian army who was working as the head waiter at the Piccadilly Hotel and moved into the basement flat of one of several boarding houses he owned with her new mother-in-law.

She had a daughter, Constance, when she was 25 but left her husband for another man when she was 38 and set up her own property management company. When this failed after three years, she sold up and moved back to her husband's basement at 146 Warwick Way, Pimlico. Whether he had died or they got a divorce is unclear.[17]

Following the outbreak of war, she joined the Auxiliary Transport Service (ATS) and married Sergeant Ronald Pepper two days before Christmas 1939. Upset when she learned that France had been forced to surrender, she often told customers at a patisserie on Baker Street run by her old friend, a Gaullist supporter, that she would be prepared to go back and fight for France. Gradually, some of SOE's staff, who also bought their croissants there, got to know her views.

Towards the end of the Blitz, on the night of 16/17 April 1941, her house was bombed, and she lost everything except her first husband's cache of money she had dug up from the basement and taken during the air raid. Her relationship under strain, she threatened to commit suicide by jumping into the River Thames but something changed her mind at the last minute. After improving her typing skills at Pitman's school, she got a job at Ebury Court, a small hotel and drinking club in Belgravia, Westminster, which was also frequented by SOE personnel.

Her French background and often expressed desire to be parachuted back to do something for France brought her to the attention of Selwyn Jepson, the SOE recruiter.

Her personnel file in the National Archives shows that, after passing the assessment course in Wanborough in May 1942, she went on the paramilitary training course in Arisaig, staying at Garramor (STS 25A), one of the hunting lodges in the Highlands. According to King, Yvonne was told not to tell anyone that she had been to Arisaig. Back in London, she joined the FANY as an ensign in July before going to Beaulieu. Although she was 45 and described by one of her instructors as a 'little old lady', she went on to surpass the other women on her course, 22-year-old Andrée Borrel, 44-year-old Valentine 'Blanche' Charlet and 52-year-old Marie-Thérèse le Chêne.

Before she was sent into France with a pistol strapped to her leg, she admitted being prepared to kill. She was reported saying,

> If a German or anyone stops me and tries to search me, there is only one thing to do. I will have to shoot him. I don't want to do that. It would be difficult to bury him. The ground is so hard … If it happens, I hope it is near an asparagus bed where the earth is soft and sandy.[18]

Concerns about her parachuting into France were overcome by SOE negotiating with a special team within the Royal Navy. At the end of July 1942, Flying Officer Thomas Russell of 138 Squadron flew down to Portreath in Cornwall in his Whitley where he picked up Yvonne and three other agents, Nicholas Bodington, the deputy head of F Section, Henri Frager, and Harry Despaigne. After refuelling, he flew them down to Gibraltar from where they were taken secretly by a felucca. Feluccas have been described as having one tattered sail, a malodorous engine, the flags of half-a-dozen South American republics in the locker, a Polish skipper, some whisky, a revolver, some camouflaged depth charges and as many secret agents as happened to be going their way.

They were landed on the beach at Antibes, near Monaco on 30 July. Yvonne made her way to Cannes where she caught the train to Lyon, where she rendezvoused with Virginia Hall, who supplied her with a forged document. From there she travelled in the coal bunker of a train to cross the demarcation line from the Unoccupied to the Occupied Zone and reached Paris.

Her mission was to work as a courier for 32-year-old Major Francis Suttill, an Anglo-French barrister who was to create the PROSPER network which covered much of northern and north-western France. Until he arrived, she worked for Raymond Flower's MONKEYPUZZLE network and then liaised between Flower and Suttill's PHYSICIAN network in the Île de France.

Based in the industrial university town of Tours, she used identity papers in the name of Jacqueline Viallat, a refugee widow from Brest, Mme. Gauthier and a variety of code names including Suzanne, Soaptree, and Leclair.[19]

Flower reported that he wanted to get rid of her as he was not impressed with her security. He claimed that she was compromising him through her contacts in Tours, which included Germans. When she was out, he visited her room and left a suitcase containing a wireless set, crystals, codes, wavelengths and schedules of hours for transmitting and a pistol. Whether he planned to denounce her to the police or Gestapo is unknown, but Yvonne was said to have returned to her room, found them before anyone else saw them and got rid of them.

Pierre Culioli, a French Lieutenant working for Flower, refused to follow instructions and as Flower considered him dangerous, he ordered a suicide pill to be sent so it could be used to kill him. As none of the group were prepared to administer the pill, a Lysander pick-up operation was planned to bring Culioli back to Britain.

In November 1942, when Culioli learned about the assassination attempt, he and Yvonne moved to Étrépagny, about 75 km north-west of Paris, and joined Suttill's network. Having attended three parachute drops, they were sent to organise further drops near Mueng-sur-Loire.[20]

Operation *Torch*, the successful Allied invasion of North Africa, resulted in the Germans taking over the unoccupied zone during November 1942, installing troops and establishing Abwehr and Gestapo headquarters in the major cities. Counter-Resistance activity was also increased.

Buckmaster noted that, once she had found her safe house, her mission was to search for suitable fields for receiving containers and other agents.

…to this end, she acquired a bicycle on the black market and installed herself in an inconspicuous little cottage in the Touraine. Her immediate chief was a French commandant, and through him, she was in touch with Prosper, about whom I have already written. I think Christiane was thoroughly happy during this time. She had plenty of scope for action, plenty of excitement, and was in great danger. She enjoyed the affectionate esteem of all those men and women who knew what she was doing and the amused tolerance of all those others who had not this knowledge.

Only the French Commandant knew that in her bicycle basket, each day as she set off on her excursions, lay a stock of explosives and a hand-grenade, for Christiane always hoped to come across a really worth-while target, and it would have been too provoking to have, say, Hitler's car at her mercy, without the means of destroying it. [....]

She and her commandant got on together splendidly; they were both single-minded people, whose sole preoccupation was to speed up the task in hand. They didn't worry about non-essentials. The parachute operations which they arranged were admirably carried out, both being invariably careful over details, and their group amassed quite a store of weapons and explosives. Occasionally Christine would go to Paris to take a message to Prosper from her chief. After such visits, Prosper would inform us by radio that Christiane had been in, and we would know all was well.[21]

Escott provided more details of her experiences behind the enemy lines:

Wherever she went, she had the gift of making friends, though what she told them varied, as she was given to romancing, which fortunately SOE did not know. Among the agents who appeared on her landing grounds were her former training friend Andrée Borrel and Gilbert Norman, both destined to join Suttill in Paris, Lise Baissac [mentioned later] to go to Poitiers, and Roger Landes for Bordeaux. They all landed in twos in September and October 1942, on a field near the farm of Boisrenard, a place recommended by Pierre Culioli. Culioli had wandered over France for some time, in fruitless attempts to escape to Britain, and eventually attaching himself to the MONKEYPUZZLE network, had forged a useful partnership with Yvonne. Unfortunately, Flower neither liked not trusted either of them, despite their efforts, and was proving a most unsatisfactory leader who tried to incriminate them in his messages to SOE.[22]

On Suttill's advice, they set up their own sub-network within his PHYSICIAN network based in South Touraine, Central France. However, as members of Suttill's networks began being arrested, they moved to Romarantin in the Solonge and expanded their network by recruiting willing helpers who she helped supply with weapons, explosives, food and money. Her headquarters was La Cercle, a cottage in the woods near Veillens, about 20 km south-west of Blois.

By March 1943, Yvonne had not only bicycled across hundreds of kilometres of the countryside carrying wireless sets and explosives, possibly some Escott suggested were in her 'voluminous bloomers', but she had also organised and attended twenty parachute drops and taken part in various sabotage operations. She had helped to blow up the 300,000-volt electricity cables of Chaigny power station south of Orléans, two locomotives in the goods station at Le Mans, high tension electricity cables, railway lines, a railway bridge and a food store in Caen.[23]

Germaine and Madeleine Tambour provided a safe house and 'letter box' in Paris for Suttill. When they were arrested in April as part of a Gestapo counter-Resistance operation, they were considered so important that SOE provided 1,500,000 francs to bribe their captors into releasing them. The operation failed when the Germans released two prostitutes instead. Sent to Ravensbrück, the Tambour sisters were among those executed before the end of the war.[24]

On 21 June, Yvonne set off in an old Citroën for Beaugency on the Loire, with Culioli, her organiser, and two recently arrived Canadian agents, Frank Pickersgill and Ken Macalister, whom they were take on the train to Paris.

When they drove through the village of Dhuizon in the Sologne, they found it full of German troops. Stopped at a checkpoint, they were all taken to the Mairie (town hall) for questioning. Managing to pass inspection, they returned to the car but Culioli had left his briefcase containing the organisation's documents on the floor behind a chair inside. It had been found, opened and realising them to belong to someone in the Resistance, a guard went out to apprehend him.

Culioli decided to make a get-away and leave the Canadians to solve their own problems. Followed by three more powerful German cars, he had to zig-zag across the road to avoid the shots being fired. Yvonne was reported to have been knocked unconscious by a bullet in the back of her head:

> Pierre saw the amount of blood coming from the wound, and since Yvonne was unresponsive, he decided to kill himself rather than be taken and tortured. He slammed the vehicle into a ditch and then the side of a cottage, but the two woke up in a hospital at Blois hours later. Yvonne was told that her injury wasn't life-threatening, and that the bullet hadn't pierced her brain, but that it would be unsafe to remove it.[25]

There was a report that she had been trepanned, a hole drilled through her skull to release the pressure of her swollen brain, and that there had been two bullets left inside. Plans to get her out failed as there had been a spate of arrests following Culioli, Pickersgill and Macalister's capture. Two wireless sets, new crystals, messages labelled 'For Archambaud' and packages labelled 'For Prosper' and 'For Marie-Louise' (the code name of Mary Herbert, Claude de Baissac's courier) were found in the boot of the car.[26]

The sympathetic doctor decided to leave the bullets in Yvonne's brain rather than operate, thinking it would only affect her balance and memory. According to Andy Forbes' 64-Baker-Street website, when she regained consciousness, 'she used the name Jacqueline Gautier, which was whispered to her by a fellow prisoner when she could not remember her own, due to amnesia after her wounds.'

After a brief time in the military hospital in Blois, still too weak to walk, Yvonne was taken for interrogation at Avenue Foch before being imprisoned in the grey, fortress-like Fresnes Prison, a few miles south of the capital near what is now Orly airport.[27]

On 15 April 1944, almost two months before D-Day, she was transferred to Ravensbrück, the infamous women's concentration camp. Arriving on 21 April, she survived almost seven months of squalid, unsanitary conditions in overcrowded huts. Fifty miles (80km) north of Berlin, Ravensbrück was built in a beauty spot, noted for its lakes and secluded villas for wealthy city-dwellers. Its site was on marshy ground, often infested with malarial mosquitoes. There were enclaves outside the camp for working parties doing factory or heavy agricultural work in the community, as well as a Jugendlager, or youth camp, where those too ill or unfit for work were accommodated. Escott gave a long account which is worth including to give an idea of the conditions many of the women agents had to endure.

The main camp surrounded by high walls was built for about 6,000 prisoners. Inside were wooden huts for living quarters containing three tiers of bunks, a few brick buildings for kitchens, showers, and a concrete cell block. Cinder paths divided the huts in front of which blossomed flowers in profusion. But there, all semblance of cleanliness and proper conditions stopped. The place was in fact known to the French as L'Enfer des Femmes, the Women's Hell.

Nearly all the prisoners were civilians, both young and old, from conquered countries either as slave labour or on suspicion of involvement with the resistance, all being imprisoned without trial, though this did not prevent them being cruelly tortured during questioning in the camp's political department. During the war years over 50,000 women, at the lowest estimate, died in this camp from dirt, disease, overcrowding, squalor, starvation, overwork and ill-treatment, apart from those who were shot or gassed or sent to die elsewhere.

When Cécile Lefort was admitted in 1943, she spent her first days in the quarantine hut, where new arrivals were kept for three weeks to ensure they brought no new infection to the camp. After being checked in, though weary from the long train journey, she had to stand several hours before being admitted to the bathhouse, where she was told to strip, and her former clothes were taken away. Here she waited naked in the cold for a further few hours under the tiny hole in the ceiling where the shower worked, and that was only for a few minutes. With a sliver of soap and a pocket handkerchief of a towel, she had to clean herself. Again a long wait and then a shock. Two men came in, one to look at her teeth and one to give her a cursory medical examination, which revealed something was wrong.

Then she was issued with prison clothing, thin and inadequate for the advancing winter, and dispatched to the quarantine hut. There, no one was to be allowed outside, though all were awakened well before dawn for bitter acorn coffee. They were crowded at the window watching while the other women lined up five deep in front of their huts, in the freezing cold and rain, the living and the dead together, and stood for the hour-long 'Appells', where they were counted and appointed their work for the day. Some were detailed for gardening, some for sewing or knitting, some for a corpse, rubbish or coal collecting, some for road mending, cleaning latrines, tree-felling or potato picking, women being used instead of horses to drag the heavy carts. Work went in shifts of 10 or 11 hours each, day and night, lights out coming at about 9 pm. Food, mainly vegetable soup and half a loaf of bread a day, was not sufficient for such heavy work. This was the life that awaited them when quarantine was finished.[28]

Pattinson mentioned that, while in the camp, Yvonne tried to colour her grey hair with a boiled onion skin that she had found but her thick hair, which had become brittle from persistent dyeing, would not change colour. Instead, she had to resort to masking her grey hair by wearing a piece of cloth like a turban.[29]

On 2 March 1945, Yvonne was moved on to Belsen, south-west of Bergen, near Celle, Lower Saxony. In Foot's *SOE in France* he added that typhoid and dysentery were widespread in the concentration camps.

Unnoticed amongst the hundreds of prisoners suffering from both these diseases at once was a Frenchwoman who called herself Mme Gauthier, who had arrived from another camp six weeks before. Her only close friend in Belsen was separated from her in the middle of March by the iron circumstances of that insensate world; she was then as well as anyone could be amid the prevailing lack of food, fuel, clothing, decency, privacy, what civilised communities call 'the necessities of life'. She 'was not in bad health, she suffered occasionally from loss of memory, but she remained in good morale, and she looked neither particularly drawn nor aged'. But she soon fell dangerously ill. When the camp was captured, she was too far gone from her diseases, or too steeped in her own cover story, or both, to mention to a soul what she had been; unnoticed to the last, she died on St George's day or the day after, and her body was huddled with twenty thousand others into one of the huge mass graves. Her name was Yvonne Rudellat.[30]

According to Escott, Belsen was a place of starvation, typhus, dysentery and death,

...where corpses, then too many to bury, lay around putrefying the atmosphere with an indescribable stench. But even here, though weak, she made friends. On about 5 April, the camp was liberated by British troops. Yvonne was still clinging to life but so deeply sunken into her alias that she drew no attention to herself. A week later, she was still alive, but too weak to move and barely conscious. Then the death pits for the essential mass graves claimed her – one unknown amongst thousands. Her death was given on or about 23 April 1945, and later confirmed by the indefatigable Vera Atkins.[31]

Buckmaster's article provided a different ending for his readers. He claimed that Yvonne recovered from her wound but was physically in bad shape after a long time in solitary confinement. When the Camp Commandant found that she was unfit to work:

...he had no compunction in sentencing her to the gas chamber. It was 'the Führer's will' – and it caused less trouble that way. Christiane had no illusions when the wardress ordered her to the baths. She knew what awaited her, but she had no regrets. She knew that her work was well done and that the flame of resistance, lighted by the patriots, would not fade. She was happy that she had done something useful, but she had no inkling of the fact that her name would be forever honoured in France.[32]

Culioli was sent to the same military hospital in Blois where he was stripped, chained to a bed and given minimal care. He too was sent to Avenue Foch where he was interrogated, tortured and then imprisoned in Fresnes before being transported to Buchenwald concentration camp which he survived. The two Canadians were also interrogated and tortured, the Gestapo wanting them to transmit messages on the captured set back to London. When they refused, they too were sent to Buchenwald and executed on 14 September 1944. The incriminating evidence obtained from their capture led to numerous arrests and the eventual demise of Suttill's PROSPER network.[33]

Yvonne was awarded the Member of the British Empire medal (MBE) by King George and the Croix de Guerre by de Gaulle's new government. Escott mentioned that it was her successes in France that led the SOE to send in more women.

It was not until 1946 that details of what happened to Yvonne and other captured agents started to find their way back to Britain. In some cases, it was not until much later. Military historian Paul McCue, who has researched the 104 French Section agents commemorated on the Valençay Memorial, reported that Yvonne, included in the list, was among a contingent of 2,500 women from Ravensbrück, largely the older or ill women, who were sent to KZ-Belsen-Bergen, supposedly to convalesce.

She arrived on 2 March 1945 and was originally in block 19, but was then moved into block 48, in an area of the camp where only sick prisoners were housed. Some eighty French women were in the block and Yvonne, still managing to maintain her false identity of Jacqueline Gautier, made friends with another woman, Renée Rosier, who survived the camp. Yvonne was still there when, on 15 April 1945, advancing British troops liberated the camp and immediately placed it under strict quarantine controls as a result of a dysentery and typhoid epidemic which was then raging among the prisoners.

Sadly, it was too late for Yvonne. She was suffering heart problems, and though a friend managed to arrange some drug injections which improved her condition for a while, she soon relapsed and continued to weaken. Even after the camp's liberation and the commencement of medical treatment by the British Army, deaths were continuing at up to 1,000 inmates a day. The scene on 17 April 1945 was described by Derrick Sington in his book *Belsen Uncovered*:

> The scene in some of the overcrowded blocks during the days following our arrival resembled Dante's Inferno. Block 48 in the smaller women's camp contained 600 Jewish women from Poland, together with about 80 Frenchwomen. There were no beds, so the women had put a blanket or some rags underneath themselves, and lay row upon row in their worn overcoats. In some parts of the room, they overlapped each other and women lay with their heads pillowed on the stomachs or legs of others. One short, bony creature was asleep in a kneeling posture when I first went inside this block. A nauseating smell of months old sweat

and dirty rags rose from the diseased and pain-ridden bodies littered there.

Tragically, Yvonne's true identity was not known to the Royal Army Medical Corps personnel battling to save the surviving inmates and consequently, she waited her turn. She was among those who had contracted typhus and was further weakened by dysentery, but in one of the greatest tragedies of the fates of the 104 agents on the Valençay memorial, it was not until around 23 April 1945 that Yvonne was moved, too late, to the camp hospital for extra care. Having survived being shot and seriously wounded when she was captured in France, and the depredations of both Ravensbrück and Belsen, she succumbed on the very point of salvation and died on either the 23 or 24 April 1945. The official cause of death was later given as 'from exhaustion'. Her body, along with those of thousands of other inmates, was buried in one of the mass graves on the site.[34]

At the end of the war, Atkins went to Germany went to Germany as part of the War Crimes Section of the British Army on the Rhine to find out what had happened to those women agents who had not returned. Research by Sarah Helm revealed that Vera was born Vera Rosenberg and, being Jewish, changed it to Atkins, her Scottish mother's maiden name when she arrived from Romania in 1937. Given her involvement with SOE, she took it upon herself to see off all those women destined for France. She had made arrangements with them to send already written letters and cards to their families and relatives on designated dates to reduce them worrying while they were out of touch. She took charge of their wills that the women made up before they left and ensured their personal possessions were looked after.

Vera's role included overseeing all aspects of agents' preparation for entering enemy territory, from the latest work and travel regulations to what clothes they should wear, what they should carry at different times of the year and in different regions of the country. She even advised them about what they should eat and how they should eat it. Although she did not accompany them on their training courses, she liaised with their instructors and met up with the women, often at West End restaurants which allowed them a safety valve, to express their anxieties and their hopes for their missions.

It was a particularly difficult task of finding the truth about the fate of the women, particularly given the secret German policy of disposing of enemy agents in what they called 'Nacht und Nebel', what the French called 'Nuit et Brouillard' and what Atkins understood as 'Night and Fog'. The parents of those missing must have gone through enormous stress not knowing what had happened to their sons or daughters.[35]

ANDRÉE BORREL

Aged 22. Parachuted from a Whitley near St Laurent Nouan (Loir-et-Cher) on the night of 24/25 September 1942. Executed at Natzweiler-Struthof. Awarded the King's Commendation for Brave Conduct, Croix de Guerre and Medaille République Française.

Andrée Borrel was born on 18 November 1919, the second daughter of a working-class family, at Becon-les-Bryuyeres, a north-western suburb of Paris. According to her account, her father died when she was 11, so, to support her mother, she left school at 14 and started work with a 'modiste', a fashionable dress designer named Mayse. When she was 16 the family moved to 58 Boulevard Aristide Briand, Paris, where she spent two years as a shop assistant in Boulangerie Pajo, a bakery, on Avenue Kleber. She then worked in Bazar d'Amsterdam, a store on Rue Amsterdam as she wanted Sundays off so she could enjoy her passion for cycling. In October 1939, for health reasons, her mother was advised to live in a warmer climate, so she took Andrée and her elder sister Leone to Toulon on the Mediterranean coast where they had family friends.

When war broke out, Andrée volunteered to work for the Red Cross in the Association des Dames de France and completed a shortened nursing course on 20 January 1940. At the beginning of February, she was sent to the Hopital Complimentaire at Nimes but was sent back fifteen days later following a decree that nurses under the age of 21 were not allowed to serve in hospitals. This decree was revoked a few days later, and on 1 March, she was sent to the Hopital de Beaucaire, between Montpelier and Avignon. When it was closed at the end of May, she was transferred to Hopital Complimentaire at Nimes where she remained until it too closed at the end of July. Although still a volunteer, for all intents and purposes she had been mobilised and was continually having to deal with discharged wounded prisoners of war who had returned from Germany.

In March 1941, while looking after wounded soldiers at St Hippolyte de Fort, a Vichy-government run internment camp near Nimes, she met and developed a friendship with 26-year-old Lt Maurice Dufour. He was a supervising officer who had been transferred to Nimes and was later to help Albert Guérisse, a Belgian doctor, who was working for MI6, the British Intelligence service. According to a timesonline article, Dufour thought she was 'a free spirit' and 'as this was wartime ... inevitably they shared both a bed and a passionate desire to liberate their country.'

According to Guérisse's Wikipedia biography, he had joined the Belgian Army and was among those evacuated from Dunkirk in 1940. Recruited by the SIS, he was employed as a conducting officer, escorting agents by boat to Southern France. On 25 April 1941, after dropping six agents on the shore at Collioure, about 2 km north of Port-Vendres, close to the Spanish border, the skiff he was in was overturned by the surf, and he could not reach HMS *Fidelity*, which was anchored off the coast. Forced to swim ashore, he was apprehended by French coastguards.

Imprisoned at St Hippolyte de Fort, Guérisse met other British officers, one of whom was Lt-Col. Ian Garrow, who, unable to escape back to England, had walked to Marseille and given himself up to the Vichy authorities. Although officially interned as an enemy alien, Guérisse was allowed to wander the city and visit the Seamen's Mission. Eventually, he met Nancy Wake, a vivacious Australian who had married a wealthy French businessman and was helping British and other Allied internees, escaped prisoners of war and others wanting to get out of occupied Europe, to escape, either by boat to Gibraltar or be guided over the Pyrénées into Spain. Then, with the financial and administrative assistance of British diplomats and intelligence officers, they would make their way overland to Gibraltar or Lisbon.

While SOE had a DF Section responsible for establishing escape routes, the British organisation that helped fund and organise the groups helping escape parties was MI9. Alan Judge, an archivist at Chicksands Military Intelligence Museum, provided a brief history:

MI9 was founded in 1939 at the suggestion of Field Marshal Sir Gerald Templer. It was commanded by Major Norman R Crockatt, DSO, MC, (Royal Scots) and was based in Room 424 of the Metropole Hotel in Northumberland Avenue, London; its charter was issued on 23 December 1939. The tasks of MI9 were to facilitate the escape of PoW; facilitate their return and that of evaders – those people on the run in enemy territory, to the UK; collect and disseminate intelligence; attempt to deny information to the enemy, and to maintain the morale of British and allied PoW in enemy camps. In particular, the system whereby intelligence was passed from PoW camps back to the UK using the codes devised for insertion into letters and parcels, proved to be most effective. MI9's tasking was divided into two: one dealt with Allied prisoners and evaders, and the other with captured enemy prisoners. MI9a handled enemy prisoners in the UK and the Combined Services Detailed Interrogation Centres (CSDIC), and MI9b dealt with escapes and evasions of British and Allied PoW. Eventually, in 1941, MI9a was redesignated MI19 and Crockatt, by now a Colonel, became the Deputy Director of Military Intelligence (Prisoners of War) (DDMI(PW)) and commanded both branches. MI9 was also reorganised with five sub-sections: 'b', liaison with the other services and interrogation of returnees; 'd', the training school set up in Highgate and later re-designated 'Intelligence School 9' (IS9); 'x', planning; 'y', codes for insertion into PoW correspondence etc; and 'z', tools and aids such as files, hacksaws, clothing and anything else which could be useful and also small enough to insert into mail and pass inspection by – or fool – the enemy censors.[36]

Although Guérisse was later captured and imprisoned, MI9 funded a successful prison break, and he then expanded his operations in the Marseille area. Using wireless sets and operators supplied by SOE, people like Garrow, Wake, Dufour, Andrée and numerous other helpers, established links with London and neutral Switzerland and helped almost 600 SOE agents, Allied airmen shot down over France, Jews and others to escape over the Spanish border into Gibraltar and then back to England.

When the network was betrayed in December 1941, Andrée and Maurice were forced to hide in Toulouse. Eventually, they escaped over the Pyrénées themselves and made their way by train and a British diplomat's car to Lisbon in Portugal. Maurice was shipped back to England, but she stayed, working at the Free French Propaganda Office at the British Embassy. It was not until April 1942 that she returned to London.

Like the other female refugees, she was taken to Nightingale Lane. After her interrogation, R. Osborne's report shed light on her experiences before arriving in Britain:

After spending a week at Tarascon at the beginning of August [1941], she went to Canet Plage near Perpignan where she first ran the Villa Rene-Therese [the last safe house before the hard and dangerous route over the Pyrénées] where the escapees were hidden while in transit for England.

This villa proved too small and at the beginning of October they [her and Dufour] rented the Villa Anita where she remained until December 1941.

Towards the end of December 1941, they received news that the Organisation in the occupied zone had been broken up owing to a denunciation and as they had to be particularly careful and as there were few people coming through, she closed the villa.

Dufour had apparently told her to go and hide out with a certain school teacher, Mr. BASSENS, near Castres, but she did not bother as a friend of hers, Madame Solange LEBRETON, who owned a Hotel-restaurant called 'Le Tennis', offered to put her up.

This woman apparently knew the work she was doing and had often helped her in obtaining food for her refugees.

She stayed with Madame LEBRETON until about 15 January 1942, when she went to Marseille to meet DUFOUR, who was expected back from the North.

Mlle BORREL met DUFOUR at Marseille on about 23 January when he told her that they would be shortly leaving for England as the police were on their trail.

While at Marseille, she stayed at the Hotel de Bruxelles in the Rue Tapis Vert.

On 1 February 1942, together with DUFOUR and another young Frenchman called Jean d'ESCRIENNE, they left for Toulouse.

This last man had apparently been working for an Organisation near Nevers and had to leave France as the police were also after him.

At Toulouse, they stayed at the Hotel de Paris, from where, on 14 February, she journeyed to Banyuls [close to the Spanish border] together with DUFOUR and the Belgian BERNARD family. The rest of her story, up to her arrival in Lisbon, is identical with that of DUFOUR. [They escaped over the Pyrénées and made their way by train and a British diplomat's car to Lisbon. (TNA HS9/455/5)]

When DUFOUR left for England by 'plane on 29 March, she moved back to Mr WILLIAMS' house in order not to be alone at the Pensac Morera.

From that day until her departure for England, she states that she worked every day at the Free French Propaganda Office at the British Embassy.

On 24 April 1942, she left Lisbon by 'plane for England, landed at Poole Airport on 25 April and arrived at Nightingale Lane the same evening.

Mlle BORREL's story seems perfectly straightforward. It is corroborated by DUFOUR who, on arriving in England, vouched for her.

She is an excellent type of country girl, who has intelligence and seems a keen patriot.

From a security point of view, I can find nothing against Mlle BORREL and recommend her release to the FFF [Free Fighting French].[37]

Dufour's experiences on arriving in Britain were quite different to Andrée's. His personnel file and research by Michael Bilton for his *Sunday Times* article about the treatment he received following his interrogation at The Royal Victorian Patriotic School, revealed that he was taken to 10 Duke Street, the headquarters of the Free French. In the basement, a converted coal cellar, 'he was subjected to constant brutal beatings and vicious cruelty' as the Free French were convinced that he was a British double agent. According to Bilton, they even threatened to kidnap and gang rape Andrée.

After being sent to join the Free French military camp at Camberley, between Reading and Aldershot, Dufour managed to escape and made his way to Andrée's lodgings at Moncorvo House, Ennismoire Gardens, Knightsbridge. When he started legal proceedings against the French authorities for assault and false imprisonment, MI5 were desperately worried that his escape and his High Court writ would name officers in MI9, the French Intelligence Service, and RF Section. Their solution was to 'shut him up', put him into a safe house, offer him £2,000 and promise that he would be able to stay in Britain after the war. He agreed, and Andrée never saw him again.[38]

On 9 May 1942, Major Robert Bourne-Paterson (F/P), F Section's Planning Officer, informed Buckmaster that he had seen Andrée with Captain Gerry Morel (F/M), head of F Section's Operations Section, that morning at '055 A.' This was the interview room for prospective agents in the basement of the War Office sparsely furnished with only two chairs, two tables, and a skylight.

> She came to this country with DUFOUR [...] Since arriving in LONDON, she attempted to join the CORPS FEMININ of the Free French movement, but they have made it a condition that she should give them all the intelligence concerning the organisation for which she was working in France. This she refuses to do, and apparently they refuse to employ her unless she does. [This sentence was highlighted in the margin.]
>
> I think that she would make an excellent addition to our own CORPS FEMININ and it should not be difficult to get her.
>
> I have arranged for F.G. [Captain Jepson, SOE's head of recruitment] to see her on Wednesday, and I propose to see her again myself, as she said that she was perfectly willing to let us have the information she refuses to give to the Free French. I am having her put through the cards.[39]

Her strong socialist views did not mitigate against Andrée, and she was duly recruited into SOE and given a commission in the FANY as an ensign on £3 a week. With her on her training was Lise de Baissac, who had been born in Mauritius but was of British descent. Like Andrée, she had escaped from France with her brother but had had to wait five months in Spain before being allowed passage by ship to Britain. She got a job on the *Daily Sketch* in London and, unlike Andrée, she volunteered to join SOE when they began recruiting women. Unusually, neither of them received the paramilitary training.

After her training at Beaulieu in early summer 1942, the Commandant reported that Andrée was,

> Of sound intelligence, if lacking somewhat in imagination. She has little organising ability and will do her best work under definite instructions. She is thoroughly tough and self-reliant with no nerves. Has plenty of common sense and is well able to look after herself in any circumstances and she is absolutely reliable. Has lost her attitude of over-confidence and has benefited enormously from the course and developed a thoroughly level-headed approach towards problems. A very pleasant personality and she should eventually develop into a first class agent.[40]

On completion of her training, she was promoted to Lieutenant on £5 a week, and F Section allocated her a position as a courier to Francis Suttill, code named PHYSICIAN, the organiser of the PROSPER network. His mission, code named WHITEBEAM, was to organise the Resistance in the Paris area and Northern France.

Suttill's correspondence shows that he felt the choice of Andrée as his courier was 'ironic' as he had hoped not to be given her. Where they had met is unknown but he told Louis Lee-Graham, another SOE student on his training course, 'that he found her attractive, so much so that the prospect of working long months with her at his side, once they were in France, to some extent trouble him, in as much as he was a married man and might find the enforced proximity a strain.'[41]

As we shall see, she did have a relationship with a member of the PROSPER network, but it was not Suttill. Provided with an identity card and food card in the name of Denise Urbain and the code name in the field of Monique, she was given a cover story which identified her as an employee of Morgans Bank in Paris. To avoid drawing attention to her mother and sister, it was close to but not exactly the truth:

Unusually for the women agents, Andrée's personnel file contained her mission papers.

You will be parachuted into France, together with a companion, during the present moon period, at a point which you have studied on the map. A reception committee will be awaiting you. This committee will lodge you and given you all details as to local conditions. You may stay with them for one or two days, but not longer than is absolutely necessary. You will ask them to give you a postbox [usually a restaurant], together with password, if necessary, where you can deposit messages for transmission to us by W/T. You will explain that very few, and only urgent messages will be sent by this means.

You will then go by train to Paris and call on 'les Tambour' (ask for Monsieur or Madame Tambour) at 38 Avenue Suffren, Paris, 15e, and say you come 'de la part de Charlot'. You will tell them to expect two friends of yours, who should be arriving a few days after you.

Les Tambour will advise you regarding the present conditions in Paris, where to lodge and where your two friends should lodge. If for some reason, les Tambour are not there, you will go to your sister, Mme Arend, 23 rue Caumartin, Paris, 9e.

You must then, without delay, establish contact with your circuit chief, Prosper, under whose orders you will be henceforward. You have discussed with Prosper how you will contact one another, and the arrangements are that he will go on the 28th of this month and every day until 5 October to a café in the rue Caumartin, the position of which you have described to him. He will wait there from midday until about 5 minutes past every day until you turn up. If this café should have been close, he will patrol its immediate vicinity for not more than 5 minutes, returning each day until contact is established. If, for any reason, your departure is postponed until next month, Prosper will wait for you every day from 22 October until 4 November, and if Prosper's departure is put off, you will wait for him on these days, unless you have received contrary instructions from us.

If you fail to contact Prosper or Thomas, you will send us a message via the friends who received you and await an answer in which we will instruct you what to do.

If you should miss your reception committee and also fail to contact Prosper or Thomas, you will be able to send us a message via Georges 60, using the following postbox:

Madame Meneau, Pavillon Belle Vue, L'Alouette, Tours. Your message should be addressed to 'Monsieur Gaspard'.

If this should not work, you no doubt be able to get a message through to us via les Tambour.

You have been given details of our use of passwords, postboxes and the security rules which must at all times be observed. You have been shown how to disguise addresses by using the Bottin system [Buckmaster described it as 'an alphabetic thesaurus of French industry and commerce, department by department, from A – to Z.' Buckmaster, M. They Fought Alone, SOE Agents in Wartime France, Norton, 1958)] and, in addition, how to use the Paris telephone directory in the case of addresses in that city, i.e., you will pick the 8th street after the real one in volume 2 of the 1939 directory, add 9 to the number of the street, put that figure before and after the name of the street, and omit the name of the town entirely.

You have also been shown our grid system of map references.

The following are the passwords of your circuit, which must never be used except with your chief and his principal lieutenants:

'Où pent-on avoir de l'essence à briquet?'

Reply: 'Du carburant, vous voulez dire.'

You know the Playfair and Benn codes.

Major H has given you a neutral postbox, an address where you can deposit long reports from your circuit for transmission by courier to us and where you can, if necessary, pick up messages from us and, finally, a safe house, which you can use if you ever need to make a getaway.

You will act as a courier for Prosper's circuit and carry out whatever instructions he may give you. He will look after your material needs as regards money etc.

You will take with you 250,000 francs.

We will pay into your account £300 p.a. at Lloyd's Bank, 145 Edgware Road. [A later report indicated that it was increased to £350 from 1 May 1943]

In view of the recent warning, we have received regarding changes in the regulations affecting identity cards in the Occupied Zone; the following additional instructions are given you.

You are to get local details from your reception committee. If they judge that you cannot go safely to Paris, you are to get into W/T communication with us through them immediately and await our instructions.

If everything is in order, you will proceed to Paris and meet Prosper at the agreed place on the agreed dates. If because of the new regulations, Prosper and Thomas cannot leave this month, we will send the following message by BBC on 1 and 2 October: (at 1915 and 2115)

'Carmen envoie ses amitiés à Eugenie.'

Should you hear this message, do not try to meet them anymore until the following moon but spend your time in Paris, preparing for their arrival in accordance with the lines indicated in your briefing.

If they should be unable to go next month also, the same message will be sent during the BBC news on 22 and 23 October. In this case, you must go back to the postbox given you by your reception committee and get in touch with use by W/T. we will then instruct you what to do.

You will leave the 250,000 francs, which you are taking to France for four circuits, in safe-keeping with Gaspard or his representative, and will call for it when instructed to do so by Prosper.[42]

Having signed her last will and testament, nominating Bourne-Paterson as her executor and her mother and sister as beneficiaries of her estate, her possessions were placed in a navy suitcase.

Having been provided with appropriate French clothing and toiletries and presumably had the chance to visit a French hairdresser and dentist, she was given her final instructions and taken to Tempsford. On 24 September 1942, she and Lise de Baissac were parachuted from a Whitley into a field 5.7 km south of St Laurent Nouan, between Crouy-sur-Cosson and Nouan-sur-Loire, Loir and Cher. The reception committee included Yvonne Rudellat and Pierre Culioli.[43]

Suttill left on 1 October with Lt James Amps and was parachuted from a 138 Squadron Halifax near La Ferté-sous-Jouarre, east of Meaux, Seine et Marne. On 31 October, Gilbert Norman alias Archambaud, and Roger Landes alias Aristide, were dropped to help Suttill as wireless operators. Andrée became Norman's courier and, over time, they developed a romantic relationship. On 29 December, as the circuit enlarged, Jack Agazarian was parachuted in as another radio operator with his wife Françine as his courier.

Buckmaster described Andrée as athletic and beautiful, often to be seen wearing a fur coat and rolling her own cigarettes. With the code name Denise, she became more than a messenger, posing as Suttill's sister. 'He let her do the talking, and she played to perfection the harassed country girl taking her farmer brother to the market in the local town.'[44]

She travelled around northern France with him, organizing sub-networks and training Resistance members in the use of weapons and explosives supplied by 161 Squadron. She also helped arrange drop zones and the escape of downed aircrew and SOE agents.

Research by Francis Suttill into his father's time in France and the downfall of his Prosper network revealed some details about what happened over the following nine months. After accompanying him in a search for suitable drop zones in the Loire Valley, she attended her first drop on the night of 17/18 November 1942 with Raymond Flower of the MONKEYPUZZLE network, Pierre Culioli, Suttill, Gilbert, and Yvonne. The drop was in a field close to a wood near Étrépagny.[45]

According to the F Section War Diary, in November Andrée's network received four containers which included 88 lbs of Plastic Explosive, twenty-four Sten guns, thirty-four revolvers, forty-six grenades, fifteen Clam [magnetic] mines and fifty incendiaries.[46] Demand for parachute silk as bedding, pyjamas, lingerie or dresses was high but instructions were given not to allow it to be used as, if found, it was direct evidence of the owner's involvement with parachutists, a crime punishable by arrest, imprisonment and death. Sometimes, their property was confiscated or destroyed.

In one of Suttill's reports to London in March 1943, his comment about her was that 'everyone who has come into contact with her in her work agrees with myself that she is the best of us all. In J…'s absence, she acted as my Lieutenant. Shared every danger. Took part in a December reception committee with myself and some others. Has a perfect understanding on security and an imperturbable calmness. Thank you very much for having sent her to me.'[47]

To give an idea of what Andrée was doing, Shrabani Basu, in her book *Spy Princess: The Life of Noor Inayat Khan*, said that in April 1943 Suttill's group had carried out sixty-three acts of sabotage, derailing trains, killing forty-three Germans and wounding 110. By June, it covered twelve départements, had thirty-three DZs and received 254 containers of supplies. They picked up 190 containers in June alone and more attacks were planned.[48]

However, lax security led to arrests and some people either accepted the Gestapo's offer of their freedom and possibly a bribe or were unable to withstand the torture and provided names, addresses and details of rendezvous. Some wireless operators agreed to transmit German-inspired messages to London which led SOE to send in agents and containers to German-controlled reception committees.

The blame for PROSPER's downfall has been attributed to the Gestapo acquiring about 200 unencrypted names and addresses of potential recruits to André Girard's CARTE network in a briefcase which was stolen from André Marsac as he slept on a train from Marseille en route to Suttill in Paris.[49]

On 24 March 1943, Roger Bardet, an F Section agent working for the CARTE network, chose to collaborate with the Gestapo rather than face imprisonment. As a result of his information, the Gestapo set up a surveillance team to monitor the Tambour sister's apartment. Germaine Tambour had been Girard's secretary, an active member of his CARTE organisation and his representative in Paris who had switched her allegiance to Suttill.[50]

The arrest of Yvonne Rudellat, Culioli, Pickersgill and Macalister on 19 June 1943 and the finding of their wireless set, codes, and documents provided valuable intelligence of other members of the PROSPER network. Jean Moulin, referred to later, had been sent in to attempt to unite the disparate Resistance groups behind de Gaulle, was arrested two days later following increased Gestapo activity in identifying Resistance members.

Andrée and Norman were said to be inseparable and were arrested together in Nicholas and Maude Laurent's house in Boulevard Lannes, Paris, on the night of 23/24 June. Interviewed after the war, Nicholas claimed to have answered a ring on the doorbell at midnight to a man asking to speak with Archambaud, Gilbert Norman's cover name. When Norman came downstairs and went out to the gate to speak with the visitor, the gate opened, a revolver was pointed at him and ten men in civilian clothes came in saying 'Gestapo'. Handcuffed, Norman was taken upstairs. Nicholas was kept downstairs and the house was searched.[51]

Suttill included Maude's account which was more detailed and shed light on Andrée's arrest:

> Gilbert and Denise were working in the office, and the table was strewn with compromising documents and the seals of all of the Kommandaturs [German Army Command Posts] in France, which were being used to stamp the false papers. Nico and I had undressed and intended to go and say goodnight to Gilbert and Denise before going to bed, but the sound of the bell changed all that. Gilbert shouted to Nico to go and answer it. He was our leader. Reluctantly, my husband did as he asked, thinking, like me, that Gilbert must be expecting someone, and we didn't know about it, though this was surprising because it was after the curfew. Nico went down the stairs that led down to the kitchen and out that way into the garden. He opened up, and I heard him call out to me, surprised and concerned, Maude, get dressed! That was his greatest concern, as

a husband he didn't want twelve men seeing his wife in a see-through slip, which happened anyway! Well, twelve Gestapo men burst in on me, revolvers raised and backed up by machine guns, shouting 'hands up.' I did nothing and was filled with anger at this violation of my home. They had already seized Gilbert and were going down to apprehend Nico. Denise tried to escape but was stopped by the threat of the revolver. Gilbert, Nico, and Denise were then taken away. Immediately.[52]

Additional information was provided by the Gestapo agent who was responsible for the arrest. He later admitted to Arnel Guerne, another Resistance member, that,

> just before midnight, i.e., shortly after Archambaud and Monique had left Guerne, a Gestapo agent came to Archambaud's house. He passed himself off as a recent arrival from London and produced the crystals which Archambaud was expecting. Archambaud was then arrested by two other Germans who entered. Monique was also arrested and prevented from swallowing the organisation code. This code was in any case already known to the Germans. The same Germans spent the rest of the night waiting at Prosper's house and arrested him the following morning on his return from Normandy.[53]

The Gestapo retrieved the fake identity cards with photographs from the office and Maude claimed that names and addresses of other members of the PROSPER group were found in Andrée's briefcase which led to many more arrests.[54]

Details of Andrée's interrogation at Avenue Foch have not come to light. Josef Goetz, the Gestapo wireless expert responsible for playing captured SOE agents' sets back to the British, claimed to have been provided with information obtained from Norman, Culioli, Pickersgill and Macalister. Ernst Vogt, the Gestapo officer who interrogated Andrée, claimed that Norman had ordered her to talk.[55]

Guerne, who met Norman in prison, claimed that he had told him that the Germans had known everything about PROSPER since December 1942 and had let it operate without hindrance. He also claimed that Norman had already agreed to a proposal by the head of the Gestapo in Paris to spare the lives of all the members of the network, except its leaders, by preventing their files being sent to the military court. In return, he had agreed to show them the location of all the arms dumps amassed by the organisation. Guerne was shown Photostat copies that the Germans had taken of all Suttill and Norman's messages to London. Realising the extent of the Gestapo's knowledge and convinced that his life was safe, Guerne also agreed to cooperate.[56]

Three uncoded messages for London were reported to have been found in Norman's possessions which he was forced to encode and transmit. Deliberately omitting his security check allowed him to let London know that he was operating under duress and that he was compromised. As the operator responsible for Norman's messages knew he was a highly accurate transmitter, they picked up the discrepancy and informed Buckmaster. Leo Marks, SOE's head of codes, reported that, without rechecking the original, Buckmaster ordered a message to be sent back to Norman informing him that he had omitted to include his security check and that 'this serious breach of security must not, repeat not be allowed to happen again.'[57]

Goetz, who had been ordered to return immediately from his leave in Berlin when Macalister and Norman had been caught, received London's message and reported Norman to have claimed being let down by SOE, that he was absolved of all responsibility and agreed to encode and decode German-inspired messages. Although he refused to transmit them, a German operator copied his fist and transmitted for him. Whether Norman knew that this led to other SOE agents and containers being parachuted direct to German-controlled reception committees is unknown.[58]

Other prisoners and her relatives shed light on Andrée's subsequent imprisonment. Robert Arend, her brother-in-law, was arrested on 19 July, sent to Schoenbeck prison and released at the end of the war. His interrogation report revealed that,

At the time of the PROSPER arrests and some time before, AREND was a refractaire and living at his parent's home at 12 Rue Champchevrier, Staine, Seine. ARCHAMBAUD [Norman] had transmitted from this house for three days sometime during June and had left a set there.

AREND's own house at 23 Rue Comartin, Paris, where his wife was still living, was used a great deal by the principal members of the group, who each had a key and came and went as they wished.

About 9.30 in the evening of 19 July 1943, while AREND was out meeting his wife at the station, ARCHAMBAUD turned up at 12 Rue Champcheverier with three Germans in civilian clothes in an open car. ARCHAMBAUD asked AREND's parents to give him the W/T set. This had never been properly hidden, because they had not found a suitable place to hide it, but AREND's father could only find four of the five parts, the fifth being put away somewhere. AREND pere therefore went to fetch his son, and told him he thought the Germans had been won over, probably by bribery, and were working for the Allies. AREND returned with his father, to find ARCHAMBAUD and two of the Gestapo in his house, the third Gestapo man remaining in the car.

ARCHAMBAUD and the Germans wanted to leave immediately but AREND pere offered them drinks and cigarettes. He then became more communicative and told them that his son was a refractaire. The Germans thereupon asked for AREND's papers and took him away to verify them. ARCHAMBAUD left with them.

AREND was taken to the Avenue Foch and locked up till the following morning when he was interrogated by a German in the room which is immediately on the right of the entrance. This man was fairly tall and wore glasses, and the interrogation was conducted in German.

Nothing very special happened at the interrogation. He was asked if he knew that ARCHAMBAUD was a British agent parachuted into France and that Denise was Andrée Borrel. The Germans said they had found a quantity of false papers when they arrested DENISE and, in fact, his own false certificat de rencensement [census certificate] had her signature.

After a certain time ARCHAMBAUD was brought in. there was a conversation about an explosive which the Germans had taken, but nothing was said about members of the group. The Germans did not ask AREND anything about PROSPER. [...]

AREND said he saw ARCHAMBAUD only three or four times in all. He did not particularly like him, but that was purely personal. He was certainly surprised that ARCHAMBAUD had come with the Germans to his parents' house, but had the impression that he had given information about the small people in the organisation in order to save the important ones.

The last time he saw ARCHAMBAUD and PROSPER before their arrest was in a restaurant in the Rue de Megador, but he does not remember the exact date.

Madame AREND [Andrée's sister Leone] who was with her husband during the above interrogation, added that she felt certain that the concierge at 23 Rue Caumartin had collaborated. She has now disappeared.[59]

In recognition of Madame Anend helping SOE with their enquiries, her husband being sent to Germany and her only getting 2,700 francs a month as a mechanical engraving machinist at the Gare de Lyon, it was recommended that she be given 10,000 francs to help support her and her baby.[60]

The first report SOE received of their arrest was not until 14 July, three weeks later. Kramer's interviews with Andrée's relatives revealed that she had managed to smuggle messages out of prison written on cigarette paper. They were folded and hidden in her lingerie and sent to her sister Leone to be washed. Some were laundered in ignorance, and it was a sympathetic prison matron who alerted Leone of their existence. Most messages were to reassure her mother and request items like a sweater, notebook, and hairpins, ending with lots of kisses. Others indicated that she had been betrayed by Gilbert Norman. He was reported to have told her to tell the Germans what they wanted to know.[61]

Buckmaster said the messages she sent to him were full of courage and the unshaken belief that she would escape.[62] According to Foot, several Germans testified that she never talked at all and treated them with fearless contempt throughout her captivity.[63]

After Fresnes, she was sent to the Natzweiler-Struthof concentration camp in the Vosges mountains, about 50 km south-west of Strasbourg. Accompanying her were three other captured SOE agents, Diana Rowden, Vera Leigh and Sonia Olschanesky.

A month after D-Day, the four women were executed by phenol injection. Witnesses later told how Andrée was still conscious as she was dragged to the ovens to be cremated. Fighting to the last, she was said to have scratched her executioner's face.[64]

A memo from F Section added that the cell chief [Suttill] was useless without Andrée, owing to Suttill's accent and that she was 'A very gallant Frenchwoman, who took all the risks and shared 100% in the dangers of the work. With typical guts, she wrote from prison exhorting her friends to be courageous. We are very proud of her.'[65]

In Gubbins' citation for her award, he stated that,

This officer was parachuted into France in November 1942 as an assistant to an organiser in the Paris area. She proved herself an able and devoted lieutenant and was appointed second in command of the organisation. Owing to her cool judgment she was always chosen for the most delicate and dangerous work such as recruiting and arranging rendezvous, and she acted as 'cut-out' for her commanding officer.

Lt. Borrel was also given the task of organising parachute dropping operations, and took part in several coups de mains, notably an operation against the Chevilly [-la-Rue) power station (near Paris) in March 1943. She distinguished herself by her coolness and efficiency and always volunteered for the most dangerous tasks. Her commanding officer has paid tribute to her great qualities, describing her as 'a perfect lieutenant, an excellent organiser who shares all the dangers'.

Lt Borrel was arrested by the Gestapo in July 1943. For her great bravery and devotion during nine months of active underground work in France, it is recommended that she be appointed a Member of the Order of the British Empire. (Civil division).[66]

Atkins's report to the War Office on what happened to Andrée and the other SOE women agents sent to Natzweiler read:

Subject: S/O D.H. ROWDEN, WAAF, 4193

A.S.O. N. INAYAT KHAN, WAAF 9901

Miss V. LEIGH, FANY

Miss A. BORREL, FANY

1. In November of last year, I received information from A.G. 3 (VW) that three women, believed to have been British parachutists, had been seen in the camp of NATZWEILER in July 1944 and had been killed there on the evening of their arrival. Enquiries were started at once and have just been completed.

2. It has now been definitely established that the four women who were killed at NATZWEILER are the four listed above and that they were killed on 6 July 1944. They were given a narcotic injection, probably Evipen, and were immediately cremated. They were unconscious but probably still alive when thrown in the oven.

3. A number of Germans involved in this horrible murder are now arrested and will be tried as war criminals. I have requested that the names of the girls should be kept out of any account of the proceedings published in the press.

4. As you know, Diana ROWDEN was arrested near DIJON on 18 November 1943, Noor INAYAT KHAN in or near PARIS in October 1943, Vera LEIGH near PARIS on 19 November 1943, Andre BORREL near PARIS on 23 June 1943. All four were kept in prison in PARIS until May 1943. On the 12 May, eight of our girls left FRESNES prison near PARIS and travelled to KARLSRUHE, where they were placed in the civilian jail for women (source – Mrs. O. Sansom, 75 Harcourt Terrace, S.W.10) The party was made up of the following: - Odette SANSOM – Left KARLSRUHE prison about 15 July 1944 for Ravensbrück, now returned to the UK.

   Diana ROWDEN [A British F Section agent], Nora INAYAT KHAN [An Indian-British F Section agent], Vera LEIGH [A British F Section agent] and Andre BORREL, left KARLSRUHE prison during the night of 5/6 July 1944 and taken to NATZWEILER. Now known to have been killed there in the evening of 6 July 1944.

   Eliane PLEWMAN [A British F Section agent], Martine DAMERMENT, Yolande UNTERNAHRER [A Swiss F Section agent] – Left KARLSRUHE on the night of 11/12 September 1944 still untraced.

5. In KARLSRUHE they were placed in separate cells, which they shared with German women, who were there either as Political prisoners or as common criminals. They received the same rations and treatment and were given occasional exercise in the prison yard. They were not ill-treated and I think that they were better off than those in concentration camps. They managed to communicate with

one another, although they were never allowed to meet. I have several times interviewed the two women who were in charge of the prison and who are still employed at the KARLSRUHE (Fraulein Teheresia BOCHER, Fraulein Hagen FRAUENG PANGNIS, Academie Strasse, Karlsruhe). They were shown photographs and recognised the women listed in para 4. Their prison records have been destroyed and they cannot remember the dates and details of the departures.

6. I have interviewed a German who had been a political prisoner in the men's jail at KARLSRUHE and who had been employed in various prison tasks (Georg KAEMSMUND [sic] of Enesstrasse 29, Weierfeld, Karlsruhe. On their arrival in the jail this prisoner gave our women the forms which they had to fill in and he then realised that they were British or French. He remembered some of their names and he also remembered that one morning in July 1944 between 4 and 5 a.m. he was taking down the prison blackout, 7 women passed him in the corridor including some of the British girls he had seen on their arrival. Gestapo officers took charge, and he saw them lead them out to a strange looking grey car, which he said, resembled a hearse (presumably the Gestapo equivalent of the Black Maria [British prison van]).

7. The camp at NATZWEILER is in France near SCHIRMECK due west of STRASBOURG and about 100 miles by road from KARLSRUHE. When they arrived there in the early afternoon on 6 July between 1 and 3 p.m., they were seen by a great many of the inmates of the camp as they walked between S.S. from the camp gates down the main prison street via the Politische Leitun (the political department in the camp) to the Hellenbau [a block of cells constituting a prison within the camp]. Amongst those who saw them are: -
Lt. Comm. P. O'Leary R.N.V.R.
Capt. B. Stonehouse,
Capt. R. M. Sheppard

Unfortunately, however, none of these saw them at a sufficiently close range to identify them from photographs but, they gave descriptions of height, colour of hair, clothes, etc. it also became known that the girls came from KARLSRUHE. After seeing a number of witnesses from KARLSRUHE Prison I am satisfied that the 3 girls who remained behind the first departure of the four and followed by the departure of Odette SANSOM are: -
Eliane PLEWMAN
Martine DAMERMENT
YOLANDE UNTERNAHRER

Photographs of Diana ROWDEN, Nora INAYAT KHAN, Vera LEIGH and Andre BORREL have been shown to a great many prisoners from NATZWEILER. The following have been definitely recognised.

Andrée BORREL – by Mr G. BOOGAERTS of 41 Avenue Endore, Punez, BRUSSELS

Vera LEIGH – by Franz BERG of Block 1.7. No. 29 3rd Floor, MANNHEIM.

8. The following account of what happened to our girls at NATZWEILER, by piercing [sic] together eye-witness accounts of the persons named in para 7 and sworn statements of Marcel RAUSCH of 48A Avenue Michel Rodange, LUXEMBOURG, and Maurice BRUYNINOXX of 26 Rue de Spa, BRUSSELS.

They were fetched from KARLSRUHE prison between 4 and 5 a.m. on 6 July 1944 by members of the Gestapo either of KARLSRUHE or more likely of STRASBOURG. They were probably first taken to the Gestapo office for final interrogation; this would account for the time taken to cover the 90 – 100 miles between KARLSRUHE and NATZWEILER on the road that goes through STRASBOURG.

9. They arrived at the gates of the Camp between 1 and 3 p.m. on 6 July. They were lead into the camp by uniformed SS officers and taken to the political department. From there they were lead to the block of cells. On arrival there they were put together in one cell, after that, they appear to have been divided up into two cells and before the evening into separate cells. Andre BORREL got into communication Dr BOOGAERTS with whom she exchanged a few words through a window. He through [sic) her some cigarettes and she threw him her money bag, consisting of a tobacco pouch, which he still has in her possession. Vera LEIGH got into a conversation with a prisoner working in the Hennebau and asked him for a pillow. Lt. Comm. O'Leary was able to exchange a few words with either Diana ROWDEN of Noor INAYAT KHAN.

It became very quickly known in the camp that four women had arrived and it was feared that they could only have been brought in for the purpose of extermination. That night all prisoners were confined to their barracks at 8 p.m. and ordered to close their windows and put up the blackouts. The fires of the crematorium were seen, and these sinister signs were immediately linked to the presence of the girls. One prisoner was watching through a peephole in his shutter and between 9 and 10 p.m. he saw two SS men (Camp overseer SAUSS and the SS NCO in charge of the crematorium (Peter Straus) go to the Hellenbau and come away with one of the women who was led to the crematorium. The same two men came back three times, at about 15 minute intervals and led away the others. The next morning the prisoner doctor of the camp, who had access to the crematorium, went into the building immediately the curfew had been lifted. He looked into the oven and saw the charred bodies of women and one unburned woman's shoe.

10. The prisoner in charge of the crematorium, a German criminal, stated that he was instructed to light the furnaces, and have them at maximum heat by 9.30 a.m. at about that time the SS NCO in charge came into the crematorium accompanied by the SS Doctor and the former camp doctor. After assuring themselves that everything was in order, the SS locked up the prisoners who were working in the crematorium into the room in which they slept. They got into their bunks and the man who on the top bunk could observe what went on outside through a fanlight and told the others what he saw. First, various camp officials arrived, and all went into the doctor's room, which adjoined the men's bedroom. Then two SS men arrived with one of the British women; she was taken into the doctor's room and a few minutes later two SS medical orderlies dragged her out and along the corridor leading to the furnace room. This performance was repeated with each of the other three women. The fourth, however, resisted in the corridor and started to scream, she was overpowered, and a few minutes later she also was dragged out unconscious. The prisoners heard the doors of the crematorium open and assumed that the women were immediately cremated.

11. I have so far only been able to interrogate one of the SS men who was present at the execution, and he denies having been there. It is possible that when the others become available for interrogation, I may be able to obtain a sworn statement from them. It will, however, be appreciated that such statements are not readily given as in most cases they would constitute a death warrant for the man was present at the murder. It is, however, certain beyond any reasonable doubt that four women met their death as described above in the camp of NATZWEILER on the evening of 6 July 1944 and that those women have now been properly identified as: -
Diana ROWDEN
Nora INAYAT KHAN
Vera LEIGH
Andrée BORREL

12. You will no doubt take the usual casualty action. As requested, I attach draft letters to P.4. Cas., FANY, HQ and next of kin.[67]

Nine SS officers at Natzweiler were tried between 29 May and 1 June 1946 for their role in the murder of the four women. When Dr Grobel, the defence lawyer, argued that 'international law allowed for the execution of irregular combatants' and that the court should 'consider this case from the point of view that it was a normal and simple execution of spies', Vera

Atkins was quoted by the press as saying that 'the women were not spies'. Apart from Atkins, the key prosecution witnesses were Albert Guérisse (Pat O'Leary), Dr Georges Boogaerts and Brian Stonehouse.

As Andrée had nominated her sister, Madame Leone Arend, 23 Rue Caumartin, Paris, 9e, as her next of kin, she was sent £580 5s 2d, being what was left in her bank account, and a completed version of Vera's draft letter:

Dear _____,

It is with the deepest regret that I have to inform you of the death of _____ in the camp of NATZWEILER on the 6 July 1944. Death was caused by an injection of an overdose of narcotic and the body was immediately cremated.

I know that after these long months of waiting, the news will come as a very great shock to you in spite of the fact that the hope of finding _____ alive has seriously dwindled since last Autumn. The investigations into this case were made more difficult by the fact that _____ was killed on the day of her arrival in the camp of NATZWEILER. She was with three other girls who had been employed in the same work, and they shared the same tragic fate.

As you know _____ was arrested on _____ near _____. She remained in various prisons in or near Paris until May 1944. On 12 May 1944, a convoy of women left FRESNES prison near Paris and in this convoy were eight English girls who were taken straight to KARLSRUHE where they were put into the city jail for women. They remained there until the night of 5/6 July when four were taken to NATZWEILER. Your ____ was among them.

[......]

The only consolation that is possible to offer is that during their imprisonment they were not subjected to any form of torture and that their end came upon them too suddenly to cause prolonged suffering.

I hope that the knowledge of the valuable contribution that _____ made towards the final victory in preparing the ground for the invasion of France will comfort you in your great loss. All who came into contact with her during the time of her imprisonment have spoken most highly of her courage and morale.

I wish to express to you on behalf of myself and all members of my staff my sincere condolences in your bereavement.

In response to Leone's enquiries as to what punishment there might be for those responsible for Andrée's death, she was told by Major Nott of the War Office that the responsible officials, who were in Allied custody, were to be tried as war criminals and charged with 'complicity in the murder of Mlle Borrel.' There was also the warning that the press might report the names of the women, but he promised 'to endeavour to arrange for the suppression of her name from any reports which may be published.'[68]

Details of the trial can be found later. After the war, Andrée was posthumously awarded the King's Commendation for Brave Conduct, the Croix de Guerre, and the Medaille République Française.[69]

ODETTE SANSOM
Aged 30. Landed by a felucca at Port Miou (about 15 km south-east of Marseille) on 3/4 November 1942. Survived Ravensbrück, awarded the George Cross and Companion de Légion d'Honneur.

The next French woman sent into France was Odette Sansom, described as 1.68 m tall, vivacious and pretty, with brown hair and eyes and a fresh complexion. According to her personnel file, she was born Odette Brailly in Amiens, northern France, on 28 April 1912, Research by Jerrard Tickell, Beryl Escott, and Penny Starns into her childhood and adolescence in France revealed that she lost her father, a bank manager, during the fighting at Verdun during the First World War. Educated at the convent of St Thérèse, the nuns found Odette difficult. Suffering from various diseases as a young girl including temporary blindness and rheumatic fever, in 1926 her mother moved her and her brother to Boulogne on the Normandy coast to benefit from the sea air. In 1930, aged 18, she married Roy Sansom, a hotel worker, and son of a British soldier who had been billeted with her family during the war. Two years later they moved to London, and when her husband joined the Army and was posted overseas, she took her three daughters, Françoise, Lily, and Marianne, to live in Culmstock, a small village in Somerset. Her mother-in-law rented a property nearby to help out.

One evening, after listening to the news on the radio, she was intrigued by an appeal for photographs of the French coast. As she had some snapshots of her and her brother on the beach at Boulogne and Calais, she added details on the back and sent them to the Admiralty. When her letter was opened, it was passed on to SOE. Her knowledge of France made her a potential candidate.[70]

In a post-war interview she admitted that, during her meeting with Selwyn Jepson, the recruiting officer, she had lost her temper when she found out that enquiries had been made into her family and early life.

In Jepson's interview file, also in the Imperial War Museum, he acknowledged that,

> Odette was a shrewd cookie and she knew at once what it was about. She guessed and said, yes, she wanted to do it. [......] When could she start?

I was rather doubtful about her capacity. Although she had perfect French and knew France, her personality was so big that [...] I couldn't see her passing unnoticed. [....]. I remember very clearly on her piece of paper I wrote, 'God help the Germans if we can ever get her near them, but maybe God will help us on the way' – because she has such a huge personality and will dominate everybody she comes in contact with. Not necessarily because she has a dominant nature, but because she just can't help it.[71]

Another motivation for accepting Jepson's offer was a Red Cross messenger telling her that her brother had been wounded and was in a military hospital in Paris. Her home had been requisitioned by the Germans, and her mother had been forced to leave, losing all the family possessions. She was probably aware that English people living in France who had not managed to get to Britain were rounded up and interned, like the Germans, Italians and Japanese living in Britain. While she enjoyed living in rural Somerset, she thought that,

If I was in France, I could already be captured along with my children, but because I was in England I had an excuse to do nothing. It would be very easy for me to do nothing, to think that way[....] But then I thought, what if everyone thought like that? [....] What if nobody risked anything?? Am I going to be satisfied just staying put with my children? I knew that I had to do something, or at least I should try to do something. [....] I thought ... there is nobody left in my family to fight for the freedom of France now. My brother was in hospital, and nobody knew where my mother was, there was just me! I thought it is my duty to do what I can. [....] If I did the training and they said that I was unsuitable, then at least in would know that I tried. There was always that feeling that I was brought up with, that one must do one's duty to honour my father but also a duty to my country.[72]

As she was separated from her husband, she arranged for her three daughters, aged 7, 9 and 10, to be sent to St Helen's Convent boarding school in Brentwood, Essex, while she was 'working in Scotland'. During the school holidays, they were looked after by her two 'splendid aunts and devoted Uncle'.

Having informed Jepson of her decision, although heartbroken at leaving her children, she was given a commission in the FANY and joined the second group of women to undergo SOE training; the others were Mary Herbert, Lise de Baissac and Jacqueline Nearne. Unusually, there were no reports from the paramilitary or parachute training instructors, only a report from Lt-Col. Woolrych of The Rings, Beaulieu:

> She has enthusiasm and seems to have absorbed the teaching given on the course. She is, however, impulsive and hasty in her judgments and has not quite the clarity of mind which is desirable in subversive activity. She seems to have little experience of the outside world. She is excitable and temperamental, although she has a certain determination. A likeable character and gets on well with most people. Her main asset is her patriotism and keenness to do something for France; her main weakness is a complete unwillingness to admit that she could ever be wrong.[73]

Her reminiscences of Beaulieu were that, although she threw her heart and soul into it, she was desperate to get into the field. The worst aspect of it for her was the physical training:

> I was never very good at it really, but the training overall was very good. The preparation of one's mind was very good. I was intrigued and fascinated by it, the pattern of it all. They even woke us up in the middle of the night to test our reactions. There were eight or ten men dressed in Nazi uniform and they staged a mock interrogation. The preparation was very good.[74]

Jerrard Tickell, who published Odette's biography in 1949, commented that when she was asked by one of her training instructors how she might handle an assailant, she responded by saying that she would run and, if he pursued and caught her, she would pinch him and pull his hair. The instructor was said to have replied, 'Ladies, it will be my unwelcome and embarrassing duty to teach you other and less refined methods of disabling would-be aggressors ... I have never before had to teach such things to ladies.'[75] While doing a jump at Ringway, she smashed her face on the side of the hole as she was jumping out of a basket, sprained her ankle on landing and was sent to an ophthalmic outpatient clinic. In another conversation, she was reported describing how she could kill a German by jabbing a pencil through his ear.

> There was never any pressure, but the training made me all the more determined to do what I could. Not because I was marvelous in any way, but because I knew more about what was happening to people

in Europe. There were some English agents who had been captured but had escaped to find their way back to England and they told such dreadful tales about what happened to their friends; so you had a good idea what could happen to you if you were caught. You knew enough to make up your mind about whether you wanted to go into the field or not. The only confidence I had, was that I was confident in myself, not to do a marvelous job or marvelous physical things, but I knew that I could endure a lot. What you don't know is what you will do when you are put to the test. I had an instinct that things could go wrong.[76]

Buckmaster decided not to send her in as a courier or wireless operator, but, like Lise de Baissac, as an organiser in the area around Auxerre in Burgundy, north-central France. Her mission was to establish herself there, locate a safe house to provide temporary accommodation for newly arrived agents and recruit people who would help.

In Penny Starns' biography, *Odette*, she pointed out that Odette's fabricated cover story was backed up with false identity cards and ration cards.

Final preparations before going into the field included a detailed checklist of her person and her belongings. No longer would she be able to display finely manicured and varnished nails since, living as a quiet widow, making her living as a seamstress, her hands had to be well worn and needle-pricked., with an indentation on her left thumb from years of wearing a thimble. Her grey flannel suit was fitted with French clothing labels. In her subdued suitcase, lilac and pale blue blouses were folded, French style, alongside some loose fitting trousers, pullovers and underwear. Her face was scrubbed clear of make-up and her dark brown hair was pulled back from her face and tied severely with a black ribbon, a token of mourning for her late husband.

Some personal effects were necessary because the absence of these always aroused suspicion. A small constructed family photograph was fixed securely in a delicate French picture frame and placed amidst her clothes. Hair brushes, combs, a hand mirror, soap, a simple red lipstick and face powder all bore the hallmarks of reasonably priced French beauty shops. A French torch, compass, and map were tucked into her case for good measure. As she observed her suitcase crammed with her new belongings, an SOE official handed her a small packet that contained her suicide pill, a gentle reminder of her dangerous occupation. With a brief nod in his direction, she placed it in her handbag. Along with her official orders, she was also given the sum of 500 francs.

At the SOE briefing station Odette had been lectured about how she should behave in accordance with her new identity. She was not allowed to act in a flirtatious manner, nor draw attention to herself at any time. [....] Her accent needed to that of an ordinary working woman and not that of a sophisticated lady. Her walk, her mannerisms, eating habits, handwriting and general demeanour all needed to conform to her new persona. She needed to be vigilant at all times and not let her guard slip in any respect.[77]

Once briefed, she learned that the original plan to send her by submarine had been abandoned as the Royal Navy commanders had never taken women on board and were unwilling to make an exception. Arrangements were made with the Special Duties Squadrons so she was taken to Tempsford, checked over and put on a Whitley bomber destined for Gibraltar. Like Yvonne Rudellat, she was to be taken by felucca and dropped on the Mediterranean coast of France. However, as the plane was taxiing up the runway, another plane landed and crashed into it. Odette was lucky to escape uninjured.

Another flight was arranged the following week, this time in a Lysander. Once settled in the passenger seat, a messenger ran across the runway to tell the pilot to abort the mission. A message had come through saying that there would be no reception committee as they had all been arrested by the Germans.

A week later, she was taken to Plymouth harbour and boarded a Sunderland flying boat. Before the plane took off, a storm blew up causing the flight to be cancelled. Desperate that she be sent on the next available plane, the following week she boarded a Whitley bomber, but was only in the air a few minutes before it crashed a few feet from a cliff edge. Not to be outdone, she was sent to Greenock, a naval port near Glasgow in Scotland, to board a troop ship, which succeeded in dropping her at Gibraltar.

Like Yvonne Rudellat, Odette was landed by a felucca at Port-Miou, near Marseille on the Mediterranean coast, on 4 November 1942. Accompanying her were two FANY Lieutenants, Mary Herbert, code named Claudine, who went to work in the SCIENTIST network, and Marie-Thérèse le Chêne alias Adéle who went to work in the PLANE network, two SOE agents George Starr, code named Hilaire, and Marcus Bloom, code named Urbain, SIS agent Tom Groome who was to work for MI9 and Gracomino Galeae, an Italian Section agent.[78]

Tickell detailed how, using the code names 'Lise' and 'Clothier', she rendezvoused as planned with 'Raoul', Peter Churchill, in the back room of a beauty salon in Marseille. This was run by Marie-Lou Blanc, who accommodated some of the women agents at her home. Churchill was a

British agent who was on his third mission in France as organiser of the SPINDLE network, operating between Cannes and Marseille.

Too busy to arrange her trip to Auxerre, he wanted her to act as his courier and asked SOE for their agreement. Posing as Madame Odette Metayer, her cover story was that she was a widow whose husband had died of bronchitis. In reality, she and her companion 'Arnaud', Captain Adolphe 'Alec' Rabinovitch, selected drop zones for the containers of arms and other supplies that were delivered by Tempsford crews. Rabinovitch, parachuted on 28 August 1942 as Churchill's wireless operator was described on Nigel Perrin's website as Churchill's 'foul-mouthed, humourless Jewish Egyptian wireless operator who was burdened with transmitting SPINDLE's enormous backlog of messages to London.'

Buckmaster agreed to Churchill's argument that Odette was 'indispensable' to him, and she should be transferred to his network. Cammaert described Sansom, Churchill and Rabinovitch as a trinity. 'If Churchill always 'assumed the leisurely manner of the connoisseur' and Odette was 'of the moment', Rabinovitch was a tough 'who clearly believed nothing and nobody.' He would snarl at Churchill, 'I don't like fucking mountains, they fucking well interfere with my transmissions!'[79]

Before SOE's F and RF Sections began supporting Resistance groups in the south-east of France, they had been most involved in propaganda rather than sabotage. However, the Resistance in that area had suffered a major setback following the arrest of Captain Francis Basin, who had been infiltrated on 19 September 1941. According to historian Ray Jenkins, thirty-one groups operating from the Italian border, along the Mediterranean coast and the foothills of the Pyrénées as far west as Toulouse, collapsed. Fearful of further arrests. SOE had no alternative but to forge links with André Giraud's CARTE organisation based in Antibes, on the Mediterranean coast between Nice and Cannes. Jenkins claimed that CARTE gave the appearance of an organised Resistance group but on closer inspection,

> ...revealed itself, unlike the Communists and the Gaullists, to be totally lacking in any political or organisational rigour. It was the plaything of a painter, André Giraud, a noisy, persuasive patriot with his feet 'firmly anchored in the clouds', a hater of Hitler, de Gaulle, Pétain, politics and the British, a lover of America: a fantasist who claimed he could raise a force of 300,000-strong nationwide yet was never guilty of a single act of sabotage. CARTE properly belonged to the high-living, surreal world of the Riviera, to an unoccupied zone mentality where the 'citizens' took

their politics from a German-controlled magazine, Signal, and where the war, already costing £15 million a day, didn't exist.[80]

It was into this mix that Odette was to added. Churchill sent her on a mission to Marseille, but when she did not return on time, he arranged for the trains to be watched, eventually replacing the man sent to keep watch at the station with himself. Both he and Arnaud were in awe of her.

In his autobiography, Churchill related how one of the rendezvous he had sent her on involved meeting a Dr Bernard to collect documents for the British, including a map of the Marseille naval base. Concerned about her security, he found her a room for the night in what he considered the safest house in town – a brothel. She spent a nerve-wracking and sleepless night because, according to Churchill, the place had been raided by the German Military Police in search of *réfractaires*, men who had avoided being called up to go and work in German factories in France or Germany. The only reason her room was not searched was that the madame – a patriot – told the police that her niece was sleeping in that room and that she had got scarlet fever.

When several contacts in the Resistance were arrested, Odette and Churchill had to make themselves scarce, moving to Arles for the winter. On the train journey there, she astounded her friends by taking a request for two francs for the 'Winter Relief Fund' to a German general sitting in the restaurant car, suggesting that he ought to contribute as it was his army that had caused the distress. To avoid creating a commotion the general paid it.[81]

There was a Resistance group based 16 km away in Faverges for which they arranged supplies. During the time Odette was operating, she helped arrange arms drops for several thousand poorly armed *réfractaires* camped out on the Plateau de Glières.

When Churchill was ordered to return to England for a conference, 'Arnaud' arranged a Lysander pick-up. In the early hours one morning while waiting at the DZ, they eventually heard its engine. Churchill was about to flash his recognition letter to the pilot when suddenly a searchlight flooded the landing strip. German soldiers, informed by a traitor in the network, approached from the bushes. Splitting up, they ran off. Not having not got the agreed signal, the pilot swung his plane around and returned to England. Running through the darkness, Odette heard dogs coming after her. Remembering her lessons on evasion techniques, she made her way to a nearby river, waded through the icy-cold water and reached the other side. Luckily, they both managed to get away.

When another DZ was suggested, the SOE's Liaison officer suggested a different one as it had already been designated for RF Section.

Consequently, they moved back to Cannes in the spring. But it was not for long. Following the arrest of two of their close contacts, they moved north into the Jura of the Haute Savoie and stayed in the Hotel de la Poste in the little village of St Jorioz, about 8 km from Annecy and 40 km from Geneva. Odette had an 'authentic' medical certificate stating that she had consumption and needed to stay above 400 metres.

Arnaud stayed up the mountain and arranged a successful Lysander pick-up for Churchill on 23 March 1943 from a field near Estrées St Denis, 10 km west of Compiegne. The incoming passengers were Francis Cammaerts code named Jockey and George Duboudin code named Playwright.[82] Cammaerts had been sent to assess the state of the Resistance in the area and report back.

The report Churchill brought back to London criticised some of the Frenchmen he had had to deal with:

> Most Frenchmen cannot bear to be in the wrong, and they still blame Britain for their defeat. The more sensible and thinking Frenchmen are pro-British. The French resisting groups are saying 'Help us now and when it is over, leave us to our own salvation.' They consider as their chief enemies those Frenchmen who have been bullied by the Germans and who have been drawn into the net of 'SYNARCHISME'. Such as the Worms group, Borotra, Chevalier and many others, they consider themselves technicians and their role to order Franc3 for the profit of Germany. In fact, they have become Germanised.[83]

Cammaerts was not impressed with the security of the group who escorted him to Paris and returned to join the DONKEYMAN network in Annecy. Worried when he found out that Hugo Bleicher, a sergeant in the Abwehr, had penetrated this network, he too moved to St Jorioz. He reported being told by Mme Cottet at the Hotel de la Poste that it was the headquarters of Peter Churchill, Odette and indeed of the CARTE organisation. 'It was public, far from silent, full of mysterious comings and goings, unsafe.'[84] As she had been left in charge while Churchill was away, she arranged a safe house for him in Cannes.

Starns described Odette as being shocked by the number of luxury goods available on the black market in southern France compared to the austerity she had lived with in Britain.

> She also despised the glamorous empty-headed wives of Vichy officials who flaunted their wealth and prestige by attending their hair and beauty salons as though nothing untoward was happening around them.

It was like another world entirely, and as a native Frenchwoman, she despaired at the shame of Vichy France. Cannes still boasted an array of beautiful, elegant houses and quaint, expensive shops.... and the people calmly went about their business, seemingly oblivious to the overriding tyranny that had swept across Europe.[85]

Within a few weeks, Arnaud received a message that Churchill was to return on 16 April, and Odette sent a message back saying she had been visited by 'Henri', identified later as Bleicher. If she could arrange a Hudson pick-up for him and his mistress to go to England, he promised her the release of the two prisoners. He also wanted her to arrange for a wireless set to be sent and claimed that he represented a group of Nazis who were planning a coup against Hitler and were keen to arrange a truce and end of the war. The message she got back from London told her that Bleicher was 'treacherous' and not to be trusted. She had to dissolve her network, cut contact with the Annecy group and move immediately to the other side of the lake.

'Arnaud' found another safe house, set up his transmitter and looked for a safe DZ. The site they chose was the snow-covered summit of Mount Semnoz, about 5 km south of Annecy. They had paced out 100 metres to the right and left to ensure there was enough room for a drop and prepared a bonfire the day before. Despite London telling her not to be part of the reception committee, she went anyway. When they heard Flight Officer Legate's 30-ton Halifax bomber approaching, the bonfire was lit with a bottle of petrol, and they flashed the letter 'F'. Legate reported that at 0052 hours on 16 April 1943, he dropped the agent at 800 feet at an airspeed of 140 mph, closely followed by five containers.

According to Gibb McCall in his *Flight Most Secret*, Odette did not know that Churchill had been ordered not to get in touch with her. She had been compromised. He was singing the Marseillaise, the song of the Resistance, when he landed in her arms. As they came down the snow-covered slopes above Lake Annecy in the pitch dark, she slipped and fell ten metres down an almost vertical gulley, knocking herself out. X-rays taken after the war show she had shattered her fifth vertebra. Overcoming the pain, she whisked Churchill off to a room in the hotel, saying that he was her husband. She did not think 'Henri' would be back for four days.

Churchill had disobeyed orders. He had been instructed to go straight to a safe house in Glaieuls, about 5 km north of the ski resort of La Clusaz. Instead, they went to the hotel and a few hours later, according to Odette's testimony, she was awoken by M. Cottett. There was a man downstairs who wanted to see her at once. Not suspecting anything untoward she went down to the lobby to find 'Henri' and several other men standing there with pistols. She was marched back upstairs with a pistol in her back.

According to Churchill, 'Henri' burst into his room with a contingent of Alpini, Italian soldiers who were controlling that part of south-east France. Some in the French Resistance and Bleicher himself claim that they were still in bed together when they were captured.

During the commotion, Odette managed to hide Churchill's wallet – containing telephone numbers of some of his contacts and 70,000 francs – and pack some warm clothes. He had previously passed on half a dozen new radio crystals, half a million francs, two Belgian automatics, a Sten gun, 200 blank identity cards and dozens of ration books to one of the reception committee. Dressed in her one and only dark-grey suit, with silk stockings and square-toed shoes, they were driven to an Italian prison.

Three weeks later, they were taken by train to Paris. During the journey, she managed to share a few moments of conversation with Churchill and pass him her tiny crucifix. Incarcerated in Frèsnes Prison, she managed to save the fresh bread she was given, only eating the stale so that she might pass on bits when she saw Churchill on the occasions 'Henri' allowed them to be together. There were days when she was taken to Avenue Foch, the Gestapo headquarters, for interrogation.

Churchill recalled in his third book, *Spirit in the Cage*, how on one occasion, when their convoy had just arrived back from an interrogation session,

> I found myself in a large open pen where the whole group was herded together under the eye of a guard while waiting for the next move. I slipped up close to Odette and as she spoke to me with her back to the sentry, a girl I had never seen before, but who was patently English to her finger tips, stood between me and the guard so that he would not see my mouth moving. Despite my anxiety not to miss a second of this golden opportunity to speak with Odette, I was nevertheless instinctively conscious of this girl's unselfish act which included a delicacy of feeling that made her turn about and face the German so as not to butt in on our privacy. I could not imagine what this refined creature with reddish hair was doing in our midst.
>
> 'Who is she?' I asked Odette.
>
> 'Diana Rowden,' she replied. 'One of us.'[86]

He reported her occupying herself while confined by working in the sewing room. As the guards were wearing a new style of Afrika Korps cap, in the ones she made, on the piece of cardboard that stiffened the peak, she wrote the words 'Made in England'. She jammed her scissors into the holes of the power point to blow the fuses and cut the electric wires so that she could get the guards to fetch the hungriest prisoners on the pretext that they were electricians, and they could be given extra food while 'on the job'. She also saved any spare cloth to make children's toys like rabbits and dolls.

> Her moral courage and fearlessness were like a fountain of strength upon which I was to draw on many a future occasion of black despair ... Odette's morale was sky-high. It was where she had put it and maintained it through her own optimistic personality, and it had devolved on other prisoners and guards alike. I began to understand what Paul Steinert meant by the regard in which he said she was held. But what I did not and could not understand was the principal reason for these words, since neither he, nor Odette, nor Henri ever told me of the sufferings she had undergone, for it was her intention that I should never know, and she had sworn those who knew to silence.[87]

In her book *Death Be Not Proud*, Elizabeth Nicholas claims that Bleicher penetrated some the 'F' Section SOE Resistance groups. As a result, not all the drops from Tempsford went as planned. She believes that the first vital penetration of SOE was in autumn 1941 by Mathilde Carré. Termed affectionately by Bleicher as 'La Chatte' because she often curled up contentedly in large armchairs, Carré was a member of Inter-Allied, a very early Resistance group founded by some Polish groups stranded in France after 1940. She was arrested but, unwilling to accept life in prison, was seduced into becoming Bleicher's mistress. He had her installed in an establishment called 'The Cattery', where she continued to work her wireless, sending German-inspired messages to London.

Rita Kramer's *Flames in the Field* details the penetration and deception, the double and triple crossing that was going on on both sides. She explained how, following the Gestapo's successful penetration of the Dutch Resistance, the head of Netherlands Section sent to the person he thought was his agent, contact details of a PROSPER agent in Paris who would help Dutch agents to escape through France. With this information, the Germans were then able to send a double agent to penetrate PROSPER and capture numerous radios and their operators. Those men and women who succumbed to German persuasion allowed the Nazis to play the same game with Baker Street.

Pretending that she was Churchill's wife and saying that he was Winston Churchill's nephew may have kept her alive. Tickell claims that, during Odette's interrogation, one of the assistants

> ...began leisurely to unbutton her blouse. She said, 'I resent your hands on me or on my clothes. If you tell me what to do and release your hands on me, I will do it.' 'As you wish, unbutton your blouse.' Having already been burnt by a hot poker on her spine, she was then told to take off her stockings and her toenails were extracted. 'To be tortured by this clean, soap-smelling, scented Nordic was one thing. To be touched by his hands was another.' Before her fingernails were removed, a higher ranking officer stopped the interrogation, but she was warned, 'If you speak about what has happened to a living soul, you will be brought here again and worse things will happen to you.' [Though] she had kept silent, she was filled with sickness and fear for she had heard of some of the other things that the Gestapo could do to women's bodies.[88]

She was said to have had fourteen interrogations, during which she refused to give any information about her friends:

> I could have told them what they wanted to know, just like that. They wanted to know where our radio operator was; they wanted to know where another British agent who had arrived some time before had been to, and now was. I'm not brave or courageous; I just make up my own mind about certain things, and when this started, this treatment of me, I thought, 'There must be a breaking point.' Even if in your own mind you don't want to break, physically you're bound to break after a certain time. But I thought, 'If I can survive the next minute without breaking, this is another minute of life, and I can feel that way instead of thinking of what's going to happen in half an hour's time when having torn out my toenails they're going to start on my fingers.'[89]

Bleicher told her that, if she was prepared to work for him as a double agent, she would be well treated. When she refused, she was told that she was condemned to death as a British spy. Never knowing when the execution was to take place, every time the door of her cell was opened, she expected the worst.

On Armistice day, when I had been in prison since April, at ten o'clock in the evening I was taken out of my cell and taken down to the courtyard of the prison. There was a car waiting with two men in uniform and the man who tortured me, who was not in uniform, said, 'Well, as you are so devoted to your country, I thought you'd like to go to the Arc de Triomphe on 11 November and see the German guard standing there.' We went, believe it or not, around and around the Arc de Triomphe. I said to him, 'You like what you are doing, the job you are doing. You are a sick man. You like doing this.'[90]

To keep up appearances she used margarine as face cream, turned up the hem of her prison skirt an inch every day so as not to let the worn part show, and used rags from her stockings every night to act as rollers in her hair. Interviewed by Pattinson about her time in the concentration camp, she said, 'I used to put them on every evening religiously in case they would fetch me the next morning to put me to death. I wasn't going to be seen going to my death without my curls.' Machine-gun turrets, searchlights, Alsatian dogs and electric wires surrounded the compound, thereby limiting any chance of escape.[91]

In Mavis Nicholson's *What Did You Do in the War, Mummy?* Odette admitted that during her solitary confinement she visualised the routine domestic chores undertaken by wives and mothers and imagined making clothes and decorating the rooms of her three daughters:

I imagined what I wanted them to wear, then I would get the pattern, then the material, lay it out, cut it out and stitch it. Every single stitch I'd sew until it was all finished. Then I would refurnish all the houses of people I'd known, starting with walls, carpets, curtains.[92]

According to Starns, Odette was sentenced to death on two counts by a court at Avenue Foch to which she replied politely, 'Then you will have to make up your mind on which count I am to be executed because I can only die once.'[93]

On 12 May 1944, she was collected in a van, taken to a beautifully decorated room in Avenue Foch and locked in with seven ill and miserable-looking women, whom she discovered were SOE agents. Provided with cigarettes and tea and milk in china cups, they were allowed to chat. No doubt the room was bugged. From there they were taken by train to Karlsruhe civilian prison. Not allowed to be together, they shared a cell with two or three German women prisoners, including anti-Nazi activists, black marketeers, and prostitutes.

On 18 July 1944, she was put on one of the 'death trains' and sent first to Frankfurt, then Halle and finally to Ravensbrück concentration camp, 80 km north of Berlin. Gleeson reported that on the way, one of the guards thumped her hard in the mouth, saying, 'I give you that for Winston Churchill – with my compliments.'

Ravensbrück was a forced labour camp where medical experiments, like testing gangrene injections, were undertaken. Her underground cell, where she was again kept in solitary confinement for three months, was within earshot of the execution yard. When the guards switched the light on to bring her rations, it blinded her. She was given a cup of watery ersatz coffee and a slice of black bread, later a bowl of thin soup made from unwashed vegetable scraps, and lastly another coffee. During the hot August days, the central heating was turned on full blast. Depending on the moods of her sadistic guards, she was starved and subjected to extremes of light, dark, heat and cold. Although burnt on her back, she never broke her heroic silence.

As the Allies approached Berlin, Fritz Sühren, the commandant of the largest women's camp ever known, believing Odette's story that she was the niece by marriage to Winston Churchill and Geneviève de Gaulle's claim that she was the niece of the French president, drove them in his white limousine as hostages to the American lines to give himself up. It was 29 April 1945. Tania Szabó, in her book *Young, Brave and Beautiful*, an account of her mother's life, tells how Geneviève, ill with pleurisy, described Odette as a 'terribly gaunt woman who seemed very old. A few stray hairs had grown again on her shaven head.' Both were still in their 20s.[94]

When Sühren told the Americans that Odette was a relation of Winston Churchill and that she had been a prisoner, she told them Sühren was the commandant of Ravensbrück. He was arrested and, although a physical and nervous wreck, she managed to seize his Walther PPK pistol and returned to England with it, along with two dolls she made out of scraps of material; it can be seen on display at the Imperial War Museum.

Speaking to the Museum in 1986, Odette described her first night of freedom from the camp as 'unforgettable. It was a glorious night, full of stars and very cold. The Americans wanted to find me a bed for the night, but I preferred to sit in the car. It was so long since I had seen the night sky.'[95]

When she returned to England, she stayed at Churchill's accommodation at 75 Harcourt Terrace, Kensington, and when she was reunited with her daughters, she learned that her husband had died whilst she was in prison.

Following her interrogation, a report was written up detailing her experiences in France, Italy and Germany which shed light on conditions in France between 1942 and 1943, the conflicts within the French Resistance and the difficulties faced by the SOE agents sent into France to help. It needs to be stressed that she had just returned from two years in captivity, much of the time in solitary confinement where she would have had time to think deeply about what had happened to her before her arrest and then during interrogation and torture. Also, SOE's interrogators tended to be male, it is unlikely she provided them with the details she would have given a woman.

SOURCE'S ARRIVAL IN THE FIELD

Source arrived in France on the night of 2 November 1942. Source went by felucca from Gibraltar with Captain YOUNG [George Starr code named Hilaire], URBAIN [Marcus Bloom], Madame [Marie-Therese] LECHÊNE [code named Adèle], Miss [Mary] HERBERT and EMILE. [According to Tillet, there were two others on the boat, Gracomino Galeo and Tom Groome, an M19 wireless operator destined for Albert Guerrise's escape line. It is possible she made a mistake as Emile was the code name of John Starr, the brother of George Starr, who returned to England on the felucca.] Her instructions were to go to AUXERRE, find a safe house there and start up a circuit. She was to meet RAOUL in CANNES, and he was to give her a contact in PARIS. They went to CASSIS near MARSEILLE, and there Source met some French people from the CARTE organisation – Dr BERNARD and LOUIS. They only stayed two or three hours at CASSIS and then went to CANNES. There was an Italian in the party who left them at Cannes. They had all been given the address of the Villa Augusta, CANNES, in London and there they met RAOUL [Peter Churchill] about 1140 a.m. on 3 November. Miss HERBERT, Madame LECHENE and Source all stayed at the Villa Augusta and the men stayed with the Baron de MALVAL at the Cilla Isabelle. Sources instructions were that RAOUL with the help of CARTE [André Girard] would get her through the demarcation line. RAOUL at once get in touch with CARTE, who was no help at all. He said that until he had a message from London, he would not do anything, in fact, he was almost rude to Source. Source told RAOUL that she did not want to stay about doing nothing and suggested that she should help him to which he agreed.

SOURCE STARTS WORK WITH RAOUL

Source then started doing courier work for RAOUL. About 6 November he sent her off on a mission to MARSEILLE where she had to contact GILS and DISELLE and to take them a message from RAOUL. She was also supposed to contact MARSAC @ MURIEL, and bring back a case to CANNES for RAOUL. [André Marsac was one of the CARTE network who had his briefcase stolen while he was asleep on a train and the contents, 200 names and addresses of resistance members, fell into the hands of the Gestapo. He was arrested in Paris on 24 March 1943, the day after Odette and Churchill.] They could not find this case for a long time and Source stayed in Marseille for one night. All this time she was living with RAOUL at the Villa Augusta, and they were working as husband and wife. During her courier work, she used to go to GOLFE JUAN and meet SEBASTIEN and VALENTIN.

At the end of November, it was decided that either RAOUL or CARTE had to go back to London, and a Halifax operation was tried on a ground near ARLES. Unfortunately, when they got there, they found the ground had been ploughed up, presumably by the Germans and probably only the day before. RAOUL, CARTE, Colonel VAUTRIN, JABOUM and Source all went to the ground and when the plane came over RAOUL made a sign to show that they were there but that the operation could not be carried out. Colonel VAUTRIN walked across the field with CARTE and got very cross and excited, and they were all very rude and said that the British were stupid. This ground had been chosen by CARTE's people and RAOUL had sent it back to London via ARNAUD. They got the field through a woman living in a village near MANOSQUE near AIX-EN-PROVENCE. This woman had a daughter about 15 who was an idiot. The woman was tall, thin with fair hair nearly grey and was over 40. Her husband was in the Army but not in France. They returned to CANNES after this and went back to work.

CARTE

About this time the men working for CARTE decided they did not want to work with him any more. They came to RAOUL and said they wanted to work with him and there was nearly a small revolution. RAOUL got into touch with London and told them of this difference and they then had special orders to send CARTE to London. They tried the operation again at the end of December in a new field near ARLES; Source believes this ground was also found by CARTE. The plane came but something went wrong with the times, and the operation could not be done. – Source thinks it was the fault of the RAF – so this field became brule ['burnt' – unusable as the Germans knew all about it] after Christmas.

They went back again to CANNES, and things were going very badly with CARTE. His lieutenant [Henri] FRAGER did not want to work with him anymore. Source's opinion of FRAGER is that he is a very good man for an army job, he is certainly very clever and did not work to achieve glory for himself as did CARTE. Even CARTE's own men did not want to work with him anymore. Source refused to work with him as his security was so bad and it was just not safe. RAOUL complained about CARTE's insecurity, and London gave orders that RAOUL should come with CARTE to London, and things could be settled. In January, they were supposed to make the operation in TOURNUS [by the River Saône, between Chalon-sur-Saône and Mácon]. This operation was only for RAOUL as by that time they had nothing to do with CARTE. He arranged his operation through the Gaullists, and they knew nothing about it until it had taken place. As things were becoming very difficult RAOUL thought he could not possibly leave France, so suggested that Source should go to London. Source accordingly went to TOURNUS with RAOUL, FRAGER, CARTE and ROGER. The latter was a Frenchman from LYONS, who was acting as a courier for FRAGER. He was tall, thin and about 26 years old. RAOUL was organising this operation. At TOURNUS the night before they were expecting the operation, RAOUL said he would go and look at the field so he took a bicycle and went off. On the field he was met by some people who asked: 'Have you got the potatoes?' He replied that he did not understand and thinking this procedure rather strange he stayed there in a corner of the field. After a time, a plane came down and he saw some people coming off and others going in. The plane was there for 2½ hours because it got stuck in the mud. By this time, of course, everyone in TOURNUS had heard about this plane, and so the field was brule and early next morning the Germans were on the field. This operation was done by the Gaullist organisation and took place about 18 January. Source and RAOUL were then living in ANNECY and ST. JORIOZ [a village in the Haute-Savoie close to the Swiss and Italian borders] was their H.Q. They moved there just before this operation. The reason they moved was mainly because of CARTE's insecurity. He was going about telling people he would get everyone put in jail. RAUL's security was very bad as CARTE and his men were so talkative that many people knew they were staying in the Villa Augusta. It was, therefore, imperative they should move. Also, there was some trouble with the Baron DE MALVAL. He was left in charge of some money, and when they asked for it, it could not be found. There was some argument, and they rather suspected him.

LOUIS THE BELGE

CARTE was now in London, and FRAGER was left in charge with MARSAC. As the operation could not be carried out, the ground being brule, they came back to ANNECY and had orders from London to try the operation again somewhere around TOURNUS in March. They stayed for two or three days at a farm at BOCCA [just west of Cannes] before they went to ANNECY. LOUIS le Belge was also staying on this farm. He was about 26, young, fair, short. The people on this farm told them not to trust LOUIS because of the way he was talking. He was working for CARTE.

CHAILLAN

Before going to ANNECY Source met CHAILLAN [Henri Bardet]. Source had met him in CANNES but did not know him well. She was not taken by him and he men certainly did not like him. MARSAC alone thought he was a good man. Source told RAOUL she did not think it was any good having a man like that and that it was mad for the men's morale apart from anything else.

KIKI

In MARSEILLE in December 1942, in the P.C. [Poste de Commandement – Command Post or Headquarters] rue St Bazil, Source met a man known as KIKI. Source believes he was working for MURIEL, but knows nothing else about him. He looked like a ruffian. (LISE was shown by the interrogator officer three photographs of KIEFFER [Head of German counter-intelligence in Paris] with some hesitation she recognised him as this man KIKI and she also said that she was certain she had also seen this man somewhere else. She thought unconnected with the work, but she could not remember where.)

ST. JURIOZ

It was about the middle of January, 1943, that they moved to ST. JORIOZ which was about six miles from ANNECY. MURIEL and his wife and their son, MIREILLE, Monsieur and Madame LEJEUNE, Roger CHAILLAN, RIQUET and a French captain were all living in a villa about 200 yards from the place in which source lived. FRAGER was living at MONTON the other side of the lake [Lac d'Annecy] and RAOUL and she were living at the COTTET's, the Hotel de la Poste, ST. JORIOZ. It was extremely bad security all those people living together in the Villa. They used to take people into their house, and the villagers thought they were Jewish refugees. ARNAUD was living at FAVERGE [about 20km south-east of Annecy]

His [Arnaud's] security was excellent, and he was an extremely good worker. He had a terrible temper but RAOUL could manage him; and RAOUL, ARNAUD and Source always got on very well together. Source's security was good since she had a medical certificate to say that she had to have a rest and live at the same altitude. They got our identity cards through MURIEL.

RAOUL AND FRAGER'S JOURNEY TO ENGLAND – MARSAL'S [sic] ARREST

Raoul and FRAGER went to England on 14 March. The operation was going to take place at TOURNUS but it was put off, and they eventually went from a field near COMPEIGNE. Source was not there for this operation as she was doing a job in MARSEILLE. M. LEJEUNE, MARSAL [*sic*] and Source believe PIQUET went to help the operation. During March Source just went on with her ordinary work. From time to time she was still going to Marseille to take and fetch messages from GILS and GISELLE because they had no radio. When she came back to ST. JORIOZ about 15 or 16 March, MURIEL had not yet returned from the operation. She thought he was coming straight back so began to worry when he did not turn up. Then M. LEJEUNE and RIQUET came back from PARIS and said that MURIEL was in the hands of the Gestapo. They brought back with them an Englishman called ROGER [Captain Francis Cammaerts, SOE agent, who was landed by the Lysander that took Churchill and Frager back to England on 23 March 1943] and Source put him in a safe place in ST. JORIOZ. Source thought they had better keep quiet about MURIEL so she told the others not to say anything and they did not let Madame MARSAC know. LEJEUNE told Source that MURIEL was sitting in a café with LUCIENNE, and someone was supposed to be coming to contact him. When this person arrived, he brought the Gestapo with him. This person had contacted MARSAC before, but RAOUL and Source did not know him or who he was. Source believes he had a sister in Paris where he was working. LUCIENNE was Mlle FROMAGOT. [Lucienne Fromageau was an SOE agent who had been working in immigration department of US Embassy in Marseille.] They had previously told MARSAC that he should not go to PARIS, but he took no notice. LUCIENNE's sister was also working for MARSAC; her name was SIMONE. She was living outside ANNECY in a hotel. No one wanted to have anything to do with CHAILLAN so the men used to come to Source for orders, and she told CHAILLAN, the FROMOGOTs and LEJEUNE that they should leave the P.C. CHAILLAN wanted to go and live in ANNECY and ARNAUD was furious about this. ROGER was lying low all this time. He was so very English that Source was worried about him and told him not to move about until he was accustomed to the place. Source used to take him out at nights.

HENRI

Source still stayed at ST. JORIOZ; and Madame LEJEUNE and Madame MARSAC were still living at the P.C. One morning Source went to ANNECY. She believes it was to contact SIMONE. She came back by bus and in the bus noticed a very strange looking man. She was with Madame FROMAGOT who was going to have lunch with her; so Source told her to go on in and she would follow this man as she did not like the look of him. She went on to the terrace outside the first floor of the hotel and had a perfect view. She saw him go into the P.C. so she followed and saw him sitting there with Madame LEJEUNE. She went into the hotel and had lunch and when she had nearly finished this man came into the Hotel de la Poste with M. LEJEUNE. M. LEJEUNE was talking in a very silly way and in a rather loud voice about their work; so she called to him and told him to be careful. This other man did not speak to her; he looked at her very hard and smiled. M. LEJEUNE came and told Source afterwards that this man was from the Gestapo but he was not a Nazi; he was a very high German officer and quite all right. He said he had a letter from MARSAC, which Source saw and which was certainly in his writing, and it mentioned the last meal they had together and the things his son used to say. The letter told them to give him a radio set which CHAILLAN was willing to do but Source was not. Source knew they had SERVAIS' [another SOE agent] set but did not trust the strange man. MURIEL tried to show that everything was alright by saying: 'Je benirais le jour de mon arrestation si mes projets se realisent...' [I will bless the day of my arrest if my projects are realised.] HENRI, the German, [Hugo Bleicher] had taken the bus back to ANNECY. CHAILLAN told Source that HENRI had told him of MARSAC's arrest and he said he wanted to get to England and see some people at the War Office and that a lot of good would come of it. He said that if they could get him and a woman called SUZANNE back to England he would set MARSAC free and take him also to England. CHAILLAN told Source he would go to PARIS and meet HENRI and release MARSAC. Source immediately contacted ARNAUD who sent a message to London telling them the whole story and asking for advice. Source got a reply from London telling them to go carefully but do what they thought best; they thought it was obviously a 'piege' [trap]. Meanwhile CHAILLAN went off to PARIS alone to meet MARSAC, and Source carried on doing courier work. CHAILLAN came back two days later. They knew they were safe for a little while as HENRI wanted to get a plane and probably wanted to catch RAOUL and FRAGER. CHAILLAN came back and said MARSAC was all right; but he said that he could not possibly stay in jail and of course the operation HENRI wanted would have to take place in order to get him out. Source did not agree with him as she thought MARSAC had only himself to blame and just have to take the consequences. Source thinks CHAILLAN wanted MARSAC back as the man obviously did not want to work under CHAILLAN and the only way he could stay and work would be with MARSAC. They did not tell CHAILLAN too much and let him think the operation might take place. England told them to lay off the German colonel so they let HENRI also think that the operation would take place; therefore, they were left alone for a while.

RAOUL'S RETURN – SOURCE AND RAOUL'S ARREST

They had a message from London asking us to go and look at the SEMNOZ [the 1,699 m. massif above Viuz-la-Chiesaz] near St. JERIOZ and to see if the operation on which RAOUL was to come back might take place there. ARNAUD and Source decided that they would not tell CHAILLAN where RAOUL was coming back and so went off to look at this ground by themselves. They got there very late in the evening. They thought it could be done so they got some wood together and put it in a dry place and went back to ST. JORITZ. Next day ARNAUD sent a message to say it was alright and that the operation must take place before the 14 March as HENRI had only given them up to the 18th. Source had to tell CHAILLAN that FRAGER and RAOUL were coming back but he had no idea where; she said she would let him know where FRAGER was arriving. ARNAUD and Source then told CHAILLAN that the operation for the German colonel would be a very difficult thing to do and he took it very badly. He apparently took a train to PARIS straight away and told HENRI that the operation would not take place, but that RAOUL and FRAGER were coming back. Source and ARNAUD did not know of course that CHAILLAN was telling this to HENRI and still thought they had until the 18th. The day before the operation Source sent ROGER to a safe place in the south of France and ARNAUD moved away. Source fixed that RAOUL and she should go to the Hotel Glaiculles at TALLOIRE [a village on the east bank of Lac d'Annecy]. On the 14th the BBC message for RAOUL came through and ARNAUD, M. COTTET and Source went off and got there about 1210 [0010] a.m. on top of the SEMNOZ. They got the fire and lights ready and about 0100 the plane came and everything went off perfectly. They received a radio set, some clothes and dynamite and had one container that they could not open. They could not get it down from the top of the SEMNOZ so put it in the cellar of a deserted hotel on the top. They got back to the Hotel de la Poste about 08:00 a.m., then changed their clothes and took the bus to ANNECY where Source was supposed to contact SIMONE. She came back before lunch, had lunch with RAOUL and they went to TALLOIRE by boat across the lake. They returned and then went by bicycle on the road to FAVERGE to meet ARNAUD who had a message for RAOUL, GILS and GISELLE, something for Captain MOREL of ANNECY and something for Source. RAOUL came back and put the message for MOREL and GILS and GISELLE on a chair. They had supper, did their work and Source told RAOUL about HENRI. About 11 o'clock she was just taking her clothes off when Monsieur and Madame COTTET came up and into the room (that struck Source as rather peculiar even though they were very friendly with them) and told Source that LOUIS le Belge was asking for her. As no-one knew RAOUL was back yet, Source told him to stay in the room. Source went down into the hall and met HENRI and some Italians [the Italians had been given responsibility for the security of this area of south-east France], and a tall thin German from the Gestapo. He had a lot of fair hair, civilian clothes, big blue eyes, was very nervy and about 32 years old. There was also a short man with a hat pulled down and a scarf; Source could not see his face and did not see him again – it might possibly have been LOUIS le Belge. HENRI offered his hand to Source but she did not take it. He said, 'I think a lot of you', but Source replied that she did not care what he thought. He told Source that she nearly fooled him. He said this was not Source's fault because her people were bad (meaning the French people had talked and been careless). He said he knew RAOUL was here and asked Source to show him the way; Source did not for a minute and a gun was stuck in her back. She thought quickly that if she screamed RAOUL would probably jump out of the window and the hotel was obviously surrounded and he might be shot, so she took him up and went into the room and just said to RAOUL: 'There is the Gestapo' and HENRI went and arrested him. Source knew RAOUL had the messages they collected that afternoon in his jacket pocket but he was not wearing his jacket and it was lying on the bed. Source managed to swap the jackets and RAOUL saw what she had done so put another sports jacket on. She also managed to slip the wallet in her sleeve. They were taken down and out of the hotel and came to a car driven by a civilian. HENRI asked them if they wanted to go with the Italians or with him and RAOUL said they would go with the Italians. Source thought that the chauffeur was probably French and might be friendly towards them so she caught her stocking in the back seat of the car and managed to slip the wallet under the back seat. She thought that it might not be found for a few days and would give the others more time to get away. She knows that the Gestapo never found the wallet. They were taken to the caserne [military barracks] at ANNECY and RAOUL and she were put in separate rooms.

LOUIS LE BELGE

Questioned as to how it came about that the COTTETS told Source on the day of their arrest that LOUIS le Belge wanted to see her, Source replied that she did not know. COTTET did not know LOUIS le Belge. LOUIS le Belge had been put up by the people at BOCCA who had had trouble with him when on one occasion he had asked for arms which they kept at the farm, and they had been unwilling to give them up. These arms belonged to RAOUL's réseau and RAOUL had given orders that nobody was to have them unless on his authority. LOUIS le Belge belonged to the CARTE organisation and RAOUL had given him no such authority. Source did not know why he was called LOUIS le Belge, but he did in fact have a Belgian accent.

COTTET

With regard to COTTET, Source felt satisfied that up to the day of her arrest COTTET had not acted in any traitorous fashion, and was not responsible in any way for the Germans coming to the Hotel de la Poste. He [Monsieur Cottet] knew nothing about RAOUL and Source's work, and all he did was to provide the hotel and was prefectly [*sic*] trustworthy. It is possible that when the Germans actually came to the hotel, he and Mrs. COTTET may have yielded to threats and disclosed to the Germans that RAOUL and Source were actually at the hotel. Thinking over the matter, Source is rather surprised that both COTTET and Mrs. COTTET came upstairs. This did not strike her at the time as they were on friendly terms.

CIRCUMSTANCES LEADING TO SOURCE'S ARREST

In Source's opinion CHAILLAN caused her and RAOUL's arrest by telling HENRI that the operation to exfiltrate him was refused and that PAUL and RAOUL's return was expected very soon. CHAILLAN knew that Source had told London that RAOUL's return must not be later than 14 April. CHAILLAN had been told this, but he was not told what the BBC message was, nor the spot to which RAOUL was going to return, because of doubts that began to ascertain about him because of his determination to get MARSAC out at any cost. Source had a meeting with ROGER and RIQUET at a patisserie in ANNECY on the morning of 12 April. At this rendezvous she told him that the operation to exfiltrate HENRI could not take place, but she did not give him the BBC message, or the precise locality chosen for RAOUL's return. Previous to this interview CHAILLAN had been told that RAOUL was to return no later than 14 April. CHAILLAN and RIQUET were very angry and abused the Organisation and the British Government, and kept on saying that something must be done and that they would tell HENRI that something would be possible. CHAILLAN said that he could get MARSAC out of Fresnes [prison] through the instrumentality of HENRI, and could send MARSAC back to England. Source told him that he was foolish and that London's orders were to keep quiet, and to wait for RAOUL, and that in any case it was better to lose one man than everything. Source advised CHAILLAN not to go to PARIS, but in spite of this CHAILLAN did go. It was on the afternoon of this day that ARMAUD [*sic*], when he heard that GHAILLAN [*sic*] had gone to PARIS, was so furious that he went to ANNECY to try to kill CHAILLAN. Source thinks CHAILLAN must have told HENRI that RAOUL was coming back not later than 14 April. CHAILLAN had complete confidence in HENRI. In Source's opinion, CHAILLAN was extremely stupid or a traitor, and he was not the kind of man one regards as stupid. When Source received the first reply from London with instructions that they were to 'act according to their discretion regard to the German Colonel', she had told CHAILLAN and RIQUET that the operation to exfiltrate HENRI might not take place until the 18 April, i.e. on the 16th, 17th or 18th. They had done this with the idea of making sure that HENRI would take no steps to arrest any of them – at any rate not until the 15 April, so that they could be sure of being free until that time. As Source points out, it is difficult to understand why HENRI should suddenly have altered the intention he presumably had to leave them free until the 18 April., and instead arrested them some days earlier. The only explanation that Source can offer is CHAILLAN's telling HENRI that the operation could not take place and that RAOUL was expected very soon. Moreover, HENRI clearly knew when they were arrested that RAOUL was there. From the day of his return to the time he was arrested RAOUL contacted nobody, and nobody knew he had come back [except the Cottets], so that unless HENRI had been told that he was coming back, he had no reason to suppose that RAOUL's return was imminent and that he was likely to be at ST. JORIOZ.

Source agrees that it is just conceivable that COTTET said: 'RAOUL is upstairs', when HENRI arrived as the result of pressure put on him, but Source does not think this is likely. Source herself is sure that she had not been watched during the days immediately preceding her arrest. HENRI himself told Source that he would have come to arrest RAOUL sooner had he not been obstructed by the Italians and Gestapo at LYONS who had made difficulties about providing transport. Source said they were definitely not followed when they went up to the mountain SEMNOZ and this, in Source's view, points to the likelihood that the arrest was due to the fact that CHAILLAN first told HENRI that the operation could not take place to exfiltrate him, so that HENRI had no reason to leave Source and RAOUL free until the 18 April, and secondly, that on his journey up to PARIS CHAILLAN might have told HENRI that RAOUL's return was expected very soon.

Another circumstance which Source points out is that she had sent ROGER to a safe place in which to lie low on the 13 April.

CHAILLAN told Source that he had met MARSAC in prison and reported that he wanted some food, but otherwise he was alright;

CHAILLAN did not give Source a report in writing about HENRI's proposals, and he did not give one to anybody else, so far as Source knows.

FURTHER DETAILS ABOUT THE ARREST

Further questioned as to who actually affected the arrest, Source said that when HENRI came to the hotel to arrest Source and RAOUL, there was a tall, thin German behind him, very nervy and jumpy, and a third man who was wearing a soft hat. Source did not recognise the third man as she only saw him for a moment and then he disappeared. She said he was the same build as LOUIS le Belge; he wore clothes that were not dissimilar, and it is conceivable that he could be LOUIS le Belge. Source said that it was certainly not CHAILLAN.

Questioned more in detail as to the arrest, Source stated that when HENRI saw Source he wanted to shake her hand and Source refused. He said to her: 'You have done a very good job of work, and you almost won the game. It is not your fault you lost.' The second man saw in the corner of the hall a case which looked as though it was a radio set. He opened it, but all he found were some rags and clothes. There was nothing compromising in it. The tall, thin man then stuck a gun in Source's back and told her to go upstairs. They went up the stairs, found RAOUL, and Source said to RAOUL: 'Here is the Gestapo'. HENRI and the tall thin man went up to RAOUL and arrested him; the third Gestapo man had disappeared by then. They then started to look in the cupboards for arms, but could not find them because they were hidden elsewhere. There was nothing compromising in the room, as everything had gone. When the Gestapo men arrived, Source and RAOUL were undressed. [Some French sources claimed that they were caught in bed together.] They were told to dress, and whilst Source was doing so she tried to think of a way of getting the pocket book (which she mentioned previously). RAOUL had the pocket book in a coat on the bed, and whilst the Gestapo were searching the room, Source managed to put a sports coat in place of this coat. RAOUL saw this and put on the sports coat. Then Source succeeded in getting the pocket book out of the coat and putting it in the left-hand sleeve of her jacket. Source said that in the pocket book were three messages which had come by radio the same day for GILS and GISELLE and also for Captain MOREL. These messages concerned Captain MOREL's work and the work of the Maquis. Source said there was something else in the pocket book, but she could not remember what it was. Source then said that either in the hall or at the entrance to the hotel they met a number of Italians. The hotel was surrounded by Italians. HENRI told Source previously that he had had to requisition

Italians to make the arrest, and also later on he told her that they had no chance of escaping because there were so many men around the hotel.

During the conversation in the room HENRI said to RAOUL: 'Do you want to go with the Germans or the Italians?' and RAOUL said he would sooner go with the Italians. Source and RAOUL knew that they would have more chance with the Italians than the Germans. When they came out of the hotel, they saw a green car, which might have been a private or a hired car and inside it was a chauffeur who looked very much like a Frenchman and was wearing a beret. Source and RAOUL left the Hotel with HENRI, the tall thin German and also a third man who was an Italian Inspector. Source cannot remember whether this man came up into the room of the hotel, and she said that she had a good look at him and would recognise him again. When they entered the car Source deliberately caught her stocking on the corner of the back seat so as to give her an excuse to touch her stocking and push the pocket book under the back seat. In doing this Source thought that the pocket book would be hidden at least for a few hours, and it would give some time for the news of their arrest to leak out, and various people would take precautions accordingly. Also, there was some money in the pocket book, and Source thought that if the chauffeur did find it, he would keep it; a third reason for her doing this was that possibly the chauffeur was a loyal Frenchman and might help them by keeping the pocket book from the Germans. Source's one idea, she said, was to keep the pocket book away from the Germans as it would give away Captain MOREL, GISELLE, and GILS.

RAOUL sat in the back seat of the car beside Source. They could not speak to each other because the Italian Inspector was sitting in the front of the car, facing backwards with a gun in his hand, and it was impossible to talk. Source is almost sure they handcuffed RAOUL.

AT ANNECY

They arrived at ANNECY and were put in Italian barracks there. They were put in separate rooms. RAOUL was put into a proper cell, but Source was put in a room with only the windows secured so that she could not get out. Source was then left until the morning.

At 06.30 – 07.00 a.m. the Italian Inspector came into her cell and said: 'Your husband is a criminal Madame.' Source said that it was something new on her and asked why. He said: 'Well, he tried to escape last night and knocked a man down, and in consequence it has been pretty bad for him.' The Inspector did not mention the name 'RAOUL.' Source said that she thought it better not to ask questions about RAOUL, because he obviously wanted her to, so she said nothing. Source was then taken to another room and the Inspector started to ask her questions about the work she had been doing, but Source refused to give him any information. He told her that her position was very bad, and that she would be made to talk. Source told him that they would not make her speak. He then said to Source in the presence of an Italian N.C.O. [non-commissioned officer] who was also in the room: 'You are very strong'. Source said that she didn't think he meant that she was physically strong, but that she was strong morally – particularly as she had asked no questions about her husband. The Inspector then left the N.C.O.'s room and Source stayed there all morning with the N.C.O.

Source said the Italian N.C.O. behaved very well to her; at midday, although Source did not ask, the N.C.O. brought her a message from RAOUL stating that he was still alive. The N.C.O. said that he was very sorry for her, and the situation was very difficult for a woman, and he would help her. Also, he said she did not look very well, and he would try and get her a doctor. Source said she stayed in the barracks some five or six days. Although she slept in the first room, Source said there was neither a seat nor water, so she spent the day in the N.C.O.'s office as he was never there. The friendly Italian soldiers gave Source news daily of RAOUL, and Source sent similar messages back to RAOUL. RAOUL sent messages as a man would to a woman he loved, and this appealed to the Italians. RAOUL said that whatever happened they must save ARNAUD as he was an excellent worker and indispensable to the Organisation.

Source was not interrogated during that week, she did not see HENRI again or anybody, but she was later told by HENRI that after the arrest he had gone with the tall thin German to a place near Chamonix [Alpine mountain resort below Mont Blanc] to show the tall thin German some of the beauties of the countryside. Source said that she knew he did not go straight back to PARIS.

GRENOBLE

At the end of seven days, Source said they left ANNECY in a lorry for Grenoble. She was in the same lorry as RAOUL, who was handcuffed. Source was not handcuffed. She noticed that he had a broken finger, injuries to his side and face, and also on the inside of his hands; he was in a very bad state. Source said that she did not know whether he had been tortured but said it was quite possible because he was in such a bad condition. RAOUL, in order to explain his injuries to Source, told her that he had tried to escape and had been very badly treated as a result. Source did everything she could during the journey to raise his spirits and succeeded, and at the end of the journey he was very much better. In the lorry Source and RAOUL were able to talk because they were the only two persons besides the Italians and the Italians could not understand what they said. At first, RAOUL did not want to admit that his name was CHURCHILL, but Source said that she did not agree with him, and the name might be somewhat of a protection, as by that time it was 1943, and Source thought that it might influence the Germans. Apart from this, Source and RAOUL decided that they would deny absolutely everything. They would, naturally, find out how much the Germans already knew. Above all things they agreed to save ARNAUD and ROGER – they were determined to save ARNAUD, not for any personal reason, but because they realised that he was a first-class Wireless Operator and they very short of Wireless Operators; and also, FRAGER could not work without ARNAUD. Source said that ARNAUD was an extremely difficult character, and was difficult to get along with, but she said she thought he was a very brave man and admired him very much, and was the best man at his work she had seen in France. Apart from his work, he was impossible, and RAOUL was the only person who could get on with him.

ARNAUD also liked Source very much, and when RAOUL was not there, he would only work with Source. Source said she always felt perfectly sure of ARNAUD and that he would die for her if necessary. She said that the three of them, RAOUL, ARNAUD and Source, formed a perfect team and could trust one another completely, and would readily lay down their lives for one another.

When they arrived at Grenoble, Source was put into a cell with two other women, and RAOUL was put in a solitary cell. Through the window of Source's cell, she could see the window of RAOUL's, and also his face. The two other women who were in Source's cell had been arrested for trying to cross the Frontier [into Switzerland], but they were released the same day. Source said that these women were of no interest, except that one of them whose name was GROS, a Red Cross Nurse living at Amiens, asked if she could do Source a service. Source asked her if she would go to ST. JORIOZ and get some clothes for RAOUL and her (Source would pay expenses), and as she was she was very short of clothes, she could take some of Source's. Source said that what she did was to get money from COTTET for the journey, kept most of Source's clothes for herself, as well as taking her bicycle, and returned dressed in Source's clothes, with just two or three things for Source and RAOUL that were of no use at all.

Source was at Grenoble for about a week without being interrogated. On her birthday [28 April] the Italians brought RAOUL to see Source for about five minutes, but they naturally could not discuss anything because they were not alone.

FURTHER MOVEMENTS

At the end of the week, one morning early, Source and RAOUL took the train for TURIN. At TURIN they took RAOUL and put him in a solitary cell in the barracks. They thought, however, the barracks would not be suitable for a woman and took Source to a convent which was being used as a place for reforming prostitutes. There Source stayed the night and was received by the Mother Superior, who was very impressed by the name of 'CHURCHILL'. [This suggests Odette was keeping up the story that she was married to RAOUL.] The next day Source and RAOUL were sent back to Nice by train in separate compartments so they could speak very little. The Italians behaved very well; they were singing all the way and gave them oranges, etc. On arrival at Nice Source and RAOUL were taken to a room in the Station where they were met by an Italian Major, who behaved very correctly to them. They were then put in a car with an Italian officer and were taken to a very beautiful villa lying at the back of Nice on a hill. Source was put into a room on the ground floor, and Source thinks that RAOUL had a room in the basement. Both stayed in their rooms, an Italian accompanying Source everywhere, and even sleeping in her room. Source said they stayed there for two or three days without seeing anybody except soldiers. Source said that she thought somebody else was in the room with RAOUL, but she was not sure. Two or three days later an Italian Inspector appeared in civilian clothes. He asked if everything was all right, and Source asked him when they were leaving, to which he replied 'very shortly'. Source said that they stayed there for 9 or 10 days altogether, and had no interrogations. They were then taken by Italian truck to TOULON first and stayed a few hours, and then two German officers came, received all their papers from the Italians, and took them in a German truck to Marseilles. At Marseilles, they took the train for PARIS, and the next day arrived at PARIS. This was about the 8th May.

SOURCE IN PARIS – FRESNES – AVENUE FOCH

WHEN Source and RAOUL arrived at PARIS, they were met by HENRI, who was waiting at the station, in company with a tall, thin man. HENRI again said he was sorry for what he had to do. They were joined by other German officers and went to a waiting car. There were three cars altogether. HENRI did not go with Source and RAOUL, but on arrival at Fresnes, whilst Source and RAOUL were having their papers gone through HENRI appeared again. He then led Source through the underground passages of Fresnes, carrying her luggage for her. HENRI took Source into a room and said to her, 'I don't like seeing you here, and if I can I shall get you out.' He then said, 'Of course you don't love RAOUL, it cannot be?' Source told him that he was making a big mistake because it was nothing to do with their arrest. HENRI said it was a pity that she was taking it like that because he could have done something for her. Source realised that although he was not saying openly that she should work with him, he was trying to get her to say that she didn't love RAOUL, so that he, HENRI, could then ask her to work with him. When HENRI saw that it was no good, he changed altogether. HENRI told Source that RAOUL was a very lucky man. He then told source that Madame MARSAC was free, after being in Fresnes for a week only.

Source said that in general she regarded HENRI as an extremely dangerous man; he does his level best to gain confidence, he asks all sorts of irrelevant questions; he talks about music etc., and would even bring one parcels and make one more comfortable so one would have to be very careful not to be taken in by him. Source remembered that on one occasion HENRI said to her: 'You are not the sort of person who would wear dirty clothes like that, do let me have one of your blouses and I will get it washed for you'. (Source had 2 blouses with her).

During this first visit by HENRI, Source said that HENRI quite emphatically said he did not like some things in the Nazi Regime and said that he would one day be put in prison for it. He said he was in prison in the last war and could have escaped but did not in order to save a British officer. He said that he just did his job as well as he could, although he did not like it.

Source said that she resisted all HENRI's suggestions during their conversation, and at the end of the sitting realised that her position was a very bad one, as it was obvious to HENRI that he was not going to get round her, and he knew that she knew his game. Source said that this first interrogation was rather like visiting a psychiatrist. It lasted for about 1½ hours. They smoked and spoke quite politely to each other, and HENRI offered to do any little thing for Source that would please her. At the end of the visit, Source was taken to a cell in the women's division. Source stated that she stayed there for 15 days without seeing anybody. At the end of 15 days, Source was taken to the Gestapo H.Q. at the Avenue Foch. She was taken to the top floor to a small room and saw a man she had never seen before. He did not speak to Source. Source says that from his appearance he was a German, then a tall, thin man came into the room. Source thinks that he was probably the same tall thin German as the one who was present at her arrest. Source cannot be sure of this because it must be remembered that she had always seen him in a coat and hat. She thinks, however, that it must be the same man. They began to talk, and Source was asked for her identity etc. The man told Source that Captain CHURCHILL was a nephew of the Prime Minister, which Source denied. He began to ask Source where ARNAUD was and mentioned him by name. He also asked about FRAGER's whereabouts and ROGER's, but Source said that she did not know. He then said that he did not believe her, and said there were ways and means of making her speak. This man spoke excellent French, and might have been taken for a Lorrainer. At this point a Frenchman came into the room, and they made Source sit on a chair and the tall, thin interrogator held Source's hands behind her back. The Frenchman then burned Source in the shoulder, with what she did not know. Source said his description was: about 5′ 7″, aged 28; thick dark hair, clean shaven, sallow complexion, very beautiful eyes and eyelashes; medium build and very well dressed as all Gestapo men are; and he had a very good shaped head, good teeth. In fact, he was a very good-looking man and very French in his movements. Source said he had a well-educated, Parisian accent. They then left Source alone for a while, and the tall, thin man said he would think of something else that might make her talk.

The tall, thin man then pointed out of the window and said to Source: 'Have a look at those happy people outside!' (Source said that why he said this was because it was spring-time and the women looked very gay in their new spring clothes, etc.) He then said: 'Why are you doing this?' Source said that her father had been killed for France and her family had suffered three times. She said that she was British, and she loved England more than she loved France. The tall man then said: '"Are you doing this for money?' but Source said that she was not, and he said it was a pity. He then showed Source the contents of her handbag (her handbag had been taken away from her) and asked her if she would like to keep something out of it. Source said that there was nothing except, perhaps, the Rosary. He then offered her the Rosary, but when she went to take it, he snatched it away.

SOURCE SEES RAOUL
Source was then taken to Fresnes. There she stayed about three weeks and was put in a cell on her own without any books and without having any exercise. Then sometime in the middle of June HENRI came to see her and as before took her to a room, the same one as before, and there she met RAOUL. Source said that HENRI was very nice to her and said that he thought she would be pleased to see RAOUL. RAOUL did not look in a very good condition, and it was obvious that he was still suffering from his previous injuries. Source could not say whether he had been tortured again.

RAOUL told Source that he thought she looked very pale, but Source said she thought it was better to say nothing and talked of other things. Source said that she could quite well go on as she was, but she was bluffing most of the time. They all spoke on general things for about two hours, and HENRI again told them the story of his being a P.O.W. Source said she thinks HENRI only made this short visit to see how things stood between RAOUL and her, and what their reaction would be to one another. Source and RAOUL behaved very affectionately to each other so that HENRI would see that she would never give in to him.

During the conversation HENRI said he was very sorry that orders were that Source could have no books and no exercise during her stay in Fresnes and asked her if he could do anything else for her. Source said that there was nothing. They then had to go back to their cells.

SOURCE IN FRESNES

After about three weeks, one night some of the women in the other rooms were talking, and one of the German soldiers heard them and thought Source was one of them. Two men and two S.S. women came to Source's room, pulled Source out of bed, and one of the women smacked Source's face twice. When Source remonstrated with them, they laughed at her. The next morning Source spoke to the woman on duty and told her that she would like to speak to the Captain-in-Charge, and gave her name as Mrs CHURCHILL. The woman went to give the message and ten minutes after, the Captain came to Source's room, full of smiles obviously very impressed by Source's name. Source told him that she was disgusted with her treatment of the night before and told him about her face being slapped twice. The Captain was full of apologies and did not want Source to think ill of all Germans, and was there anything he could do for her to make up for it? He said he would send a parcel; (which he did), and also he would go and see Captain CHURCHILL and tell him that she was all right. He talked to Source for about twenty minutes. His description was: Fatherly type; aged about 56-57; grey hair; blue eyes' about 5' 6". Source said that if necessary she had ways of finding out more about this man. [His methods of torture were not specified.] He then went away and gave instructions for a German woman to look after Source. This woman came once a week to see if Source was all right and in time they became very friendly. This German woman was an educated person who had been a governess to some very good families before the war, and she took a great liking to Source and was very impressed by Source's name. She said that she wanted to get a job in America or England after the war, and did not want to return to Germany. Source said that this woman knew a lot about everybody in Fresnes, and could be contacted through Madame JEANNE, Hotel Litre, MONTPARNASSE. She would be very useful, but she would have to be approached very carefully. She might give information to Source, but otherwise, approach might be difficult.

Her name is Rosie Scherer and her description: aged about 43 years; height 5´4˝; has very little dark brown hair and wears it short; blue-green eyes; very bad teeth, big feet; spinsterish type; speaks very good French. Rosie SCHERER would also be able to give information about HENRI. (She would probably know him under the name TASCHNER).

Source said she thought she was treated kindly because of her name. [Marsac was reported to have told Bleicher that Churchill was related to the British Prime Minister, which might explain Odette's treatment.] She even received a few books from the Captain and the German woman.

Source remained in Fresnes for seven months. During her stay there she managed to get in touch with a woman called BETTY, who was the wife of Johnny HOPPER, who was also in Fresnes. BETTY was a Canadian woman who worked in intelligence for Johnny HOPPER. [British saboteur, robber, and assassin arrested operating independently in Normandy. (http//:home/clara.net/clinchy/ hopp1.htm)] Source said that BETTY had talked a lot to the Gestapo and received special treatment from them, and given away everything to them. Her description was: Aged 31-32; 5´6˝; pale complexion; very thin; brown hair; blue eyes; wears her hair in a roll all the way round; she was very friendly with all the Germans and they, including the Commandant, used to make a great fuss of her. Source said that she used to take drugs and was quite crazy. Source thought that BETTY had done a great deal of harm.

AVENUE FOCH – EMILE

At the end of July Source was sent to the Gestapo H.Q. Avenue Foch again. She went to the first floor and was met by a man whom Source thought looked rather like [Hermann] GOERING [Head of the Luftwaffe]. She said he was very big and had lots of decorations. He addressed Source as Madame CHURCHILL and was very polite. They went up to the top floor and were met by a new man. This man, Source said, was about 5´8˝; thin, dark; Source said that from the colour of his complexion he looked as though he suffered from stomach trouble; aged about 40-45; well-dressed in civilian clothes; he was a German. He asked Source whether she would like some tea. He asked Source questions about Miss HERBERT and Madame LECHENE [the SOE agents who had arrived in France with her], but Source would say nothing. He then went out, and Source was left alone.

Then the door opened, and a man came into the room carrying some sketching material, etc. under his left arm. Source recognised him as EMILE, who had been working in CANNES. [EMILE was the code name of John Starr, an artist who was exfiltrated in the same felucca Odette arrived on. Returned to France in May 1943, he ran the ACROBAT network in Saint-Etienne until his arrest in November 1943.] Source said his description was: Short; not thin; had a moustache; sandy hair; blue eyes; aged about 30; so far as Source can remember he limped on one leg. He was quite well dressed in flannel trousers and a blue jacket and a beret and looked very fit. Source said she was very surprised to see EMILE there, and as he came into the room with papers etc. under his arm she gained the impression that he was working there. Source said that when EMILE entered the room he was smoking a cigarette, and she did not take any notice of him. EMILE was followed by 'GOERING' and the man who had questioned her before. They asked her if she knew EMILE, but Source said 'No.' They then said that was very strange because he had come back in the same felucca as Source. EMILE said to Source: 'Yes, we have met before. I have been working with RAOUL in Cannes. I came back a few months ago, and there you are, I am here!' He then told Source not to worry; everything was going along all right, and the war would soon be over. Source then realised that something was wrong, otherwise EMILE would not have spoken like that in front of the Gestapo. Source then said: 'You must understand that I did not recognise this man because I met him only for a few minutes at 2 o'clock in the morning and I was getting out of the felucca, and I did not worry about the people getting in.' The Gestapo accepted this as a reasonable explanation and did not worry Source any more on this point. EMILE then said to Source: 'What about Fresnes, can you take it?' Source answered: 'It is all right, I can take it.' Source then said that this went on for about ten minutes. EMILE then went off, and Source said she could not understand why he was there and thought something was very wrong. The Gestapo men then asked her: 'What do you know about that man; he was working in CANNES with RAOUL?' Source told them that she did not know anything about him, RAOUL had never told Source anything of what he had done before, and she had not asked him about it. The Gestapo man then said that they naturally supposed that as Source was French, she had been persuading RAOUL to come to work in France, and then went on to say that they would both be dead very shortly. They said that RAOUL had a chance, but Source hadn't any. The Gestapo man added that Source ought to be killed once for France and once for England, but Source retorted that they could only kill a woman once.

Source then asked if RAOUL had a chance and the Gestapo man said that they had been asking for an exchange for RAOUL, and they said that they thought it would be quite all right because RAOUL was an English officer and was a CHURCHILL. But they said that it would not be in her case as she was a woman, and what Source had been doing was not a woman's business or words to that effect. Source then said to the Gestapo man: 'Can you tell me anything about this exchange, and for whom are you asking?' The man said 'HESS'. [Rudolf Hess, Hitler's deputy Fuehrer, had flown solo to Scotland in May 1941 reportedly to negotiate peace but was arrested and imprisoned.] (Source then said that she remembers HENRI, the first time he saw her in Fresnes, asking whether she thought the British would exchange HESS for RAOUL, to which Source had laughed and said 'No'.) Source did not say anything when she heard the Gestapo's proposition.

FRESNES

Source was then taken back to Fresnes, but she still remained in solitary confinement. A few days after HENRI came and visited Source. He spoke to Source and Source got the impression that he was trying to give her confidence so as to persuade her to work for him. After a short time, HENRI brought RAOUL into the room. RAOUL was there about 1½ hours, and a general conversation took place. On reflection, Source said that she was not certain whether RAOUL was there on that occasion, but nothing of any particular interest was said. At the end of this time, Source was conducted back to her cell. She received some books and also a few parcels through Miss Scherer and the Captain.

About 18 August HENRI came again and took her to the same interviewing room as before. He always saw her in this room. RAOUL was present as well and also another German officer, who said nothing. This meeting with RAOUL lasted from half an hour to an hour. HENRI asked Source if she would like to go out for the day, and said he would take her to Paris with some friends, leaving her there and bringing her back in the evening. Source refused but said possibly RAOUL would like it. HENRI then said to RAOUL: 'Would you like to go out?' At any rate, nothing came of it as far as Source was concerned, and she never went out. From that time Source was left severely alone by HENRI, who did not come to see her again, although when he came to Fresnes he used to enquire from Miss SCHERER how Source was getting on.

Source stayed in solitary confinement in Fresnes until 15 October 1943. She received two parcels from the FOLs [?] in PARIS. On one occasion Source saw M. FOL when he came to Fresnes with HENRI. Source said FOL might well be able to give information about SUZANNE, HENRI's mistress. His address is 8 bis Chaussee de la Muette, PARIS, 17. RAOUL had known FOL long before the war, but apart from this Source knows nothing about him, and in any case would prefer RAOUL to be asked about him. By the 15 October Source looked ill and was in a very bad state. The German Captain said to Source that it was too cold to be alone in a cell, and he would put her in a cell with two other girls whom he would choose himself. Source was accordingly moved into a cell with two girls. Her cell-mates were changed from time to time as they were not prisoners who were in Fresnes on serious charges. Through them Source was able to get news out, and pass messages to her mother and M. FOL, telling them she was still at Fresnes and all right. Through these girls, Source heard further news of EMILE at the Avenue FOCH. One of the girls on returning from her first interrogation at the Avenue FOCH said that it was a curious thing, but there was an Englishman at the Avenue FOSH [*sic*]. Source asked her to tell her all about him. The girl then described EMILE correctly and stated that he was a prisoner there; well looked after and he made portraits and was having a good time with a woman who was doing work there. She also said that EMILE had said to her: 'Don't worry, the war won't last long.' She had been alone with EMILE for a time, and it was during this time that EMILE had said to her that she was not to worry, etc. The girl added that the Englishman had a wireless set of his own, rather like a small white box, and that he had told her that the Germans were keeping him at the Avenue FOCH because in that way they could get news of things from England before anyone else. This girl knew nothing about Source or her work. She herself had been doing some Resistance work with some French organisation. The name of this girl was Lucienne DELMAS, and she can be found at the Hotel Dantin, PARIS. (Source added that DENISE and MARTINE could give further information about EMILE.)

FURTHER INTERROGATION AT AVENUE FOCH

On the 11 November Source was again interrogated at the Avenue FOCH by the same interrogator, namely the small ill looking one. He showed her some photographs, including a photograph of URBAIN, and also a man who worked for MURIEL in MARSEILLE. (He lived at the Rue St. Jacques at MARSEILLE and Source thinks his name if ANFOU.) Source stated that she did not recognise any of them.one of the photographs Source says might have been one of the men who came with Source in the felucca [probably Tom Groome, Pat O'Leary's wireless operator]. The interrogation was short and lasted for about an hour. The interrogator asked Source what she thought of Col. Buckmaster. [Clearly some captured SOE agents had talked.] After the interrogation, Source was put in a room alongside until the evening, and then taken by car to the Rue des Saussies where they changed cars again and Source was driven round the Arc de Triomphe. Another Gestapo man came in the car with them, whom Source thinks was French. They said to Source: 'You are French and would like to see the Arc de Triomphe.'

OTHER PERSONS IN FRESNES

They then took Source back to Fresnes and Source was put back into a cell. In PARIS Source got information about LUCIENNE, and she heard that LUCIENNE was in Fresnes and well. Source also heard that Madame LEJEUNE was in prison. Source also learned that MIREILLE [who had lived in a villa at St Jorioz near Hotel de la Poste] had been freed some three weeks after her arrest, and after her release had gone straight to her family in the country, and by so doing had caused the arrest of a number of people, herself being brought back to prison with them.

About this time (towards the end of October) Source also heard that CHAILLAN had been arrested and that one day very soon after he had been taken from Fresnes for interrogation by the Gestapo, he had managed to escape from the car in which he was being transported. Source heard about the arrest of EUGENE [Maurice Pertschuk, F Section agent operating PRUNUS network in Toulouse until arrested 12 April 1943 (https://fr.wikipedia,org/wiki/ Maurice_Pertschuk)] and his secretary YVONNE, and was told that they had been betrayed by one of EUGENE's lieutenants, whom Source thinks was a Frenchman and a name something like NOBLE. According to what Source was told, this man had betrayed them beforehand and not as a result of any pressure or duress. He himself had not been arrested and must have belonged to the Gestapo. Source herself had met this man whilst at TOULOUSE in the beginning of 1943, and thinks that RAOUL knows more about him. She remembers that he was dark, young, well-dressed, with curly dark hair, and so far as Source remembers he limped. There was, however, a second man, older with grey hair, but Source thinks it is just possible she is confusing this other man. On one occasion Source had dined with this other man and a third man, a Commercial Representative, who also worked for EUGENE at Toulouse.

On the occasion of this visit to TOULOUSE Source had met an agent from the UK who was tall and wore a moustache. He is known to RAOUL. This agent had tried to get back to England through Spain as the Police were after him – Source thinks French police. Source saw him in a café in TOULOUSE, and he pointed to a man and woman saying that they belonged to the Gestapo, and he was very friendly with them. This alarmed Source and she accordingly left TOULOUSE. Source points out that her memory is very indistinct about these matters, and the above is all that she can remember.

In about November Source succeeded in sending a message to MIREILLE and received back a message to say that Roger CHAILLAN had succeeded in escaping. This confirmed what Source had already heard before, as stated above, with regards to CHAILLAN's escape. Source heard that MIREILLE's position was not bad, as she worked as a kind of stewardess for the prisoners in Fresnes; indeed, Source saw her doing this work. In Source's opinion, MIREILLE was very stupid. Some days before Source's arrest MIREILLE had been in a buffet at ANNECY with two men unknown to Source to whom MIREILLE said that she was working for the Intelligence Service. Source entertained no suspicions against her and merely thought that she was very indiscreet. A courier of EUGENE heard MIREILLE say this, and he was so alarmed that he came to find ARNAUD and Source and told them. In consequence of this, Source went direct to ANNECY and told MIREILLE that if she was so stupid, she would have to clear out altogether. In Source's belief, MIREILLE was CHAILLAN's mistress and would have done anything for him. CHAILLAN was a very determined man.

Source lived in the same cell until the end of January 1944. LUCIENNE DELMAS was interrogated on several occasions and on each occasion said the same thing about EMILE. About the end of January, Source was also told about EMILE by Simone HERAIL of NARBONNE. Lucienne DELMAS told Source that EMILE had said to her that he had tried to make an escape, and had been shot in the leg. When Source saw EMILE she thinks he had a stiff leg. He was on excellent terms with the Gestapo officials who slapped him on the back and called him 'mon vieux' [old friend].

On 12 May 1944, when Source left for Germany, she again saw EMILE at the Avenue FOCH. He was then in rather bad shape and was much thinner. Seven other women who were being transferred with Source also saw him. They were all sitting in a top floor room in the Avenue FOCH when EMILE came in. Source said to him: 'How are you?', and 'Did you know that your brother has gone to Germany?' Source said this under the impression that URBAIN was EMILE's brother, and had gone to Germany. EMILE said a few words to DIANE [Diane Rowden, F Section wireless operator for John Starr, arrested in November 1943.] a woman whom Source met in Fresnes, but Source did not overhear what he said. This woman Source describes as: ill-looking, red-haired, about 30 years of age. She had come from England and belonged to some Organisation, having been arrested in 1943. Source knows no more about her. RAOUL and Source had gone to the Rue des Saussaies on the 6 February 1944, together with DIANE. It was while talking on this occasion that Source discovered that DIANE belonged to an Organisation. RAOUL talked to her, and he would know more about her. The object of this visit to the Rue des Saussaies was simply to take fingerprints, etc. In view of their impending departure for Germany, and there was not very much opportunity for them to talk together.

About the end of 1943, Source saw MARSAC. He was in what is known as a Jardin Cellulaire. This was a cell-like garden around which the prisoners walked for exercise. This was the only occasion on which Source saw MARSAC. She called out his name but he made no answer. Source said he looked very ill and he was in a bad state, and Source has no knowledge as to what happened to him.

Source for some time was in contact with Roger RENAUDY of Cannes who had known RAOUL and had been in contact with him for the purpose of their work. He acted as a kind of a Steward for the prisoners at Fresnes, and through him, Source was able to get news. RENAUDY told Source that RIQUET had been sent to Germany.

For some time, Source had been suffering with a swelling in the throat. Source requested treatment for this and the Commandant of the prison asked the Gestapo for Source to receive some treatment, but they replied that the treatment would only be allowed if Source was in danger of death.

Source has no knowledge of what happened to Lucienne DELMAS but thinks that she must have been sent to Germany, as her case was a serious one.

GERMAINE TAMBOUR
Source often heard this name through RAOUL or ARNAUD, but knew nothing of her.

BARON DEMALVAL
Source said that MALVAL thought that RAOUL had involuntarily given him away. RAOUL managed to bring about MARSAC's liberation by saying that he (RAOUL) had refused to work with MALVAL because MALVAL was too old. [When de Marval was released he provided details of Odette's imprisonment.]

FRAGER
Source knew FRAGER well and said he was an excellent soldier type.

ROGER BRAY
WHEN Source was at ST. JORIOZ a few days before her arrest Roger BRAY turned up in a magnificent car. He appeared to be devoted to FRAGER but did not like CHAILLAN (as nobody did because of his manner). Questioned about his car, BRAY said it belonged to a very rich friend of his who had at his disposition all sorts of papers for passing frontiers. RAOUL and Source thought this was very strange and distrusted BRAY. Another thing was that BRAY used to telephone and even phoned Source asking for her in the name of 'LISE'. He was tall, thin, fair, and always wore a check jacket; he was about 25-26 years old, blue eyes, high-pitched voice.

About the 25 January 1944, nearly everybody that source knew in Fresnes left for Germany. There were about 100 prisoners who went, including EUGENE's group.

PAUL HEINHERST

Source mentioned this man who was an Aumonier [chaplain] at Fresnes, and who was very well behaved and helpful to prisoners. He was 5; 11, well-built, had a fresh complexion; spectacles; fair brownish hair cut short; clean shaven; about 35; in the uniform, Source thinks of a Captain. He was the Prison Chaplain. The Gestapo got to hear how kindly he was treating the prisoners, and in consequence forbade him to visit the men. Further information about this man can be obtained from Madame Le FAUCHEUX, 203, Boulevard Raspail.

She did a lot of work for the prisoners and sent them packets etc. she was an old lady and HEINHERST was in contact with her as she could do things for the prisoners which he could not manage. HEINHERST could probably give information as to the whereabouts of HENRI (BLEICHER).

SOURCE GOES TO GERMANY

On the 12 May 1944, Source left Fresnes for Karlsruhe where she remained until July 1944. On the 18 July, she left Karlsruhe for Frankfurt where she stayed a week in the prison and on the 25 July went to Halles. Here, as there was no room in the prison, Source, together with 37 other women, mostly Ukrainians, were put in the Grenier [attic] of the prison. The only sanitation here was one old basin with a little water, and they had to sleep on the floor; whenever anybody moved, the dust flew up and choked them. Here they stayed two or three days, and Source was savagely struck by a man who worked here, who asked her if she were an English woman. He struck her twice. His description was: Big strong man with blue eyes and brown hair – practically all shaven off. He belonged to the regular police. Source saw this man in the courtyard of the prison beating up an Englishman, who could scarcely stand up. He was banging this man's head against the wall. Source could easily recognise this man if confronted with him.

RAVENSBRÜCK

On the 26 July Source left for RAVENSBRÜCK where she arrived on the 27th. Here Source was put into an underground dark cell as a punishment. This was because of the invasion of the South of France which had just taken place, and the Germans knew from someone who had been arrested after Source (Source does not know who it was) that Source had a plan of the Naval base at Marseille. In fact, Source had obtained this from GILS and GISELLE and ARNAUD radioed particulars of it to London. Source had kept the plan and hidden it, but the Gestapo did not find it. [How they learned about her having the map was not revealed.] At PARIS the Gestapo had tried to make Source tell them where she had got the plan, but source refused to say and maintained that the plan had been burned. This was given to Source as a reason for her punishment at RAVENSBRÜCK.

She stayed in this underground cell for three months and eight days. After six days she was told that she would have no food to eat and for five days she was given nothing at all. At the end of the five days, Source was found on the floor delirious. She was then given some soup and told that she had been punished by mistake. By that time Source was very ill and the swelling on her neck was very bad. The Camp Commandant then came and saw her, and she was taken out of the cell and her throat X-rayed – this was about 6 October 1944. As a result of the X-ray, Source was told that she had tuberculosis. Whereupon she demanded to see the X-ray plates which they refused to show her. Source was then put back into the same underground cell. Then Source made a great fuss, and when the Camp Commandant came, she demanded to see the plates. He said that he would take her and show her the plates. Apparently the doctor had said that if Source had stayed in the cell, she would be dead in two months. Source believes that she managed to frighten the Germans by saying she was not German, etc. [?] At the Kommandantur Source was shown the plates, and it was apparent that she did not have tuberculosis. The Camp Commandant in question was SHUREN [*sic*], source has this man's address and photograph [how she had these was not explained] and can furnish the address if called upon. From that time Source was given Infra-Red Ray treatment, and treatment for her hair which was all coming out. She also received Vitamins and was put in a fresh cell, and moreover, taken out each day between December 1944 to January and February 1945. SHUREN did this without consulting the Gestapo, but Source was convinced that this was not done through any tender feelings for her, but simply to protect himself from retribution.

At RAVENSBRÜCK Source knew a German officer, Michel BRINCK, who lives at INNSBRÜCK. Dr. BITTERLICH of INNSBRÜCK can give information about this man. BRINCK was in prison in RAVENSBRÜCK in the cell next door to Source's. BRINCK was in prison because he belonged to a group of intellectuals. He was a Doctor of Philosophy and a friend of the Archbishop of Berlin. He was entirely opposed to the Nazis. He did not belong to the Nazi Party and the group to which he belonged had for its aim to overthrow the Nazi regime. Four others of the group were shot. BRINCK speaks English and French well; he is 33 years of age, 6′ tall; has a round red face, is thick set and has blonde hair – bald in the front. He has a scar in the face from a wound he received in Russia. Source gradually got to know him and to have confidence in him, and they passed news to each other. Source kept two letters which she received from him and sewed them in a dress which Madame PEROUSSEL, wife of a Barrister in TUNIS has now got. Madame PEROUSSEL knew the letters were sewn in the dress, and she probably has got them. Source kept the letters to show BRINCK's frame of mind, and they were about general subjects. BRINCKS's fiancée was Fraulein BITTERLICH, daughter of Dr. BITTERLICH, above mentioned. BRINCK has written a great many books and Source mentions him because she thinks he would be very useful to the Allies.

Source left RAVENSBRÜCK on the 28 April 1945. On this date, the Germans evacuated the whole camp because of the approach of the Russians. They were to be … [the rest of the document is missing] [96]

Given her delicate physical and psychological state, Buckmaster arranged for her to receive medical treatment, which, in Churchill's opinion, saved her life. Her doctor's reports in her file confirm the torture detailed during her interrogation, and he estimated her disability at 70 per cent.[97]

In recognition of her role in the French Resistance, de Gaulle's new government awarded her the Chevalier de la Légion d'Honneur, the highest military decoration in France. Peter Churchill wrote a detailed account of his imprisonment and interrogation and corroborated Odette's story in the SOE's attempts to get her a British honour.

Cammaerts confirmed that, thanks to Odette not revealing his address, he was able to remain unmolested in Cannes for three months and 'carry on my work without hindrance. I can also certify that Ensign SANSOM knew of contact addresses for Captain RABINOVITCH and that none of these addresses were given to the Germans and that Captain Rabinovitch was able to leave France unmolested.'[98]

Simone Herail, who shared a cell with Odette in Fresnes between 15 October 1943 and 11 January 1944, stated that,

In the name of Mrs CHURCHILL, Miss Odette SANSOM had for many months been detained in solitary confinement in that prison, and when she came to live with me her health was seriously impaired by this inhumane procedure so dear to the Nazis; her weakness was extreme; she could no longer even eat the small amount of filthy and repugnant food which was given to us.

On some days, she had not the strength to leave her paillasse [straw-filled mattress] but at no moment did her courage or her determination to struggle to survive, falter.

Foreseeing that she would be sent to GERMANY, she regretted only one thing; that she would not be able to go on serving freely what she called her two countries – Great BRITAIN and FRANCE.

Convinced that she would certainly be shot, she said that she had for a long time accepted the sacrifices of her life which she had wished to dedicate without reservation to the service of her country.

An example of this order is unforgettable.[99]

In Gubbins' citation for her MBE, he stated that she worked for six months in difficult and trying conditions.

The circuit to which she was attached was large, and she travelled widely, maintaining liaison between the various groups, delivering operational messages and transporting W/T equipment. She was frequently stopped and searched by Police and Gestapo and always showed outstanding coolness and complete disregard of danger.

During March 1943, while her commanding officer was away on a visit to England, she took his place and proved herself a competent organiser. She personally arranged and supervised several parachute deliveries of arms and equipment. She also organised the reception of her commanding officer at very short notice and in a dangerous area, when he returned to France by parachute early in April.

Ensign SANSOM was arrested soon after this operation and spent more than two years in captivity in France and Germany before being repatriated to England in May 1945. For her courage, self-sacrifice and devotion to duty it is recommended that this officer be appointed a Member of the British Empire.[100]

In 1946, she was the first woman to be awarded the George Cross by King George VI. In Gubbins' citation, he said that she 'displayed courage, endurance and self-sacrifice of the highest possible order.' Having convinced the Germans she was married to Churchill throughout fourteen interrogations,

She also drew Gestapo attention off her Commanding Officer and on to herself by saying that he was completely incompetent and had only come to France on her insistence. She took full responsibility and agreed that it should be herself and not her Commanding Officer who should be shot. By this action, she caused the Gestapo to cease paying attention to her Commanding Officer after only two interrogations.

In addition, the Gestapo were most determined to discover the whereabouts of the wireless operator who had been working with her Commanding Officer and of another senior British officer whose life was of the greatest value to the Resistance Movement. Ensign SANSOM was the only person who knew their whereabouts. The Gestapo tortured her most brutally to try to make her give away this information. They seared her back with a red hot iron and when that failed, they pulled out all her toe-nails; but Ensign SANSOM continually refused to speak and by her courage, determination, and self-sacrifice, she not only saved the lives of these two officers but also enabled them to carry on their most valuable work.[101]

In 1947 she married Peter Churchill, and they spent almost a decade together before they divorced and she married George Hallowes in 1956. In 1949, Jerrard Tickell published *Odette: Secret Agent, Prisoner, Survivor* and the following year the British film *Odette* was released starring Anna Neagle and Trevor Howard. With the media interest in her story, there were disputes and debates about the veracity of her accounts, with Foot suggesting that her stories about being tortured were fabricated to sensationalise her story. Churchill successfully sued him. Odette claimed to have identified double agents in F Section, but there were no relevant pages in her personnel file. In a post-war interview, she commented on the espionage, treachery, and betrayal she experienced:

It is a game that I suppose is a good game for certain people. A game of youth, you have to have ideals. You have to have the mental strength and the physical fitness for it. But it is not possible for it ever to be a clean game.[102]

Following Odette's death on 13 March 1995, Tickell's biography was reprinted in 2008. The following year Penny Starns published *Odette: World War Two's Darling Spy* and in 2011 Kate Vigurs produced *The women agents of the Special Operations Executive F section – wartime realities and post-war representations*, a fascinating analysis of the post-war accounts of Odette and other agents' biographies and autobiographies as well as their coverage in newspapers, in films and on television.

Three survivors interviewed by Pattinson described being badly beaten. Testimonies of locally recruited French Resistance workers note that some women had electric currents run through their nipples, electrodes inserted into their vaginas, their nails extracted, their breasts severed, and some were raped by guards, sometimes in front of their male colleagues.

Being robbed of one's dignity after having been stripped, shaved and been given shapeless prison clothing and a number, was mentioned by many survivors. Lillian Kremer, who researched the Jewish survivors of the Holocaust, said that women were

>...shamed and terrified by SS men who made lewd remarks and obscene suggestions and poked, pinched and mauled them in the course of delousing procedures and searches for hidden valuables in oral, rectal and vaginal cavities.[103]

Prisoners were forbidden to exchange their camp clothing, to dress well, to wear make-up or to style their hair – they were defeminised. Many had to cope with diarrhoea, cystitis, malnutrition, excessive exercise and lack of sanitary products. This maltreatment often led to menstruation stopping. Tania Szabó reported that 'those for whom periods continued, through intentional lack of hygienic material to prevent the menses flowing down the legs of the women... they suffered great distress and humiliation.'[104] Some were worried that bromide had been put into their soup to stop them from having children.

One poignant account, told by Geneviève de Gaulle, a captured member of the French Resistance, was celebrating her birthday. She had been given a birthday cake made from compressed breadcrumbs which had been kneaded together with several spoonfuls of a molasses-like substance they called 'jam' or 'jelly', twenty-four twigs were used as candles and leaves picked from the banks of the nearby swamp decorated the edges.

In the accounts of all these women there were very few records of them taking advantage of their 'L' pills. It could well have been that they were convinced that, if they kept to their cover story, they would be able to bluff their way through, even survive the torture. Marcus Binney summed up the role of the SOE women in *The Women Who Lived for Danger*:

>In an organisation that recruited numerous outstandingly brave and resourceful men, who repeatedly carried out the most hazardous missions in enemy-occupied Europe, constantly facing the threat of betrayal, arrest and torture by the Gestapo, these women were to show corresponding valour, determination and powers of endurance, serving alone or in small groups. Without hesitation, they risked their lives on an often daily basis. For this, they had no previous military or professional training, as many of the men had. They had to be alert, quick-witted, calm and unruffled while constantly acting a part. Women had never had such a role to play before, yet again and again, they surprised their comrades with their astonishing mastery of clandestine life.[105]

'ANGELA'
Landed by Lysander near Saumur (Loire) in autumn 1942.

Sometime in the autumn of 1942 one of 161 Squadron's pilots flew 'Angela', a 17-year-old FANY radio operator/courier, out of Tangmere with 18-year-old Derrick Baynham to a landing strip in the unoccupied zone of France, near Saumur, south of the Loire. Intriguingly, neither name has appeared in the mainstream SOE literature which suggests that, if the account is true, it was an SIS mission.

According to Baynham's obituary in the *Daily Telegraph*, he had been awarded the George Medal for bravery when he was only 17. Fifty years later, in his short, pamphlet-style memoir of his recruitment, training and SOE mission, entitled *'Never Volunteer,' Said My Dad*, he referred to his accomplice as Angel but admitted towards the end that many names he used were fictitious to protect their identities. They met at Thame Park, one of the SOE's country houses where they had intensive wireless training courses.

The previous day a young FANY called Angela had come up to me in a very anxious state saying that she had answered an advert for a bilingual secretary, and was now being trained as a radio operator in Morse, and in various subversive activities. She had no idea of what she was being trained for. I told her that I had no idea either. I did not mention the German Uniforms in the QM [Quartermaster] Stores.

...We were then moved to a similar country house – Chicheley Manor – near Newport Pagnell. Here we had further wireless training, including setting up various Spy sets in the nearby country and transmitting back to base, using one-time pad codes.

...I was told to choose a Wireless trained courier to go with me. This was because as a man it would be difficult for me to move around without being noticed, and although my French was reasonable, it would not have fooled a French Gendarme for long. I decided to ask Angela, as she had been educated in France, and her morse was brilliant. Also, I had grown rather fond of her, which seemed to be mutual. Not a very professional approach, but she readily agreed, and I was given permission to brief her on the details of my mission, or at least the part of it that would affect her.

Later that day I began to have misgivings. She was not eighteen yet and would have been described in my day as 'stunning'. It was certainly a very dangerous mission and the chances of getting back to UK were evens at best. I suggested that she talked it over with the Senior FANY, and postpone her decision until I the following day. She said that she would not change her mind, but would do as I said. The following morning the Senior FANY asked to see me in her office. She said that she had told Angela that she would be in good hands, and after all that is what we had been trained for. If she wanted to change her mind, she could be a UK Operator and nobody would ever blame her. She then said that Angela was quite sure of herself, and trusted that I would look after her and not get her into any trouble. I replied that we were both very well trained and would know what to do. She said 'That's not what I meant' and she had the courtesy to blush!!!

I went off to find Angela and thanked her for her confidence in me. She threw her arms around my neck, kissed me, and said that she was quite sure that we would be lucky. A bit overcome, I said that we should not rely on luck but on our training....

We were to fly in a Westland Lysander by night from RAF Tangmere in a few days' time. We were then kitted up in civilian clothes, but something had to be done about Angela's striking good looks. Such treatment was deemed unnecessary for me!! When she reappeared some hours later with a schoolgirl's haircut, she looked about fifteen at the most, and would have been classified in the Army as 'Jail Bait'.[106]

Their mission was to report to Baron Philippe de Vomécourt's VENTRILOQUIST network operating around Limoges and find out what had happened to three missing agents, to investigate if a radio operator who had included errors in his messages was being forced to send under duress. They had to see if there was an informer in the circuit and to eliminate him or to arrange his elimination. They also had to spot new talent in France to be returned to the UK by Lysander for training, to 'recce' and report on new small industrial enterprises being relocated from cities to make weapons components and to plant bogus information to entrap informers.

Things did not go quite according to plan. When they landed, the expected agent they were supposed to meet had already been arrested.

That night we took it in turns to keep awake with torches at the ready, guns loaded. When my turn to be awake came, around 3 am, Angela woke me up. I could see that she had little tears running down her cheeks, she apologised and said that she was cold and frightened. I said cheerfully I hope, 'you need not apologise – I am not too happy myself – so join the club.' I wiped her tears away and stroked her poor shorn hair until she drifted off to sleep. In fact, there were a number of options available to us, but I would discuss them with her when we were both awake. I suddenly remembered that we both had a half bottle of Navy rum with our goodies. What better time as I thought it must be the 'Dog Watch'. Life was not so bad after all![107]

Despite help from a local farmer and his wife, they did not manage to make contact with VENTRILOQUIST and only narrowly escaped capture by the Milice. The blue-coated, brown-shirted, blue-bereted Miliciens were the Vichy government's security police, established January 1943. While Baynham set up his wireless in a pigsty; Angel went to the local market with a message. Suddenly,

> I heard a noise behind me. I thought that it was Angel – it was a member of the Milice holding a pistol in my direction. I had made an elementary mistake; I could not reach my own weapon! He told me to stand up and keep my hands in the air. Suddenly, there was a loud shot; I thought at first that I had been hit, but it was he who folded up and fell to the ground. Then in tripped Angel as I was about to finish him off. 'Don't fire' she said, 'there is another one, and you might alert him.' In fact, he was already dead. ... She [said] that she saw a van arrive, which was parked in the farmyard. There were two Milice in it, one of whom was still sitting in the front reading a paper. The other had gone off to have a look around.... She carefully followed him, and when she came to the pigsty, she quickly took in the situation and shot him through a window.
>
> We had to get rid of the other one. So Angel acted as bait, and lit a small fire, to heat up some water, in full view of the van. The unfortunate occupant had not heard the single shot, and when his accomplice had not appeared back, got out, and looked up on the hillside. He saw Angel about 800 yards away and set off to investigate. As he approached Angel, I was hidden behind a hedge about 15 yards away and shot him before he had even had time to say anything. All this might seem to be rather cold-blooded, but we could not take prisoners, these were the rules of the game in SOE. We carried him up to the pigsty, and laid him out next to the first victim, I went through their papers and found that their names were those of two of the worst bullying Vichy collaborators in the Town, with a history of arrests and shootings.[108]

When the bodies were found, a search of the surrounding area ensued which discovered the hidden radio set they had brought with them. The locals told them that two men were keeping watch, waiting for their return. Rather than killing them, Baynham decided to knock them out for twelve hours with an injection. He claimed they had been supplied by the RSPCA and had been a fully paid up member ever since.

> I beckoned Angel to come up by my side and checked that her pistol safety catch was not on. We slid forwards on our stomachs until we were almost up to the spot where I had seen them on my morning recce. I suddenly recognised two bodies lying only a few feet ahead...... They were both

asleep, and their weapons were lying on the grass. I stood up over them gun in hand, and told Angel to quietly wake them, up, but not to shoot unless I did. As they woke up and realised their predicament I made them lie face down, limbs outstretched. They pleaded for their lives as Angel frisked them for any arms – they both had pistols which Angel removed...... I called up the two helpers and supervised the tying up operation which was probably overdone, even to the extent of attaching lines to their feet and wrists between two separate tree trunks so that they could not attempt to untie each other. Angel then injected them in the thighs; we assured them that the jab was just to put them asleep for a few hours. We did not gag them, as we did not know how to do it without risk of suffocation. How to tie up people was not on the syllabus in my SOE training![109]

The tense circumstances of their mission threw them together in a way which led to the inevitable question as to whether they should develop their relationship.

However, when I woke up at about noon she had put her arms around me, pressed her cheeks which were wet with tears against mine while quietly sobbing. I did not quite know what to do – I just asked her to talk to me. She said that as we approached the Milice she had a fear that almost paralysed her. She had felt that we would most certainly be killed, and we would have died without having shared ourselves with each other when we had the chance. I forget what my responses were, but they were to the effect that when we had got through our mission our time would come, and would be all that more precious for waiting. It's hard for me to explain now – I loved and adored Angel – we both expected that we would be caught eventually to be tortured and executed, but maybe we would get back one day to England, marry and have a little family together. The stakes were too high to risk wrecking our future by giving in to immediate satisfactions; Angel had to be my prize when we had accomplished whatever was required of us.[110]

Not long afterwards, they moved to Périgueux where Angel developed a chest infection. Quite seriously ill, Baynham arranged for her to be looked after by Roman Catholic nuns in a convent where she stayed until 1945. When he returned to England, he was commissioned into the Royal Signals and served overseas where a grenade wounded him. He was briefly taken prisoner but escaped and was Mentioned in Despatches. When he returned to England after the war, he made enquiries after Angel, only to discover that she had managed to get back to England, had married and had two children. He kept her identity a secret, even on his deathbed in 1999.

MARIE-THÉRÈSE LE CHÊNE

Aged 52. Landed by felucca (converted fishing boat) at Port Miou, about 15 km south-east of Marseille, on the night of 3/4 November 1942.

The last French woman to be sent in 1942 was Marie-Thérèse le Chêne, whose husband and brother-in-law were also F Section agents. Nothing about her family background was included in her personnel file, which, perhaps because they were a husband and wife team, was included in his. He was Major Henri le Chêne, born in London in 1891 to French parents who had taken British citizenship and he worked as a hotel proprietor and an administrator in Kenya. Marie-Thérèse was born in Sedan in the Ardennes on 20 April 1890. After escaping with Henri and his brother Pierre on the last boat from Bayonne in 1939, she was recorded as living at 23 Nottingham Place, Marylebone, London, working in hotel management and as a cook in Elton hospital near Peterborough.

Refusing to join the BCRA, de Gaulle's secret service, she was recruited by SOE on 16 May 1942, a few weeks after Henri and Pierre's departure to France as agents. According to Escott, she was in the first group of women to be trained.

The Commandant's report from The Rings (STS 31) at Beaulieu stated that she was,

> A very intelligent and quick-thinking woman who is full of initiative, energy, and considerable determination. She is shrewd and experienced and has a strong character. Somewhat excitable and talkative, which, unless kept under rigid control might prove a danger. Usually, she shows considerable foresight but occasionally jumps to conclusions and acts impulsively. Has an independent and confident nature with a bent for defying authority. It is probably safe to say that she is alive to her own shortcomings, and her determination and courage will see her through any commission she is given.[111]

Henri was recorded as leaving for the field on 31 March 1942 to organise sabotage and propaganda for the PLANE network initially in the Lyon area and later in Clermont-Ferrand and Périgueux. Tillet records him as, code named Victor, being landed by a felucca named Seawolf near Théoule-sur-Mer 16 km south-west of Antibes on 22 April with Jean Menesson and Lt Maurice Pertschuk, code named Prunus.

Her brother-in-law, Pierre le Chêne, code named Grégoire and Aspen were parachuted near Loches, Indre and Loire, on 2 May. He went to Lyon to work as a wireless operator with Georges Duboudin's SPRUCE network.[112]

Marie-Thérèse was taken by destroyer to Gibraltar and accompanied Yvonne Rudellat, Odette Sansom, Mary Herbert and four men on the felucca to Port-Miou on 4 November 1942. Escott gave the date as 31 October, but this could have been when she left Britain. Also known as Marie Thérèse Ragot and Wistaria, her mission was to work as Henri's assistant and courier, carrying messages and documents to various Resistance groups.

Research by Escott revealed that, after she had made her way to Cannes, the Germans took over the Unoccupied Zone, making their headquarters in Lyon, where Pétain's government was based and many of SOE's agents operated. Buckmaster changed his plans for her. As the situation had become very dangerous, Virginia Hall had found Marie-Thérèse a safe house:

> ...in an insignificant corner of Lyon city. It turned out, however, that Marie-Thérèse had [?] it, as the scope of her work had altered when she met Henri and learned of the reasons for her last-minute change of orders and the new dangers facing them.
>
> Henri had arrived in France in 1942 prepared for a tour of sabotage and propaganda, but after his first visit to Virginia Hall, he had decided that Lyon felt unsafe and changed his area and work. He still kept his eyes and ears open for information, helpers and suitable landing and dropping zones for aircraft, but most of these were far outside the city in the less populated areas to the west between Clermont-Ferrand and Périgueux. Here, by moving and splitting his network into two he could use either town as his new headquarters. This change of plan had worked quite well and he found that there was much more support for spreading propaganda in the smaller towns and villages, since they provided workers for the area, with the added benefit of being able to recruit elderly women of between fifty – sixty into the network, who made the best couriers, as they tended to arouse less suspicion.
>
> Marrie-Thérèse's work changed from courier to distributing anti-German leaflets and tracts, many of them printed under the very noses of the Germans. Of course, there were messages as well, and she was often heavily loaded with bags and parcels, which grew larger and heavier as her travels grew longer. It was helpful that the main-line passenger trains still ran on time, though there were fewer of them, and she soon set herself to find friends at most destinations, where she could stay safely overnight after curfew. Then, chatting in the big fire-lit kitchen with the family, picking up useful information from them, they would often bring out their forbidden and carefully hidden

wireless to listen to the French news on the BBC and follow the course of the war.[113]

Marie-Thérèse's travels took her down to Marseille where she contacted members of an escape organisation who were able to make good forgeries of Spanish documents needed by those wanting to escape through Spain. Through them, she learned of members of the CARTE network in Antibes, Cannes and Toulon. Through Henri, she learned of the workers at the Michelin rubber works in Clermont-Ferrand deliberately making inferior quality tyres for the Germans which needed regular replacement, thus guaranteeing them continued employment and avoiding them being sent to Germany as forced labour.[114]

On a trip to Paris taking documents to various Resistance members, she was surprised to discover that some of the leading figures were Jews, Communists and trade union members who had put aside their political differences to work together for the liberation of France.

She later admitted that her favourite area was the Dordogne. She liked the simple, agricultural lifestyle, where farmers made extra money selling food surpluses on the black market. The remote village of Domme, about 50 km south-west of Périgueux, was Henri's main DZ where supplies of sabotage material and London-prepared propaganda materials could be stored in the many caves in the hills.

Some of the propaganda leaflets she arranged with the chief engineer of the tramway marshalling yards in Lyon to be distributed among the workers and the passengers on the trams.

In December 1942, the deteriorating weather and the stress of her courier work was compounded by news that Pierre, her brother-in-law, had been captured by the Gestapo while operating his wireless set. Following further arrests, including some in Henri's network, he decided to halt his activities and return to Britain. Marie-Thérèse's condition and the winter weather made an attempt to cross the Pyrénées impracticable so until an alternative was arranged, she was found another safe house.

When she recovered, she went to Paris where she met Henri Déricourt, F Section's new Air Movements Officer, who promised to let her know when a pick up became available.

Back in Lyon, she met Robert Boiteux, who had been parachuted near Ance, Rhone, to take over the SPRUCE network on 1 June 1942. Based in the hills north and west of Lyon, an area she knew well, she agreed to do courier work for him and took part in railway and canal sabotage.

As she had mentioned Déricourt to Boiteux, when he realised the situation was getting too dangerous, he asked that a Hudson pick-up could be arranged. Using references Marie-Thérèse provided for a field north-east of Angers, about 1 km south-east of the village of Soucelles, Déricourt arranged it.

Completely burnt out, Henri left Marie-Thérèse and returned to Britain via Gibraltar on 14 May 1943 where, after debrief, he was given a desk job in the political intelligence department.[115]

On the night of 19/20 August 1943, she and nine others, including Boiteux, were taken to the field where they had to wait for Déricourt to turn up. When the plane landed, the two passengers got out with their luggage, including Erwin Deman to set up the VAR escape line, the others got in and the pilot flew them safely to England.[116]

Once debriefed and reunited with her husband, she went to see some of her old friends, one of whom reported her to Lt-Com. John Senter, head of the Security Section.

On 21 August, Senter informed Buckmaster that Marie-Thérèse had told someone who knew nothing whatever about their organisation that 'she worked for the Secret Service in Baker Street and that she went to France in a destroyer and had recently returned from that country. I feel that this is a bad breach of security and would therefore be obliged if arrangements could be made for Madame le Chêne to be seen at Orchard Court.'[117]

One of Buckmaster's subsequent memos revealed that Marie-Thérèse had spoken with the mother of one of the FANY drivers. He called her to see him about it and three days later informed Senter that,

I saw this woman at Orchard Court this morning and warned her that I had a very serious matter to tell her about. She showed immediate signs of nervousness. I then accused her of the indiscretion referred to you by you on 21.8.43 and she started to bluster. She then said it was totally untrue, burst into tears and proceeded to give a diatribe on the iniquities of me and everybody connected with the organisation. I warned her that if it were in fact true and she had denied it being true she would be liable to an even graver charge if the case was proved against her. This made her think. While still maintaining cum lacrimis that it was totally untrue she began to hedge and said that wicked people had a down on her and had invented this clever story in order to put her in prison. As the remarks so obviously could not have been invented I am afraid that we must conclude that she is a silly old woman who is telling lies and I ask that she be treated as such. Her work in the field was not outstanding but it is fair to concede that her mission was not a very big one. I suggest that she should be formally reprimanded and I leave it to you to decide what other steps if any should be taken against her. I am not averse to her being given more serious punishment which I think she thoroughly deserves and I should not be willing to employ her again.[118]

The following day, without providing the details of her security breach, Selwyn Jepson informed SOE's General Section that 'We are unable to return her to the field as she is "blown" and we have no other employment for her. Her security is very bad. May I please have your views as to the method of disposal wherest [sic] I will institute a disposal form.'[119]

Disposal in those days meant the administrative arrangements that had to be made for her employment to be terminated, the balance of her wages paid and, depending on the circumstances, assistance provided in finding another job. Acknowledging that her lapse in security was due to 'sheer stupidity and thoughtlessness', Flight Lieutenant Miller of the General Section contacted MI5 asking if they would keep an eye on her as he was worried she might 'harbour rather bitter feelings against us'.[120]

Keeping an eye on her could have included: opening her post; listening to her telephone calls; bugging her accommodation and following her to identify who she was in contact with.

On 2 September, Mrs Pateman of Training Section informed the head of Security that Marie-Thérèse was being interviewed by Mrs Marion Gamwell, the head of the FANY, presumably about the prospect of employment. However, it appeared that she had had a further chat with Mrs Stringer, the mother of Mrs Bateson, the FANY driver to whom she divulged her SOE work. Convinced she had ignored Buckmaster's severe reprimand, Pateman stated that she had consulted with Buckmaster,

...on the question of Mrs Lachene's [sic] operational knowledge and it does appear to be considerably more comprehensive than is usually the case when an Agent returns from the field. She was working with Marie [possible Pearl Withington whose code name was Marie] and came to know at least 20 and possibly 30 of our agents out there, involving some 10 circuits. In addition to this she does, of course, know all the F Section HQ staff and the location of various schools. Beyond this knowledge of personnel, she has been in a position to see a great deal of the methods and techniques with which we operate in the field. F [Buckmaster] agrees that if Mrs Lechene is indeed as irresponsibly indiscreet as these reports suggest she constitutes a very grave danger to us from the security point of view. She seems to us exactly the sort of person who is, because of her complete inability to hold her tongue about her work, a potential source of valuable information to any enemy agent who might come upon her. It really does seem as though she cannot realise how valuable her knowledge is and how easily a practiced seeker after information could extract it from her without her realising what was happening. On the side issue of Mrs Stringer, Mrs Bateson tells me that she is seriously perturbed by her mother's capacity to gossip and inability to understand even the elementary principles of security. Mrs Bateson is quite sure that her mother did not know before she made the Lechene contact that her daughter was driving for us and that it was the association of Baker Street and the Secret Services which enabled her to conclude that her daughter was in the same organisation as the Lechenes.

It was AQ/F [code-letter for officer in the FANY personnel and civilians' Section] who first told me about the letter Mrs Bateson had received from her mother which started all this; as I told you yesterday I asked AQ/F to let Staff Commander Gamwell know that it would be undesirable for her to see Mrs Lechene in connection with a possible job. You will, of course, know best how this matter should be handled but Mrs Bateson herself suggested that as far as her mother is concerned she thought it would be a good thing if someone saw her and tried to bring home to her the danger of careless talk.[121]

In a subsequent memo, MI5 were asked to be careful not to let Mrs Stringer known that it was her daughter, Mrs Bateson, who had brought her mother's indiscretion to SOE's attention.

MI5 took the matter very seriously and duly sent Major Glover, the Nottingham Regional Security Liaison Officer, to interview Mrs Stringer. His report detailed how he,

...visited the Red Cross Convalescent Home at Elton [near Peterborough] on Sunday 5.9.43 at 3.30 p.m. having previously telephoned to Mrs Stringer in the morning stating that I wished to see her on a confidential matter. Mrs Stringer was waiting for me on arrival and I informed her that I wished to discuss a serious case of leakage of information in which her name had cropped up. I explained that I understood that Mrs Lechene had recently visited the hospital as a guest and informed Mrs Stringer and others of her recent employment. Mrs Stringer became somewhat agitated and immediately asked if the interview could be adjourned and continued in front of the Commandant. I enquired her reason and she explained that the commandant knew just as much as Mrs Lechene as she did and her knowledge was, if anything less than that of the commandant. On being informed of this I thus interviewed the Commandant in the presence of Mrs Stringer. The commandant was Lady Alethes Eliot, wife of Major P.C. Eliot now serving in the 97th Kent Yeomanry Field Regiment, M.E.F. [Middle East

Forces.] She is the daughter of the Countess of Buxton. I repeated to the Commandant my reason for the visit and explained to them the seriousness of the matter and my desire to ascertain precisely what they knew and the persons likely to be aware of any information passed on from Mrs Lechenne [*sic*]. After two hours of extensive conversation (verging on interrogation) the story is as follows. Elton House was taken over in 1941 by the Red Cross. The Red Cross run it on strict lines and I think have on average about 100 patients. The nursing staff consist of about 26. Lechene was a French national employed as a cook and arrived at the hospital in 1941. She became, very naturally, very friendly with the nursing staff, and I imagine was extremely popular. She came there, I believe, because Mrs Coxon is a sort of guardian to Mrs Lechene. Mrs Coxon is an intelligent and superior type of woman. In 1942, January or February, Lechene told Mrs Coxon that she was proposing to do a hush-hush job for the War Office and would be going abroad. Mrs Coxon states that she immediately believed that Mrs Lechene would be going to France in view of her French nationality, although Lechene did not tell her. Lechene saw the Commandant to ask for her release as cook and explained that she was accepting a post of a hush-hush nature with the War Office and would be going abroad. The Commandant stated that Lechene was going to France by underground means, although the Commandant cannot today recall whether Lechene told her or whether it was her own guess. At any rate the Commandant told no one and did not discuss this with Mrs Coxon; nor, states Mrs Coxon, did she mention Lechene's project to anyone herself. [...] Mrs Coxon states that she was kept informed periodically by letter from the War Office Room 238 Hotel Victoria, stating that Lechene was well. She received periodical information of this nature, which she passed on to the Commandant. Lechene on her return to this country, first of all telephoned to Mrs Coxon to say she was back in England and later telephones to ask if she could come down to stay. [....] Lechene's request to stay was approved and [...] she arrived last Sunday 29 August. She received, I imagine, a very good welcome. The commandant held a tea-party in her room. The Commandant says that to the best of her recollection the conversation with Mrs Lechene was very much based on enquiring the conditions in France at the present time and at no time did Mrs Lechene say how she travelled to France, what her job was in France or her method of obtaining it, nor did she disclose any details about her Service Department. She did, however, freely discuss conditions in France and people she met, including the German authorities and I think, quite naturally she was pressed for much information and to express an opinion on how the war was going on and how soon it would be over and whether the French were with us, etc. I enquired how many others knew of Mrs Lechene's adventures and the Commandant thought that all the staff knew, as a result of her visit., that she had been to France and had returned. The Commandant said that whereas she herself had treated Lechene's mission as something most secret and had divulged it to no one, now that she had returned and had come down to stay she gained the impression that the secrecy had been lifted. It did not occur to her that Lechene was committing any breach of the Official Secrets Act by talking about her impressions of France. Mrs Coxon did not satisfy me that she was telling the truth when she stated that she did not know what Lechene's work was. I taxed her pretty thoroughly on this and she reacted rather badly. I am prepared to say that in my opinion Mrs Coxon knows a good deal more about Lechene and the organisation and this is supported by the fact that Lechene wrote a letter to Mrs Coxon on last Friday 3.9.44 [clearly opened by MI5 and then resealed and reposted] thanking her for the hospitality extended at Elton on her visit. She stated that she was meeting interesting people in London, but was marking time waiting for further instructions. Her letter then went on to talk about mutual friends and then had the following sentence: "Darling I will let you know as soon as I know what my future plans are." I asked Mrs Coxon what she understood by this and she was unable to offer any explanation. At this stage the Commandant informed me that she had written to her husband, Major P.C. Eliot and in trying to find something to say had mentioned the fact that Lechene had recently returned from France. She thought she had also mentioned this to her mother, the Countess of Buxton, as Lady Buxton had also met Lechene whilst staying at Elton. I put to Mrs Stringer the question as to whether she had communicated to anybody the visit of Lechene to the hospital and she denied flatly that she had done so, and with her eyes opening wide and putting on an innocent expression said she could not think of anybody who would be interested. I pointed out that the Commandant had recalled that she had mentioned Lechene's visit to her mother and her husband and had Mrs Stringer any relations who she might have told. Her reply was that she had a daughter, Mrs Bateson, but she had certainly not communicated with her and then; as an afterthought, she said, "I did, however, give Mrs Lechene a letter of introduction to my daughter. My daughter is in the MTC [Motor Transport Corps] in London and I thought it would be so nice for the two to meet". In view of the undesirability of letting Mrs Stringer or the other ladies know the source of our information I did not press the matter further, although Mrs Stringer was lying pretty hard. My impression of the Commandant was extremely favourable. I thought she was a most sensible and intelligent person and truthful. (the only person I had that feeling about whom I saw). I therefore subsequently saw her alone and said I was most anxious that the whole affair should be hushed up and forgotten and I asked the Commandant if she could assist me in seeing that all the females who were present at the tea-party could be interviewed by her and impressed to hold their peace in connection with the Lechene affair. The Commandant agreed to do this and as she struck me as a very good disciplinarian I felt she would be better than I. I am satisfied that as a result of my interview I have put the fear of God into Mrs Coxon and Mrs Stringer who I regard as being the only really dangerous people; Mrs Coxon because I think she knows a good deal and Mrs Stringer because I think she is a garrulous old lady, although I do not think she knows very much ... To conclude, I should like to say in favour of Mrs Lechene that it seems to me that although she committed the offence of telling her friends that her work had taken her underground to France and had brought her back safely I could not elicit from any of her friends any evidence that she had told them of the nature of her work. I left feeling satisfied that none of them knew except Mrs Coxon. Mrs Coxon, you will remember, was the guardian of Mrs Lechene and was devoted to her, and I think she may be in the know. Even so I have absolutely no evidence to confirm this opinion.[122]

On receiving Glover's report, Senter reported back to Jepson that she was not to be trusted, recommended that her employment be terminated and that she be given a very strong security talk before her departure, adding that 'suitable steps are being taken to keep an eye on her private address.'[123]

Before being informed of the result of the enquiry, Marie-Thérèse wrote to Buckmaster expressing her concerns:

Breach of security is too serious an accusation to be made or passed over lightly, and I ask with all the respect due to your official position that this letter be forwarded to the head of our department. Three weeks ago you accused me of a breach of security in that it had been reported to you by an M.T. driver that within ten minutes of your general warning to all present in your office had said that: – "I had travelled to France in a destroyer." At the moment of accusing me of the breach of security above-mentioned, you asked for my written undertaking that I was not guilty of such a breach; to my indignant verbal denial of such a slander, you stated you would make further enquiry and inform me accordingly.

Faced with three weeks' silence on the above-mentioned subject, I insist that my slanderer or slanderers be brought before the head of our department repeat before me that which you informed me that they had reported to you.[124]

Buckmaster considered it a stupid note and asked Security Section what steps they wished him to take 'to get rid of this of this problem as soon as possible.' Gubbins was informed but it was stressed that there was no evidence that she had disclosed the places she had visited, names of people she worked with, the routes she took or the nature of the work. Therefore, prosecuting her with the intention of interning her for the rest of the war was not considered possible or desirable. 'I recommend her release to civil life after a stern warning and further advice how to conduct herself.'[125]

She was given formal notice of dismissal on 4 October but she refused to sign an official document relating to two sections of the Official Secrets Act without the presence of her husband. When an appointment was arranged for them to meet Jepson at 6 Orchard Court, Captain Lechene contacted him saying that, because of 'the physical strain of her "sejour"' abroad added to the emotion of her last distressing cross-examination, his wife would not be able to attend any further interviews and asked him to communicate with him by telephone to 'discuss any reasonable demands you may wish to formulate.'[126]

The Political Intelligence Department was informed of Captain Lechene's correspondence and it was then revealed that, during his internment in Jaraba camp in Spain on his escape to England, he had been indiscreet in telling a fellow prisoner that he had spent seven months doing propaganda work in France on behalf of MI5 and the British Government and gave him an envelope containing a list of Frenchmen who he had been working with, including their political tendencies. He also mentioned the names of 'two contacts of his in France, one his brother, and the other a Captain GREER, known as RAKE. He gave certain particulars of a mission in Paris which his brother had been sent to do, though his brother, he said, had been caught and shot at Lyons.'[127] It was stressed that this report was uncorroborated but it went on to state that he was inclined to drink and another note read, 'Temperamental and unreliable, especially when not closely controlled. Fond of the bottle. Dangerous man.'[128]

Both were invited to Room 055 at the War Office where, although she continued to argue that she was innocent and that she had been framed, the necessity of keeping quiet about her work for SOE was made quite apparent. Buckmaster later admitted to Senter that,

...there has never been a worse and more flagrant case than the Madame Lechene case to which I called your attention upon its happenings. Both she and her husband are extremely glib and smooth people and quite clearly have persuaded the MI5 officer that the accusation was not a serious one. It is not often, I am sure, that Country Section officers request the utmost 'rigours of the law' in respect of security breaches but this was one of the few cases for which I could find absolutely no extenuating circumstances. Owing to the time which has elapsed I have little doubt that Madame Lechene has kidded herself into the belief that she said little or nothing but I am absolutely certain and have positive proof that the offence was a grave one, in so far as offences of loose talk can be considered grave. I naturally do not wish to pursue this unfortunate incident further now that both Lechenes are unconnected with SOE but I do think that this present note should be put on record and if you agree communicated to MI5 here, if ever, is a cast-iron conviction for loose talk in the most critical circumstances.[129]

French Women Infiltrated in 1943

FRANÇINE AGAZARIAN
Aged 29. Landed by Lysander near Asionne, south of Poitiers, (Vienne) on the night of 17/18 March 1943. Mentioned in Despatches.

According to SOE records, eleven women were infiltrated into France during 1943, but only two were French. Françine Agazarian, a French volunteer FANY, was the first. Born Françoise Andre in Narbonne on the Mediterranean coast on 8 May 1913 to French parents, she was working as an English-speaking secretary in 1940.

Arriving in London on 1 September 1941 with an Emergency Certificate, she was interrogated, and MI5 reported that to get to England, she had used a marriage of convenience to Sergeant William Reynolds of the Royal Signals Corps, who claimed he was an escaped prisoner of war. It turned out that he was a bigamist, so the French ceremony was declared null.[1]

She reported to the police that she was anxious to marry a former fiancé, Jack Agazarian, who was living in London. She gave her address as 805 Chelsea Cloisters, SW3. Where she had met Jack was not stated, but, according to his personnel file, he was the second of six children born to an Armenian father and a French father. Educated in France and England, he became a British citizen and joined the Army when the war started, but his French language and having lived in France attracted the attention of the SOE recruiters. He was in training as a wireless operator. She was 28 years old when they got married.[2]

Commissioned as an Ensign in the FANY, she was sent to Wanborough Manor for assessment. In early December, her instructor reported that she was quite at home with the other French students, 'popular, genuine, full of interest in everything, usually cheerful, but rather apt to get moody for a short time after the results of the "Quiz" have become known if she has not done well.' A fellow student described her as 'une excellente camarade.'[3]

A subsequent report a few days later expressed concerns about her security, that she was 'temperamental, might blow the gaff in a fit of jealousy. On the other hand, is quite reticent about herself.' She was still unwilling to talk about her past life a week later, and her instructor reported that she 'might be indiscreet in a fit of pique.'[4]

The finishing report graded her as 5. Her physical training has 'much improved; possesses stamina in spite of her apparent thinness. She was keenly interested in fieldcraft and for weapon training she had 'picked up rudiments of weapons taught, including the .303 Vickers M.G. [machine gun] and 2" Mortar; inclined to get flustered but by no means timid or gun shy.'

She followed the subject of explosives and demolitions with interest and although taking part, her knowledge was 'rather vague and inaccurate.' No work was done on signaling and communications; she had begun to grasp elements of map reading, but her reports were 'slap dash and untidy. Lacks perseverance.' The instructor's remarks were that she 'has worked conscientiously and keenly throughout the course, and on the whole, has made great progress. Her lack of patience, however, and her temperamental attitude make her very careless at times. She is easily discouraged and often gets flustered, though never nervous, with weapons. Not without intelligence, and with more restraint would achieve better results.'[5]

The Commandant, Major de Wesselow's report was that she was: 'Intelligent and keen; no fear of firearms. In a strange milieu has sometimes exhibited temperament and caprice. Moody, jealous; unattractive to men. Under pressure by her excellent mentor and husband, got down to it halfway through the course and has since shown mettle and stamina. Unimpressive by comparison with the two others who came here temporarily but admittedly game.'[6]

There was no indication she went on a paramilitary or parachute training course and no evidence she attended a course at Beaulieu. There were no details about her mission, only that she was sent into the field on 17 March 1943.

Tillet reported it as a double Lysander operation on the night of 17 March. The field was near Asionne, about 4.5 km north of Marnay, south of Poitiers. She was accompanied by John Goldsmith, Lejeune and wireless operator Robert Dowlen. With identity papers in the name of Madame Françine Fabre and code named Marguerite and Lamplighter, she went to join her husband who had been parachuted in on 29 December 1942 with a mission to work as another wireless operator to help the PROSPER network.

Her mission was to be a courier with this and the PHYSICIAN networks, passing and collecting information and delivering money, forged documents, and weapons to members in the Paris area. According to Escott, it was felt she would work well with her husband despite her frail appearance, temperamental personality and possessive nature.

Although in the same network, my husband and I were not working together; as a radio operator he worked alone and transmitted from different locations every day. I was only responsible to Prosper (Francis Suttill) whom we all called François. He liked to use me for special errands because, France being my native land, I could get away from difficulties easily enough, particularly when dealing with officialdom. François was an outstanding leader, clear-headed, precise, confident. I liked working on his instructions, and I enjoyed the small challenges he was placing in front of me. For instance, calling at town halls in various districts of Paris to exchange the network's expired ration cards (manufactured in London) for genuine new ones. Mainly I was delivering his messages to his helpers: in Paris, in villages, or isolated houses in the countryside. From time to time I was also delivering demolition material received from England. And once, with hand-grenades in my shopping bag, I travelled in a train so full that I had to stand against a German NCO. This odd situation was not new to me. I had already experienced it for the first time on the day of my arrival on French soil when I had to travel by train from Poitiers to Paris. A very full train also. I sat on my small suitcase in the corridor, a uniformed German standing close against me. But, that first time, tied to my waist, under my clothes, was a wide black cloth belt containing bank-notes for Prosper, a number of blank identity cards and a number of ration cards; while tucked into the sleeves of my coat were crystals for Prosper's radio transmitters; the crystals had been skillfully secured to my sleeves by Vera Atkins herself, before my departure from Orchard Court. My .32 revolver and ammunition were in my suitcase. The ludicrousness of the situation somehow eliminated any thoughts of danger. In any case, I believe none of us in the field ever gave one thought to danger. Germans were everywhere, especially in Paris; one absorbed the sight of them and went on with the job of living as ordinarily as possible and applying oneself to one's work. Because I worked alone, the times I liked best were when we could be together, Prosper (Francis Suttill), Denise (Andrée Borrel), Archambaud (Gilbert Norman), Marcel (Jack Agazarian) and I, sitting round a table, while I was decoding radio messages from London; we were always hoping to read the exciting warning to stand by, which would have meant that the liberating invasion from England was imminent.

When Françine got to Paris, she rendezvoused with Julienne Aisner, who had an office on the Champs Élysées. After spending a night in her studio apartment, she moved to another in Rue de Colonel Mol, which Julienne had rented for her. Jack spent time there when he was not transmitting from other safe houses. To prevent the concierge making too many enquiries, she was told that they were escaping a jealous husband. On her travels, she grew familiar with the German and French police controls, checkpoints, stops, and searches. Suttill sent her to various Mairies to take cleverly forged time-expired ration cards or local papers to exchange them for the real thing.

Gleeson reported how she was very nearly caught by the German's Operation *North Pole*. Having captured wireless operators and their sets, some were coerced through torture and bribes to collaborate. Messages were then sent through to SOE requesting arms, ammunition, money, the latest wireless sets, money and more agents so that the Germans knew exactly when and where they would arrive. Herman Giskes, the mastermind of this radio game, having successfully penetrated the Dutch Resistance, was sent to repeat the operation in France.

Two German agents pretending to be British were sent down one of the escape lines from Holland, through Belgium into France. When they approached one of the networks in Paris, without having their credentials checked, they were given the name of a café near the Sacré Coeur in Montmartre. They were introduced to the Agazarians, Andreé Borrel and two members of the Resistance playing poker. Accepted as genuine agents, they infiltrated their network and arrests followed.

When people started to disappear, arrangements were made for Françine, Jack and some other members of the Resistance to be lifted out. The prospect of being caught and her constant travelling had worn her down. She lost weight and became pale and nervous. Although she felt that she ought to continue her work, the SOE insisted that she return. A note in her file stated that 'LAMPLIGHTER returned to the U.K. after ten weeks in the Field, as she was unfit.'

On 16 June 1943, when the two Lysanders landed in a field near Vieux Briollay, 3.5 km west of Villeneuve, about 12 km north-east of Angers, Diana Rowden code named Paulette, Noor Inayat Khan, code named Madeleine, Cecile Lefort, code named Alice, Charles Skepper code named Bernard, and another agent got out. Françine, Jack, and three others boarded the planes with their luggage and were safely returned to England.[7]

They moved into 276 Russell Court, Russell Square, and, following debrief, rest and recreation, Jack was allocated another mission and he left on 22 July leaving Françine on her own.

A month later, an SOE officer noted that 'her operational work has come to an end, and I am afraid we have no other job for her. She will be quite content, I think, to be returned to civilian life. She has no up-to-date operational knowledge, and her security I expect you will agree, has always been good. Her status is that of a FANY, having been embodied by M/F [SOE's Training Section] on our behalf.'[8]

A few weeks later, she was interviewed about the security situation regarding her husband and was reported as 'very unlikely to conduct herself in a way which might jeopardise his existence. She is a serious-minded girl, moreover, who realised the importance of the work involved. She quite understands why she is not being used again and is quite happy about it. She shows no sign of being disgruntled in any way but hopes that she can continue to be used as a FANY. If she can be found such employment, there will certainly be nothing to fear as to her security.'[9]

Arrangements were made for her to be taken on as a driver/orderly at Gardener's End, Ardeley, near Stevenage (STS 19). This was one of the requisitioned houses used by the Polish Section and, although undocumented, she probably escorted Polish agents to Gaynes Hall prior to the flight and then to Tempsford.

She continued working there and at Pollardswood Grange (STS 20b), Chalfont St Giles, near Chorley Wood, until three days after D-Day when she was transferred to Maryland, SOE's code name for its forward base in southern Italy.

While at Gardener's End and again in Italy, she was involved in several lapses of security. On 6 December, a report was forwarded to Captain Rees at the War Office.

On 27 May 1944, Capt. NEKOLA, a 29 [Czechoslovakian], who had been resident at XIX, arrived at XXB and asked to see Vol. AGAZARIAN. Capt. NEKOLA had been friendly with Vol. AGAZARIAN while she was stationed at XIX, and, according to information received from other FANY personnel, Vol. AGAZARIAN gave to Capt. NEKOLA, on her departure for XXB, the open address of the Station. In extenuation, she might plead (a) that FANY are allowed to use the open address (but not, of course, with students), and (b) that she had no idea that Capt. NEKOLA would use the address for anything but correspondence.

At the time of these reports no action was, I think, taken from HQ, because Vol. AGAZARIAN was already under instructions to move to Italy, and it was ruled that she was beyond our control. FANY personnel at XVIII [Frogmore Park, Watton-at-Stone, Hertfordshire] and XIX were, however, reminded of the restrictions on the use of an open address.[10]

Six days later, Flying Officer Miller, head of vetting, records and training at SOE HQ, sent the following note to Lt Hover-Millar, one of the SOE officers responsible for Italy.

The following breach of Security is reported to you so you can bring it to the notice of the responsible FANY officers or take such other action as you think necessary.

Station 19 is one of our Polish training schools. The C.O. is Captain Emmings. Some time ago, Captain Emmings was talking to a FANY employed there as a cook. She said that 'Pica' who was a Czech body who had been some time at Station 19, was back. Emmings later passed this information to MP [Lt. Col. Perkins, Berkeley Court] who was astonished as it had only just come through to HQ. MP naturally asked Emmings the source of his information. Emmings then asked the FANY cook, who is Volunteer Clover Turner, the source of her information. Volunteer Turner stated that it was Volunteer Mrs. F. Agazarian, who had written from Italy saying she had met Pica.

It is understood that FANY personnel censor their mail which is sent through the open post and which therefore may or may not be uncensored in transit. It is certain, however, that a mere statement in a letter that the writer 'had met Pica' would not offend against censorship rules. An SOE censor, knowing who Pica was, would erase such a statement from a private letter as it is clearly undesirable that the movements of our agents should be discussed socially between our personnel.

As I say, I leave this matter entirely to your discretion. You may think that this is an example of an unconscious breach of security which might, therefore, serve as a general reminder to all those who censor their own letters.[11]

She was duly reprimanded but whether this was before or after she learned what had happened to her husband is unknown. He had been captured along with Suttill and Borrel, survived six months of interrogation, torture, and solitary confinement, and was executed on 29 March 1945 alongside Dietrich Bonhoeffer, the Lutheran pastor, at Flossenburg concentration camp, Bavaria, near the border with Czechoslovakia.

When Françine was informed of his death, she was with a group of FANYs stationed at Paradiso, ME 54, the SOE's forward camp near Brindisi in Italy. From here, the RAF were flying out to drop containers to the Resistance groups in northern Italy, Yugoslavia, Albania and Greece. Margaret Pawley, one of the other FANYs in Italy, recalled seeing her out in the gardens of the house they shared, kicking the gravel, trying to come to terms with her loss.

Just as the boat passed the Scilly Isles on Françine's return to England, she was asked what she was going to do. Her reply was that she was going back to France to see if she could find out who betrayed her husband.[12]

When she got back to London, Françine trained in a beauty culture salon and informed Vera Atkins that, 'I think all will be right as I like it very much.'[13] Like most of the other women agents infiltrated into France, she was cited for an award. Major General Gubbins' citation stated that,

> On 18 March 1943, Ensign AGAZARIAN was infiltrated into France in the PARIS area to act as a courier to an established circuit and to encode and decode wireless messages.
>
> In the course of her duties, she was responsible for keeping contact between these scattered groups of the circuit, a task which entailed continuous travelling throughout an area where police and Gestapo activities were intense and travel checks an everyday occurrence.
>
> Despite these dangerous conditions and in the face of a number of arrests of other members of the circuit, she fulfilled her task most conscientiously and with complete success until the 16 June when she returned to the United Kingdom.
>
> For her courage and sense of duty shown for a period of three months under most dangerous and exacting conditions, it is recommended that Ensign AGAZARIAN be Mentioned in Despatches.[14]

Jack was posthumously Mentioned in Despatches and awarded the Legion d'Honneur and Croix de Guerre. Noreen Riols, an F Section secretary and later one of the administration staff at Beaulieu, thought Françine never recovered from her husband's death and every year visited Flossenburg to commemorate the massacre. She reported that,

> one afternoon in March 1945, a few days before the Americans liberated the camp, in order to wipe out all trace of them, the remaining twelve F Section agents were viciously flogged then hung, side by side, three at a time, with piano wire attached to a meat hook and suspended from the wall where the plaque [commemorating the SOE agents executed] was unveiled. This was a favourite form of execution practiced at Flossenburg, and in other concentration camps. It was particularly barbaric since it took the victims twenty minutes to die by slow strangulation. [...] Jack Agazarian, one of the last of the twelve agents to be led to the slaughter that afternoon, managed to smuggle out a note for his wife. He told her what was happening and wrote: 'I am in the last cell so they will be coming for me very soon. I just want to thank you for everything and tell you that I love you.'[15]

Whether Françine identified his betrayer is unknown. She later remarried and died in 1999 before the unveiling in 2007.

JULIENNE AISNER

Aged 43. Landed by Lysander near Le Port, 13 km south-east of Tours (Indre & Loire), on the night of 13/14 May 1943. Awarded the King's Medal of Commendation.

The second Frenchwoman sent into France in 1943 was Julienne Aisner. She was born Julienne Simart in Anglure, a small agricultural village near Troyes, Marne, on 30 December 1899. When her father joined the police, the family moved to Chalons-sur-Marne, about half way between Dijon and Mâcon, During the Great War, he served as an official with the British Expeditionary Force.

Nicknamed Ju, she studied to become an English teacher and, according to Escott, grew up to be 'an exceedingly beautiful and attractive woman, small and full of energy with a round face, softly curling hair and large liquid dark eyes.'[16] While teaching in the Lower Rhine, she met Joseph Lauler, an Alsatian, who had emigrated to America but returned as a Lieutenant in the US Marines fighting with the American Expeditionary Forces. In September 1923, they moved to Indianapolis, USA, where they married, and she entered Butler University. Two years later, their son Louis was born. In 1929, following her husband's death in a car accident, she went to live with her parents in Lebanon.

When her father retired, the family moved to Hanoi in Vietnam and joined her sister, whose father-in-law owned a chain of cinemas. While teaching English at St Peter Institute in Hanoi, the tropical climate made her ill so, in 1933, she returned to Paris, found work as a scriptwriter and lived in a flat on Place des Ternes.

During this time, she met and married Robert Aisner, a Polish Jew, and moved to Auteuil, in the western suburbs of Paris where she was introduced to Henri Déricourt, a French Air Force test pilot. He was later to become F Section's Air Movements Officer in Northern France.

Just before the Second World War started, she used her family connections in Hanoi and became a partner in Hérault Films, a small company with an office at 1 Rue de Berri, overlooking the Champs-Élysées.

When her husband was mobilised in September 1939, he was caught and imprisoned but managed to escape and make his way, first to North Africa and then to the United States. Settling in Hollywood, he helped produce propaganda films for the Free French, was a technical adviser for the anti-Nazi Warner Brothers' film *Casablanca* and co-wrote *The Cross of Lorraine*.

From Julienne's office windows, she was reported to have witnessed the arrival of German troops in Paris, the shooting of hostages and the rounding up of French citizens for work in German factories. Worried about the future for her son, she arranged for him to be put on the SS *Washington* in Bordeaux, the American ship sent to repatriate its nationals, and sent him to live with his aunt in Indianapolis.

Slapping a German officer in the face for making improper suggestions led to her being held in Cherche-Midi internment camp for two months in 1941. On her release, she divorced her husband who left her with the film business and by November she had developed her friendship with Henri Déricourt and they were reported to have had an affair. How long this lasted is uncertain as she was later reported to have developed a relationship with Jean (Charles) Besnard, a barrister who had valuable contacts in the business community and was working with the Resistance. Whether Besnard and Déricourt were involved in helping one of the escape lines is unknown but in August 1942, Déricourt managed to use one through Marseille and reach London.

Although MI5 expressed doubts about him, he was reported to have been recruited by MI6 and introduced to F Section. After months of training, on 22 January 1943, code named GILBERT, he was parachuted from a Halifax near Fréville du Gâtinais, 30 km south-east of Pithiviers, central France.[17]

Déricourt's mission was to organise secret aircraft landing operations in the Loire area and the infiltration and exfiltration of agents and personnel. To assist him, F Section sent in two wireless operators, Gilbert Norman in October 1942 and Jack Agazarian in December.[18]

When a tramp visited her, it took her some time to recognise that he was Déricourt. He wanted her to find him somewhere to stay once he returned from Marseille with his wife. This she agreed to do and was later persuaded to use her cover to help welcome, find seven safe houses and acclimatise new agents in Francis Suttill's PROSPER/PHYSICIAN and later the FARRIER/GILBERT networks in and around Paris. The whole operation was financed with SOE money.[19]

Her cousin, Mme Bignon, helped provide false identity papers and ration cards which her husband 'acquired' from the Mairie in Saint Ouen. In communication with London, she was allocated the code name Claire and her cousin, Madeleine.

On 18 March 1943, she was sent to Poitiers for her first parachute drop. It was a double Lysander pick-up, and she returned with Françine Agazarian, Jack's wife, who had been sent to work as a courier. On meeting Jack, Julienne arranged to have his chest X-ray retouched to show that he had an ulcer and acquired a forged hospital certificate to ensure that he was not picked up by the Germans for forced labour.

As arrests were increasing and recognising Julienne as an efficient helper, Déricourt arranged to have her sent to England for SOE training. Having told her business partner and staff that she was going on a month's holiday, she was taken by Déricourt to a field 1 km north-east of La Chatre-sur-le-Loir and 40 km north of Tours, Sarthe. In the early hours of 16 April, Hugh Verity picked her up in his Lysander and flew her to England.[20]

Evidence of her time in England has not come to light. There is no record of any MI5 or MI6's interrogation report and no record of her attending any of the SOE training schools. According to the Special Forces website, she was given a commission as a volunteer FANY.

It may be that the SIS organised her visit, but they do not release any of their files to the public and neither confirm nor deny their involvement in undercover activities. It seems very likely that she would have been sent to Beaulieu for the clandestine warfare training and then briefed to be sent back as a courier. After the war, she admitted being briefed by Vera Atkins at Orchard Court and having wireless crystals secured in her sleeves to give to Prosper's wireless operators.

According to Verity, he landed her by Lysander at Azay-sur-Cher, near Tours at 0100 hours on 15 May. Accompanying her in a double Lysander operation was 40-year-old Vera Leigh, another volunteer FANY code named Simone, weapons instructor Sidney Jones and wireless operator Marcel Clech. Once they and their fourteen suitcases and packages were unloaded, Suttill climbed on board and Verity took him to England.[21]

As well as the crystals, she also brought forged bank-notes for Prosper's network; some blank identity and ration cards; a .32 revolver and ammunition. On getting back to Paris, she used new identity papers in the name of Madame Marie Clemence, the same code name 'Claire' and, depending on whom she met or corresponded with, was known as 'Jeannette', 'Dominique', 'Eminente', or 'Compositor'. She carried messages between various members of the Resistance in and around Paris. She also worked closely with Besnard, who was helping the FARRIER network in the west of Paris and, over the following months, their relationship developed and they got engaged.

Nicholas Bodington, a friend of Déricourt from before the war, bought the small café Mas in Place St Michel for her to run. It was to be used as a contact point for agents seeking to escape from France and also to evacuate RAF pilots or Resistance members who needed taking to England. Noor Inayat Khan, a wireless operator in the PHONO network, transmitted from this café when she was evading capture in Paris in August 1943.[22]

Noor was allegedly betrayed for 100,000 francs along with her set, codes and transcripts of decoded messages. Her set was successfully played back to London resulting in seventy-nine operations yielding seven men, 491 containers and 126 packages all received by German organised reception committees.

One awkward task Julienne had to manage was ensuring that Madame Gouin, the wife of one of General de Gaulle's ministers, was sent to England with all her luggage. On the night of 19 July 1943, knowing this well-known woman would be recognized if she travelled by train, Julienne hired three velo-taxis to take her to the Azay-sur-Cher drop zone and then managed to squeeze her and the luggage into Flight Lieutenant McCairns' Lysander.

Another tense situation developed when her business partner was thought to have developed tuberculosis. She arranged for him to be sent back to a hospital in Briançon, a mountain town in the Hautes-Alpes, where he had previously been treated. The Gestapo were suspicious and when they turned up to arrest him, found him ill in bed with a high temperature, so they left him. Returning the following day, he was no longer there. Tipped off, he had been helped to disappear and was looked after by the maquis.[23]

Suttill's arrest in August 1943 sent shockwaves through numerous Resistance networks but Julienne managed to avoid capture. Some people suspected that Déricourt had betrayed them so the SOE ordered him to return to London for questioning.

According to Verity, he flew a Lysander to pick up Déricourt and his wife, Jeannot, on 9 February 1944. She came on a shopping trip to London and was described as short, plump, having brassy hair and travelling in a very expensive-looking fur coat. Déricourt expected to parachute back with her within the week, despite her having had no training nor taken an active part in the Resistance.

He was returned to France, but not until after the war, to stand trial as being a German agent responsible for the arrest, torture and death of numerous French and British agents but was released through lack of evidence. Vera Atkins was certain he had worked for the Gestapo and is reported never to have spoken again to Bodington, who made a statement in court about Déricourt's good character.[24]

It is now acknowledged that he was, in fact, working for MI6 and used his SOE role as a cover. He claimed at his trial that the SOE allowed agents to be captured to distract the Germans' attention from the Allies' invasion plans. There was a rumour that the Germans had paid him four million francs for his information and that, after the war, the plane he was flying over Laos crashed in mysterious circumstances, and a quantity of opium was found on board.[25]

In spring 1944, Jean Besnard became worried that he was being followed. Warned by a colleague that he faced arrest, he liaised with Julienne, who was reported to have been very ill. She closed the café and told the concierge of her apartment to look after it until she returned. Taking separate trains, they met up at a safe house in the suburbs and then made their way to another field in Azay-sur-Cher. On 5 April, in a double Lysander pick-up, she and Besnard went in one and Adher Watt, a compromised wireless operator and two downed airmen went in the other.[26]

During her debrief, she wrote a mission report, following which she was questioned about it. The interrogation report provided details on conditions in Paris in early 1944, in particular, the tensions of working in the Resistance when hundreds of arrests were being carried out.

At the very beginning of March 1944, source received a telegram from the UK asking her to come here. On 3 March 1944, just after the receipt of this telegram, occurred the first of the incidents at the bistrot in rue St Andre des Arts [near Place St Michel and bought by Bodington]. These incidents are described at length by source in the report she made prior to her interrogation. She was therefore questioned on points mentioned in the report which required elucidation.

On 3 March two strange men came to the bistrot; they were completely unknown to the barman. Although the gave the exact password, the barman felt that there was something peculiar about them and when source saw them later, she had the same impression. [According to Foot, only the first part of the password was given: 'je voudrais parler à la patronne'. The speaker forgot the second part: 'de la part de ma tante à Marseille'.[27]]

THE BISTROT

Asked about the clientele of the bar, source stated that they are mostly people of the district, workmen and tradesmen, also a few personal friends of source herself. Sometimes other cafes are used for rendez-vous; that depended on the arrangements made by CLAUDE [Déricourt]. The place of rendez-vous was often changed, but it was always CLAUDE who made the contacts; occasionally he would ask source to make contacts for him. The bistrot, which was situated at 28 rue St. Andre des Arts, Paris, VI, had been used since the beginning of September. It had not been used much for organizational purposes.

GEOFFROI

Source stated that GEOFFROI [Andre WATT] did not work very successfully. He had great difficulty in transmitting, although he could receive messages all right. After the visit of the two strange men to the café, source instructed GEOFFROI

To send a message on the subject to the UK. The message made no mention of TOINOT [?].

The two men were obviously Frenchmen and spoke without an accent. Although they gave the correct password and asked for the patronne, the barman was suspicious of them and telephoned source who came to the bistrot. As they had mentioned 'MARSEILLES', source asked them if they had come about some Black Market transactions as she had been receiving some goods from MARSEILLES. They said 'No', and asked whether she did not help people to escape from France. She answered in the negative and said she could not understand why they had come as she had had no letter from TOINOT. The men never gave their name; they were men of ordinary appearance, rather shabbily dressed and had a definite 'air policier'. Seeing that source refused to give anything away, they produced a slip of paper marked at the top 'De Londres', and bearing an instruction to go to the bistrot, 28 re St Andre des Arts, and giving the correct password. Source returned the slip of paper, saying that she could not understand the whole thing. Finally, the men left. On her way to the Metro source noticed someone waiting there who eyed her as she passed but did not follow her. In case he should have been following her, source got off at the wrong station and went back on the other line, explaining to the ticket collector that she had mistaken her station.

Source was very perplexed by the whole affair; that night she collected certain documents, i.e. courrier, false identity cards and ration cards and JEAN [Besnard, her subsequent husband] took them to a safe place. During the days that followed, several strange people came to the bar; most of them asked for vin rouge which gave the impression that they were policemen. These people never asked any questions; they came in for a drink and then went away.

The first two strangers reappeared at the bistrot but on the following Tuesday afternoon (7 March 1944). Source and JEAN were leaving their apartment when they noticed two men walking up and down the street in opposite directions. One of the men followed source and JEAN to the Metro; source went on to her office and the man followed JEAN, but was shaken off at the Etoile Station when an alert sounded and a certain amount of confusion ensued.

TOINOT

On Saturday, 11 March, the barman rang up source's apartment and, thinking it was another Gestapo trick; source decided not to speak to him. In case it concerned some of their friends who were in danger, JEAN decided to investigate, explaining to the barman that Madame was not well. The barman explained that the visitor had arrived at the café asking for the patronne and giving the password. He was told to say that Madame could not see the stranger as she was ill, but a few minutes later he rang again to say that the visitor insisted on seeing Madame. JEAN decided to go to the bistrot and found a man who called himself TOINOT and who said that it was urgent that he could see the proprietor of the café. JEAN played the jealous husband, pretending that he took the stranger for one of Madame's former boy-friends. He described TOINOT as being tall, blond, with a ruddy complexion and a scar on his cheek; he spoke with an Alsatian accent. He explained that he had sent two friends to make contact for him the previous week when he had to leave PARIS and that doubtless they had explained themselves badly. He stated that he was a French officer, but gave no proof of his identity. JEAN said that he was unable to help him and was also sure that Madame could not help him in his desire to get to the UK. Finally, JEAN gave him his office telephone number, telling TOINOT to ring him up on the following Wednesday. JEAN wanted to make a few researches in the meantime, especially as he has a cousin by the name of TOINOT and thought the incident might be connected in some way with her. As GEOFFROI was having great difficulty with his [transmission] work at this time, it was impossible to inform London of the incident immediately. Source prepared a long message on the subject, but when it was eventually sent, GEOFFROI had to cut it down considerably as it was too long and the difficulties of transmitting were great. [To avoid the 'gonios', slang for gonionometrists or detection finders, locating the transmission, morse messages had to be short enough to be sent in less than 15 minutes.]

Source and JEAN tried to lead a normal life, hoping thereby to allay suspicion. They considered that if the man called TOINOT was merely anther refugee, he would never ring up JEAN as arranged. If the police had been looking for one of the ordinary customers of the bistrot, the matter would probably clear itself up without their interference.

Asked for further details about the telephone call overheard by JEAN when someone was heard to say 'L'Historie marsellaise est morte', (this incident had been related by GEOFFROI to the interrogator), source explained that on the night of the visit of the two strangers to the café, JEAN and GEOFFROI took a bundle of documents from the flat to a safe place. After they had been safely deposited, JEAN telephoned to source from a café (not the bistrot at rue St Andre des Arts) to reassure her that everything was alright. While telephoning, he overheard the above-mentioned remark made by a man in the next telephone box, but source is convinced that it was pure coincidence and doubtless the remark did not refer to the visit of the two men to the bistrot, but merely to some Black market transactions.

After the visit of the two strangers to the café, JEAN had asked a policeman friend of his to follow him one day when he had numerous business calls to make as he thought it might be possible that he was being shadowed. Nothing happened that day, but in the evening, this police inspector met another [policeman] whom he knew in the vicinity of the bistrot and asked him what he was doing there. The other replied that he had been instructed by the Renseignements Generaux (who work in liaison with the Gestapo) to watch the bistrot, although he did not know why.

M. GUESDON DE ROUSSEL

On Thursday, 23 March 1944, JEAN told source that he had heard that the Germans were convinced that he (JEAN) was playing an important role in underground activity. One of JEAN's clients, a M. COMTE, had asked JEAN's assistance in the publishing of a work called 'L'Armorial de France' of which the author was a certain M. JOUGLA. M. JOUGLA, during his researches at the Bibliotheche Nationale, had spoken to M. GUESDON DE ROUSSEL and mentioned that JEAN was going to help in the publishing of his work. At the mention of JEAN's name, M. GUESDON DE ROUSSEL immediately advised M. JOUGLA to move his business to another lawyer as JEAN was to be arrested during the next few days. Apparentntly M. GUESDON DE ROUSSEL is a Gestapo informer. He also told M. JOUGLA that the Gestapo had one of their men watching JEAN's movements. Source stated that, on receiving this piece of information, and in view of the strange events that had preceded it, she and JEAN would have disappeared to the country for a time. However, the telegram asking her for her appearance in the UK had arrived before this, and that was what made them decide to come out. The first telegram asking her to come out was sent on 1 March 1944 and another in the same sense came shortly afterwards. It was never explained to her why her presence was required over here. If GEOFFROI had not come out, source thinks he would certainly have been arrested; suspicion always falls more heavily on a man than on a woman. GEOFFROI was certainly more compromised than source.

After hearing through M. JOUGLA that the Gestapo were on his track, JEAN decided that he and source should leave PARIS. It was too late to do anything that night but, after arranging a few things, they left the following day for a friend's house. They told no-one they were leaving the country. They asked GEOFFROI to telephone their apartment, but although he rang on three successive days, there was no reply. The maid must either have been out or have been arrested; she did not know that her employers were going away. The employees at source's cinema agency [Hérault's Films] and JEAN's legal business knew nothing about these events, and doubtless they are carrying on as best they can in the meanwhile. Unfortunately, GEOFFROI had no time to telephone the offices. JEAN has some 4,000 clients.

Asked when she last saw the barman, source replied that it was several days before she left. She visited the café several times after the strange events already recounted, but the barman said that there had been no further developments. From the time of the visit of the two men until she left PARIS, source tried to behave as normally as possible in order to avoid attracting attention or appearing suspicious. Several strange people turned up in the bistrot from time to time, but none of them stayed long or asked any questions. Source did not inform the barman that she and JEAN were leaving PARIS; she places the utmost confidence in this man who has worked very well and caused no trouble at all. He has never handled radio messages and has not even seen one.

Source stated that she is anxious to know if such a person as TOINOT really exists. She is certain that the man who presented himself at the Bistrot as TOINOT is in contact with London as the message shown to her by the two strangers looked exactly like the many radio messages she has handled from time to time. She is puzzled as to how TOINOT, and subsequently these two men, got hold of the password of the bistrot. The men said that TOINOT could not come himself to the bistrot on the first occasion as he had gone to LYON. As he was back within a week, (he turned up at the bistrot a week later) source thinks that it was strange that he should have crossed the demarcation line twice in a few days, especially if he was anxious to get out of the country, probably because he was being followed. Source thinks that if this man TOINOT was really in contact with London by Radio, he would have asked for a confirmation of this message after the first contact proved fruitless.

Another incident which source considered rather strange was the announcement of a radio message over the BBC about 17 March 1944. The message was for BESNARD, which is JEAN's surname. It was obviously a coincidence but proved disturbing to JEAN and source at the time.[28]

ROGER

Source was questioned about ROGER [Roger Bardet, Henri Frager's deputy] by F Section on her arrival, which rather surprised her. Source stated that ROGER did not know the password of the bistrot. Source saw ROGER for the first time in October 1943 just before the departure of PAUL (Louba) for the UK. [Paul was Frager's code name and he was André Giraud's deputy and friend of André Marsac.] About two months later she saw him again when he told her that he was cut off from all contact with the UK and handed her a message to send through GEOFFROI. Source passed the message on to GEOFFROI but the latter found work so difficult at the time that he was unable to send the message. Shortly afterwards, news came from the UK that ROGER had been arrested, and GEOFFROI accordingly burnt the message. The bistrot was not used for several days, but it was soon learnt that ROGER had turned up again and had not been arrested. Shortly afterwards GEOFFROI was amazed to hear over the BBC the very message which ROGER had asked him to send when he was supposed to be cut off from all contact with London. Source and GEOFFROI were somewhat annoyed that ROGER should have pretended to be cut off from London when he obviously had another means of contact. Source saw ROGER only once after this. They met at the end of February or beginning of March 1944 when ROGER handed over some courrier which source brought along with her to the UK. She saw him for a few minutes in the Metro during the evening rush hour and had not time to ask him how he managed to send the message. He could not have sent it through ABELARD [code name of Maurice Dupont parachuted in on 20 October 1943[29]] as GEOFFROI was transmitting for ABELARD and, in any case, ROGER did not know ABELARD.

Source considers ROGER a serious type; he has been arrested several times. Source did not work in his group and never had any long conversations with him. ROGER's chief, PAUL [Henri Frager], had caused many difficulties for CLAUDE.

SIMONE

Source knew SIMONE [Vera Leigh], FELIX [Sidney Jones] and BASTIEN [Marcel Clech] as they had all stayed with her in PARIS after their arrival. Source gathered that BASTIEN was PAUL's W/Op and that SIMONE was to work for FELIX. SIMONE arrived in PARIS with source herself and as SIMONE had nowhere to stay, source allowed her to live in rooms at her office. She stayed there for two months and source did everything possible to help her. She found a flat eventually which belonged to a woman who was going away for some months. After the affair of PAUL's accusations against CLAUDE, SIMONE left this flat and found another. The last time source saw her – about 10 or 12 October 1943 – she looked very ill and asked source to recommend her to a doctor. She apparently had a touch of pleurisy. The flat she was living in was very cold, and as fuel was very difficult to obtain, source made arrangements with her supplier for SIMONE to obtain some wood. Source asked her if she wanted new monthly ration tickets but SIMONE said that she would obtain these through FELIX. Source did not see her again for some months and one day ROGER came to the bistrot with the news that SIMONE was missing, and it was assumed that she had been arrested. [She, Sidney Jones and his bodyguard were arrested when they met in the Café Mas on 30 October 1943.] apparently she had not turned up to a rendezvous with FELIX and nothing more had been heard of her. Source thought that she may have been involved in a street accident or be ill in hospital. Source does not know whether SIMONE has a sister who works for the organization. SIMONE was very nervous during the first days after her arrival in the Field, but source went out with her on visits to the dressmaker, etc. and helped her to regain confidence. FELIX was also very nervous when he first arrived and refused to go out for the first few days.

BASTIEN
ROGER passed on the news that BASTIEN had been arrested, but source knew no details.

COLONEL HEINRICH
Source has heard the name Col. HEINRICH [cover name of Abwehr Sergeant Hugo Bleicher], but knows nothing more.

PAUL'S ALLEGATIONS AGAINST CLAUDE
One night last summer, source met SIMONE about 11 o'clock when the latter said that she must see Major Bodington as soon as possible as she had an urgent message from PAUL. She refused to pass on the message, insisting that she must speak to the Major personally. PAUL saw the Major shortly after this and then, some 2 or 3 days later, an interview between the Major and CLAUDE took place. This interview was at source's office in the Champs Elysées. Asked if she was present during the conversation between Major Bodington and CLAUDE, source stated that she was. She later corrected this statement and said that she was not actually present at the beginning of the conversation; she was working in an adjoining office at that moment. She heard the Major tell CLAUDE

that he had heard 'une drole d'historie', [funny story] namely that CLAUDE had passed some of the courrier to the Germans. CLAUDE did not seem unduly surprised at the allegation but thought the whole thing seemed a little strange. He rejected the idea as foolishness and tried to recall exactly what courrier he had sent. He told the Major that he had sent a report from PAUL, which he had read. The Major told him that he ought not to have done this, but CLAUDE stated that it was perfectly in order for him to read this report since it was not sealed and therefore not secret; furthermore, it dealt with possible ways of escape from Fresnes and CLAUDE thought he might find the information useful one day. The Major apparently made no accusations himself against CLAUDE but merely passed on what he had heard. After CLAUDE left, source discussed the matter with the Major and the latter expressed his opinion that it was impossible to believe that CLAUDE could be guilty of such treachery. He asked source's opinion of CLAUDE and MARC [probably Maurice Clement who arrived on 16 October 1943 with Adher Watt[30]], but never mentioned the name of PAUL.

A long time after these conversations took place, source told SIMONE about them. SIMONE said that CLAUDE had reported the conversation to the Gestapo, which source found difficult to believe. SIMONE had obviously told PAUL about Major Bodington's interview with CLAUDE, and no doubt ROGER also knew of it since he worked with PAUL. Source made a long report on the matter at the time. SIMONE told her that the Gestapo were going to arrest her (source), and she became nervous. She found it difficult to work under such conditions.

THE INCIDENT ON THE LANDING GROUND

ROGER came to the rendezvous at the bistrot instead of PAUL, who was to go on the operation and source saw him there. Source thinks that several bodies left on this operation. CLAUDE was furious because PAUL sent ROGER to the rendezvous when he intended coming on the operation himself. They apparently quarreled on the landing ground, and CLAUDE told source all about it afterwards. Source did not tell CLAUDE that SIMONE had informed her that she (source) was to be arrested by the Gestapo. She kept this information to herself.

When ROGER turned up at the bistro in December (1943) he was shabbily dressed and explained this by saying that he had been working very hard. Source was not very surprised at his appearance as ROGER had never been very smart; he was just a little more untidy than usual that day.

PAUL

SIMONE told source that PAUL was in contact with the Gestapo, but source does not know whether this is true. SIMONE added that source was hindering CLAUDE in his work and that she would be arrested before long. Source could not see how she was hindering CLAUDE in his work and told SIMONE that they must just wait and see whether she was arrested; she said that she would prefer to go on working and risk being arrested than hear all the various rumours which were going about. SIMONE never named PAUL's contacts in the Gestapo, but source did hear that there was a certain Colonel 'B' who worked either for the English or the Germans and was in some way connected with PAUL. Source asked SIMONE whether PAUL's contact in the Gestapo was the well-known Colonel 'B', and she noticed that SIMONE changed colour. Thoroughly tired of these stories, source refused to discuss the matter further with SIMONE and changed the subject. Source does not know any details about Colonel 'B', but thinks he plays an important part in something or other.[31]

Colonel 'B' was reported to have been Oberststurmbannfuhrer, Karl Boemelburg, head of the Gestapo in Paris, who some claim gave his pre-war friend Déricourt four million francs in return for the date of the Allied invasion. Déricourt is reported to have handed over satchels of courrier to be photographed by the Gestapo before being handed back for despatch to London. He admitted cooperating with Boemelburg in exchange for protection for himself, his family and his agents and claimed that forty-three agents were infiltrated and sixty-seven exfiltrated from France without any of the aircraft being shot down. There were claims, however, that the Gestapo arranged to have drop zones watched, and agents successfully followed, despite their security training at Beaulieu, to their safe houses and rendezvous. Buckmaster is claimed to have admitted in 1984 that Déricourt was a double agent who was worked against the Germans by Dick White, deputy head of SIS's B branch which was responsible for Security.[32]

Source was somewhat upset by the accusations she had heard against CLAUDE, especially as he is a friend of some years standing. She was so confused by the different stories that she couldn't decide whether CLAUDE, SIMONE or PAUL was guilty, or whether it was all or none of them who was implicated. She took all possible precautions and carried on with her work. About this time she was typing a copy of a long, important document which had no connection with the war and which was to be sent by courier; she made up her mind that it would arrive intact in the UK. No other copy of the document existed in France, and she considered it her duty not to let anyone else see it. She had only typed half of it when the operation took place, and the courier was despatched. CLAUDE saw her typing and evinced great interest in her work, saying that as the courier had gone, he would take the document to MARSEILLES with him and send it from there. Source was slightly annoyed by this and said she preferred to send it in the normal way at the next moon. It was a small incident and source thinks that his attitude was probably due to the precautions taken by her as a result of the various rumours which were going around at the time. CLAUDE often visited MARSEILLES; his wife was from there. MARC and JEAN CLAUDE are carrying on during CLAUDE's absence; source does not know them at all.

MARC

About this time also SIMONE began to suspect MARC as well as CLAUDE. Source told her it was foolishness and that she was tired of hearing these different stories from SIMONE. Source thought it possible that SIMONE may be confusing MARC with ROGER as both were tall and very dark. SIMONE, however, said that she had great confidence in ROGER and source said that she was equally sure of MARC. Source thinks that MARC was, like CLAUDE, a pilot, he always seemed to work well, but the others found it difficult to co-operate with him as he always refused to use a boite aux lettres. The operation in the beginning of March was spoilt because of MARC's refusal to have a boite aux lettres. Source tried to contact him several times by telephone, but it was hopeless. MARC never came to the bistrot. Source did not help at operations. At the beginning (March 1943), she helped CLAUDE when he had no-one else to help him, but that was the only occasion.

COVER STORY

Source found her private business a good cover for her clandestine work. She went to her office for an hour or two every day and apparently lived a perfectly normal life. She contacted GEOFFROI almost every day at an agreed rendezvous. If GEOFFROI had anything for CLAUDE, he would tell source who slipped a note into CLAUDE's flat telling him that GEOFFROI had a message for him.

When Simone was arrested, FELIX [Jones] disappeared, and no-one has seen him since.

OTHER BISTROTS USED

Asked what other bistrots were used to make contacts, source stated that she was sent once to the Monte Carlo in Avenue Wagram to meet an old woman called ADELE [?]. She also went once to La Lorraine, but no-one turned up. She went three times to a little café near the Porte Champerret, but once again no-one came. It was CLAUDE who arranged the contacts and he had asked source to go there. Source does not know the café Biard or the Bar Boissiere. She stressed the difficulty and danger of making contacts in cafés. One must go to the café at the same time for several days in succession if the body does not turn up on the first occasion. A man or woman sitting about in a café, obviously waiting for someone to turn up, always attracts attention. A couple can do this easily without being noticed, but for a single person it is too dangerous. Source prefers to make contacts in a crowded underground station or a large shop. Even the underground stations are now more dangerous than previously. There are many rafles [large scale police arrests of young men] in PARIS at the moment. Source recently saw 18 buses full of people taken away for verification of papers after a rafle in the Champs Elysées.

INNKEEPER aka HONORE aka STEPHAN [Denis John Barrett code named INNKEEPER was parachuted on 11 April 1943 with Ben Cowburn, the organiser of the TINKER network. (Tillet, op.cit.)], wireless operator to ABELARD [Dupont], went to the bistrot to make contact before he left the Field [on 15 November 1943]. Before she left, source warned everyone that the bistrot was brûlé so that even if a genuine person went there for contact, no assistance would be forthcoming.

Source runs several flats in PARIS for the use of agents who arrive and want to stay there a short time. It is very difficult to find a flat in PARIS now. This difficulty is increased so far as agents are concerned as identity cards must be produced and registration affected. Source was able to obtain some flats on a sub-letting basis from acquaintances who were leaving town for a month or two.

Asked for the names of all agents who had visited the bistrot since it began to be used in September last, source gave the following list: – INNKEEPER, ANNETTE (Yvonne Cormeau parachuted on 22 August 1943], ABELARD, ROGER, MATHIEU [?]. SIMONE knew about the bistrot through ROGER. When the message arrived for PAUL about his departure from the Field (i.e. end of 1943) it was incomplete; some details of the password and address were missing. SIMONE showed source the message and they decided that it was indeed source's bistrot to which it referred. Although it is thought that SIMONE is now arrested and there is a possibility that she has spoken, she could only give away the address of the bistrot but not the password as this has been changed since her arrest. Only the barman, source, JEAN and London know the new password, and the first time it was used was on the occasion of the visit of the two strange men. ROGER certainly did not know it; he did not even know the old one as the message, as explained above, was mutilated. If SIMONE had not known source personally and had been able to confer with her on the subject of the mutilated message, the arrangements regarding PAUL's departure might have miscarried.

SOURCE'S RETURN TO THE FIELD

Source is anxious to go back to work in the Field but stresses that she must avoid the PARIS area at all costs as she is obviously blown there. She is prepared to go to the provinces where she is not known.

All round the coast of France people are being evacuated now; they are allowed to take only 30 kilos of luggage. Only those who have relatives in PARIS are allowed to go there.

Source reiterated her desire to clear up the mystery of the two men who came to the bistrot on behalf of TOINOT and gave the correct password.

Source mentioned that there is a Gestapo H.Q. in the Rue des Saussaies in PARIS.[33]

Foot reported that the day after her return to France, an Alsatian RF agent arrived in England, code name Toinot. When his situation had become too dangerous, he and two companions made their way to Paris but met with no success when they used the password at the rendezvous and had to use an alternative escape line.[34]

When she was finally released from questioning, her interrogator noted that she was 'very much all there. I should imagine very cunning. A not so young woman, not particularly smart but she seems to have been a good agent. At the moment was more concerned about her boyfriend than anything else. Not a highly reliable witness. Expect she was being paid by both sides.' Nevertheless, despite these misgivings, F Section arranged for her to be given an honorary commission in the WAAF and, to hide her identity in England, she was provided with identity papers in the name of Julienne Ploye.[35]

Interrogated by the Security Services, she was described as 'extremely intelligent and possibly very cunning. Appears to have been a very good agent.'[36] They informed Captain Miller that MI5 had cleared her and that she should be handed over to F Section for renewal of training.[37]

On 29 April, she and Besnard got married in Marylebone and lived at 20 Cranley Place, South Kensington and did not return to France until after liberation.

It is possible she was unaware that Roger Bardet, a member of the Carte organisation who had been turned by the Germans and betrayed many agents and Resistance members, reported that Julienne was Déricourt's mistress, had worked for the Germans and that she had a postbox in a bar, Rue St Auche des Arts, and Rue de la Harpe, which was used by the Germans to trap agents. [38] SOE believed otherwise.

Buckmaster's citation for her to be awarded an OBE was that,

> Assistant to FARRIER, she made all the arrangements for the accommodation of officers who arrived in France by Lysander and Hudson. She was also involved in providing specimens of false papers, especially new supply cards which were sent to be copied in the U.K. She rented two apartments and a bistro where different resistance members were able to meet their contacts. She continually sent very interesting reports and identity papers etc., and some targets for the RAF. She helped many officers, notably SWINEHERD [Wireless operator Adher] WATT to be installed in Paris and find places for him to transmit during October 1943. Despite an agonizing illness, she continued to work until his return in U.K. She is now very ill ... Very courageous and hardworking, she gave a lot of help to numerous officers at her home. Always smiling and full of good will, she is beloved by all the service and much appreciated by everyone she knows. Admirable precision and caution, she has rendered real service to her country. [39]

Gubbins wrote a citation for her award which read:

> Madame Julienne Ploye worked for two years with the Resistance Movement organizing a ferry air service to this country. She herself came to the U.K. in April 1943 and returned to France in May 1943 after a short course of training. She remained in the field until May 1944 when she returned to England to report.
>
> During her two years' service she provided safe houses, papers and contacts for a number of agents, all of whom speak highly of her efficiency and discretion. She also supplied valuable information and reports and ran a 'boite' used for rendezvous at which she personally attended daily. Her efforts made possible the smooth infiltration and exfiltration of a very great number of persons.

She shouldered all the risks connected with this very dangerous work, to which she devoted himself [*sic*] with untiring energy and loyalty. It is recommended that she be awarded the King's Medal for Courage in the Cause of Freedom.[40]

Interviewed after the war, she attempted to clarify the situation about her work:

Although in the same network, my husband and I were not working together; as a radio operator he worked alone and transmitted from different locations every day. I was only responsible to Prosper (Francis Suttill) whom we all called François. He liked to use me for special errands because, France being my native land, I could get away from difficulties easily enough, particularly when dealing with officialdom. Francois was an outstanding leader, clear-headed, precise, confident. I liked working on his instructions, and I enjoyed the small challenges he was placing in front of me. For instance, calling at town halls in various districts of Paris to exchange the network's expired ration cards (manufactured in London) for genuine new ones. Mainly I was delivering his messages to his helpers: in Paris, in villages, or isolated houses in the countryside. From time to time I was also delivering demolition material received from England. And once, with hand-grenades in my shopping bag, I travelled in a train so full that I had to stand against a German NCO. This odd situation was not new to me. I had already experienced it for the first time on the day of my arrival on French soil when I had to travel by train from Poitiers to Paris. A very full train also. I sat on my small suitcase in the corridor, a uniformed German standing close against me. But, that first time, tied to my waist, under my clothes, was a wide black cloth belt containing bank-notes for Prosper, a number of blank identity cards and a number of ration cards; while tucked into the sleeves of my coat were crystals for Prosper's radio transmitters; the crystals had been skillfully secured to my sleeves by Vera Atkins herself, before my departure from Orchard Court. My .32 revolver and ammunition were in my suitcase. The ludicrousness of the situation somehow eliminated any thoughts of danger. In any case, I believe none of us in the field ever gave one thought to danger. Germans were everywhere, especially in Paris; one absorbed the sight of them and went on with the job of living as ordinarily as possible and applying oneself to one's work. Because I worked alone, the times I liked best were when we could be together, Prosper (Francis Suttill), Denise (Andrée Borrel), Archambaud (Gilbert Norman), Marcel (Jack Agazarian) and I, sitting round a table, while I was decoding radio messages from London; we were always hoping to read the exciting warning to stand by, which would have meant that the liberating invasion from England was imminent.

In acknowledgement of her work, the British government awarded her the King's Medal for Courage. The citation for her Croix de Guerre stated that 'For one and a half years she sheltered more than fifty officers British and French being sought by the Gestapo, taking daily risks in cold blood.'[41]

Returning to Paris after the war, she died of breast cancer in 1947.

French Women Infiltrated before D-Day 1944

MARGUERITE PETITJEAN

Aged 24. Parachuted from a Halifax near St Uze (Drome) on 29 January 1944. Awarded the Companion de Légion d'Honneur and Croix de Guerre.

By January 1944, Germany had forty-six divisions in France, partly as a defence against the threat of an Allied invasion but also to allow German units an opportunity to refit and retrain. The Abwehr and the Gestapo's counter-espionage sections had, with the assistance of the Milice and paid French collaborators, successfully infiltrated some Resistance networks and hundreds had been arrested. Consequently, the situation for new agents had become much more dangerous.[1]

Given the collapse of the PROSPER network and the importance of the Allied invasion, SOE set up and supplied forty more networks in France before D-Day. A number of trained French women agents were infiltrated to help them.

The first Frenchwoman sent in 1944 was 23-year-old Marguerite Petitjean. On the night of 29/30 January Wing Commander Speare of 138 Squadron dropped Petitjean with three other BCRA agents from his Halifax on a drop zone, code named Ajuster, near St Uze in Drôme, about 60 km south-west of Grenoble.[2] Her name was listed in Foot's *SOE in France* as an RF agent but her story does not appear in any SOE or Resistance publications.

Her personnel file revealed that she was born in Strasbourg on 24 October 1920 but there are no other details of her early life. Her cover story was that she was a nurse. According to her obituary in the *Miami Herald*, she had trained as a nurse during her teenage years and volunteered to be a Red Cross ambulance driver when war broke out,

'But a single act of cruelty propelled her to become a World War II soldier. Bassett [her married name] witnessed a Nazi officer shoot a little girl who lived in her town. The incident inspired her to join the French Resistance.'

The role she played in the Resistance is unknown. There was nothing in her personnel file to explain why she suddenly arrived at Prestwick Airport from Algiers on 1 October 1943.

Contributions to her web page on the francaislibre website indicated that she had been active in the Resistance and needed to escape but gave no details.

Once debriefed, she was recruited by RF Section, who needed more women to work with de Cheveigné. He stated emphatically that the only training she should be given is a course at Beaulieu.'[3] Training Section were told that she had been selected by the Colonel to work for him as a courier in the réseau he proposed to establish. The Security Section reported that they had found no issues with her but commented that, 'Her case is unprecedented.'[4] What was so unprecedented remains a mystery.

Sent to Clobb Gorse (STS 37b) at the end of October, her instructor commented a fortnight later that,

> She is intelligent, well-informed, quick, shrewd and full of common sense. She has imagination. She is keen, worked hard and displayed considerable initiative and drive. She has a strong character, knows what she wants and is determined to get it. She is domineering and sometimes intolerant. She would not be likely to be influenced by sentiment. She is probably quite ruthless. Her personality is strong, and she has plenty to say for herself. She knows how to be pleasant and agreeable. She is a good mixer and should be generally popular. She is an amusing raconteuse with a strong sense of humour. She has natural powers of leadership and organising capacity. She should make a good courier, but would be capable of undertaking more important work. Codes: Routine practice needed.[5]

Taken to Ringway in the middle of November, she completed three jumps but was only awarded Third Class.

Major Edwards, the Commandant at Ringway, commented that Sgt (Mrs) Anderson, Marguerite's conducting officer

> looked after her student well and went through all the ground training but did not jump. There was little wind throughout the week, and the fog necessitated the use of the balloon. In his opinion, Marguerite was

'Intelligent, keen imagination and worked hard. Has a domineering personality. Will make a good courier, but could undertake more responsible work. Routine practice needed.'[6]

The original plan was for her to be dropped on her own during the December moon period as liaison officer to RF agent CYLINDER, the organiser of para-military action in area R (south-east France). As well as a fake cover story, she was also provided with a fake ration card, birth certificate, clothing coupon, identity papers in the name of Michelle Pradier and a student union card.

However, the winter of 1943/44 was so severe that the runways at Tempsford were so deep in snow that flights had to be cancelled until they could be cleared. This meant her flight had to be postponed until the next moon period. The team she was to be sent with included Yvon Morandat, an organiser code named Arnolphe, René Obadia, a sabotage instructor code named Pioche and Eugene Deschelette, code named Ellipse.[7] In Duke Street she was given her code name Binette and appointed captain.

According to Wikipedia, 30-year-old Morandat served with the Alpine troops in 1939, participated in the Norwegian Campaign in April and May 1940 and on 18 June came to England. Working with the Free French, he was attached to de Gaulle's cabinet.

In summer 1941, he was entrusted with contacting the trade unions and Resistance movements in Southern France. Instructed by Commissioner André Diethelm, he was parachuted from a Whitley in November 1941 to meet leaders of the Christian Youth, French Confederation of Christian Workers, General Confederation of Labour and prepare for the arrival of Jean Moulin.

42-year-old Moulin had been the regional administrator of Chartres before the war, the youngest in France. Imprisoned by the Gestapo as a communist, a failed suicide attempt left him with a scarred neck. Once recovered, the Vichy Government ordered all left-wing officials to be sacked. When he refused, his employment was terminated so he joined the Resistance. Brought to England in September 1941, he met de Gaulle and other exiled leaders with a view to establishing a political resistance movement.

When Moulin arrived in France in January 1942, with Morandat's assistance, he spent over a year trying to create the National Council of Resistance. Captured in June 1943, he was interrogated and tortured by the Gestapo in Lyon and Paris and died on a train on the way to Germany on 8 July.

Morandat was brought back to England on 17 November 1942 in a Lysander operation with General François d'Astier de la Vigerie once Henri Frenay and General Emmanuel d'Astier de la Vigerie, Francois's brother, had disembarked with six wireless sets and a Eureka set. Their mission was to unify Franc-Tireur, Libération and the Combat Resistance movements.

The Eureka and its partner Rebecca were some of the new technology developed by British boffins to assist the SOE's agents on the ground direct the Special Duties Squadron' planes to their DZ. Most Halifaxes and Stirlings were fitted with 'Rebecca', a long distance directional air-ground radar device that homed on to a ground-based 'Eureka Transmitter'.

Jim Peake, a 138 Squadron navigator, described Rebecca as a radio beacon consisting of a black box with a retractable 11 ft (3.3 m) aerial. They were lowered out of the back of the plane and had to be wound in before landing. Some planes had two bi-pole aerials attached either side of the fuselage. The battery-operated light-weight Eureka transmitters could be set by the ground operator to create a radio beam down which the aircraft could fly. Inside was also a self-destruct detonator to avoid them getting into enemy hands. The beauty of the Eureka was that it used very little power and could be used to guide an aircraft to a dropping ground without the use of lights or flares. It was only switched on when the approaching aircraft had its Rebecca switched on. Pilots could easily guide the aircraft to within 100 yard (91 m) of the box. They had a range of at least 30 miles (48 km) at 2,000 ft (609 m) so navigators did not need to use GEE, a meter showing the location of a wireless transmission, or map reading.

Brave French steeplejacks positioned two of these Eurekas, nick-named 'Boot' and 'Shoe', on the pinnacles of Rheims and Orleans cathedrals. This was a great navigational help, as the pilot did not have to fly close to these heavily defended cities. Towards the end of 1943, Eureka beacons were planted in three of the great French forests. Although they were unmanned, a local reception committee would be ready to pick up any containers that were dropped on these 'targets' should they not have been successfully dropped on their dedicated DZ.

While working for Morandat was Marguerite's main mission, she also had to liaise with Alexandre Parodi who had been tasked by de Gaulle with setting up an action network and preparing the local resistance for D-Day.

Forced to hide when the Gestapo found incriminating documents in Paris, in 1943 he managed the clandestine Committee of Press and

Information, made plans for the post-liberation press and helped found the Resistance's financial committee.

In January 1944, de Gaulle asked him to be a general delegate of the Committee of National Liberation and when Marguerite arrived he was liaising with the National Council of Resistance, the Provisional Government of the French Republic in Algiers and various resistance groups.

In the same month that Marguerite arrived, Parodi was appointed the general delegate for the French Committee of National Liberation. in the Occupied Zone. He participated in the liberation of Paris and in August 1944 became minister of liberated territories and organised the implementation of the new civilian authorities. Exactly how Marguerite worked for him has yet to come to light.

On the day Marguerite's flight was finally confirmed, an RF officer contacted the team's conducting officer telling her that,

> I forward herewith a gun for ARNOLPHE. Please note that this is a 25 calibre, the ammunition for which is now in extremely short supply.
>
> Baker Street [shooting] range had no ammunition at the time, and this agent was unable to test his gun. Therefore, he should test it at STS 61 [Gaynes Hall].
>
> Please make it clear to the agent that he only has been issued with 15 rounds and consequently, if he prefers, he may take in exchange one of the extra 32 calibre gun [sic] in your possession which is issued with 50 rounds of ammunition.
>
> I am giving you herewith 50 rounds of ammunition of 32 gage [sic] for the spare gun in your possession should the agent want it.
>
> With regard to BINETTE, she may have either a small revolver or a 32 but not both. In all I give you three extra 32s, so you are now in position to cope with both these agents.[8]

Provided with 50,000 francs, she was told that more would be available according to her needs. Having been taken first to Gaynes Hall, STS 61, the team were then driven to Tempsford for the flight.

The reception committee waiting for them was headed by Henri Faure, head of the 'Section Aterrissages-Parachutages' (SAP) who had heard the BBC message confirming their flight, 'We will go over the dune with four friends.' Despite the thick fog, he was able to guide the navigator to his DZ using one of the Eureka sets.

They all arrived safely except Déchelette who broke his right ankle. After partially recovering from his injury, he was obliged to carry out his mission and established the R5 Action Network around Limoges, made contact with Georges Guingouin of the Limousin Maquis and other Resistance and political groups, arranged training, appointed leaders in the FFI and allocated resources in the preparation for D-Day.

Michel Augeard in his *Melpomene se parfume á Heliotrope*, reported that the local resistants were initially unhappy to accept Marguerite's role as their sabotage instructor. 'We have learned to look after ourselves; we do not need specialists.' But they were quick to appreciate this woman who knew how to win their sympathy. She was to become the first and only female assistant to Louis Burdet, the Regional Military delegate for R2.[9]

Burdet was reported as managing the Hyde Park Hotel in St James, London, which was frequented by members of the French Resistance. As Burdet's sympathies for de Gaulle were well-known, he was recruited, trained as an agent and he acknowledged after the war that his SOE training had saved his life.

Code named Circonference and Cylindre, Burdet was landed on 8 February 1944, when Flight Lieutenant Johnnie Affleck flying 161 Squadron's Hudson got stuck in a muddy field, 4 km west-south-west of Bletterans in the Jura. Once he and six RF/BCRA agents got out, there were great worries as the wheels of the plane would not move. The four returning passengers, including Raymond Samuel, code named Aubrac, his heavily pregnant wife Lucie and their son, had to wait two and a half hours for the local villagers and their team of horses to pull the plane to firmer ground to allow it to take off. Very luckily, it managed it without the gendarmerie or Gestapo arriving.[10]

Burdet organised resistance in the R2 region centred on Marseille where he helped unite communists and extreme right-wing conservatives under de Gaulle as the best means to defeat the enemy.

Marguerite's obituary, mentioned earlier, provided details of her mission, claiming that, while in England, she received special training by the Royal Air Force.

...she learned how to parachute and perform dangerous acts of sabotage. When she returned to France, she made her first jump near Lyons and eventually completed 17 missions. Bassett's [Marguerite's married name] assignments supported military actions to disable enemy bridges and power stations. She suffered multiple injuries, including a fractured skull and spine, and her life was often in grave danger. During one sabotage mission, she was captured by two enemy soldiers, her family said. Bassett waited until they fell asleep and then tied them up while holding her .32-caliber gun, which she nicknamed Josephine and kept throughout her life. Bassett's missions were so successful that the Germans placed a 10-million-franc ($500,000) price on her head.[11]

On Marguerite's page on the francaislibre website, Liz Evans added her translation of Jean Fernand's book, 'J'y étais'. He was head of SAP, landings and parachutes drops, in the Apt region of the Vaucluse.

Marguerite Petitjean, alias Binette, which was her nom de guerre, was parachuted, if my memory serves me well, into the department of the Drôme near Valence. In the proper sense of the word, she was the exact replica of a spy. She was in effect an artful saboteur, and expert in all types of sabotages. She was a close collaborator of Circonférence alias Colonel Burdet, chief of the team Action in the South zone.

On reflection I think we can say of this girl, that at the time she was just 20 years old, that her beauty wasn't the equal of her courage.

As a saboteur she was actively hunted by the Gestapo and outwitted all the traps that they set for her. Her command post was at Marseille where she received her orders. Under the pressure of certain events, she found herself in a delicate situation. It was very urgent that she left Marseille. One day I was given a gift, by her roundabout route she ended up being washed up in Apt.

Given that she was in need of rest after a sustained period of tension, both of the nerves and of her morale, I decided to put her out to grass in a safe place, and billeted her at the home of Rose Grégoire who we called 'poussette' [pushchair].

In this haven of tranquillity, she recovered well and sharpened her convictions to carry on.[12]

Chrystel Huq's research into Burdet's role, published on the Alliance Française de Londres' website, identified an attack on an industrial plant at Gardanne near Marseille as one of many he helped coordinate. Knowing that the D-Day landings would spark a rapid German response, attempts were made to sabotage transport and radio communications in order to delay the Panzer divisions in the south of France reaching the Allied forces. He was also engaged in the counter-scorch planning, preventing the Germans from sabotaging the Mediterranean port cities when the American and Free French Forces invaded the south coast. As Marguerite was engaged as his courier, she undoubtedly would have been involved in sabotage operations in the build up to D-Day, including Plan

Vert (rail and road sabotage), Plan Violet (telecommunications sabotage) and Plan Tortue (attacking armoured vehicles).

The exact circumstances of her leaving France are unknown. According to Foot, she crossed the Pyrénées in August 1944. On her own or part of a group was not specified. From Spain she must have crossed to Algeria because on 21 August, four days before Paris was liberated, a request was sent to London that she be returned to the UK from Algiers to report on her mission in the south-east of France. She arrived back on 5 September 1944, but her report has yet to come to light.[13]

Whether it was during her time in France or on her journey back to London is unknown, but she met Harry Hood Bassett, a First Lieutenant in the American Army Air Corps. Returning to France, on 23 June 1946, they got married the Cathedral of Notre Dame in Paris and moved to Florida where she had three sons. She was reported to have 'cast off her military fashions and immersed herself in the elegant fashions and milieu of high society.'[14]

In recognition of her work during the war, she was awarded the Legion d'Honneur and, according to her obituary, was also a five-time recipient of the Croix de Guerre, the French award for bravery. In 1959, Allen Dulles, then director of the CIA, honored her and other Second World War heroes at a reception at his home. Melissa Bassett, her daughter-in-law, described her as 'an extremely kind and loving woman. But at the same time, she was very stern. You really saw the soldier in her.' She died in 1999, aged 78.[15]

Patrick Bassett, Marguerite's son, added this following comment to the francaislibre website saying that,

As my mother, I grew up with many tales of her exploits during the war and met and remembered many dear friends of hers from that era. There are even tapes I recorded of her describing her missions and war memories. There is no doubt that my mother was fearless in the face of danger and yet had such love of family and friends that you would never have known her determination during the war. As a proud Alsatian, she would often tell us the Germans called them 'wooden heads' for their stubbornness. I have to agree. I have many a war memory tale of hers that depicts that determination. She accomplished so much during the war but didn't carry outright hostility toward Germans after it. Her quote was 'forgive but don't forget'. Many artefacts from her war years are still with my brother Harry and I. Her war pistol, a Colt .32 calibre, named by her as 'Josephine' was held by my deceased brother George. Its whereabouts are unknown following his passing. She was an amazing mother with a war history like few others.[16]

JEANETTE GUYOT

Aged 24. Parachuted from a Halifax near Loches, 70 km north-west of Châteauroux (Indre & Loire), on 8 February 1944. Awarded the Croix de Guerre with Palm, Medaille de Resistance, Chevalier of the Légion d'Honneur, Order of the British Empire, George Medal, the Sussex Medal and the American Distinguished Service Cross

Jeannette Guyot was born on the 26 February 1919 in Chalon-sur-Saône, about 150 km north of Lyon, Saône and Loire. Details of her early life have yet to come to light except that she finished her elementary education at 17 and looked after her parents who lived in Sevrey, a village a few kilometres south of Chalon-sur-Saône.

Research by Pierre Tillet revealed that both parents were active in the Resistance during the war. Her father, Jean-Marie Guyot, was a timber merchant who became a First Lieutenant Forces Françaises Combattantes (FFC) but was arrested on 5 February 1943, imprisoned in Chalon-sur-Saône, deported on 15 January 1944 and died in Cham, Bavaria. Her mother, Jeanne, was a seamstress who also became a First Lieutenant in the FFC. She was arrested ten days after her husband, imprisoned in Chalon-sur-Saône, deported on 30 January but survived and was repatriated on 11 April 1945.

With the demarcation line between the Occupied and the Unoccupied or Free Zone less than 100 km to the north, from the end of 1940 until August 1941, Jeannette worked with Félix Svagrowsky of the AMARANTE network. She became a 'passeur', a guide who used her 'ausweiss' border pass to accompany people to meet boatmen who took them across the River Saône.

Whilst engaged on this clandestine work, she met Gilbert Renault. He and his brother had refused to accept Pétain's surrender and went by Norwegian trawler to England on 22 July 1940. One of the first men to volunteer after de Gaulle's speech on the BBC's French Service, Renaud was persuaded by Andre Dewavrin, to return to France and organise an information network.

How he was infiltrated is unknown but he helped set up the Confrérie Notre-Dame Network (CND), and from August 1941 Jeannette became his liaison officer. CND supplied the BCRA with military, economic and social intelligence about the Germans' activities in France and the Vichy government.

She continued to accompany people and carry documents from Paris to Chalon-sur-Saône until February 1942 when she was arrested on one of her journeys. Imprisoned for three months in Chalon-sur-Saône and Autun, about 50 km north-west, she did not break under interrogation and nothing could be proved against her. When she was released, despite the Germans withdrawing her 'ausweiss', she continued to take about a dozen people across the demarcation line each month.

There was a report that she crossed the Saône near Sevrey. This could have been to avoid German controls on the A6, the main road from Paris to Lyon, and use quieter roads on the eastern side of the valley.

However, following betrayal by Pierre Cartaud in June 1942, many members of the CND were arrested, forcing Jeannette to move from Paris to Lyon. There she met Jacques Robert who was Lysandered out on 27 April and, having been briefed by RF Section, parachuted back on 3 June 1942 to set up the PHRARIE network. It was rated by Dewavrin as the 'most extraordinary' of all the Free French networks, had several subgroups whose activities encompassed intelligence-gathering, sabotage and helping downed Allied airmen and French civilians to escape from France.

She worked for Robert but, as further arrests were made and she was on the Gestapo's wanted list, her exfiltration to England was arranged.

On the night of 13 May 1943, F/Lt McCairns of 161 Squadron, landed his Lysander in a field, code named 'Planète', near Les Fontaines, about 2 km south of Luzillé (Indre & Loire). SIS agent Baird got out and Jeannette got in with Francois Chatelin and Jean-Louis Chancel.[17]

The following day, like all refugees arriving in Britain, she was interrogated by British Intelligence to ensure she was not a German agent and then by Captain François Thierry-Mieg, head of the BCRA's counter-intelligence unit, who wanted to question her about her work in the Resistance. A copy of his interrogation report is found in her personnel file at the Service Historique de la Défense (SHD) Vincennes.

1. I did my studies at Chalon sur Saone up at the age of 17, I got the elementary patent. after I did not work, I 'm still with my parents. I still live in Sevrey.

2. I worked for the Fighting French until 1941. First with Jean-LUC [Gilbert Renault]'s organisation then with Denis [Jacques Robert]'s PHATRIE organisation.

   B. From which date did you start to work officially?

3. From September/October 1941.

   B. During all this time didn't you have any contact with the official organisations?

4. No.

   B. You did resistance work by yourself, by what means?

5. I stayed by the demarcation line and 'passed' a number of people with CESAR [Félix Svagrowsky]. He lodged at my grandmother's. Madame Guyot, who was living in Sevrey. At that time, he had seen

an opportunity to use my services to help pass people across the demarcation line.

B. When did you get to know CESAR?

6. About January 1941.

B. What did he propose you do?

7. To pass people across the demarcation line. As I had a border pass, I could cross really easily. CESAR sent me people to get across.

B. What were the conditions for recognising these people?

8. He was known under the name of FELIX. All who came from FELIX, I got them across.

B. Did CESAR ever Give you a real identity?

9. SVACROVSKY. I believe that he was a mechanic in real life. He was born in France, in Lyon.

B. Where was the centre of his operations?

10. SEVREY. He had stayed there from September 1941. At that time. he had commenced working with PAUL, who worked for our organisation. I passed him many times.

11. From January 1941 until September 1941 I worked on behalf of CESAR. All those he sent came from FELIX. CESAR had fixed his residence at my grandmother's in SEVREY. I was uniquely in charge of passing prisoners.

B. Were you aware of what CESAR's work schedule was?

12. No. at that time, I didn't know. I did when I encountered PAUL. [Roger Dumont]

B. Do you think that CESAR worked for an organisation or did he work on his own initiative?

13. I think it was his private initiative.

14. CESAR was the only one I was in contact with at that time. He moved often and had just come from PARIS.

B. How did CESAR come into contact with the people you passed?

15. I don't know. In general, the people came by themselves.

B. Do you know whether CESAR made contact with these people in PARIS who found prisoners to be passed?

16. I don't know.

B. How did you meet Paul?

17. He wanted to cross the demarcation line. At that time, he had false border passes; it was very easy. Actually, he had been in prison, working for Jean-LUC.

B. What is his real name?

18. I don't know.

B. What did he do?

19. He was a tennis coach in PARIS; I don't know for which club. PAUL introduced himself, coming instead of FELIX. He had crossed the line many times. He certainly knew what to do and proposed that I passed the people from his special réseau. I could tell already that he was part of Jean LUC's organisation.

    Having realised that I could render services, he asked me to be part of his organisation. I went to PARIS with him and CESAR.

    B. Did CESAR work with PAUL?

20. No. We started to work together. The three of us went to PARIS and were introduced to Jean-LUC at his tennis court. I don't know its whereabouts, somewhere by the entrance to MUETTE Metro. It's a little club on Rue Nicolo, near Avenue Paul Doumer, I believe. It had a unique covered tennis court on the third or fourth floor of a large modern building.

    B. Who is this Jean-LUC?

21. He's very large, but I don't know anything about him, his real identity of where he lives. I've often met him outside but always under the name of Jean-LUC. He seems to me to be the chief of the organisation.

    B. What happened at that time?

22. We discussed what we could do about the passages and then it was arranged. In my case, I decided to continue my work; that's to say facilitate the passage into the Free Zone and carry certain documents.

    B. What were the conditions like for the people presented to you so you could recognise them?

23. They were brought personally, by PAUL or by Jean-LUC.

    B. Concerning the passage of documents, what did you have to do with them?

24. PAUL, Jean-LUC and other smaller agents like PIERRE [Paul MAUGER] and CAPRI [Pierre CARTAUD], they were actually in prison. I also knew PACOT [François FAURE].

    B. Did you stay a long time in PARIS?

25. I was doing the line, sometimes I was on one side, sometimes on the other. My mission was to go to PARIS, find the prisoners or the documents. In PARIS, I shared an apartment at 13 rue Verniquet with César SVAGROVSKY.

    B. Were you introduced to the prisoners at rue Verniquet or given the documents there?

26. It varied all the time. Sometimes in a café, sometimes in a square. I introduced myself to the prisoners and took them the next day.

    B. How long did it last?

27. Some time, until I went to prison. I was arrested on the demarcation line in February 1942.

28. In fact, I passed people and documents after I got out of prison. When they came, I generally had appointments to rendezvous with them at my grandmother's house which was in the Free Zone. As I had a border pass I was able to go from one side to the other.

    B. In this role that you played, PAUL and you, and Jean-LUC as chief, what was CESAR's role?

29. CESAR always did the parachute drops and landings in the Occupied Zone, on the Brittany coast.

    B. Did he find many?

    Yes.

    Always on behalf of Jean-LUC?

    Yes.

    B. He worked alone?

    No, with the BRITON [Léon SABAZEC], and one time with BOB [?].

    B. Did you know everyone there?

    Yes, I'd often seen them in PARIS, they often came to the house. BOB and the BRITON worked strictly with CESAR. BOB shared the work; I believe it was specially the parachute drops and landings, while the BRETON did the repairs [ensure there was no evidence left in the fields]. Their field of activity was in Brittany and in the Loire region.

    B. Is that all you can tell me about your work with CESAR?

    Yes, because his work was completely different to mine. There were certain times when I was in the house in PARIS which I had to type reports, but that was all.

30. In February 1942 I was arrested on the demarcation line, unfortunately by the Germans. It was beastly, I had taken one of our agents to a passeur [guide] who made the crossing by boat, I had accompanied him, I had to go through a post [check point/control point] and at that time a patrol arrested me. The agent was in serious trouble as he had a false identity card so spent three weeks in prison. I was thought to be involved as a guide and spent three months in prison. I spent three weeks in Chalons-sur-Sâone and the rest of the time in Autun.

    B. Were you badly treated by the GESTAPO, they didn't try to make you talk?

    Yes, they wanted to know the name of the guide; they were rude, they put me in a cell, but they didn't hit me.

31. When I left prison, they took my border pass, so I had to stay in the occupied zone. I stayed in PARIS and continued my activities.

    B. When?

    Straight away.

    B. Weren't you worried, didn't you have the impression that after your arrest they would be keeping a watch on the route to SEVREY?

32. No, because it wasn't always the same route. The demarcation line passed a few kilometres north of SEVREY.

    B. During this time did you 'pass' many people?

33. Yes. I'm not able to say exactly how many each month exactly, a dozen or more. They were uniquely people in the organisation. I didn't know them particularly.

    B. Those you knew therefore were CESAR, JEAN-LUC, BOB, the BRETON and PAUL?

34. I also knew MALOUIN, radio, and FAVELONNE [Lucienne Dixon], who replaced PAUL when he was arrested by the Gestapo. I also knew Madame JEFF, who was a friend of PAUL and worked with him anyway, she was married to an American.

    B. What was PACOT's role?

35. He was introduced to me as second in command to CESAR.

    B. De CAPRI?

36. I don't know well what he did exactly; he had a most significant role. He is the one who 'sold' all the others. I believe his father was a captain in the anti-Bolshevik Légion.

    B. How had he been recruited?

37. I don't know exactly.

    B. And FAVELONNE?

38. FAVELONNE worked with PAUL. In the end, he was arrested as well. Madame JEFF has also been taken.

    B. And you continued your work during this time?

39. Up to June 1942. At that time, the Gestapo came to the house. I had to type a report for Jean-LUC, it was really long. I had a rendezvous at 4 o'clock, but I was not able to go. I was given another at half past ten and went to rendezvous with CESAR, just back from PARIS. When we came home, four civilians were waiting on the stairs in the court with the concierge. When they saw us, they demanded our border passes and followed behind us. When I saw them, instead of taking the stairs, I continued walking. CESAR followed me and we went to the cellar, looked for a way out but couldn't find one. At this time, there were [wireless] transmitters in the cellar and all sorts of compromising material. We left the cellar the next morning at 6 o'clock and waited for people to leave and go to work and followed them. We saw no-one on the stairs, but when we got to the door, officers appeared and demanded identity cards. The concierge was magnificent. The Gestapo had asked him where we were, and he told them we were in the apartment below. He knew what we were doing, didn't help us but was very sympathetic.

    B. Do you know how the Germans became suspicious of 13 rue Verniquet?

39. Yes, it was de CAPRI who told everybody. He had been taken. Anyway, I believe that now he works for them. As it is, all the networks have been forced to move. These hadn't been arrested: MALOULIN, FAVELONNE, PACOT, PIERRE; Jean LUC had to change his apartment, CESAR and I were saved.

    B. Are you certain that CAPRI denounced you?

40. Certain, no, but it is believable.

    B. What happened to them?

41. I think that they have been officially condemned to death. I knew it two months ago.

42. There was the famous PHEOBUS who also 'sold' a lot of people. I don't know him. When he was in prison, if he was asked if he knew such and such a person, he said 'Yes'.

    B. When was he arrested?

43. Not very long after PAUL. I have the impression that it was him who 'sold' Paul.

    B. Do you know the circumstances under which PAUL was arrested?

44. Vaguely. I know that he was arrested in a restaurant he often used to go to.

    B. And you've got the impression that it was PHEOBUS who 'sold' him?

45. Yes, when he was confronted with him and asked if he knew him, he said: 'Yes.' PAUL has been condemned to death. I learned this two months ago. The others, PIERRE, PHEOBUS, PAUL, PACOT, MALOULIN, have all been condemned to death.

    B. What about the rest of the organisation?

46. Not much. Jean-LUC, the BRETON; Madame JEFF was arrested at the same time as PAUL, or some days later. I believe she's been released and reprieved.

    B. Why?

47. Certainly to see if she'd do anything. At that time, they were not searching that much.

    B. In fact, then it's you, Jean-LUC, CESAR, and the BRETON.

47. There was also a liaison agent named LEON [Maurice Barbe].

48. At the time, I was living with an agent in the security named PASCALINI, at 10 Boulevard Murat. He wasn't part of the organisation, but he was sympathetic. Cesar and I stayed with him for a month. Then we decided to re-cross the demarcation line as we wanted to come to England. There was also the BRETON and LEON. We cross the line at ANGOULEME, the four of us, with a guide named ANDRE. I didn't know him at all; it was Jean-LUC who pointed him out. We then spent some time on the coast of

RIBERAC; I can't remember the name. One time in the Free Zone, I returned to my parents' home in SEVREY.

49. CESAR and LE BRETON left for North Africa in July. It was very difficult for a woman to pass clandestinely in a boat. They went to ALGIERS, ORAN and from ORAN to GIBRALTAR. They came here, rested for three or four months and then returned to France.

B. Did they have the necessary papers to go to North Africa?

50. No. They were hidden in a boat which took them to MARSEILLE. They went from ALGIERS to ORAN, ORAN to GIBRALTAR and from there they went back.

B. Did they come to see us or the English?

51. Both.

B. You have the impression that they were working for an English organisation.

52. No. I stayed for some time with my parents and, as Lyon was not very far, I went shopping, and by chance, I met DENIS.

B. CESAR wasn't arrested at the same time as the others, was he?

53. I don't know. I lost all sight of him.

B. But it was him who introduced you to the guide at ANGOULEME.

54. Yes. I know he changed apartments, but I don't know if the Gestapo have been to his new place.

B. Where is he now?

55. Here's here [in London], I've seen him.

B. Why is he here?

I don't know. I haven't asked him. After the arrests, he gave me the name of the guide, but I've not seen him since.

B. So, you met DENIS in LYON?

56. Yes, by chance, in the street. I'd never spoken to him before, but I knew him. He was the third in Jean LUC's organisation. I saw him all the time. I don't know what type of work he did, probably intelligence. I saw him in PARIS.

B. Under what other name is he known?

57. JACK, DENIS and actually ARTHUR. When I met him, he asked me to continue his work with him, which I soon did.

B. When you first met him, who were you working for?

58. For him personally. He had lost contact with Jean-LUC. At that time, I was liaising between LYON and NICE, with COTY [Jean-Louis Chancel]. I did not know him at all.

B. Had he worked with CESAR before?

59. No, it was the PHATRI organisation. I liaised only between DENIS, COTY, YVONNE and GERVAIS. I met DENIS nearly every day outside LYON. In the beginning, it was at 2 Place OLLIER, in an

office, it was in a particular building. Then we rendezvoused in the street. I was given the job of passing intelligence information.

60. One time I went to NICE. I had trouble with the French police. I had a false identity card in the name of Melle GEORGES.

B. What was your name in Jean LUC's organisation?

61. Jeannette.I never changed it.

B. The Gestapo must have known the name of your family. When you went back home, weren't you worried that your parents might be worried?

62. No. I never thought of that.

B. In NICE, how did you communicate with COTY?

63. Outside. He went to the station at the same time every day. I was sure I could meet him at that time. COTY was the second in DENIS's organisation; he was in the intelligence service. He transmitted the intelligence to DENIS, who was in LYON. DENIS stayed a bit in LYON; then he went down to NICE and at that time I had returned to LYON because I'd had some trouble with the police. It was December 1942.

64. I was in a hotel. There had been a 'rafle' [large scale arrest] of evaders [people attempting to leave France]. Their identity papers were being checked, and as my card was false, they came to my room to ask me to explain it. They asked me if I was ready. I told them, 'No. I'll be an hour.' Then they told me to go and see the Commissioner in an hour, so I left for CANNES. There I met COTY, who told me to leave.

65. I went to LYON where I worked with GOBELET. He was part of DENIS's organisation

B. Was he part of Jean-LUC's organisation?

66. No.

B. What was his real name?

68. M.de PIERREBOURG. He was a tissue wholesaler, 20 or 22 rue de Constantine. At that time, I liaised between LYON and VICHY. At VICHY I saw BERTHE, I didn't know who he was, and VALETTE. I went to VALETTE's house who had a publicity office at 29 rue de Mascaret, VICHY. I liaised between BERTHE and VALETTE on one side, and with GOBELET on the other. All three depended on DENIS, who was their chief.

B. Since when did this organisation call itself PHATRI? What does its name mean?

68. I don't know.

69. I worked with them until March 1943. During that time. I stayed continuously with GOBELET.

70. We were also involved with the Lyon police. I was in contact with all the National Security. They had set up an organisation alongside the

National Security, and it was these members of National Security who provided the intelligence for GOBELOT. The chief was M. CHABERT, principal Security inspector in Lyon. He had M. PELISSON, ICARD, FAUCHEUX, LACHASSAGNE; they were all inspectors. I don't remember the others' names. There were more or less a dozen. I especially knew those I pointed out to you. I went to the Security Office and specially occupied myself there. They made the register of identity cards; they had all the intelligence on the Gestapo I needed. It was GOBELET who set this up.

71. This organisation still exists. There was an event with GOBELT and DENIS, and I believe that GOBELET doesn't work there anymore following something that happened with DENIS. GOBELET received lots of money, and he gave very little to the organisation. I had already done a lot to make it bearable DENIS had a lot of work, but not a lot of money to give the organisation; I believe this is the reason why there was discontent between them.

72. GOBELET had asked to go to LONDON with his family; this had been refused. He went to see M. CHABERT and asked if he could stop work. I also went to see M. CHABERT, asked him to continue and pass on the service to DENIS. CHABERT had entered an arrangement with MARC, DENIS's third in charge. At that time M. CHABERT had been appointed chief, he had a little organisation, he centralised all the intelligence and sent it to DENIS. GOBELET ceased work completely. I lost all contact with him.

73. The next day I got into trouble. I was at M. FAUCHEUX's house, and the Gestapo came to search it. They came and rang for the porter, asking for Jeannette. I didn't know what was happening. Certainly they had been given the address. If GOBELET and FAUCHEUX knew the address, I didn't know. I didn't open the door. It was a day when M. FACHEUX was on night shift; his wife had left on holiday. Normally I would have been on my own, but I was with CESAR. He went to look at the door and then left by the balcony. I've seen him since March. We got over the balcony and escaped through a construction site next door. At that time, I went to the house of another Security inspector, M. ICARD; he was very kind; he lived at 20 rue, Jerome. M. FAUCHEUX lived at 10 rue Nicolai. I went to ICARD's house and that day I ceased all contact with the organisation. I was 'burnt' [The Gestapo wanted to arrest her].

B. What was your personal impression of GOBELET?

74. He had very little will. He received a lot of money. I don't know how much.

B. How much did you receive?

75. 7,000 francs a month at that time. When I was with Jean-LUC I got 4,000 a month.

B. Did CESAR return to France to work for PHATRI?

75. Yes. He worked for the DENIS réseau [network] and independently. He was always there. I saw him with COTY and FRANCOIS.

B. And DENIS?

76. He had an incident not long ago. He had been arrested by the police. He had been to NICE and returned to LYON with the courrier [intelligence reports]. There had been a rafle [large scale arrests] on the train, and he was arrested. Two or three days later COTY left the area. He actually went to PARIS. I believe that he came here [London] the next month.

B. CESAR continued to work with the DENIS group. He formed his own réseau.

77. There was the CHABERT group in LYON; MARC liaised with in the CANNES and NICE areas. YVONNE was with MARC; I don't know what she did, liaison probably. CHABERT worked with MARC at this time.

B. What did you do?

78. I went to see ICART and ceased all my work. Afterwards, I went to someone else's house and stayed there a month until the time of my departure [for England]. I was helped a bit by CESAR, but most was done myself as I was his courier.

B. What do you know about your parents' arrest?

79. I'm not very well informed about this.

B. What caused it?

80. PACOT had started to talk [providing the police/Gestapo with information] two and a half months ago; by that time my parents had been arrested.

B. Have you the impression that PACOT's a bastard?

81. No. Not at all, he's very good, but I believe that he wasn't able to resist the torture; he had a son. I believe he was tortured in from of him. I suppose that the arrest of my parents is linked with this, and by carelessness. I'd left my parent's address at the house. I was the only person in my family who knew where to find me. At that time, I was in TOULOUSE.

B. What did you do in TOULOUSE?

82. I was there with M. GOBOLET to facilitate the release of two young people from St Sulpice prison. I was back with him at that time.

83. It was from their parents that I learned of the arrest of my parents. I don't know under what incrimination; I simply know they are missing. My grandmother, she's 80, has been interrogated, so I stopped having any contact with her because she was old already. I have not tried to make contact with my parents. I've done absolutely nothing. I'm worried about their imprisonment, naturally.

B. So you decided to leave?

84. I wasn't me who decided who decided to leave. It was DENIS.

    B. Who organised your departure?

85. CESAR. They came looking for me, and I left by plane during the night, in the area of CHÂTEAUROUX on a landing strip prepared by CESAR. Three of us left, COTY, FRANÇOIS, and I. DENIS didn't leave. COTY was to leave the following night. They will cross, and DENIS will come here [? England].

    B. Who's FRANÇOIS?

86. He left for another réseau, MARCO POLO réseau.

    B. Had you seen often him before?

87. Yes, because I stayed at his house in LYON for some time.

88. We left on Wednesday 14 May and brought the courrier. A small young man called BILLARD got out of the plane [a Lysander]. I didn't know him. We got in. The plane took us to an aerodrome in England [RAF Tangmere]. Then we were taken to M. BERTRAND's house [Bignor Manor, near Chichester, West Sussex] in the country. We were very well received and from there we were taken to London. The English took us directly to the French Office on Duke Street on Wednesday night.

    B. Do you know whether any members of DENIS's organisation were a bit suspect?

89. No. There was nothing about GOBELET being a little suspect. The others weren't. COTY is very good, MARC as well. They were also very good in Jean-LUC's réseau.

    B. What's the general situation in France like?

90. It's not brilliant. At the moment, there's a very bad feeling about the young men being forced to leave and work in Germany. In my view, they're not very brave. The first ones were not very happy, for a normal life they needed 10,000 francs a month. Mostly they averaged 2,000 a month. In general, what helps is that their family in the countryside send them food. Mostly they've had enough of actual politics; they don't all have the same opinion about the occupation; they're beginning to understand a bit of the situation. They love Pétain less than de Gaulle in France, but this had made a bad impression, and there is disagreement.

91. In the police, there are two groups, those who are for and those who are again. It's very clear. Those that are against are as bad as the Gestapo – vis-à-vis the French population, the German soldier is alright.

    B. Have you heard anything about shooting hostages?

92. Yes. They take hostages at every turn, but it's not published. At this time there are a lot of people who've disappeared in France, one doesn't know what's happened to them.

    B. Have you heard anything about the measures the Germans and French are taking about the gas?

93. No. I've heard nothing about it. I have heard about what measures they're taking against the invasion, by the security inspectors. The people of LYON have been ordered to leave all their doors open to allow free entrance and exit, all those against it would be shot immediately etc. But for the gas, nothing.

B. Do you know of any French Germanophiles?

94. I know one. Charles ABBET, he owns the Olympia bar, rue des Ramparts des Ninay in LYON. He received enormous tips from the Germans. I know he works for the Gestapo, and the intelligence.

B. One last question – apart from the mail transmission and intelligence work for Jean-LUC and others, have they sought to form shock troops?

95. I don't know. We carried transmitters in paniers to LYON. CASENAVE [Jean Fleury] was working on it; I don't know where he lived. He received his instructions from LONDON. I haven't seen any other English people.

OPINION OF THE COUNTER-ESPIONAGE SECTION

Melle GUYOT alias JANIN made an excellent impression. Her declarations appear honest. A Visa No. It has been issued accordingly.[18]

Having proved her bona-fides, Jeannette enlisted in the Free French Forces under the name of Jeannette Janin and worked with 'Colonel Rémy' who had been brought to England by a trawler from Finistère on 6 January 1943.[19]

Part of the Allies' plans for the invasion of France was the SUSSEX Plan, a joint operation by the British Secret Intelligence Service (SIS), the American Office of Strategic Services (OSS) and the BCRA.

Small groups, normally made up of two men, called SUSSEX teams, undertook the same training as SOE agents and were parachuted into Northern France. Their missions were to collect and send back information on the German order of battle and their troop movements by identifying the different units and counting the amount, type, and direction of their rail and road traffic. The information was then passed back to Allied Command via S-phone to the radio operators on board overflying Mitchell bombers of 226 Squadron. These planes returned to their base at RAF Hartingbridge, now Blackbushe Airport, where the information was passed on to High Command. The SUSSEX teams were a prelude to the Carpetbaggers' Red Stocking missions over Germany.

With the assistance of Kenneth Cohen of SIS, Francis Pickens-Miller of OSS and other BCRA officers, Colonel Rémy recruited French men and women who had reached Britain from Spain and North Africa following their interrogation at the 'London Reception Centre'.

According to the Le Plan-Sussex-1944 website, two French women, Lt Jeannette Guyot and Sub-Lt Evelyne Clopet, were part of two Sussex teams. On 13 November 1943, under the command of the British Major Guy Wingate and American Colonel Malcolm Henderson, the first recruits undertook a ten-week training course at Drungewick Manor (TS-7), near Hersham, Surrey and, as numbers increased, at Praewood, a large country house near St Albans, Hertfordshire. Courses on military intelligence techniques were run by SIS and OSS instructors

As much of the railway network in Northern France had been put out of action by saboteurs, the agents were all issued with bicycles and taught to drive motor bikes and cars. Their syllabus also included night map reading, skills they would need back in France.

According to the ossreborn website, their British and American instructors divided them into thirty teams, normally two men, an organiser and a wireless operator. They were issued with 'L' pills and 25,000 francs each and 150,000 for the team. The wireless operator was issued with an American TR-1 and/or a British Mark VII set, batteries and bicycle generator and equipped with a double-transposition cipher with a flash code. This was a group of numbers, each of which represented a word or phrase designed for transmitting military intelligence.

Included in the Allies' planning for the invasion was Operation *Jedburgh*, the parachuting of over thirty uniformed three-man teams including a Frenchman from the BCRA, an American or Canadian from OSS and a British SOE officer, to conduct sabotage and guerrilla warfare and lead the French Resistance in co-ordinated attacks against the Germans.

Before their flight, the Jedburgh teams were accommodated at 'holding stations' including Grendon Hall, Northamptonshire, which was close to RAF Harrington where the USAAF Carpetbagger missions were flown out from, and Farm Hall, about half an hour's drive from RAF Tempsford, where the Special Duties Squadron was based.

According to the Le Plan-Sussex-1944 website, Jeannette's regular requests to Rémy to be allowed to be trained for the Pathfinder missions were eventually granted and she and 22-year-old Evelyne Clopet were given paramilitary and clandestine warfare training at Praewood and parachute training.

Given a commission as a Lieutenant, 25-year-old Jeannette was one of the first two SUSSEX teams to be infiltrated. Her organiser was Captain Georges Lassale and she was to act as his courier and wireless operator. The organiser of the other team was Major Marcel Saubestre, code named Marcel, with Lt Pierre Binet, code named Lucien, as his wireless operator.

Although the mission was ready to depart in January 1944, continuous bad weather and human error prevented their departure during that moon period. The reasons were explained in the OSS history of the SUSSEX PLAN.

An Actual Dispatching

Since it gives a good picture of the procedure involved in a dispatching operation from the viewpoint of the staff who got the agents ready, the following account by Major O'Brien of an unsuccessful attempt to dispatch four agents – the original Pathfinders – is included. This was a British operation.

I picked up Marcel, Lucien and Jeannette at Palace Street and after a very hasty lunch in an ABC, we met K [Kenneth Cohen] of SIS and Jean (the W/T) at TS ... [probably Praewood]. We arrived at Tempsford at about four thirty on Saturday afternoon. Farm Hall is a large, old and very comfortable house, presided over by Mrs Watchon, a WAAF officer, who is very efficient and full of charm. She has a large staff of WAAFs, who do the cooking and serving at the Hall. Everything is done there to make the agents comfortable. [There was no Farm Hall in Tempsford. There was a Farm Hall on West Street, Godmanchester, about 12 miles north of the airfield and used to accommodate French agents and Jedburgh teams before departure from Tempsford or Harrington.] The house was rather full of other agents and dispatching officers since there were to be 29 planes departing that night. We were led to a large bedroom where we left Jean to change from battledress into civilian clothes, while Jeannette, Marcel, and Lucien came with K and me into the billiard room, where we went over their identity papers and examined all the contents of their pockets to make sure they had no papers or objects such as cigarettes, matches and so forth, which would link them up with England. The net result of this operation was that K and I came out of the room with our pockets stuffed with matches and cigarettes.

Then we went for high tea, where a sharp distinction was made between passengers about to take off and dispatching officers, the agent getting a fried egg in addition to what was served the others. After tea, we went to the third floor of the house where a sergeant in charge of the supply room issued our friends the objects they had picked out from the shelves. These consisted of French cigarettes and matches, bandages, medicaments of various sorts, chocolate, tins of rations, knives and arms. K of SIS had already brought four .25 automatics and ammunition for them, so we ignored the side arms. We had difficulty in persuading Jean not to take a spring cosh. I gave them such a sales talk about the .69 grenade that they each took one.

At about 7 o'clock we got into the car again and drove out to the field, which is about 12 miles from Farm Hall. There were four or five cars making the trip due to the large number of parties departing that night. As soon as we arrived at the field, we were led to a Nissen hut where our group was alone. In general, the groups are kept separate, the only unfortunate thing being the limitations in accommodation at Farm Hall. Inevitably people meet on the stairs or at tea and see who is going out. For instance, Charles recognised a man in another party as someone he had met at Ringway.

In the hut, the Pathfinder equipment was ready in large bags marked 'Calanque', the name of the operation from the viewpoint of the dispatchers. NCOs dressed our four agents in their strip-tease suits [heavy-duty overalls with two zips down the front for ease of removal] and parachutes and mud boots. During the dressing, the same non-coms served the agents with rum, plying cup after cup. Jeannette did not take any. Squadron Leader Bonzie showed K of SIS and me the Etat-Major map with the pin-point [drop zone] marked on it. Apparently until that moment, K of SIS had not been informed of the exact pinpoint.

The pilot came in, by the name of [Wing Commander] Hodges, and was introduced all round. By the time Jeannette was dressed, it was apparent that she could easily break an ankle with her small shoes swimming in the over-large mud boots, so we had to remove her parachute and strip-tease in order to take the boots off, on the theory that it was worse for her to hurt herself than to get covered with mud.

I loaded and issued the .25 automatics. By this time the four agents had every available pocket stuffed with their equipment, including automatics, grenades, cigarettes, and flashlights. The last objects issued to them were thermos bottles of coffee and packets of sandwiches which they carried to the plane in their hands.

We then drove a few hundred yards out onto the field to the Halifax. It was already tuning up and after about ten minutes of standing about and repeated farewells, the passengers all climbed in.

This plane was engaged in three operations and was carrying no fewer than nine passengers and 19 containers or packages. This discovery earlier in the evening annoyed K, who phoned through to Commander C, but it was impossible to make any change. Our operation was scheduled as the last and was given priority over the others.

The morale of our four agents was excellent throughout all the preparations; the only one to show any nervousness was Marcel, the oldest of the group, and his nervousness manifested itself in a slight querulousness and tendency to issue orders to his three companions. However, there was nothing frankly disagreeable about this to anyone. Although the agents had to sit about for some little time in their uncomfortable costumes, particularly the first one or two to be dressed, nevertheless they continued smoking and talking cheerfully with everyone. They definitely had the impression that they were being coddled [well cared for in terms of food, drink and entertainment]. In connection with our future operations, I would suggest that we do this kind of thing as much like the British as we can, but that, in addition, we avoid a

An 1944 aerial shot of RAF Tempsford, the airfield from which most women agents were flown. (Courtesy of the East Anglian Aviation Society)

Above: Westland Lysander used to take and pick up agents and VIPs from Tempsford (and RAF Tangmere on south coast). Note the ladder attached to the fuselage to allow passengers quicker access and the additional fuel tank to increase its range to the south of France. (Hugh Verity, *We Landed by Moonlight*)

Below: An agent receiving her last kiss before boarding the plane to the Continent. (Courtesy of Pierre Tillet)

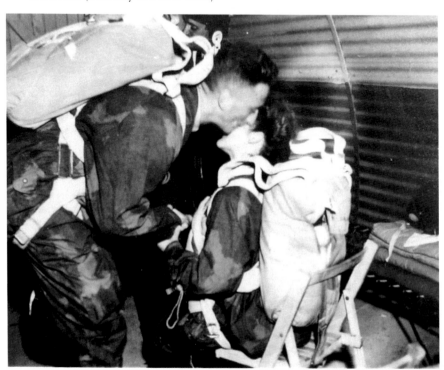

Above: The control tower at RAF Tempsford. (Courtesy of Peter Haining)

Right: Practising landings inside a hangar.

Below: An American B24 Liberator Bomber. They were used to parachute agents and containers into occupied Europe. The same planes were used from Algiers to drop agents into southern France. (Courtesy of the US Air Force)

Odette Sansom was landed by felucca (converted fishing boat) at Port Miou, about 15 km south-east of Marseille, on 3/4 November 1942. She survived Ravensbrück, and was awarded the George Cross and Companion de Légion d'Honneur. (Courtesy of the National Archives, TNA HS9/648/4)

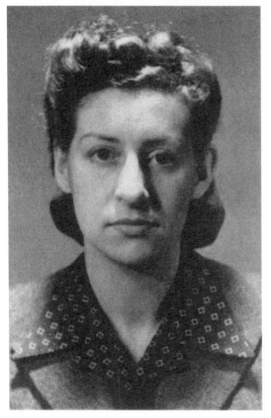

Denise Bloch was landed by Lysander near Baudreville (Eure & Loir) on 2 March 1944. She was executed at Ravensbrück, and posthumously awarded the King's Commendation for Brave Conduct, Companion de Légion d'Honneur, Croix de Guerre and Medaille de Resistance. (Courtesy of the National Archives, TNA HS9/165/8)

Andrée Borrel parachuted near St Laurent Nouan (Loir-et-Cher), on 24/25 September 1942. Captured, she was executed at Natzweiler-Struthof. She was later posthumously awarded the King's Commendation for Brave Conduct, Croix de Guerre and Medaille Republique Française. She is pictured here in her FANY uniform. (Courtesy of the National Archives, TNA HS9/183)

Andrée Borrel's code sheet. (Courtesy of the National Archives, TNA HS9/183)

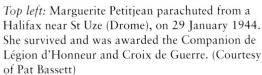

Top left: Marguerite Petitjean parachuted from a Halifax near St Uze (Drome), on 29 January 1944. She survived and was awarded the Companion de Légion d'Honneur and Croix de Guerre. (Courtesy of Pat Bassett)

Left: Françine Fromont parachuted from a Whitley near Montpellier (Languedoc-Roussillon), on 3/4 March 1942.She was executed at Fresnes Prison, Paris. (Courtesy of Donal O'Sullivan)

Below left: Julienne Aisner was landed by Lysander near Le Port, 13 km south-east of Tours (Indre & Loire), on 14/15 May 1944 and survived the war. She was awarded the King's Medal of Commendation. (Courtesy of Justin A. Davis)

Below: The women of the SOE were not the only ones to help in the liberation of France; pictured is Simone Segouin, a member of the French Resistance who was reported to have captured 25 Nazis in the Chartres area, in addition to killing others. (Courtesy of the US National Archives and Records Administration)

Above: Arisaig, Inverness-shire, north-west Scotland, where the French women received paramilitary training. (Courtesy of Alan Weir under Creative Commons 2.0)

Below: Royal Victorian Patriotic School, Wandsworth, London, where, from January 1941, MI5 interviewed refugees to determine if they were enemy agents and gain intelligence about conditions overseas. Potential recruits for F and RF Sections were identified. (Courtesy of Mike T under Creative Commons 2.0)

Above: Dunham House, (STS 51a), Altrincham, Cheshire, where agents were accommodated whilst they had their parachute training at nearby Ringway aerodrome. (Courtesy of Iain Cameron under Creative Commons 2.0)

Left: Brickendonbury Manor (STS 17) near Hertford, where agents, including Jeanne Bohec, received industrial sabotage training. (Courtesy of Neil Rees)

Below left: Bignor Manor, Chichester, West Sussex, where about 200 French BCRA agents were provided with accommodation before their flight from RAF Tangmere. (Courtesy of Charles Drake under Creative Commons 2.0) sudden change in treatment at the time when agents arrive at the dispatching center. In other words, let us begin coddling them during the briefing period at the Freehold [probably Sunnyside House].

Our plane left at exactly 9 o'clock, the scheduled time. It was preceded and followed by other Halifaxes, there being about one every three or five minutes. Most of them were bound for France, but at least one was bound for Norway and another for Denmark.

K of SIS and I went to bed and were awakened at 0530 hours with the news that the plane had returned with our party, having dropped the other two parties. The other operations were easier than ours from the pilot's viewpoint because they were blind droppings [with no reception committee]. We got up and dressed at once, and by 6 o'clock our friends had returned to Farm Hall where we talked with them.

The pilot was sure that he had found the pinpoint, and he had made three runs over it without seeing the ground lights, Altogether, he was in the neighbourhood for twelve minutes. The plan, as outlined by the dispatcher in the plane, was for Jeannette to jump first, then the packages, Lucien second, Jean third and Marcel last. Jeannette and Lucien were to take their place on the forward side of the opening ['Joe hole' – the American term for the opening in the fuselage through which the parachutists jumped], with the packages on the tail side. As soon as the packages had gone, Jean and Marcel were to take the place vacated by the packages. All of this had to be arranged before departure because of the noise in the plane during flight. Hence, during the unsuccessful operation, Jeannette and Lucien were occupying their action stations for forty minutes. They could look down through the hole and see the passing countryside 500 feet below them. The moon was bright, and they saw meadows, woods, houses and a road, but saw no lights.

The passengers returned to Farm Hall from their eight and a half hours of flight and went up to bed at once, after eating some sandwiches and drinking some more coffee. The operation did not take place Monday night because of weather.[20]

With the support of the French Resistance, their mission, Operation *Calanque*, was to prepare for the arrival of fifty-two SUSSEX teams which were to be parachuted into Northern France between April and September 1944; to locate dropping grounds for the parachutists and their equipment; to help build up caches of arms and equipment; to prepare safe-houses where the new agents would be accommodated upon their arrival and to receive and dispatch them to their areas of operation.

After arriving in Paris with Lasalle, Jeannette visited her cousin, Madame Kiehl, who ran the 'Café de l'Electricite' at 8 Rue Tournefort in

Montmartre. There she got to know others in the Resistance and a few days later moved into Madame Andrée Goubillon's apartment, whose husband had been imprisoned and who owned the café.

In an interview after the war, Madame Goubillon told the BBC, 'I knew which kind of work she had come to make, and when she asked me... if I were ready to help her, I answered yes without the least hesitation. Although the café was located beside an office of the Gestapo, I knew what I wanted to do; I was not afraid.'[21]

After Liberation, she renamed it 'Cafe Sussex' because Sussex agents used to rendez-vous there.

Over the following seven months, with the help of the second team, they found twenty-two drop zones, organised seventeen drops, along a line from Brittany to Alsace. Some DZs were used twice. She was also involved in finding almost a hundred safe houses to accommodate fifty-three subsequent 'Sussex' teams. Pierre Binet and Etienne Ancergues were arrested and shot in Forest d'Othe on 19 August 1944, two days before the Allies captured Paris.

From 1 October 1944 until 30 June 1945, Jeannette was allocated to the Direction of the Studies and Researches. She then returned home to Sevrey and married Marcel Goucher, the leader of one of the other Sussex teams.

In recognition of her contribution to France's liberation, de Gaulle's government awarded her the Chevalier of the Légion of Honour; Croix de Guerre with Palm and Medaille de la Resistance. Field Marshal Montgomery, Commander-in-Chief of the 21st Army Group, in his citation for her to be awarded an OBE stated that she was, 'Parachuted early Feb-1944 (First SUSSEX agent to jump), worked as principal liaison agent of the "Pathfinder" Group. For seven months revealed highest qualities of initiative, daring and endurance.'[22]

The British awarded her the George Medal, the second highest civilian gallantry award as military awards were not awarded to women. The only other woman agent who was given this award was Nancy Wake.

Jeannette was one of only two female recipients of the US Army's Distinguished Service Cross, the second highest American award after the Medal of Congress. The other was Virginia Hall. President Roosevelt's citation provided more light on Jeannette's mission for the OSS.

As the principal liaison agent of the mission, she travelled widely over the northern France and contacted a large number of agents. Lieutenant Guyot travelled by various methods of conveyance with luggage, which, if it had been opened by the Gestapo, would have resulted in her torture and death. Because of her great courage and initiative, she undertook the most dangerous assignments, such as reporting on Gestapo activities and verifying reports of the arrest or execution of any of the 'Sussex' agents.

Lieutenant Guyot's work and conduct were beyond all praise and exemplify the highest traditions of the Armed Forces of the Allied Nations.[23]

Gilbert Renaud wrote prolifically about the Resistance and referred to Jeannette in his *Mémoires d'un agent secret de la France libre*, Raoul Solar, 1946–50. After the war, she led a quiet life, avoiding publicity and died in Chalon-sur-Saône on 10 April 1916, aged 97, leaving two daughters and a son. She was the most highly decorated Frenchwoman during the war, but it was the British press that first published her obituary.

DANIELLE REDDÉ

Aged 32. Parachuted from a Halifax near Montluçon (Allier) on 9 February 1944. Awarded the Member of the British Empire Medal, Croix de Guerre and Companion de Légion d'Honneur.

The next French woman to be infiltrated was 33-year-old Danielle 'Eddie' Reddé, a member of the Corps Auxiliaire Féminin. Foot listed her as the first of nine RF Section women to be parachuted into France. Two others were landed by Hudson.[24]

She was born in Châtillon-sur-Seine, a southwestern suburb of Paris, on 7 October 1911 and grew up with her parents, both painters, at 32 Rue des Ponts. After leaving school, she joined the Post Office in 1932.

At the beginning of the occupation, she was assigned first to Dijon and then to Lyon. According to the World War Two Escape Lines website, she was working as a telephonist in Lyon when she met Australian agent Tom Groome. He worked as a wireless operator in Pat O'Leary's escape organisation, having been parachuted into France in October 1942. She then worked as his courier, helping to get French, Belgian and British escapers and evaders out of France and into Spain using the identity papers of Félicité Kermarec, Simone Fournier and Camille Fournier.

On 11 January 1943, she, Groome, and some of the men they wanted to get out of the country, were arrested at a house in Montauban, about 60 km north of Toulouse. Groome had failed to set a look out while he was transmitting and was caught by German direction finding equipment.

Taken to the Gestapo HQ at Hotel Ours Blancs in Toulouse, Groome jumped out of a window trying to escape. Although he was recaptured, Danielle managed to escape in the commotion and in March crossed the Pyrénées on foot with Nancy Wake, an Australian who had also been working for Pat O'Leary, and several others involved in the French Resistance. Subsequent evidence suggests that she suffered badly at the hands of the Gestapo during her imprisonment, but her personnel file gave no details.

On 4 June 1943, she arrived at Greenock Docks, near Glasgow via Perpignan, Barcelona, Madrid and Gibraltar and, following debrief, ten days later she joined the BCRA and was recruited into the Corps Auxiliaire Féminin.

According to her personnel file, she was 1.68 m, had brown hair, chestnut eyes, and no distinguishing features. Her cover story was that she worked for a wine merchant in Lyon.

She had been selected by Colonel de Cheveigné to work as a wireless operator in a new network he was creating. Whether de Cheveigné was a nom de guerre is unknown, but there was a 21-year-old Maurice de Cheveigné parachuted blind from a Halifax about 3 km south of Thoissey, Ain, on 30 May 1942. He had worked for three years with an American Radio Corporation before escaping to Britain and was a French Air Force radio instructor. Recruited by SOE, he needed very little wireless training, only paramilitary, parachute and clandestine warfare courses. Code named Salm, he was given 100,000 francs to fund his mission as a wireless operator to Jean Moulin, who had been parachuted on 1 January 1942 to try and unite important political figures in both the Occupied and Non-Occupied zones.

In April the following year, he was appointed chief of clandestine wireless operations in France and, according to his citation for a King's Medal for Courage, 'recruited and trained wireless operators, inspected centres and dealt satisfactorily with all difficulties in regard to material and security.'[25]

On 15 June 1943, he was brought back to Britain by Hudson with Resistance leaders Henri Frenay, Paul Rivière, Raymond Fassin and four others and prepared for another mission.

Recruited as a wireless operator, Danielle was trained with two other French women selected to help de Cheveigné, Eugénie Gruner and Yvonne Gittus. Their stories can be read later. Although she was given the cover name Edith Daniel, she was known to her friends as 'Eddie' Reddé.[26]

Her overall assessment at Winterfold (STS 7) was C, average. Her intelligence was rated at 8, Morse and mechanical were good but instructional was poor. Her instructor commented that she was

A pleasant, serious, intelligent girl with imagination, forethought and practical sense and a fervent desire to get back to France. She is rather self-effacing, and her general outlook is rather a pathetic one. She is, however, thoroughly reliable and conscientious and out to do her best. She is at present in a state of nervous tension and is obsessed by her experiences with the Gestapo in France. She has the aptitude and personal knowledge for

W/T, and if trained not too hurriedly under psychiatric supervision in which the C/S concurs, she should become very suitable for return to the field.[27]

A note in her file indicated that she 'certainly knows a great deal about home-made explosives and should be useful in the field where she is anxious to go as soon as possible. A short stay at STS 6 will be beneficial. She will then be fitted to go to whatever specialised School is considered the most appropriate.'[28]

While waiting for her security to be checked, she spent a few weeks at West Court (STS 6), one of the SOE's requisitioned country houses near Finchampstead, Wokingham, Surrey.

Major Dunn-Hills reported that 'she has done a little silent killing' but had been ill in bed most of the first week. She did no fieldcraft but was a very good shot with a pistol 'better than most of the men.' She did very little on the explosives and demolition course, knew little about map reading but impressed him with her W/T skills. She had learnt Q code and procedure and sent at 17 wpm and received at 14.[29]

At the end of the training, Acting Lieutenant Hodson added that, 'She is very much better and has profited by her stay here. She is leaving here tomorrow to continue her training as a W/T. She is very keen to get on with her training so that she can get back to France and get to work. She is a good type of Frenchwoman, rather more artistic than practical and inclined to be sentimental. I think her security mindedness is good, and she realises how important security is.'[30]

His final report before being sent to Thame Park for wireless training was 'not too physically fit, but as far as ability goes, is ready for STS 52, A very good pistol shot.'[31]

After a fortnight's preliminary wireless training, her instructor commented that, she 'Sends 17, receives 19 wpm. Had difficulty in technical subjects, but knows her set well and has quite a good style. A very hard worker and should be successful in the field. Slow at codes but reliable.'[32]

A subsequent unsigned note while she was at Ringway reported that,

Mademoiselle Daniel, in my opinion, is both mentally and physically very tired and depressed. She seems apprehensive of her future work and very sensitive. Her left wrist which she has strained in some sort of way should be attended to as this might handicap her in future jumps.

I was very impressed by her low 'morale' and feel that she is in need of mental and physical rest as her low spirits might act as a drag on the other people that she might be working with. She has a very loyal and straight character, a kind heart and understanding of people. She is very patriotic, most security minded and very pro-British. She has a definite inferiority complex and has to be encouraged in her work, but I feel sure that she would go to any lengths in serving her country and her ideals. She seems unable to understand why she is not working for the 'Service Anglais' and I think it would help her morale if an explanation could be given.[33]

She completed her parachute training with two jumps, and then having celebrated Christmas, her clandestine warfare training continued on Boxing Day at Boarmans (STS 36). A fortnight later, her report stated that she was 'not intelligent, but has common sense and some practical ingenuity. Fair imagination, Keen and worked hard. Lacks self-confidence; is serious minded, enthusiastic, methodical and persevering. Well-disciplined and agreeable personality. Inclined to worry and needs encouragement. A good student who would do her best work under a chief who would be patient and encourage her. Codes: Taught Innocent Letter, based on Playfair, with conventions. Secret Censorship. Understands the systems but has not a good memory. Considerable practice is required.'[34]

Her FANY conducting officer reported that she 'worked hard during the whole course and appeared to benefit greatly from the lectures and practical exercises. I found her very well balanced in every way, but she is inclined to lack confidence in herself without any justification. She did not express at any time any regrets for undertaking this work and I was most impressed with her splendid morale. She did, however, mention a fear of talking in her sleep, which I did notice but this seemed to me to be incoherent. She did appear to me to be overtired and to require several days' complete rest.'[35]

Whether she was allowed a few days off was not mentioned but, as the weather that winter was severe, her flight was postponed until the February moon. During the wait, she escorted another student to Ringway where she undertook another jump.

Code named Morroccin/Marocain, an RF officer briefed her for her mission which was subject to the approval of the Military or Civil Delegate of the Action Committee in France. On the night of 14/15 February, she was to rendezvous in Lyon with two Resistance leaders, code named Latin and Phénicien, and work as the latter's wireless operator in the South Zone. Her personnel file identified she subsequently worked with Bohémien. As yet their identities have not come to light.

On 9 February 1944, she was parachuted near Montluçon, about 80 km north-west of Clermont-Ferrand. Clark mentioned five Halifax flights that night and six agents being dropped with 34 containers but made no mention of Danielle.[36]

Her mission had three distinct phases. Firstly, from February until the end of June she was to be in the region around Saint-Etienne, Loire and Haute-Loire trying to create and test a réseau which, despite advances and various efforts, had been limited by a fearful population and a business community who spoke well but promised little.

Secondly, from June until the end of July, she was to be around Morestel, Isère, which had a number of Resistance areas. Its population was devoted to the Resistance; there was little traffic, and any arrests would need a strong force. Maure and Phénicien were mentioned.

Thirdly, from the end of July until September, she was to go to the Lyon area where the Allied victories would give hope and courage to the weak, but there would be difficulties with the surviving transport system. For a long time, there was only one accessible location, situated 800 metres from a German car repair shop, which would restrict possibilities. On 15 September, she had to rendezvous with SFU 4 (possibly Special Forces Unit) in Lyon.

Research by Julien Etienne Moulin, a journalist for *Le Parisien-Aujourd'hui en France*, revealed that Danielle was an inseparable friend of his aunt, Marguerite Soulas, an important Resistance member in Saint-Etienne. Marguerite allowed Danielle to transmit messages to the Free French from her house, the pharmacy on Rue Gambetta.[37]

After the American and French Forces landed on the Mediterranean coast in August 1944, their northern advance eventually overran Danielle's area, and she returned to England on 24 October.[38]

Having been debriefed, she was prepared for another mission, this time in Asia. On the Mémoire et Espoirs de la Résistance website, it mentions her arriving by ship in Calcutta on 3 May 1945. Her mission included wireless communications with Siam, what is now Thailand. Both the SOE and the French were active in the Far East at that time.

Before long, she accepted another mission, this time as Sous-lieutenant Simone Fournier to work with the SOE in liberating Allied prisoners of war held in Japanese camps in Indochina.

On 22 August, this time code named Edith Fournier, she and Lt Klotz parachuted into Thakhek, Laos, just over the border from Thailand. She was to work as his radio operator. Details of her work were included in her citation for a bravery award.

During the period under review, 16 August – 15 November 1945, this officer, the only woman to drop by parachute into Japanese occupied territory, was attached to my HQ together with Lieut. KLOTZ with whom she was serving as a radio operator. Their orders were to locate and do all possible to help locate French and Allied P.W.s or civilians in the area of THAKHEK F.I.C. [French Indo-China]. They dropped 'blind' on 22 August and landed in broad daylight within a few hundred yards of a Japanese column which at once pursued them. They only escaped with the greatest difficulty, and under fire, but nevertheless salvaged all their W/T equipment, Sous-Lieutenant Fournier herself carrying a load which most women would have found impossible.

For several days, they lived in a cave in the hills near THAKHEK during which time S/Lt FOURNIER worked 'skeds' to RANGHOON day and night every two hours in attempts to make contact, but she was unsuccessful owing to atmospheric and other conditions outside her control. On 5 December 1945 she accompanied Lieut. KLOTZ to THAKHEK to visit some 50 French civilians, mostly women and children who were interned there by the Japanese and were in danger from the Annamese. In spite of the very great and obvious risks both from the Annamese, who were well armed and very dangerously excited and from the Japanese who were taking the line that they had not surrendered to the French, S/Lt FOURNIER insisted on accompanying Lt. KLOTZ to THAKHEK. They entered the town in daylight, visited the internees, ascertained their immediate needs and by their presence, calmness and encouragement, vastly raised their morale. On leaving the town, these two officers were surrounded by an armed and excited crowd of Annamese, who attempted to arrest them and tried with menace to deprive them of their pistols. At this moment, they were undoubtedly in the gravest peril, and the slightest hesitation or sign of fear by either of them would certainly have caused the instant death of both. However, with contemptuous disregard for their own safety and with an air of complete confidence and assurance S/Lt FOURNIER refused to hand over her pistol and, together with Lt KLOTZ pushed her way through the Annamese. The later opened fire on them but soon ceased without having hurt either. After this incident, these two officers removed themselves to my HQ where they continued their work under my command. From that time until the middle of October she remained with me. During this time, she worked or rather overworked unceasingly. Her help was indispensable in the evacuation of the French internees from THAKHEK to NAKHAUN THANOM and in looking after them afterwards. In addition, she worked tirelessly trying to contact RANGHOON and also helping my own W/T operator in his work. At this time, the excessive quantity and complicated nature of the work of this mission and the acute shortage of personnel to deal with it, demanded abnormal efforts from everybody. S/Lt FOURNIER's contribution exceeded anything that could have been expected of even the strongest woman. She rendered such invaluable service that without her I do not know how the Mission could have carried on. The murder of Lt KLOTZ by Annamese on 27 September shook her profoundly, but she refused to let it interfere with her work. In the very difficult and trying days that followed, her great talents, energy, loyalty and devotion to duty were beyond all praise. [39]

While she was in the Far East, de Gaulle awarded her the Médaille du Combattant Volontaire de la Résistance, the Médaille commémorative des services volontaires dans la France Libre, the Croix du Combattant, the Croix de Guerre avec Palme, and Chevalier de la Légion d'Honneur.

In commending Danielle for the Croix de Guerre des théâtres d'opérations extérieurs avec Etoile d'Argent, Colonel Roos and Capitaine Goudry said that on 14 December 1945 Danielle parachuted with her radio into what they described as a very dangerous part of Laos with no reception committee. Despite being wounded on landing and surrounded by hostile forces, she showed calm and composure. Thanks to her constant efforts and devotion, she saved numerous human lives and participated in the evacuation of all the French from the province where she was working and transmitted vital military and political messages. However, the wound she got on landing resulted in her being hospitalised in Bangkok.[40]

On 29 March 1946, having recovered from her injury, she was sent from Saigon to China. This mission involved dealing with all the social problems raised by repatriating the French women and children who had been interned in Shanghai, separated from their husbands.

In 1948, she interrupted her career in the army and returned to her original administrative job with Postes, Télégraphes et Téléphones, (PTT) the French administration of postal services and telecommunications. Given her extensive knowledge of Indochina, the Ministry of France Overseas sent her back to Saigon to head a unit of radio-electricians. In 1949, she was appointed chief of BCR in Vietnam (Laos) and Deputy Chief of 1st class Postage Radio. Transferred to Laos in 1951, she helped established the country's radio-electricians unit.

When she returned to France, she was assigned to PTT Vieux-Moulin, Oise, but, missing the action, in May 1955 she joined the Military Air Force and in October was sent back to Siam.

After further study, she was appointed the chief radio-electronics operator by the Minister of State for the Air Force, before settling in Perse-Beaumont, Aix-en-Provence, where she died on 1 July 1962.

For her work in the Far East, Danielle was awarded a Citation à l'ordre du Corps d'Armée. The British awarded her the Medal of the British Empire as well as an honorary Colonial medal. In 1953 she was given the Médaille en Argent du Million d'éléphants (à titre militaire) dans l'Ordre du Règne du Laos, the Médaille militaire and Médaille des Evadés.

MADELEINE DAMERMENT
Aged 26. Parachuted from a Halifax near Sainville, 33 km east of Chartres (Eure-et-Loir), on the night of 28/29 February 1944. Executed at Dachau. Awarded the King's Commendation for Brave Conduct, Companion de Légion d'Honneur and Medaille de Resistance.

Madeleine Damerment was born in Tortefontaine, Pas de Calais, on 11 November 1917, the second daughter of a senior civil servant in the French postal and telegraph service.

After a while living in Monastir, Tunisia, Charles Damerment was appointed postmaster in Lille, where Madeleine's younger sister was born. After finishing École Premiere Superieure 'Sevigne' in Roubaix, close to the Belgian border, her father got her a job as a clerk in the Post Office.

Following the German occupation, she and other members of her traditional Catholic family worked with Michael Trotobas on the PAT escape line. Trotobas had been born in France, joined the British Army, fought in Northern France and was evacuated from Dunkirk. Recruited and trained by SOE, he was parachuted near Argenton-sur-Creuse, Indre, with Ben Cowburn, wireless operator André Bloch, J. P. du Puy, George Langelaan and Victor Gerson (Giliana's husband) on 6 September 1941.

Part of Trotobas's mission included working with Gerson to make arrangements for helping escaped Allied prisoners of war and downed aircrews to cross the demarcation line into unoccupied France, particularly to Toulouse and Marseille. From there, members of Dr Albert Guerisse's PAT escape line helped them cross into Spain where MI9 helped them get back to Britain.[41]

While helping in this work, she met 19-year-old Roland Lepers, and a British escapee, 34-year-old Sergeant Harold Cole. She accompanied them on several trips, subsequently getting engaged to Lepers. Cole was accused of embezzling MI9's funds and, avoiding the escape line organisers, he ended up being captured by the Germans in 1941.

According to the historian, Iain Adamson, Cole collaborated with the Gestapo and denounced many important people in the Resistance, including the leaders of the PAT line. At least 150 were arrested, a third of whom were executed.[42]

After a number of arrests in late-1941, Roland got her away from her house before the police arrived and arrested her family. They went south to Tulles to wait until their escape could be organised. Having to separate in Barcelona, she was caught and spent several months in an internment camp until the British Consulate arranged her release. Eventually, she reached Lisbon and was flown out on 27 June.

On arriving in England, she was sent to Nightingale Lane. In her interview with Security Officer P. Van Dyck, she provided details of her experiences in France and Spain. Her report was particularly valuable to MI9 who would have used the intelligence to brief other agents and RAF crews about evasion as well as other escape line organisers and workers.

This woman studied at the Primary and later Secondary School in ROUBAIX where her father was at the time holding a responsible position with the postal and telegraph service.

She left school at the age of 16 and has remained with her parents ever since. She also obtained a job at the post office as a clerk through her father's connections.

From soon after the collapse of France, the family DAMERMENT became active members of an organisation whose main object was to assist French prisoners of war, and before Madeleine actually realised what was happening she found herself to be taking a very keen interest in this sort of work and in the welfare of the French prisoners of war and their escape.

Many stray soldiers were roaming about the LILLE district or were in hiding with various families.

One day a man named DELMOTTE, a young student at the Roman Catholic High School who made himself generally useful at the Centre d'Acceuil functioning in Lille, came to see her at her father's place together with an Englishman by the name of David BIN (she was not very certain of the spelling of this name) and begged them to help this man.

This case was to be the start of a series of similar escape cases of British subjects, in which young Madeleine was to take such a prominent and important part later on.

Her father was a man of good social standing, highly esteemed in local government circles, a personal friend of the Mayor of LILLE and besides holding a position of responsibility at the General Post Office. Her mother was on the committee of various benevolent societies and welfare centres and under this convenient cover was actively engaged in assisting the escape of Frenchmen and also British subjects, affording them shelter, very frequently in her own house, putting them up with reliable friends or providing food and clothes.

Madeleine became very interested in BIN's case, whom she was determined to get away safely. She called on her friend Mademoiselle MIMEBOIS, who lived in the rue de Cambrai and whose people had a greengrocer's shop. There the family MIMEBOI were also frequently sheltering and helping prisoners of war. She took David BIN along to these people who eventually disposed of him and got him safely away.

Shortly after this Madeleine got hold of another young Englishman of about 20 years of age, who had been very badly wounded, she put this young boy up at her father's house.

It was during this young man's stay with her parents that a man called GRENUE, residing on the Grand Boulevard, informed her that the Germans had found out all about their activities and strongly advised her to get out of LILLE. As the Authorities had already called on her parents twice in connection with certain suspicious activities which they thought were going on in their house, she got more or less nervous and decided to leave her parents. This was, she thinks, November 1940.

In order to get through the Red Zone [about 1,200 square kilometres of northeast France designated after First World War as physically and environmentally too dangerous for human habitation due to the number of unexploded bombs, destroyed buildings, human and animal remains] she got herself a false Identity Card which she obtained from the owner of a café in the rue de Douai, which was owned by a man called JACQUES. She said that this man was later rounded up and found out by the Germans; the identity Card was in her own name, but it showed that she was regularly domiciled in PARIS.

She crossed the Red Line by train in PERONNE, and the demarcation line she crossed near VIERZON. This was accomplished with the help of a postman who crossed over this line sometimes two or three times a day, and on learning that her father and herself were connected with the post office, this postier helped her across the demarcation line.

She first of all went to TARBES and visited her [elder married] sister [Janine Larque] there. During her stay there she also went to TULLE (CORESE [sic]) and visited Mr and Mrs JOUHARD, residing at 46 Avenue Victor Hugo. She also visited Pauline TETSSANDIER who is a daughter of the JOUHARD family. Together with this young lady she also went to NICE and MONTE CARLO. This was more of a pleasure trip than anything else and made in order to recuperate. She stayed at the Hotel Regine in NICE.

She managed to keep in contact with her parents and was greatly relieved to learn that nothing serious had happened to them so far. She therefore decided to go back to live, but was unable to fix up the papers necessary for this journey. After she had informed her people [in the escape line organisation] she received a telegram from her parents asking her to get in touch with two men who would meet her at the Hotel Regina, facing the railway station in TOULOUSE.

These two men were to take her back clandestinely to the north of France. She arrived in TOULOUSE about the 25 April and at the appointed place she met Sergeant Harold COLE, known as PAUL, and Englishman, and a Mr Roland LEPERS, a Frenchman to whom she was later to become engaged.

Together with these two men and her younger sister Charline, who was with her at the time, they returned to LILLE. When she arrived, she found a full house. There were indeed about 10 British people in hiding there. Many British women in these days were being sent to special camps and [sic] tried to conceal themselves with private people.

At her house, she found a Mrs GARNER with her three girls, a Canadian lady with her two sons and three British soldiers, Robert MACLEYLAND and another two who were known as JOHN and RENY. JOHN and MACLEYLAND had been hidden for some time in a hospital in HAESEBROEK.

Madeleine was, of course, astonished to see as many people, and there was not even room for her in the house.

The man PAUL was in turn a friend and in very close contact with M. DUPREZ. DUPREZ lived in LA MADELEINE, a little suburb of LKILE and he was working at the Mairie [Town Hall] there. In this capacity, DUPREZ made himself very useful in providing food, clothes and cards for the British prisoners of war in hiding.

She observed that both her parents were very active in helping wherever this was possible. She was more or less dragged into the whole business by her parents and it was very often her duty to collect these British prisoners from various places and then take them back either to her house or to pre-arranged abodes. in this connection she mentions the house of Mme MOISE in the rue Jean Maillot at LA MADELEINE, Mr and Mrs Potter, rue Chanay, Mrs Planque, living in WAMBRECHIES, and the house of Mrs CARDEN, rue de Marquette, WAMBRECHIES. Madeleine was engaged in this sort of work, which needless to say entailed immense risks until she had to leave FRANCE.

It was soon after she returned home that she became suspicious of the man, COLE, known as PAUL. She tells me that he got himself entangled with a number of women and that his mistress was a certain Mme Suzanne Deram. Mme Suzanne, in the beginning, was a very beautiful woman who also did good work, but the couple lost their heads when PAUL, who was in charge of certain escape organisations, mainly concerned with bringing prisoners of war from the north of

FRANCE to MARSEILLES, instead of using the money for this purpose, apparently kept it to himself and spent it on this woman and probably other women. Besides PAUL came to the house of Madeleine's father very frequently and squeezed everything out of her mother that he could. He not only asked her for money but even for clothes which he said were wanted for British airmen.

PAUL and his mistress were leading a most extravagant existence and one day when Madeleine called at PAUL's place she said she found there a real store full of food provisions and clothes, enough to provide for a squad of men.

Roland and PAUL were working in close contact with the MARSEILLES organisation, but PAUL was more or less in charge of the convoys. Towards the end of October and the beginning of November, PAUL and Roland left with 13 men, including a British Squadron Leader by the name of BUFTON, a Sergeant-Pilot and a wireless operator. Their destination was MARSEILLES, and the journey was safely accomplished, but M. DUPREZ was also waiting in MARSEILLES and wanted to square up with PAUL, who had during the last month embezzled considerable sums of money which were given to him, she thinks by a man called [Lieutenant-Colonel Ian] GARROW. These sums ran into 10s of thousands of francs.

All this led to a split between the man PAUL and the rest of the organisation and Roland shortly afterwards got himself into difficulties and was arrested while he was staying at the Hotel PARIS-NICE, MARSEILLE.

The man DUPREZ thereupon returned to the north of FRANCE with another man called Andre MASON who, it had been decided should take the place of PAUL in the future.

A man known as M. JOSPEH, who belonged to the MARESEILLES organisation then came to LILLE and told DEPREZ that somebody should be sent to MARSEILLES at once to try and liberate M. Roland, as it was not known for what reason he had been arrested. Madeleine thereupon decided that she would undertake the journey and this mission.

She crossed the Red Line clandestinely at Abbeville with the help of Abbe CARPENTIER, who had given her the necessary papers, and to her astonishment, she learnt that Roland was not detained in MARSEILLES, but in ABBEVILLE. She managed to get in touch with him somehow and to establish that he had merely been arrested for clandestinely passing into unoccupied FRANCE.

In order to clear himself, Roland Lepers had put up a cooked story to the German interrogators, whom he told that he was at the time on his way to PARIS where he was employed as a waiter in the restaurant DUPONT in the quartier St Maritaine. In order to convince the Germans of this Madeleine went to PARIS to this restaurant DUPONT, where PAUL and the prisoner generally put up and asked the manager there to give her a written statement to confirm the story of Roland LEPER. PAUL happened to be in the restaurant dining with women and he refused to give madeleine the statement she was after. PAUL eventually split the beans there as well and she was obliged to return.

She had, however, discovered that PAUL was now entirely unreliable and dangerous. Roland was liberated as the penalty for his offence is generally a light one.

She naturally told the organisation in LILLE that she had seen PAUL, of whose arrest she learnt later when she was at Mme VOGGLIMACOI's place, a coiffeuse at 2 rue le Turenne, LA MADELEINE. PAUL it appeared had been arrested with his mistress, Mrs DERAM. This old course was a disaster which resulted in the arrest of M. DUPREZ and another man named CHEVALIER and others working for the organisation. M. DUPREZ, however, had sent a warning to Madeleine and told her to leave occupied FRANCE at once.

On or about 22 December 1941, she left with Roland, who had now become her fiancé, and her object was to settle down in unoccupied FRANCE with her sister. Before she left, however, she went to ROUBAIX where she stayed for a short while with Mrs TALMAN at 18 rue Ingres. There she met the man MAZON, who had taken PAUL's place.

They arrived in MARSEILLES towards the end of December, and they told the organisation there what had happened up north.

The couple were put up with a friend there, Mme THSANDIER whose husband was a cinema director at TULLE, but the organisation in MARSEILLES thought it would be far better for Madeleine to get out of France altogether as the Germans might even be able to get hold of her there. It was therefore decided to come to this country. [There was no indication what funds she had available to make the journey, whether it was her own money, her parents, or given to her by MI9.]

She left TULLE in March 1942 and crossed the Spanish frontier with the help of the escape organisation in TOULOUSE. A man called MARIO was looking after her and besides herself, there were about 4 or 5 other people in the party. They all went to BANYULS first and crossed the PYRÉNÉES with the assistance of a guide, reaching BARCELONA on or about the 10 March 1942.

In BARCELONA Madeline and Roland were obliged to part, owing to arrangements made by the British there. She was billeted with a private family there and left BARCELONA on 10 March in a British Consular car for MADRID, where she was allowed to stay in the house of Mr CRESSWELL [an MI9 officer]. This latter then fixed up an emergency set of false papers and made arrangements for her to travel to BADAJOZ.

There she was to pick up a guide but was unfortunately arrested in the train on the 24 April, because her papers were no longer valid. She spent two days in prison there and was then sent back to MADRID where she was locked up for about two weeks in the cellars of the Securidas people. The treatment she had there was extremely rough and degrading to the utmost.

On 6 May she was allowed to be transferred to the prison VANTAS, from where she was released on the 30 May. Madeleine immediately reported to the British Embassy, who put her up at the Hotel MORA where she remained about 8 days.

On the 6 June as she was paying a visit to the well-known aumonier [chaplain], LE CLEF, the police entered this man's house and although she had been concealed in an adjoining room, LE CLEF was asked to produce his visitor. It happened that the police officer who came to LE CLEF's house was the same man who handled her case in BADAJOZ and MADRID. He recognised her at once and she was arrested again and thrown into the horrible cellars of the Securidas, from which she was released on 12 June 1942.

Mr CRESSWELL then took her up again and made her stay at his own place. There she was given a British Emergency Certificate, and she was taken to LISBON in the diplomatic car, with an officer of the British Embassy.

She arrived safely in LISBON on the 20 June 1942. In LISBON she stayed with Mr and Mrs JOHNS [he was MI9's representative in Lisbon] who had been informed about her and on 27 June she was put on a plane taking her to this country where she arrived at BRISTOL Airport on 27 June 1942.[43]

Further questioning about Lepers and Cole followed and a similar report can be found in her personnel file. In conclusion, her interrogator commented that, 'My personal impression of this lady is very favourable and her story quite interesting, although under a great nervous strain, she was unable to coordinate her statements.'[44]

She went to live at Rycote Park, Milton Common, near Oxford, where she was employed as a French teacher. Whether her employer was involved in MI9 or SOE is unknown. Having got in touch with Lepers, she found out that he no longer wanted to marry her. The engagement was broken off, and they went their separate ways. Lepers joined the RAF.

Allocated the cover name Martine Dussautoy and given a commission as an ensign in the FANY, she was described in her personnel file as 5 ft 4 inches tall, short, fattish, light brown hair, brown eyes, snub nose and having an appendix scar. Her hobbies were music, reading and riding.

Sent to Scotland for paramilitary training, Captain Dixon-Robertson, her signals instructor at Inverie (STS 24), determined that, only being considered fair for sending and receiving messages, she was unsuitable for work as a wireless operator. Captain Smith reported that for physical training she was a 'keen and hard worker with good stamina.' She had a good grasp of the principles of close combat, worked well and was aggressive. For rope work, she was reported to have had fair muscular strength and good coordination but required more practice. She worked well and showed keenness in fieldcraft although she found the theoretical side difficult. For weapons training, she was reported to have improved and was 'now a fair shot with pistol and carbine, but is lacking in aggressiveness.'

She was very good at explosives and demolitions, both in theoretical and practical work.

'Extremely keen and make up splendid charges.' For signalling and communications she 'made a very good show at the beginning but fell away. Not very keen, but did her best.' She was very good at writing route reports, being 'accurate and painstaking. Fairly good at reading, and would develop with practice.' For schemes and tactics, she was considered to have been a 'very hard-working member of a band on all schemes and has a good knowledge of tactics as well as a fund of common sense.' She was not very interested in boat work but 'worked well and acquired a fair knowledge of elementary small boat handling and of knots.[45]

Captain Parson, the Commandant, reported that, 'I have not a great deal of faith in this student. Although she has a good brain, she is too temperamental and not sufficiently impersonal for a first-class student. She has, however, a good sense of humour and a certain amount of charm and intelligence.'[46]

After celebrating her first Christmas and New Year in England, she was sent to Beaulieu, for a clandestine warfare course. Major Wedgwood, an instructor at the House on the Shore (STS 33), reported in the beginning of February that,

She is quite intelligent, practical, shrewd, quick and resourceful. She has imagination and cunning. Although she seemed keen, she did not always work very hard.

Her character is strong, but she is self-centred, rather irresponsible and sometimes impatient and turbulent. She is temperamental, and personal relationships play a considerable part in her life. She seemed deeply attached to her friends.

Her personality is vivacious, and she can be pleasant when she wants to be, but she is also inclined to be malicious and sullen when she does not get her own way. She has a strong sense of humour.

This student should make a satisfactory subordinate under a strong leader, but she would need careful handling.

CODES. Taught innocent Letter based on Playfair, with conventions. Double transposition. Letter One-time pad and secret censorship. Further practice required.[47]

To avoid her family in France being compromised should she be arrested, her cover story, that she was a telephonist, was close to but not exactly the same as her real life.

Given the code names Solange and Dancer, her mission was to work as a courier with Major France Antelme, code named Renaud, the organiser of the BRICKLAYER circuit in the Le Mans area.

On 29 February 1944, she parachuted from a 161 Squadron Halifax near Sainville, 33 km east of Chartres. Accompanying her were Antelme and his wireless operator, Captain Lionel Lee, code named Mechanic and DAKS. Although not mentioned in Tillet's list of infiltrations, her personnel file reported that she was also dropped with Henri Garry, but he had been arrested in France on 18 October 1943.[48]

Three days later, the SIS reported that all three agents had been arrested as soon as they landed. The Gestapo who had been waiting for them took them to Fresnes prison. On 6 June, this was confirmed in a message from a German-controlled circuit.

Subsequent investigations revealed that, in June 1943, the Gestapo had captured Francis Suttill, the head of the PROSPER network operating in the Paris area, and many members of his group including Gilbert Norman, one of his wireless operators, with his set. Norman was taken to No. 84 and reported to have been forced to transmit German-inspired messages back to SOE's London HQ. To let them know he was operating under duress, he was said to have deliberately omitted his second security check.

London's reply that he had made a mistake by forgetting the check alerted the Gestapo that he had tricked them. Whether he voluntarily gave them the second check or had it tortured out of him is unknown but the Germans were able to 'play' his set back to London, allowing them to order weapons, ammunition, explosives and sabotage devices, supplies, money, more agents and up-to-date wireless and ground-to-air communication equipment. They were able to provide London with the details of the DZ and the date and time their reception committee would be waiting, and apprehend them with their machine guns, Alsatian dogs and handcuffs.

It is worth noting that the Germans controlled about a dozen SOE wireless sets in France prior to D-Day. (Communication with historian Declan O'Reilly.)

Another SOE wireless operator captured in Paris in October 1943 was Noor Inayat Khan. Her wireless, codebook and copies of all her messages were found in her apartment which allowed the Gestapo to play back her set as well. Again, SOE did not pick up that it was German-inspired messages they were receiving.

Madeleine, Antelme and Lee were not the only SOE agents captured as a result of this playback; fifteen others were. Subsequent evidence shows that they were taken first to Avenue Foch for questioning and then to Fresnes. Exactly what happened to Madeleine over the subsequent two months is unknown. However, Antelme and Lee were tortured and eventually transported to Gross-Rosen Concentration Camp where they died.

On 12 May 1944, Madeleine, Andrée Borrel, Odette Sansom, Eliane Plewman, Yolande Unternährer, Diane Rowden, Noor Inayat Khan, Vera Leigh, and other captured SOE agents, were taken by train to Karlsruhe, a journey of about 560 km, where they were put into the civilian jail for women. They remained there until the early hours of 12 September.

Kramer interviewed a German woman prisoner with whom Madeleine shared a cell and was told that during the heavy RAF raids on Karlsruhe, she clasped her rosary beads and prayed. Sometimes they sang to keep her spirits up and exchanged stories about their homes and families. Her German cell mate had been imprisoned having been informed on for telling a joke about Hitler in the street.[49]

Atkins, assisted by an SAS team who wanted to find out what happened to some of their colleagues, succeeded in locating witnesses involved with their deaths. In her report on Madeleine, she stated that,

I have seen the following witnesses apart from Mrs Odette Sansom in connection with their stay in Karlsruhe: -

Frau Becker and Fraulein Hager, in charge of the women's jail, Karlsruhe, as well as the 3 temporary wardresses all of whom remember the girls. I have also seen Fraulein Hedwig Muller, 28 in Gruen, Karlsruhe-Rueppurr, who shared a cell with Madeleine Damerment whom she knew as Martine Dussautoy. I enclose a letter from Hedwig Muller which she asks should be forwarded to Martine's mother.

I also saw Frau Else Sauer of 3 Nachtigalerweg, Rheinstrandsiedlung, Karlsruhe, who was in Martine's cell the night she was fetched away. I attach Frau Sauer's sworn statement. From this, it will be seen that she also knew Eliane Plewman at the same time as Martine.

I also saw Nina Hagen of 5 Ortizner Strasse, Durlach, near Karlsruhe, who shared a cell with Yolande Beekman [Unternährer – a Swiss F Section agent]. I attach a translation of her deposition.

Whilst in Karlsruhe prison the girls were not ill-treated; they were put into separate cells which they shared with one or two German prisoners – most of them appear to have been political rather than criminal prisoners – and there is no doubt that Hedwig Muller, Else Sauer and Nina Hagen struck up a very real friendship with our girls and that they did everything possible to help them by sharing their food parcels and having their laundry washed, etc. Nevertheless, they had, obviously, a very hard time of it and they became very anxious when first the four girls and then Odette Sansom disappeared, and they could find out nothing about their fate. They were locked in their cells during the heavy raids on Karlsruhe and apparently showed amazing courage and cheered up their cell-mates, all of whom spoke of them with the greatest admiration.

On the afternoon of 11 September, Frau Becker received instructions to prepare the girls for departure early next morning and she went round to each of the cells and returned to the girls their personal belongings and told them that they would be moving off the next day. At about 0130 a.m. on 12 September they were called out of their cells by an elderly male warder who was on night duty and were taken down to the reception room where they were collected by Gestapo officers. I have interrogated various members of the Karlsruhe Gestapo and in particular, the two officials who accompanied the girls to Dachau [about 330km]. Their accounts of the journey differ in several respects, but I am satisfied that, in broad outline, the following took place: -

The girls were driven by car, accompanied by 3 Gestapo officials, two of whom have been identified as Kriminalsecretar [Max] Wassmer and [Christian] Ott, to the station at Karlsruhe or of the nearby town of Bruchsal and caught the early train for Munich, arriving in late afternoon. Here they changed trains and caught the last train to Dachau, some 20 miles North-West of Munish [sic]. They arrived after dark and had to walk to the camp which they reached about midnight. They were handed over to some camp official and spent the night in the cells. Between 8 and 10 the next morning (13 September) they were taken to the crematorium compound.[50]

In *Unearthing Churchill's Secret Army*, Grehan and Mace quote Ott's testimony after the war about what happened next,

The four prisoners had come from the barrack in the camp, where they had spent the night, into the yard where the shooting was to be done. Here he [his colleague Max Wessmer] had announced the death sentence to them. Only the Lagerkommandatur and two SS men had been present.

All four had grown very pale and wept; the major [Madeleine Damerment] asked whether they could protest the sentence. The Kommandant declared that no protest could be made against the sentence. The major then asked to see a priest. The Kommandant refused this on the grounds that there was no priest in the camp.

The four prisoners now had to kneel down with their heads towards a small mound of earth and were killed by the two SS, one after another by a shot through the back of the neck. During the shooting, the two English women held hands and the two Frenchwomen likewise. For three of the prisoners the first shot caused death, but for the German-speaking English woman [Beekman] a second shot had to be fired as she still showed signs of life after the first shot.[51]

When the Allies first learnt of their deaths is unknown. It was Vera Atkins who obtained much of the information about their execution and immediate cremation. She also obtained details of the fate of the other seven SOE women executed by the Germans. Once back in England, she undertook to make the arrangements to inform Madeleine's mother and sister about the details of her death, stressing that she and the other girls were not ill-treated in prison, that the news of the invasion and Allied advance had buoyed up their morale, and they never lost courage nor their faith.

The Mother Superior of the French Sacred Heart convent in Hitchin, whom Madeleine had named as her executor, was also informed and told that it was not known whether the death sentence was read out before she was executed but that 'until the end she was cheerful and of good faith and that while suffering equal hardship she was spared the horrors of a concentration camp. Madeleine worked and sacrificed her life for the Allied Cause, and this will not be forgotten by all who knew her both here and in France.'[52]

After the war, the French government posthumously awarded her the Légion d'Honneur, Croix de Guerre and the Médaille de la Résistance.

The British awarded her the King's Commendation for Brave Conduct. She is recorded on the Brookwood Cemetery Memorial in Surrey as one of the SOE agents who died for the liberation of France. She is also listed on the FANY memorial at St Paul's Church, Knightsbridge, London and on the 'Roll of Honour' on the Valençay SOE Memorial in Indre. On the south wall of the crematorium at the former Dachau concentration camp, there is a plaque commemorating Madeleine, Eliane Plewman, Noor Inayat Khan and Yolande Beekman (Unternehrer).

JEANNE BOHEC
Aged 25. Parachuted from a Halifax near Alençon, (Orne), on 29 February 1944.

The next Frenchwoman infiltrated into France was Jeanne Bohec, a 25-year-old RF Section sabotage instructor, one of the very few women to be trained at Brickendonbury. She was the first of ten women the RF sent into France and was flown out of Tempsford on 1 March 1944, to work with the Resistance in Brittany leading up to D-Day.

Her personnel file reports her as born in Tourlaville, an eastern suburb of Cherbourg, Normandy, on 16 February 1919. A family source claimed it was Plestin Greves, near Lannion, Brittany. She grew up accompanying her father and grandfather on trips around the coast.

In her autobiography, *La Plastiqueuse à Bicyclette*, she described herself as a 'sailor girl' and commented that if she had had XY chromosomes she would have lived her life on the sea. Her ambition, however, was to become a mathematics teacher but, on leaving school, she worked as an assistant chemist in a gunpowder factory in Brest, preparing to do a degree in Chemistry. She writes,

> August-September 1939. The war!
> We have long felt the future. Since I was old enough to think, I think I knew what was waiting for us, that sooner or later we would get it. And I felt concerned as much as any man in France. (...) I felt a very acutely the desire to participate in this war, to do something, but what?[53]

On the day the German troops arrived in Brest, the 21-year-old left for England in a tug boat. Arriving in Plymouth on 21 June 1940, after her debrief she was sent to Anerley School, formerly the North Surrey District School, near Bromley, South London.

To improve her English, she went to work as an au pair looking after an English couple's baby.

She claimed not to have heard General de Gaulle's call for the French people to resist, but she wanted to do something to help. On 6 January 1941, she was among the first five women to be accepted into de Gaulle's Corps Volontaires Françaises. Trained as a nursing assistant, she reported that, 'I hated it. I had chemistry and scientific training and had worked with gunpowder. I hadn't escaped France and joined up just to fold bandages.'[54]

She took lessons in stenography, but insisted on being able to put her knowledge of explosives to good use. Promoted to corporal in the FFL, the Free French Forces, she was eventually posted as a technical secretary to the armaments section in Carlton Gardens.

By spring 1942, she was transferred to the French College's engineering department laboratory, researching the best ways of using chemicals bought from a pharmacy as explosives. All her colleagues were hospitalised at one time or another for burns. Their formulas, to this day, remain secret.

While working at the laboratory, she was introduced to Henry Frenay. He had been a leading member of the Resistance who had helped start the National Liberation Movement and Combat, wrote for Verités, an underground newspaper, and escaped to England in 1943. De Gaulle appointed him a minster of prisoners, refugees and deportees and he must have visited the laboratory to observe the work done by Jeanne and her colleagues.

When she asked why the Resistance could not be taught in France, she was told that no women were sent as agents.

> I kept banging my head against the wall. But then I am from Brittany and Bretons are stubborn. So I asked and asked, to the point where they finally said, all right. I was the first woman to be taken by the BCRA and sent to France.[55]

After repeated requests, in late-sumer 1943, the RF Section changed their minds. She succeeded in persuading them to let her use her explosive skills to train BCRA agents about to be dropped into France.

Sent to Winterfold (STS 7) for assessment, she was the only woman in a group of seven. Her report graded her as C with an intelligence rating of B. Although she failed her Morse code and got 'Poor' for Instructional, she got 'Good' for mechanical.

> An intelligent practical girl of diminutive stature with common sense and composure. She is quick and observant and seldom at a loss for ideas. She is at present inexperienced and has not yet acquired the requisite balance in her relations to others, but she is well able to hold her own and should improve with training. In view of her special knowledge,

which should be checked, she might make a useful adviser, otherwise courier. It is not considered that she would make an instructor.'[56]

Sent for paramilitary training to West Court (STS 6), Acting Lieutenant Hodson described her as speaking French and English fluently, having chemistry and explosives as hobbies and knowing Brittany well between Morlaix and Lannion, Brest, Augers and Le Havre. She was

a strange little lady. I should think she is less than 5 ft [1.5 m] tall but a regular little tomboy, and seems to enjoy being thrown about by the boys. As soon as she comes into a room she starts scrapping with one or other of them. She is well-educated [with a] Baccalaureat and preparing for a chemist's degree when war broke out. She has been in the French ATS since 1941 and speaks English well. Her hobby is making homemade explosives. I should think she is a capable, determined little person and well able to look after herself. She is intelligent and quick witted.

I understand this student is leaving STS 6 tomorrow Friday to continue her training in another school. She seems to me to be a capable and intelligent young woman and is very keen on her work and anxious to get into the field. From the security point of view, I think she is perfectly reliable.[57]

Major Dunn-Hills added that for physical training she

'has done silent-killing and has learnt quite a lot on this subject. She is much below average in size and strength, but appears quite fit.' She did not do any fieldcraft but for weapons training she was reported to be 'quite an accurate shot with the pistol.' For Explosives and Demolitions she was said to have has 'a great deal of experience, and a complete knowledge of the manufacture of explosives. She did little map reading and no reports but did well in signalling classes, receiving at 9 w.p.m. and sending at 10 w.p.m.

She obviously has a very complete knowledge of explosives. She has shown moderate interest in the methods taught at this school. She would make an excellent instructor in home-made explosives. She is extremely keen to get on with the job as quickly as possible... I think she can be taught little else in that or any other subject here.'[58]

On 3 October 1943, she was sent to Hartford House (STS 32a), Beaulieu, for Group B's clandestine warfare training where her instructor reported her as

intelligent, shrewd, quick and practical as well as being highly educated. She has a considerable imagination. She is keen and worked hard, is thorough and has plenty of initiative. She has a strong character, an equable temperament and seems to have plenty of determination and courage. Her loyalty is beyond question, she has a pleasant, unassuming personality, is not at all shy, is a good mixer and has a strong sense of humour. She should be popular everywhere. She has some powers of leadership and could be relied upon to do well at any job within her powers. Her inconspicuous appearance should be an asset. CODES: She requires further routine practice.[59]

Margaret Collins Weitz reported Jeanne saying how,

The training left me sceptical about my own chances against a strong, determined man, but perhaps someone caught off guard would find it hard to overpower me. In any case, the training gave us confidence in our potential and a combative spirit that would be essential to us. [...] The English were fine. The only discrimination came from the men in the BCRA, who initially did not want women involved. I believe this is because France is a Latin country. Even today, it is difficult for women to get equal treatment. Men go to war; women stay home.[60]

During her parachute training she was the only woman in the group and, being small, had to have the harness specially adapted. According to her report, she did three drops between 17 and 22 October, including one at night and was graded 2nd class.

With her previous experience and an additional note suggesting that she 'would make an excellent instructress in Home Made explosives', on 26 September she was sent to Brickendonbury Manor (STS 17), near Hertford, for a week's course in Industrial Sabotage. She was the first and only Frenchwoman sent on such a course. When it was finished, her instructor commented that she was a 'capable and competent instructress. Weak in theory of chemistry. Practically up to LAB standards.'[61]

When she finished her training she was promoted to Second Lieutenant with a mission to train Jean-François Clouet des Perruches's GALILEE network in Brittany in using explosives. On being given her equipment, she crocheted a better secret compartment in the purse she was issued with, threw away her 'ladies' handgun and the 'L' pill, deciding that God would help her keep quiet if she was tortured.

Given the code names *Rateau* (rake) and *Pinasse* (flat-bottomed boat), her mission papers ordered her to go to France as an instructor of sabotage in the Region M3, Brittany. 'She will also be responsible to make a special investigation of manufacturing explosives in different regions. She will be sent on her own to contact our agent FANTASSIN,

Military Delegate in Region M who will give her the contact details of other Military Delegates.'[62]

Fantassin was the code name of Raymond Abeille, who had been dropped on 12 September 1943 near La Grande Place, 2 km north of Rivareenes, near Tours.[63] She was provided with 50,000 francs and told that more would be sent according to her results and to her needs. She was also provided with identity papers in the name of Geneviève Marie Guichard, and a cover story according to which she was a governess.

Marguerite Petitjean, her wireless operator, code named Hoe, had been dropped in January 1943. Jeanne, having been briefed for her mission, was taken to Gaynes Hall (STS 61) on 21 February to await her flight. After two flights from Tempsford had to be cancelled due to bad weather, on 29 February her conducting officer noted that Jeanne had already been supplied with a gun which was presumed to have been left at Gaynes Hall. 'However, to make sure, I am giving you a Suavage 32 with 50 rounds of ammunition. This gin [*sic*] has been tested several times and belongs to an agent who has been scrubbed [not sent].' As her pills and jumping kit had also been left, 'Mrs Irwin has a package of pills for Semoir which Rateau can jump with if she is willing to do so.'[64]

On that night, Flight Lieutenant Ashley of 138 Squadron dropped her, the only passenger, from his Halifax near Alençon, between Le Mans and Caen, Normandy.[65] The reception committee was organised by Clouet des Perruches, code name Galilé, who had not expected such a petite young woman. She reported him saying, 'What's going on? They're sending us children now!'[66]

After being taken to Paris, she got the train to Brittany in early March and bought a bike. To get around all the Breton departments, she cycled everywhere and by the beginning of April had set up her first 'training school' at Loudéac. Saboteurs were taught the best use of 'plastique', the French term for plastic explosives, for attacking the Germans and in particular how to frustrate their attempts to thwart the D-Day landings.

She reported that there was still time for her to get a suit and dress made. 'Dressing, sleeping, and eating properly are also elements of a clandestine life.' She repeated the explosives training in numerous localities over the next few months and became known as the 'plastiqueuse avec bicycle'. Demonstrating her expertise, she was involved in the 'Green Plan', attacks on the railway between Dinan and Vannes. As the detonators had not been included in the container with the explosives, she made a thirty-minute one herself.

She took part in the defence of Saint-Marcel, decoding their instructions from London. When the message came through to keep the German forces from getting to Normandy, she coordinated several parachute drops, but this team would not allow her to use a machine gun to help force the German troops out of Quimper. Her Maquis companions would have let her. 'I was considered a comrade – one of them. It was the men in uniform, the professional army. They couldn't accept the idea of a woman carrying guns.'[67]

In appreciation of her assistance, she was named the secretary of the regional chief of the Free French Forces in Finistère. When Quimper was liberated on 8 August, she returned briefly to London before returning to France and becoming a maths teacher and later mayor of the 18th arrondissement in Paris.

Although she did not receive a British award, in 1963 she was given the civilian award, Commander of the Order of Merit, a level lower than the Legion d'Honneur. In 1999 she published her autobiography, *La Plastiqueuse à Bicyclette*. She died on 11 January 2010, aged 90.[68]

DENISE BLOCH

Aged 28. Landed by Lysander near Baudreville (Eure & Loir) on 2 March 1944. Executed at Ravensbrück. Awarded the King's Commendation for Brave Conduct, Companion de Légion d'Honneur, Croix de Guerre and Medaille de Resistance.

Denise Bloch arrived in London from Lisbon on 21 May 1943, with identity papers in the name of Danielle Wood. Taken straight taken to Nightingale Lane for interrogation, it appears likely that SOE was aware of her arrival as Vera Atkins was sent to interview her. She claimed to have been sent by George Starr, one of F Section's agents operating in south-west France but the report he had entrusted her with to bring to London, she claimed had been confiscated during her escape through Spain. Following the interview in which she was keen to pass on as much of its details as she could remember, Atkins sent a report to Buckmaster informing him that,

> She struck me as being perfectly sincere, very eager to deliver her message and return to the fight. I have spoken to D/CE.5 [Major Baird of the Security Section] this morning and asked him to Y-box her report and have her interrogated as soon as possible and handed over to us on her return. [...]
>
> She left France at HILAIRE's request, about 1 May, in order to carry to us HILAIRE's Report, which, as you know, has been confiscated in Spain. Apparentntly his position is almost desperate as he is quite out of touch with London. He asks most urgently – hoping that it might be still done during the May Moon – for a W/T operator and for funds.
>
> HILAIRE is living at CASTELNAU-sur-l'AUVIGNON, about 8km. from CONDOM in the region of AGEN. He is very popular in the

neighbourhood where he is regarded as a gentleman farmer. He is very friendly with the Mayor and holds the position of 'Adjoint au Mairie'. He is about to obtain an official Card as 'Inspecteur pour le Ministère du Ravitaillement'. Apparentntly the neighbourhood is a very healthy one as all the Mayors and Officials are very pro-Allied, and HILAIRE has established amongst the peasants some very reliable reception committees, notably at CASTILLON and CONDOM. Unfortunately, so far there has been only one reception. In order to keep up morale, the goods then received were split into small lots and distributed over as wide an area as possible. It is essential to give these simple people proof positive, in tangible forms of arms and comforts, if they are not to lose faith, and it has been a very great disappointment that no deliveries were made to CONDOM, in spite of the fact that the message (VICTOIRE EMBRASSE JOSEPH) was sent out on several occasions. The reception committees on these grounds stand by during the whole of the Moon period.[69]

The name Danielle Wood was given her by MI6 officers in Spain to ensure the French authorities were unaware that she was in England. Born in Barault, Paris, on 21 January 1916, she was the only daughter of Parisian Jews, Jacques Bloch and Suzanne Levi-Strauss. She grew up at 51 Rue de Passy, Paris with three brothers, Jean-Louis, Jean-Claude, and Jean-Pierre, born eight years after her. Educated at Louveciennes, she learned English as a second language.

Research by Nigel Perrin, the author of *Spirit of Resistance*, an account of SOE agent Harry Peleuvé, revealed that, when the war started, Denise's father and two elder brothers served with the French army. Her father and Jean-Louis were captured and imprisoned by the Germans, but Jean-Claude returned to France and later joined the Resistance.

Over the next two years, Denise gained her first experiences of leading a secret life, as she, Jean-Claude and their mother adapted to living as Jews under Nazi rule, using false papers and constantly changing addresses to avoid police and Gestapo attention. By the summer of 1942, the situation in Paris had become extremely dangerous, and the family decided to move to the relative safety of Lyon, then still in the southern 'free' or unoccupied zone of the country. They left at the right time, just evading the Vel d'Hiv round-up: one of the worst atrocities in the city's history which resulted in the deportation of more than 12,000 Jews to the death camps. Adopting the surname 'Barrault', Denise, Jean-Pierre and her parents (her father had been released from captivity the previous year) were safely smuggled across the demarcation line.

As her account of her Resistance work used the code names of the agents she worked with, Pierre Tillet's list of infiltrations and exfiltrations and other sources have been used to identify most of them.

She lived in Paris until moving to Lyon on 17 July 1942 where she worked as secretary to Lt Jean-Maxime Aron, code name Joseph, at Citroën's car plant in Lyon. Aron led the Jewish Resistance network and, helping him in this work, she met Réne Piércy, code named Etienne, the chief of Resistance in the city. Later she helped Captain Henri Sevenet, an F section agent code named Rodolphe, who had been parachuted on 25 August 1942 near Chedign on the Dauprat-Sevenet's estate, about 10 km north of Loches, to set up the DETECTIVE network. This group oversaw the Tours-Poitiers railway.

Through Aron and Sevenet, she had contacted two other Jewish SOE agents, Lt Maurice Pertschuk and Lt Marcus Bloom. Pertschuk's mission was to set up the PRUNUS network in Toulouse. Bloom landed with George Starr and worked as his wireless operator.[70]

She also helped find Brian Stonehouse, an F Section agent parachuted near Tours on 1 July 1941, with a wireless set, accommodation at Chateau Hurlevent near Lyon. When Blanche Charlet, another F Section agent arrived by felucca at Agay harbour on 1 September 1942, she moved in with Stonehouse and a romance developed. However, he was careless in transmitting for so long that the D-Fers were able to detect his location, and he and Blanche were arrested on 24 October. He was put in solitary confinement and endured interrogation and torture before being transferred to Fresnes Prison. He was later sent to Saarbrücken and Mauthausen concentration camps, a Luftwaffe factory camp in Vienna and then to Natzweiler-Struthof camp in Alsace, where, it is claimed, he saved his life by drawing sketches of the camp commandant, the guards, and their families.

Blanche, having lost her lover, made an unsuccessful suicide attempt but, with the help of a prison wardress, got hold of pistols and spare keys and escaped in a mass break-out from Castres Prison with Suzanne Charisse, another Resistance member. They went into hiding, eventually being picked up by a boat on the Brittany coast in April 1944.[71]

Pertschuk was arrested during a rafle in Toulouse on 12 April 1943. As this was a police round-up of young men to be sent to work in Germany, Denise hoped he had been regarded as a Frenchman and held by the French police.

What was called the 'La Relève' was introduced on 22 June 1942 where one French prisoner of war would be returned to France for every three men who volunteered to go and work in Germany. Every week about 20,000 were picked up on the streets of Paris. The Germans expected

500,000 in the first six months. When it failed to raise the expected numbers, in February 1943, the Vichy government was compelled to introduce the Service du Travail Obligitaire (STO), compulsory work service. All French men had to register their birthdates. Those between nineteen and thirty-two were sent to work on the Atlantik Wall, in factories in Germany or on the Russian front as many German men were engaged in military duties. To avoid being called up, many young men left the towns and cities to go to live in the countryside and forming groups which became known as the Maquis. As a result, lone men were unusual on French streets.[72]

When Pertschuk did not reappear, there were worries that he might have been forced to denounce members of his Resistance group. Subsequent evidence showed that he was transported to Buchenwald concentration camp and executed on 29 May 1945, thirteen days before it was liberated.

On 3 November, Denise, Aron and Sevenet were on their way back from Marseille with details of potential drop zones when Aron was arrested at Lyon station. They had decided to split up on leaving the train, and although she got safely through the main exit, Aron was caught by twenty-five Gestapo officers controlling the side exit. Sevenet, who was just behind him, was not stopped. Aron had been betrayed, and the Gestapo found a photograph of him in his flat. Tillet reported that he was shot by the Gestapo on 11 May 1943 in Loyettes where there is a commemorative plaque.[73]

Denise appears to have also been denounced. The Lyon police had intercepted a telegram she sent to her mother telling her of her arrival, and although the family home was searched, nothing was found. She and Sevenet were met by Amadée Contran who hid them in Mme St Victor's house in St Laurent de Chamousset, near Lyon. A week later, they moved to Villefranche-sur-Mer, a small fishing village on the Mediterranean coast, where they hid until January 1943. The only trip she made was to Nice to have her dark hair dyed blonde.

When the weather got warmer, she moved to Toulouse where Sevenet introduced her to Sergeant Maurice Dupont, code named Ivan, a former French army officer and organiser of the DIPLOMAT network. He arranged for her to escape over the Pyrénées but the attempt was thwarted by deep snow and enemy patrols. Back in Toulouse, she was introduced to George Starr.

When Piércy was arrested about 20 April 1943, Starr took over what was left of both organisations and, as Denise considered his French had too much of an English accent, she acted as his adjutant and courier. She reported that he knew the location of all the depots where the SOE's arms and ammunition had been hidden.

Having lost access to the finances Pertschuk had provided, Starr needed assistance. Worried about the prospect of further arrests, he sent Denise down one of the escape lines with a report to take to London. It was too long to transmit by wireless as, by then, ten minutes was the maximum time operators were recommended transmitting to avoid detection by goniometrists. She did not mention that Dupont accompanied her in her report. Vera Atkins explained to Buckmaster that,

> It would appear, however, that HILAIRE himself is in great danger owing to the many arrests all round, and he may also be gravely endangered by the loss of his Report. It was written en clair and addressed to ROOM 055A. It requested a W/T and further deliveries during the May Moon at CONDOM T.25, CASTILLON Y.30 and one other ground. It also gave the messages attached to these Grounds. HILAIRE also requested a Lieutenant.[74]

The Germans were executing anyone found providing shelter to English parachutists, whom they called 'terrorists', and offering 10,000 francs to anyone providing information leading to their arrest. Anyone found listening to the BBC or being involved with or supporting the Resistance was arrested, interrogated, possibly tortured, imprisoned or sent to concentration camp. While bribery, the use of large sums of money, including gold, to secure their release did happen, it was not common.

The report of Denise's interrogation shed light, not just on what life was like in Southern France in 1942 and 1943, but also on the difficulties faced by members of the Resistance while operating in the field and the worries they had when colleagues disappeared.

CELESTINE AND CHRISTIANE

Source was in LYONS at the time of the arrival of CELESTIN and CHRISTIANE at FEYZEN [*sic*]. [Captain Brian Stonehouse, code named CELESTIN was parachuted near Tours on 30 June 1942 to work as a wireless operator in the Lyon area. Valentine Charlet, code named CHRISTIANE, was landed by felucca at Agay harbour on 1 September 1942 to act as his courier and take over the work of Virginia Hall, an American SOE agent who had to escape over the Pyrénées.[75]] Feyzin is a southern suburb of Lyon, where, according to Perrin, he transmitted in an attic for three hours which allowed the D-Fers to locate him.] She knows that he [Stonehouse] was arrested because she met him in the street with two men, and when she followed them, she saw that he was taken to a police station. She is absolutely certain that she left LYONS on 26 October 1942 to go to MARSEILLES, so she is sure that the date of CELESTIN's arrest was either the 24 or 25 October. She did not see CHRISTIANE, but is convinced that she was arrested at the same time; she had heard two different versions of her capture. The first was that she had been standing beside CELESTIN when he was taken, and the second was that she was caught when she went down to the car to meet him.

It was thought that CELESTIN was actually working [on his wireless set] when he was arrested. The Frenchman who was hiding with him was taken at the same time, and source believes he was shot as well. CELESTIN knew of the organisation in MARSEILLES, but she did not think he could have been aware of any individual names because he worked with her organisation for only two months. He arrived about the middle of September, began working that month, and was caught in October, therefore he was working 2½ to 3 months (this is source's own arithmetic).

One of source's functions was to look after CELESTIN and accompany him about because he did not speak French very well; she acted as courier between him and JOSEPH. He [Stonehouse] was extremely good at drawing and always carried a sketchbook with him, in spite of the fact that she was continually telling him that it was dangerous. She used frequently to carry it under her own arm. On one occasion several members of the organisation had lunch together and afterwards she was asked to take CELESTIN to RODOLPHE's room. On the way he said to her in English in the middle of the street, 'After the war you must come to Scotland to see my house'. She thought he was very homesick and was too young for his job. [According to Escott, Denise's father tried unsuccessfully to bribe the guards for their release.]

The sequence of arrests was as follows:- CELESTIN and CHRISTIANE sometime before [*sic*] 24 October, L'ALLEMAND in MARSEILLES at the beginning of November, [L'ALLEMAND was the code name of Adrien Hess, one of de Vomécourt's agents who was involved in intelligence gathering and sabotage operations along the Riviera.] and then JOSEPH and they attempted one of herself in LYONS. She had been told by a lawyer that CELESTIN, CHRISTIANE, a man who was hiding CHRISTIANE and another whom she did not know, had all been shot. HILAIRE also said that he knew this, but did not tell her how he came by the knowledge. She was sure that the organisation would have heard if they still had been alive. She thought that they, like ETIENNE and EUGENE, were taken by the Gestapo, but that JOSEPH was arrested by the French.

L'ALLEMAND

After CELESTIN's arrest source went to MARSEILLES, where she met L'ALLEMAND. She had heard of him from JOSEPH, but it was the first time she had met him, and the first time she had been in MARSEILLES.

She did not know his full name and address, only his telephone number. She knew nothing about the circumstances of his arrest, except that she was present when JOSEPH rang him up on 2 November when a strange voice answered him. JOSEPH made an appointment, but instead of going to the rendezvous waited in a café next door. L'ALLEMAND never arrived, so they concluded that the telephone must have been answered by the Germans. Source met him for the last time at seven o'clock on the evening of 31 October, when he came along to her hotel and gave her GAUTHIER [de Vomécourt]'s report about landing grounds, etc., which she did not read as it was not her job. She thinks, therefore, that he must have been arrested either on the evening of the 1 November or perhaps on the morning of 2 November. She was quite sure that neither CELESTIN nor CHRISTIANE could have given him away; then added that she did not know about CHRISTIANE, but she was extremely discreet and never talked, so it was very unlikely. Source did not know CHRISTIANE's address in spite of the fact that she lunched with her every day in LYONS. She suggested that possibly CHRISTIANE passed through MARSEILLES when she first came to France, and something might have leaked out then.

JOSEPH

RODOLPHE met JOSEPH and herself in MARSEILLES with others for JOSEPH not to go back to LYONS. Although she had a feeling that something was wrong she volunteered to go in his place, but he insisted on accompanying her because she was a woman. On the way, RODOLPHE remarked to JOSEPH that he must not be caught with the papers on him, and volunteered to reconnoitre at the station in LYONS to see that the coast was clear. At first JOSEPH agreed, but finally, he refused to allow this. When they reached the station there were twenty-five people waiting for them. JOSEPH went out through the smaller entrance, where a control had been placed armed with his photograph. They were obviously waiting for him because after his arrest the control was removed. She saw him being taken away in a car. RODOLPHE, who was just behind him, was not noticed.

It was purely a matter of luck that she should have elected to leave the station by the larger entrance, where there was no control. There were eight men waiting for her, but as they had no photograph of her she was able to walk straight through. She admitted that she had sent a cable to her mother addressed to the office at 2 rue St Helene, in which she had said that she was arriving on Tuesday (3 November). As the police had been in possession of the office since the 31 October, they received the telegram and went to her mother, who said she did not know what her daughter was doing. Therefore, the police knew through her that she and

JOSEPH were coming, but they expected her with JOSEPH, and it was sheer luck that they had arranged to leave by separate exits which save her.

The police had been to JOSPEH's flat, taken everything and caught her friend, Madame? She thought they were able to identify him because of photographs of himself with his wife and children which he kept at his flat. The police also searched her mother's flat, but they failed to open the suitcase in which she had GAUTHIER's papers. They went to MENDELSOHN's flat, where there were about six or seven photographs of herself. It was because the police had these photographs that she changed from being a tall, sturdy, broad-shouldered and dark haired to a tall, sturdy, broad-shouldered blonde.

In source's opinion organisations are usually 'blown' through the wireless operator; he gets caught and the police find names and addresses amongst his papers. CELESTIN had a paper on which was a message to be sent to HILAIRE telling him to contact her at the rue St Helene, and she believes this is how they got everybody.

ADOLPHE

ADOLPHE [?] was arrested in MARSEILLES on the 2 November and taken to LYONS. When asked why he was arrested she replied that she did not know; they had been waiting for the excitement to die down before making enquiries.

MENDELSOHN

MENDELSOHN was a brother to her rather than anything else; she also had to engage herself to him because of her work. [He was another of Jean Aron's contacts.] He was very anxious to help the organisation and asked her to give him the chance, so as RODOLPHE was in another part of France and their staff was at that moment depleted, coupled with the difficulty of finding suitable recruits, she introduced him, and he was accepted. RODOLPHE at that time was expecting the arrival of HILAIRE.

After the arrest of MENDELSOHN, RODOLPHE and her father went to see the lawyer who was handling his case. At that time, the French had his dossier and said they would do their best to keep it as long as possible. HILAIRE has told her that he could secure the release of JOSEPH, MENDELSOHN, GAUTHIER and CHASSE [?] for 1,500,000 francs, the money to be sent directly to him.

EUGENE

Source did not know EUGENE [Pertschuk] very well, as she had lunch with him only three times, and saw him on perhaps three other occasions.

She was unable to say where he lived, or what name she went under, but knew that he had no occupation. She described him as follows:

Aged 28, about 5'10" or 5'11", very thin, looks half dead, face as if cut in wood, filthy dirty hair falling over his nose, could easily pass as French, looks like an artist's model. Bears a strong resemblance to the French actor, Jean Louie BARREAU.

The last time she saw him was in TOULOUSE on Monday 12 April when she had lunch with him. He was all right then, but rather worried. She acted as a courier between AGEN and TOULOUSE on Mondays and Thursdays, so she went to their usual café for lunch on the following Thursday, but he never came. She made enquiries from the proprietress but was told that he had not been seen since the Monday. Source then went in search of a woman who worked in a factory in addition to helping EUGENE but was told that no one had seen her since the previous Tuesday. Source believes that EUGENE must have been arrested on that Tuesday (13 April), but it is not known whether he was taken as English or French; HILAIRE is trying to find out, and he is also looking after the thirteen-year-old daughter of the factory worker. HILAIRE and she went to their private address in AGEN and waited for two days, as they knew that is EUGENE escaped he would go there, but he never came. She is quite sure that EUGENE would not have given away this address because he had it written down under a false number and false name of the town. This house belongs to a Spanish woman who is married to a Frenchman and hates the Germans. She met one of the organisation at a factory, and will do anything to help them. She gave HILAIRE the key to her house and permitted him and source to use a room there when they wanted to – 'we took it in turns to go there'.

HILAIRE

HILAIRE actually lives in CASTELNAU, where there are only about 200 inhabitants, half of whom are working for the organisation. The other half are very stupid and are under the impression that HILAIRE is an extremely rich man and just wants to get away from the war. There is no poste de gendarmerie. HILAIRE is at the Mairie, and is to be provided with a card as a food inspector, stating that the Germans must give him help if he requires it! HILAIRE should be told if the organisation does not intend to use the field at CASTELNAU, because there is no electricity, and it means that he has to travel 9km there and back each night to see if it can be used. He thought that the field was good, and could not understand why it had not been used more, but she had heard that it was very difficult to find. She herself had waited there many times for a plane. On one occasion a plane circled round for some time but failed to find the place, and eventually flew off. The next day the people in CASTELNAU who were not connected with the organisation reported that they had counted 27 German planes over that night.

The last time source saw HILAIRE was at AGEN on the 29 April, the day before she left France. She described him as being in a 'terrible mess'. He needs someone to help him as soon as possible, because he is now the only one left to control five departments (he is taking on LYONS and TOULOSE), and is he is arrested there is no one else. It was arranged at first that EUGENE was to give money each month to HILAIRE and herself, but this arrangement of course broke down with the arrest of EUGENE, and when she left HILAIRE he had only about 15,000 francs left.

He particularly asked source to request that the following articles should be sent to him by the next container:-

3 shirts

3 pairs of pants

2 pairs of pyjamas

Socks

Handkerchiefs

Toothbrush (they are unobtainable in France, and nail brushes, etc. are very acceptable.)

Soap (wanted very badly)

He asked that these articles should be put in one half of the comforts parcel. He would be especially glad of leather for soling shoes, as the organisation cannot afford to pay 3000 or 4000 francs for shoes. Extra shirts are also needed for the other men because they must look decent as they are then looked after better.

VICTOR

When asked if she knew anyone named VICTOR source replied at first that she did not, and enquired if the interrogator were thinking of HENRI [Sevenet], the real name of RODOLPHE. She added later that possibly VICTOR might be a tall, fat man working in the organisation in LYONS, and with whom she once had lunch.

URBAIN

Source never met URBAIN [Bloom], and had no idea what happened to him, except that he was probably arrested. He was EUGENE's radio contact near TOULOUSE, but she did not know where. The day after she left, HILAIRE was going to find out what had happened to him, but she thinks we would have heard if had been successful. There was no one else near EUGENE in the GAUTHIER organisation.

ETIENNE

There was only one person of this name; he was more or less the chief in LYONS. ETIENNE's wife knew all about the organisation, but fortunately, the Gestapo were unaware of this, and when she [Denise] left, HILAIRE was intending to interview her and obtain all her information.

THE RELEVE

TOULOUSE is a very dangerous place to be just now. The authorities will suddenly close a street and take all the young men in it for the releve, without even allowing them to go home. The actual arrests are usually made by French in uniform, but the German officials are just behind. This has been going on for the last five or six months. When she was more or less hiding in TOULOUSE, she heard people screaming and saw two men being taken in this way. The Gendarmerie are frequently helpful; in fact, when they received the containers in AGEN they used a car provided by the Gendarmerie.

It is most important that any agents sent to France now should not look younger than 25, whether they actually are or not, or otherwise they will certainly be taken. HILAIRE asks that the man sent to him should look between 28 and 40, and should speak French really fluently, as the Gestapo are now apt to take foreigners on principle, regardless of whether they have anything against them or not. The trouble with the Gestapo is that it is manned by Germans who have lived in France for twenty or twenty-five years and speak the language perfectly; even French people frequently do not realise that they are speaking to a German. She herself met two or three men in TOULOUSE and was astonished when she heard afterwards that they belonged to the Gestapo. HILAIRE speaks French extremely well, but all the same she could tell at once from his accent that he was English; for this reason, she always travelled everywhere with him. In the country he could pass with a peculiar accent with less difficulty than in the more sophisticated towns.

WIRELESS

Another reason why HILAIRE asks for a helper who speaks fluent French is that he knows of about 15 farms in villages around AGEN where the radio could be worked in turn; but this would obviously be impossible if the operator did not know French well. The set would be worked for only ten minutes at a time, and even if the Gestapo D/F'ing vans rushed to the farm, the operator would be well away when they reached it. HILAIRE considered that this was the only way to work properly. It was no use trying to send long reports by wireless; the best plan was to find a courier like herself. In particular, HILAIRE has many new fields about which he would like to advise H.Q. He asked that the operator sent to him should have two sets – a mains and a battery one. He would be able to get the accumulator charged by a man they know who works at a garage in AGEN. And who always does repairs to sets.

The members of the organisation always carried the set round quite openly in a suitcase. On one occasion when source was doing this she arrived to catch a bus, and saw that there was a control of papers by German and French. She selected a typical German – a tall, stupid-looking man – and amused him by asking in very bad German is he would hold her suitcase while she bought a paper. She then went to the bus and showed her papers, saying laughingly to the man that when she came back he would know her and would not need to look at her papers again. She then returned to the man holding her suitcase, collected it and got into the bus without any trouble.

On another occasion AMEDEE [?] had his suitcase opened, but explained the contents by saying that he was a doctor on his way to give therapeutic treatment. They always managed to wangle their way through somehow.

SUPPLY OF ARMS

HILAIRE particularly asked her to warn the organisation to be very careful to whom they sent arms. The Francs Tireurs and Liberation are both Red, and he is convinced that they would use the arms for themselves to secure power. They might perhaps help to clear the Germans out, but afterwards, they would hide the arms and hold on to them. Each organisation in France is thinking about its own position after the war.

ISSUE OF SOURCE'S CARTE D'IDENTITE BY DEUXIEME BUREAU

When staying with Mrs CHURCHILL [Odette Sansom] source met a cousin of GAUTHIER, who knew someone at the Deuxième Bureau in LYONS who was prepared to issue RODOLPHE and herself with new cartes d'identite. They were warned that they must tell the truth as RODOLPHE stated frankly that they were working for the English and that everyone had been arrested except for themselves. To her surprise, the Deuxième Bureau consented. She and RODOLPHE took a great risk, but at that time they had no other way of obtaining new cartes d'identite; now they have a man at CASTELNAU, who will forge them.

STAY AT VILLEFRANCHE-SUR-MER

Source arrived at VILLEFRANCHE-SUR-MER on the 10 November (later in the interrogation she said the 11th). And stayed until 2 January, during which time she did no work at all. She twice saw RODOLPHE [Sevenet] at the villa, and AMADEE [Contran] came to see them at the New Year.

He actually stayed with his family in NICE, but visited the villa for dinner. She herself never went out except into NICE to have her hair dyed, but she did not know anyone in the town. She left because RODOLPHE came to fetch her, telling her that she must go at once as she was 'brulé'. She did not know RODOLPHE very well as she had not met him frequently, but she thought that he always seemed a bit nervous for his job.

FIRST ESCAPE ATTEMPT

Source went with AMEDEE and RODOLPHE to TOULOUSE and spent three days at MONTAUBAN, where AMADEE left her. She described him as 'A beautiful worker, but a queer boy'. He was very prudent, extremely clever, and always managed to get through. RODOLPHE introduced her in TOULOUSE to DUPONT, who took her by bus to OLORON, where she was to attempt to cross into Spain. But DUPONT was stopped twice as he was reconnoitring for her, and the snow was much too heavy for her thin shoes, so he took her back to TOULOUSE, where she met HILAIRE, who had then started working in AGEN. HILAIRE told the other members of the organisation to take care of her, and she began working again.

JOURNEY FROM FRANCE TO THE UK

When it was heard that EUGENE had been caught HILAIRE decided that someone must go to England to report, and as source's English was good enough for her to pass as an English girl in Spain it was arranged that she should go. HILAIRE told her that he had obtained a route by which she would have to walk only 3km on flat ground to cross the Pyrénées!

She left AGEN on Thursday 29 April, for TOULOUSE, and then went on to MONTREJEAU, where she spent the night. She travelled for three hours the next day by train through 17km if the zone interdite to CIRS DE LUCHON, where she knew she could contact the chef de gare. (She did not mention that she was accompanied for any part of this journey by IVAN [?], compare R.P.S. [Royal Patriotic School] report No. N.L. 249.) The chef de gare, who thought she was English, said she was mad, but took her into a little room where she told him that she was carrying papers which she must get through. He told her that she must walk 600 yards past several patrols to get to the Hotel des Trois Ormeaux, but fortunately, she did not see any Germans. When she met the proprietor of the hotel, he put her in a room where she hid all day until he found her a passeur [guide]. She left at 12.30 a.m. and walked for seventeen hours in the snow, with bare legs and wearing a thin, half-length coat. Crossing at 3,300 metres, she reached the first town, BAUSEN, at 3 o'clock in the afternoon (source's own arithmetic). Her guides were excellent; one accompanied her, and the other went on ahead to see that the way was clear. At one point she was so cold that they stopped to make a fire for her. HILAIRE had told her to pay 5000 francs for her passage, so she gave one 3000 and the other 2000, but they would have helped her just the same if she had had no money. On the way, it started snowing, and she was afraid she would get lost and inadvertently wander back to France.

She remained in BAUSEN for three days, as she had arrived on a Saturday after the bus had left and so had to wait until the Monday, but she was glad of the rest. [Perrin mentioned that Starr's report was confiscated by the Bausen police.] She then proceeded to VEILLE and thence to VERIDA, where she was fortunate enough to find the British Consul in BARCELONA on a short visit. She had dinner with him the same day (5 May), and he gave her a paper [salvo conducto] which enabled her to go direct to MADRID, where she arrived on 8 May. She was there for five days and was then sent to GIBRALTAR, which she reached on Saturday 15 May. after three days there she left for LISBON and arrived in London on 21 May. The whole journey, therefore, took only 20 days.

Source considered that is HILAIRE had to escape from France this would be a very good way for him to go. He should go to the Hotel des Trois Ormeaux in CIRS DE LUCHON, say that he is a friend of the tall, fair English girl, and ask the proprietor to give him the same guides.

ESCAPE OF FOUR ALLIED AIRMEN
In MADRID source stayed in the same hotel as four airmen, two American and two English, whom she had previously met in France. The two Americans, Kay Ford and Del MARKLAND, were shot down in France. They did not know a word of French and looked obvious Americans, but they managed to buy themselves a French carte d'identite and put on some photograph. They wrote in English across the card that they were American airmen who had been shot down and were trying to get to Spain. They showed this card to the police in a train near TOULOUSE, and the police helped them, even to the extent of giving them money. They met someone who asked HILAIRE to help them to escape, and he, having carefully verified the fact that they were what they appeared to be, and not Germans in disguise, gave them the same escape route as was used by source, the only difference being that as they did not speak French they had a guide through the zone interdite instead of going by train. Source confirmed that it was necessary to have papers to pass through this zone. HILAIRE obtained the escape route from a farm which sheltered the Americans.

The two English airmen, Alan OGILVIE and Ralph ANDRSON, escaped through EUGENE. They were told to contact an English girl

[?], married to a Frenchman, who worked in the Gestapo headquarters in TOULOUSE. They walked straight up to where this girl was sitting at the counter and started talking to her in English, fortunately, they were not noticed, and the girl was able to help them.

POSSIBILITY OF SOURCE'S RETURN TO FRANCE

Source is extremely anxious to return to France and believes that it would be quite safe for her to work in LYONS as she has been living in AGEN for the last eight months. She was told by Captain Gibson [?] that she is known to the Gestapo, but she cannot believe this is true; if it is, HILAIRE should be brought out of France immediately as, owing to his bad French, she accompanied him everywhere, and their names were frequently written in the same book (hotel register?). she does not think that the Gestapo would have allowed her to escape if they had known her, and as she had lived in the same place for the last five months they would have had ample opportunity to arrest her if they had so wished. The police are looking for so many people that they are unable to concentrate on one person for more than two or three months. She managed to meet her mother in a small café three months ago, and at that time her parents were already telling everyone that she had escaped to England. She lived under the name of Katrine BERNARD, but had a second carte d'identite in the name of Chantal BARON. When asked whether the Gestapo would know her under her own name or as Katrine BERNARD, she replied 'Ask Captain Gibson'.[76]

Following her interrogation, Mr F. Miller, one of the Security Section officers, sent a memo to Buckmaster about Miss Danielle Wood, informing him that,

I have interrogated this lady at length this morning, and I am quite satisfied as to her loyalty. I am not competent to express an opinion as to whether her security is good enough to permit her being sent back to the field, which she ardently desires to do; and in view of the criticisms of her behaviour while in hiding at Villefranche made by Sarraut, the wisdom of sending her back would appear to be doubtful. On the other hand, I accept her account of what she did both at Lyons and at Castelnau, where she was associated with HILAIRE and of the escape across the Pyrénées, on which basis there is no doubt either to her courage or to her determination.

I am satisfied as to her loyalty chiefly because she faced squarely the difficulties which arose from the fact that 'L'ALLEMAND' was arrested in Marseilles on the 2 November some days after the arrest of

CELESTIN and CHRISTIANE at Feyzen, but the arrest of the former cannot be traced to the arrest of the latter. Miss WOOD was emphatic that CELESTIN, even if he had known of the existence of an agent of the organisation in Marseilles, would certainly not know either his identity or his address, and refused to accept the suggestion that CHRISTIANE could have known either or would have disclosed her knowledge if she had had it. If Miss WOOD had been instrumental in the arrest of L'ALLEMAND, it is scarcely conceivable that she would not have attempted to suggests that that casualty occurred through the prior arrest of CELESTIN and CHRISTIANE. Further, her account of her movements is borne out in every particular by both SARRAUT [?] and SEVENET, neither of whom appear to have much use for her. Lastly, her account of her escape across the Franco-Spanish frontier bears, in my view, the stamp of truth. If this were a concocted story it would not depend on such phenomenal luck as she had in getting into the Zone Interdite by train without a permit and yet without detection.

These are the chief points which, I think impel one to accept her story, but I would add that her demeanour in giving it was impressive.[77]

In her file was a copy of a digest of reports of sentences carried out by the French courts that MI6 had picked up from radio broadcasts and other sources. On 29 June 1943, La Croix reported that the State Tribunal at Lyon had passed the following sentences for anti-nationalist activity: Aaron and Denise Bloch, ten years' hard labour, Denise Bloch being sentenced in abstentia; Dedieu, four years' imprisonment and a 12,000-franc fine; Mendelssohn and Ches, one year's imprisonment and 12,000 francs fine. Vomécourt, Shess and Crevoisier got three years' imprisonment and 6,000 francs fine. The court sat in camera [no members of the public present].[78]

Initially, Selwyn Jepson opposed her request to be sent back to France because she was 'blown', known to the Gestapo. Perrin identified a further problem:

To make things worse, one of the French Section's staff, Nicholas Bodington, began complaining that she was causing a security risk by hanging around their offices at Orchard Court and needed 'to be disposed of' immediately, suggesting she should be 'let loose into civilian life' and found a job with 'something like the Ministry of Information, or the BBC'.

Exasperated by F Section's objections to sending her back, Denise forcefully argued that she'd lived in Agen for months under the name of 'Katrine Bernard' without attracting any Gestapo attention, and if anything Starr was at this moment in more danger, walking around speaking French with an obvious English accent. It took another month before Jepson changed his mind, finally being persuaded that by the time she finished training, her name would have probably dropped off the Gestapo's wanted lists. However, according to another agent, she remained contemptuous of SOE and its conduct, only promising to 'do her work in the Field to the best of her ability, in the hope that she will live through it and tell us all, afterwards, what she thinks of us.'

Denise gave up her temporary alias of 'Danielle Wood', and became a new recruit at the end of July under the name of 'Danielle Williams'.

Rather than sending her back to the area where she might be recognised, it was decided she should be given a commission as an ensign in the FANY and trained as a wireless operator.

After a few days' assessment at Winterfold, she was given a grade C with an intelligence rating of 8 and good mechanical skills. 'An experienced woman with a knowledge of the world. She has courage and determination and a thorough understanding and hatred of the Boches. Has complete self-assurance and is capable of handling most situations. Has a feeling of physical inferiority which limits her athletic activities. Keen to get back into the field and under a male organiser would make a very good W/T operator or courier. Is not physically suited to the training of Group A [paramilitary training school in Scotland].

The Board agreed to her being sent to Thame Park where she showed aptitude and interest. As well as physical exercises, potential wireless operators were given a 16-week specialised radio, cypher and security training course. They had to learn how to use and repair sets, tap out messages in Morse at 18–22 wpm and use codes and checks to verify their transmission.

Arrangements were made for her to accompany Captain Robert Benoist, who had fought in the Great War, flew as a fighter pilot in *Armée de l'Air*, worked as a flying instructor and was a Grand Prix racing driver. When William Grover-Williams, one of his fellow racing drivers who had escaped to England, returned in May 1942 as an SOE agent, Benoist helped him collect weapons and ammunition dropped in Rambouillet Forest and stored them at his home in Auffargis, Ile-de-France. With the assistance of Jean-Pierre Wimille, Benoist's former Bugatti co-driver, they organised sabotage cells in Grover-Williams's CHESTNUT network. He had tried to create a new network, named CLERGYMAN, but had found the countryside around Nantes unsuitable for DZs and, having had a wireless operator arrested, was unable to arrange more drops. On

19 August 1943, he was brought to England in a Hudson operation with nine other passengers. One of them was Marie-Thérèse Le Chêne, who had been working in the PLANE network.[79]

Having been debriefed and trained as an F Section organiser, Benoist was to be sent back to rebuild the CLERGYMAN network, assisted by Denise, code named Ambroise.

At the end of February, she was sent for parachute training but, according to her instructor at Dunham House, she did not impress.

Alternative arrangements had to be made so, on 2 March, accompanied by Benoist, she was taken to Tempsford, from where Flight Officer 'Dinger' Bell flew them in one of 161 Squadron's Lysanders to a field 1.5 km west of Baudreville, east-south-east of Chartres.[80] They met up with Wimille to restart what Benoist claimed was the 2,000-strong CLERGYMAN circuit and stayed at Villa Cécile on Benoist's estate at Sermaise, near Rambouillet, southwest of Paris.

Their mission was to bring down the high electricity pylons that crossed the river Loire at Île Heron and linked the hydro-electric power stations in the Pyrénées with Brittany as well as to sabotage the telephone and railway system around Nantes. This would disrupt German communications before D-Day. Over a period of three months, she sent thirty-one messages back to London and received fifty-two. She also started passing on her skills to André Garnier, Benoist's son-in-law.

An indication as to how extensively she travelled on her missions was the number of aliases she used. Harrison recorded them as 'Micheline Claude de Rabatal', 'Chantal Baron' and 'Katrine Bernard' with the code names Criniline and Line.

With all the activity following D-Day, Benoist ordered his network's main members to Villa Cecile where, on the evening of 18 June, he received a call informing him that his mother was dying in Paris. Before he left, he told his friends that if he did not come back the following day, they should all scatter.

He was arrested, but when Denise and the others received the news, they did not expect the Gestapo to arrive so quickly. Perrin's research revealed that,

> For some reason, they all appeared to take [it] as a joke, an inexplicable reaction which soon proved to be costly. The next day was dull and wet: Wimille drove Denise to a nearby farm to send a wireless message, and afterwards she walked up the road to the train station in the hope of spotting Benoist or Charlotte [?], but there was no sign of either. Even

at this stage, it seems that no-one at the villa thought of heeding their organiser's advice from the previous evening.

At about 8.20pm they were starting to prepare dinner when they heard the sound of approaching vehicles, and moments later about a dozen cars rolled up to the house, carrying Germans in civilian clothes. According to Garnier, the Germans were already aware of Denise, shouting 'Line, Line, où est Line?' She, Charlotte, Mme Tayssedre and Mme Wimille were caught in the kitchen, while L'Antoine, Robert Tayssedre and Garnier were soon handcuffed and escorted away. Wimille had been the first to run and managed to evade capture by submerging himself in the stream behind the villa, where he stayed hidden for two hours with only his nose above the water. Before leaving, the raiders set the villa alight, and the convoy of prisoners watched it burning to the ground as they set off for Paris.

Benoist was already in custody, having been arrested the night before. As with other circuit collapses in France, the absence of an obvious traitor immediately sparked off various accusations and counter-claims, but who actually gave them up was never proved. [...]

The German interrogator, Ernst Vogt, read a report to Garnier that identified 'Charles' and 'Corrine' – F Section agents Philippe Liewer and Violette Szabó – as responsible for giving away Benoist's address. This looked plausible, as Liewer had met Benoist in Paris some months before. However, bogus reports were used to confuse captured agents, and this one contained a simple error: although Szabó had been captured earlier that month, Liewer had not.

All those arrested were taken to the Sicherheitsdienst (SD) headquarters on Avenue Foch, but exactly what happened next to Denise isn't clear. John Starr, an F Section agent and long-term resident at Avenue Foch, later said that Denise was allowed to see Benoist in his cell on the fifth floor, but little more is known about her movements. As a wireless operator, she would have been interrogated about codes and the locations of her sets, and one source suggested that she may have personally led the Germans to her radio posts. For the past year, the SD had been deceiving London by playing back SOE's captured wireless sets, which resulted in agents being unwittingly dropped to German reception committees, but Denise had no further contact with London. In fact, the last CLERGYMAN drop came the day after her arrest, when a new assistant for Benoist, Louis Blondet, parachuted to an enemy reception: fortunately, one of the group called out to Blondet in German by mistake and Blondet immediately shot him, making his escape in the ensuing confusion [...]

After questioning, Garnier and several others were transferred to the Gestapo prison at Place des Etat-Unis. Some were later deported, but Garnier was released and Madame Wimille managed to escape. Further arrests followed around Sermaise over the next few days, and most of CLERGYMAN's arms were captured.

Denise was transferred to Fresnes prison but few details of her time there have come to light. Escott claimed that the Germans learned nothing from her. Bob Starr reported seeing Danielle, as she was known, being allowed to see Benoist in his cell.[81] On 8 August, with the Allies approaching Paris, the Germans took Denise, Violette Szabó, Lilian Rolfe and thirty-seven male SOE prisoners to Gare de l'Est and crammed them into third-class carriages for transport further east. Although the train was halted during an RAF attack, none of the prisoners were able to escape without being shot by the guards. Violette, still chained to Denise, got hold of a tin cup and crawled to the adjoining men's compartment. In Bruce Marshall's *White Rabbit*, he narrates how captured SOE agent Yeo-Thomas,

> ...felt deeply ashamed when we saw Violette Szabó, while the raid was still on, come crawling along the corridor towards us with a jug of water which she had filled from the lavatory. She handed it to us through the iron bars. With her, crawling too, came the girl to whose ankle she was chained.
>
> This act of mercy made an unforgettable impression on all. She spoke words of comfort, jested, went back with the jug to fill it again and again.
>
> "My God that girl had guts,' says Yeo-Thomas. 'I shall never forget that moment,' says Harry Peulevé.[82]

In Tania Szabó's biography of her mother, she reported them

> giving sustenance and life to a good number of men in two wagons. It was exhausting. Poor Denise was almost dropping, and Violette was keeping her going with words and a helping hand, taking the weight of the large can they found and refilled it over and over again from the water closet used by the soldiers.
>
> The bombing stopped, the soldiers returned from their hiding places in ditches alongside the railway track. They shot some dozen prisoners, beaten half to death. Violette and Denise also caught the butt of a rifle each, sending them hurrying back to their carriage knowing that by their actions alone many of the men were somewhat refreshed.

The courage and example of these two dirty, starving girls gave the men courage to endure their own agonies and kept some of them alive for a while longer.[83]

Escott reported Buckmaster saying that one of the other prisoners who escaped death in the camps told him that Violette gave him half a bottle of wine abandoned by the guards, saying, '*Bon courage. Les alliés sont aux portes de Paris. Rassure-toi.*' After various stops, they were driven to a 'fly-blown' concentration camp of Neue-Bremm Saarbrücken, where Denise shared a large shed with women of all nationalities, including Yvonne Baseden, another captured F Section agent. The men were sent to Buchenwald where Benoist was executed a few weeks later.

On 24 August, Denise, Violette and Lilian were sent to Ravensbrück, the women's concentration camp known to the French as *l'Enfers des Femmes* – Women's Hell. Less than a fortnight later, she was sent to a camp in Torgau, east of Leipzig, where conditions working in an aircraft factory were described as relatively good.

In October, despite deteriorating health, she and some inmates planned an escape but it was foiled at the last moment. On 19 October, they were transferred to a derelict camp outside the gates of Königsberg on the River Oder. Still in her light summer clothes, she was forced to fell trees and do heavy building work for a new airfield. Over the winter, she developed gangrene and Lilian was admitted to the camp hospital seriously ill.

Details of what happened to Denise, Violette Szabó and Cécile Lefort, another captured F Section agent, were obtained following Vera Atkin's enquiry as to their fate after the war. She interrogated Obersturmfuhrer Johann Schwarzhuber, the SS Camp overseer at Ravensbrück, who testified that,

...I had delivered to me toward the end of January 1945 an order from the German Secret Police, countersigned by Camp Superintendent Suhren, instructing me to ascertain the location of the following persons: Lilian Rolfe, Danielle Williams [alias Denise Bloch] and Violette Szabo. These were at the time in the dependent camp of Königsberg on the Oder and were recalled by me. [All of them were in a pitiful state and Lilian too weak to walk.] When they returned to the camp, they were placed in the punishment block and moved from there into the block of cells.

One evening they were called out and taken to the courtyard by the Crematorium. Camp Commandant Suhren made these arrangements.

He read out the order for their shooting in the presence of [various names of camp officials, including the doctor]. I was myself present. The shooting was done only by Schult, with a small caliber gun through the back of the neck. They were brought forward singly by Cpl. Schenk. Death was certified by Dr. Trommer. The corpses were removed singly by internees who were employed in the Crematorium and burnt. The clothes were burnt on the bodies...

All three were very brave and I was deeply moved. Suhren was also impressed by the bearing of these women. He was annoyed that the Gestapo did not carry out these shootings...[84]

There were reports that a German doctor checked bodies to see if they had any gold fillings he could extract before they were put in the crematorium furnace. Escott gave the date as 27 January 1945. Denise was 29 years old and there is no known grave.[85]

Before SOE learnt of her fate, Buckmaster arranged for her to be Mentioned in Despatches. After her family in Paris were notified of her death and of the War Crimes Tribunal, some of her belongings and correspondence was sent back. In a letter sent to Miss Atkins, she was told that,

We've safely received a kitbag and small valise containing kit and toilet necessities belonging to my sister-in-law Denise Bloch and also the parcel of letters and personal belongings that you kindly sent to us.

Could I ask you to please continue sending any communications and parcels that there may be to me and not to my mother-in-law? Both my parents-in-law are sick people now and it is no use upsetting them. They have just received from London a letter telling of Denise's death by shooting. If this news if official, could you possibly send me an official document certifying her death and the will which is in your keeping so that we may have it opened by our family avocat. All this is very sad, but I'm glad to be able to help the family by doing the disagreeable jobs; after all it's not so hard for me as for them.[86]

This was duly done. She was given several posthumous awards, including the King's Commendation for Brave Conduct, the Croix de Guerre avec palme, the Légion d'Honneur and the Médaille de la Résistance. The SOE plaque at Ravensbrück includes her name and she is also listed on the FANY memorial at St Paul's Church, Knightsbridge, London, the Brookwood memorial in Surrey, and the F Section memorial at Valençay in France.

YVONNE FONTAINE

Aged 30. Landed by motor gunboat on de Vilin Izella beach near Beg-an-Fry (Finistère) on 26 March 1944. Awarded the Medaille de Resistance.

Yvonne Fontaine was born on 8 August 1913 in Longuyon, Meurte et Moselle, about 40 km north-east of Verdun, close to the border with Belgium and Luxembourg. According to the information that she gave the MI5 interrogators when she escaped to London in November 1943, her father, Prosper, died when she was 10 and her mother, Charlotte Bogert, remarried and went to live in Troyes, about 130 km south-east of Paris. She was sent to school in Lyon, Bordeaux and Longuyon and left when she was 15. She married Jean Sandon, an Italian, in 1931 and lived at 39 Rue Georges Clemenceau for two years until she divorced him and moved in with her parents.

When they moved to Brousseval, she stayed in Troyes and found work as a staff supervisor in a factory owned by a radiologist. In September 1939, she left, refusing to work under the orders of a German. In 1940 she worked as a manageress of Ets. Marot Teintures, a dyeing and dry cleaners works, but left on 13 June, following the German occupation and went into hiding with some friends. Through financial necessity, she returned to her former work in September.

> Until April 1943 she continued her job and did not take any part in any [resistance] organisation work. She said that she disapproved of most of the de Gaullist movement, her reasons being that she considered that many of the people were too politically-minded and self-seeking and that the majority of them talked too much, endangering both themselves and their organisation. In April 1943 was approached by a friend who asked her to help him, to which she consented. This was her first contact with any clandestine activities... About 6 September she organised the evacuation of about 20 American aviators in all, men who had made forced landings by parachute in the district ...[87]

Escott's research revealed that Yvonne lived in a busy industrial area which, with all its road, rail and canal connections to Paris, became one of the RAF and USAAF targets at the beginning of the war. When Allied planes were shot down, downed pilots and aircrew, if they avoided capture, were often helped by local French families. Yvonne worked with Pierre Mulsant's TINKER network south-east of Paris, a group which organised shelter for such men. Provided with food, clothing and money, often in containers dropped by the Special Duties Squadrons, their guides escorted them along one of the escape lines, either to the Brittany coast or the Swiss or Spanish border.

On 11 April 1943, Ben Cowburn, code named Germain, was parachuted south of Blois to revive the TINKER network. Accompanying him was Denis Barrett, his wireless operator.

They met up with Mulsant, a timber merchant, code named Paul, who, assisted by Robert Stein, his stepbrother, used his stepfather's fleet of lorries for picking up containers after the curfew. Through Mulsant, they met Yvonne, who agreed to join them in their operations.

In Escott's *The Heroines of SOE*, she commented that,

> Quick-witted and trustworthy, Yvonne easily slipped into the role of courier to other networks, as well as TINKER. Now known as Nenette she travelled everywhere – Piney, Romilly, Chartres, Tonnere, the forest of Chatillon and even, but rarely, to the PHYSICIAN network in Paris, carrying not only messages but sometimes sabotage materials.[88]

Among her network's successes were sprinkling itching powder on the shirts and vests of German submarine crews when they had been washed at the laundry where she worked. This resulted in submarines not being able to operate for long as the crew needed medical treatment to control the itching.

On the night of 3/4 July 1943, they destroyed six railway engines and put another six out of action in a locomotive roundhouse in Troyes. In Marcus Binney's *Secret War Heroes*, he mentions her acting as Ben Cowburn's courier in the revived SPIRITUALIST network around the Seine-et-Marne department to the east and south-east of Paris and described her as

> ...an ardent patriot, quite fearless and ready for anything. She worked in a laundry, and for her SOE work he paid her 2,000 francs a month. Thanks to Nenette, Cowburn did not feel in need of a woman courier from London ... Nenette had found a 'nice, safe restaurant where they could get meals without tickets, ironically named the Paul l'Allemand, opposite the town theatre.'[89]

According to Escott, she helped organise five drops over two months which provided her group with a total of sixty containers packed with Sten guns, rifles, grenades and explosives. Following Cowburn's successful sabotage of the rail transport around the important junction town of Troyes, the ensuing clampdown by the Gestapo forced her to lie low. When a fleet of Flying Fortresses flew over Troyes on their return from bombing Stuttgart, seven of them were shot down. Of the thirty American crew who bailed out, eighteen were rescued by local people and Yvonne helped make arrangements for them to escape into Switzerland.

The German response to the Resistance activity was to offer large financial rewards for information leading to the arrest and conviction of those involved. Money talked, and it is claimed that several leading resisters were caught as a result and revealed information under interrogation and torture. Sending German agents disguised as evaders who needed getting out of the country, allowed them to infiltrate the PHYSICIAN network and arrest hundreds of Resistance members in July 1943.

The SOE ordered Cowburn to return in mid-September 1943 leaving Yvonne working for Mulsant and Barrett. However, as the Gestapo closed in, Henri Déricourt organised a Hudson pick-up from a field 1 km south-east of Soucelles, northeast of Angers.

She left Paris on 1 November and made her way to Soucelles. In the early hours of 15 November, Lt Hodges of 161 Squadron landed his Hudson on the landing ground with five SOE agents: André Maugenet, Paul Pardi, Jean Menesson, Eugène Falangue, Victor Gerson, and one BCRA agent, H. J. Fille-Lambieand. Eight passengers boarded including Yvonne, Mulsant, Barrett, Cammaerts, Pierre du Passage, Rechenmann, François Mitterrand, the future President of France, Jakub Adam Edward Michalak and allied airmen.

Unknown to them, the landing and departure were watched by Waffen SS Sturmbannführer (Major) Hans Josef Kieffer, the senior German counter-intelligence officer in Paris during the German occupation. His men arrested the three men who went to see them off and followed and then arrested Maugenet, Pardi, and Menesson.[90]

Interrogated on arrival, her report shed light on what conditions were like in France immediately before her departure and provided details that SOE may have found useful in their sabotage planning as well as for the Training Section preparing to send more agents into the field.

She had been introduced to GERMAIN by Dr. MAHEE, the leader of a local GAULLIST group, whom she had known all her life. She kept a flat in TROYES for the purpose of permitting GERMAIN to meet his Agents in safety. This flat had two exits, and a safety signal was always used. It consisted of shutting a certain window if the rendezvous was not to take place. Source was never present at these meetings. She used to go out and leave the flat unlocked., and GERMAIN would have his meeting and leave before she came home. As the Circuit is fairly concentrated, she did not have to make many journeys, and in the course of her work, she only met GERMAIN, ANDRE (his lieutenant), HONORE (his W/T operator, who once made a transmission from her flat, but did not keep a set there), ABELARD, who was GERMAIN's successor in the Circuit, and CINEMA.

DR. MAHEE

Source speaks very highly of the Doctor, who is an old friend of hers. Unfortunately for him, his first efforts at resistance work were with the GAULLISTS. Most Agents agree that the indiscretions of the GAULLISTS are almost legendary, and that though they mean well, they have no idea how to set about serious resistance work. The Doctor's former Chief was WAUTERS, another very unfortunate association from the security point of view. In fact, it is probably through the indiscretion of some well-meaning person that DR. MAHEE is in prison today. He was arrested at TROYES in July, and has been interrogated several times since by the Gestapo, at approximately weekly intervals. The first two interrogations were quite normal, but Source believes that subsequent ones have been very unpleasant. His family has been allowed to see him at intervals, and also the maid, who is source's informant, and who is a loyal and reliable woman, had been allowed to pack up some clothes and take them to him. Source does not think that Dr. MAHEE will have given anything away. However, JEAN PONTRON, a GAULLIST arrested shortly after the Doctor, may, it is believed, have given something to implicate him further.

WALTERS

Everyone who met WALTERS in the Field seems to have disliked him, on account of his tactless, boastful and indiscreet talk. Source says he was rather a rough diamond, although certainly courageous, and would probably have been more suitable for sabotage ad coup-de-main raids than for the organisation and leadership of a circuit.

GERMAIN

Source admired him a lot, and thought he was quite a remarkable man. She said he had a resourcefulness and polish that his successor definitely lacked.

ABELARD

He took over from GERMAIN when the latter returned to this country. He is a courageous young man but not so popular in the organisation as his predecessor.

THE PROCUREUR DE LA REPUBLIQUE (Dept. d l'AUBE)

This is a very good man and has often helped the Circuit in the matter of Identity papers etc. he has also been very useful in the disposal of large quantities of airmen shot down in the area.

TEXTILE AND CLOTHING FACTORIES AT TROYES

Source worked at Troyes in the Dyeing and Cleaning works MARAUD. This is also a laundry, and the owner of the business has a big German contract at the moment, which he is hoping to have renewed in January when it will expire. Material for shirts and underclothing is received from the manufacturers in its natural bleach colour, and they dye it olive green, for German army requirements.

She gave the names of 10 manufacturers on the TROYES district, who get contracts from the Germans every few months, and during these periods work exclusively on production for the German armed services. They make hosiery, shirts, lengths of material, etc., and when it is a question of a German contract, the raw materials are always forthcoming. She believes they come from Germany.

The factories: MAUHAUFFE, de LOSTAL and GHILLET are the three largest and most important working for the Germans. PONON, MELANGER, BERARD-ROLET, BARFRET, DEGREZ, RHET-ARCHIVES, BON-BON and Le PRINTEMPS, also have German contracts. She has been in many of these factories in the course of her work. No special passes are required to enter any of these, but naturally one would be stopped by the doorman and asked whom one wished to see.

Source does not think the material of German uniforms is as good as the material she has seen over here.

THE RELEVE

In Source's opinion, very few young Frenchwomen have volunteered to go and work in Germany. And these are mostly from the lower classes. The Releve is not compulsory for women,

1. NEW REGISTRATION DECREE IN FRANCE

Source believes that at the beginning of November a new decree was issued, ordering all unmarried women in France, over the age of 21, to register for work either in France or Germany.

2. CONTROLS

Source has never been controlled when travelling, and never seen anyone else being controlled. (This is just luck, as she admits). She says that it is definitely much easier for a woman to travel in France than for a man; the great thing is to present a normal unflurried appearance, and not to appear furtive or nervous. If asked to take a radio set to PARIS in a suitcase, source would be quite willing to do so, as she thinks she would not be exposing herself to any great danger. One can fool the French Police (i.e. tell them that a radio set is a new kind of electric massage apparatus), but not the Gestapo.

3. DOCUMENTS

Source has always used her real Identity Card, and never had a false one. She had not Carte de Travail, as this is not necessary for a woman. The Identity Card was issued to her by the Prefecture.

4. PUBLIC OPINION

Americans are now vastly disliked in France, owing to their high altitude bombing raids. The R.A.F. are increasingly popular. It used to be the other way round. (A woman friend of Source, who had been subjected to the American bombing of NANTES (where they hit everything except the enemy squadron in the port) says that she would help an English airman who had been shot down, and cut the throat of any American she found.)

5. COMMODITIES

(a) TEXTILES

Can only be bought with special permits in addition to ration cards. There is no wool at all, unless it can be found on the black market, and there it is very expensive. (Source remarked that the women of France still seem to be extremely well dressed, and does not know how they manage it. The working classes of France are, and always have been, very poor and underpaid, and now they are still more so because the small rise in wages is totally out of proportion to the immense increase in prices. It is only a small section of the population that can afford to shop in the Black Market.) A certain amount of Lyon silk is still being manufactured, but the dyes are not as good as pre-war ones.

Perfume is a Black Market commodity only, and even the famous brands have no lasting aroma.

(b) SHOES

A lot of wooden soled shoes are now being made, rubber being only obtainable on the black market. In some cases, women's shoes are being made with wooden soles two or three inches thick. Good leather is very hard to get.

(c) CIGARETTES

Are quite easy to get if one can afford them. They cost Frs. 150 per packet; Frs. 300 for British and American

(d) WINE

The monthly ration is 4 litres per head, and one must take what the dealer has. It may cost anything between 125 – 300 Frs. per bottle.

(e) <u>MILK</u>

Issued only to children. Costs 12 Frs. per litre when obtainable.

<u>BLACK MARKET PRICES</u>

Dinner	Frs. 600 – 1000 (an ordinary meal can be had for 50 Frs.)
Meat	Frs. 80 – 150 per kilo
Butter	Frs. 400
Sugar	Frs. 80 – 120
Woman's suit	From 8,000 Frs.
Men's suit	From 2,000 Frs.
Silk stockings	Frs. 250 Frs. per pair

Source bought ration coupons as it is necessary to do so if one wishes to entertain.

<u>SUGGESTIONS FOR AGENTS GOING INTO THE FIELD</u>

Agents going into the Field would do well to take a supply of chocolate (particularly for members of reception committees to take home to their children.), coffee, soap (soap in France is of such poor quality now) and olive oil for cooking purposes. It is quite impossible to get this now. Agents should see that about 20 coupons are cut from their clothing books before going into the Field, as it is hardly normal to have a book still intact at this date.

Source also suggests that organisers going into the Field should be provided with false seals and stamps of the local Prefecture, so that they can issue Identity papers quickly in cases of need, without having to send photographs back to England and wait a long time for the completed Card.

<u>STANDARD CLOTHING</u>

Source was very worried that Agents arriving from this country seem to have standard underclothing. Apparentntly GERMAIN and ABELARD had several shorts that were identical. Also, all English Agents seem to be dropped in the same kind of striped pyjamas. Source saw the pyjamas of several Agents on their arrival, and they all had blue stripes. She feels that if more than one were in the same prison, the Gestapo would notice the similarity, and realise that they were both Agents. Otherwise, the personal effects given to Agents are quite satisfactory. It is still possible to get studs, cigarette cases, etc. in France.[91]

After being debriefed, her MI5 interrogator commented that 'Mme Fontaine was perfectly straightforward under interrogation and it is not considered that there is anything against her from a security point of view.'[92] Her report included her code name, NENETTE and provided physical measurements.

Given a cover-name of Yvonne Fauge and a commission as an ensign in the FANY, she was sent to Winterfold for the SOE's assessment course. Her instructor graded her B, gave her 5 for intelligence, rated her Morse as good and remarked that she was

> A very plucky, determined girl with a sharp quick mind and a confident manner. She has little time for theories and is essentially practical and effective in effort. A fervent patriot whose motives are of a high order. Displays independence and dominance and leadership qualities which were never disputed by the group. At times very high spirited and even quick tempered but au fonde very tolerant. Should make a good Assistant to Organiser. Would prefer to work for her former chief.[93]

Considered suitable, she was sent to Meoble (STS 23a), Morar, Inverness-shire, a remote requisitioned shooting lodge, for paramilitary training. Her conducting officer, Acting Lieutenant Gordon, found out that her hobbies included camping, cycling and lectures on travel and that she had been married twice. She made no mention of the second marriage in her interrogation report. In Gordon's opinion, she was,

> The most interesting person here and probably the most intelligent. A lively and indefatigable talker, easily outshining the ancient mariner, her conversation is not, however, of an indiscreet character, but bears on her emotions, bruises, aspirations, and amusements. Fancies herself as 'une sportive' and is fond of recounting the great distances she can swim by her own peculiar methods of natation. Likes a great deal of attention from those whom she is pleased to call 'les boys!'[94]

Her first Christmas and New Year in Britain was spoilt as she was in hospital for over a week with a bad leg. On her return, Gordon was pleased that she enlivened the group with her high spirits.

A fortnight later, having completed the course, Gordon commented that,

This student has, I think, much enjoyed her visit here. She is a little remorseful now that she has not worked more seriously. She is a very delightful person, polite, anxious that things should be correct, and with a standard of civilized behavior lacking in some others. She is very considerate of other people, and absolutely reliable, intelligent and agile-minded. The only non-English speaking person here, her behavior has been most charming and helpful throughout the course.[95]

What was not mentioned was her sabotage and explosives training, skills that she was later to use in the field. Her instructor commented that her injury had led her to miss much of the course which meant she did not have enough thorough knowledge. However, she was,

'Very quick, mentally, with a temperament very susceptible to encouragement and indeed, the reverse, but is not persevering and is too casual.' The Commandant added that she was, 'A very temperamental person. Can work hard when she wants too but is much too inclined to allow her attention to wander and take things much too casually. Has missed at least 50% of physical work, schemes, etc., owing to leg injury. I think she could be useful if the right job were found for her, as she is quick-witted and shrewd and keen to do a useful job.'[96]

Although students progressed from Scotland to Ringway, she was instead sent to The House on the Shore (STS 33) at Beaulieu for clandestine warfare training. At the end of February, her instructor commented that,

She is intelligent and cultured and at the same time has good practical ability. She is shrewd, quick and cunning and her imagination is good. Although she seems very keen on her work, she is not particularly industrious. If she thinks that she knows the subject or that it is not much use to her, she displays little interest. Her character is strong, and she seems determined, but she is egocentric, spoilt, stubborn, impatient, conceited and anxious to draw attention to herself. She is temperamental and on account of this might not always prove reliable. Her personality is strong, but she is moody. When she likes people or thinks they will be useful to her, she can be gracious, sociable and charming, although she is always dominating. On occasions, however, she can and might work well as a subordinate to someone who she liked and trusted. She would, however, always require strong leadership. It is essential that she is associated with those with whom she is prepared to work. Otherwise she might prove unsatisfactory. Codes: This student understands the principles taught. Further practice required.[97]

Desperate for more female agents, Buckmaster ignored these concerns and agreed to send her back. Her personnel file mentions her returning to the field on 21 March 1944 and Tillet records her being dropped by motor gun boat on de Vilin Izella beach, south of Beg-an-Fry, Finistère on 26 March 1944. It is possible she left London on 21 March and did not set sail until the night of 25/26 March. Once she got out, Colonel Ivan Gerard, a Belgian army officer, got in and was taken back to Britain.

She made her way to Paris and rendezvoused with Mulsant, who had been given the cover-name Paul Guerin and code name Minister. He had been landed by Hudson on 3 March with Barrett, cover-name Stephane, and code named Innkeeper, to create what became known as the MINISTER network.[98]

Using identity papers in the name of Yvonne Fernande Cholet, code named Mimi and also using the names 'Yvonne Dumont', 'Nenette' and 'Florist', she was taken by Mulsant to a safe house in Melun, about 40 km south-east of Paris.

She began by locating safe drop zones for container drops and agent landings and finding men to join reception committees. Using the skills taught at Beaulieu, she showed them where to set up guards, how to lay out lights to guide the pilot bringing supplies. Often, she led these night-time operations. Between April and May 1944, she organised five receptions and helped collect sixty containers. She also took and received messages from Barrett and Mulsant.

When Mulsant moved his operations to Nangis, she had to move and was accommodated at Marcel Ballaguet's bakery. With D-Day approaching, she was busy travelling by train, tram, lorry, bus and bicycle between Bray-sur-Seine, Nemors, Donnemarie-à-Moutois to Paris and other towns and villages. On 17 April, she welcomed a three-man team of American officers and another on 10 May. Their mission was to co-ordinate the Resistance for the invasion.

According to Escott, when the local doctor who was involved with the Resistance told her that he had been asked to provide details of her private life, he advised her to keep out of circulation. Disaster struck in late-July 1944 when she accompanied a Resistance group to help a uniformed party of SAS (Special Air Service) troops trapped in the forest of Fontainebleau. They had just been parachuted in but had run into difficulties and radioed Barrett, asking for assistance. German troops attacked them and although Yvonne managed to escape, Mulsant, Barrett, and other comrades were caught.[99]

In her report, she claimed that the cause of their arrest,

…was entirely the fault of sending in SAS parties in uniform in an area which was very closely patrolled by SS troops who immediately became aware of their arrival and went to the area where they had been dropped. The SAS had by this time withdrawn to a safe area. MINISTER was not aware of this and went to contact them and her with his W/T INNKEEPER were immediately arrested. FLORIST had not direct news of what has happened to either MINISTER or INNKEEPER but is under the impression from rumours that she heard in FONTAINBLEAU that they have been taken to GERMANY.[100]

Subsequent evidence shows they were taken to Rue Saussaies in Paris, interrogated and tortured but did not betray their network. Deported to Germany on 8 August 1944 with thirty-seven other agents including Yeo-Thomas and Robert Benoist, they were taken to Buchenwald in Thuringia and shot on 5 October with eleven other prisoners, shouting, 'Vive la France.'[101]

The MINISTER network continued with no organiser. Yvonne knew what needed to be done but missed not having radio contact with London. Despite this, underground telephone lines were cut, overhead lines were brought down, trees were felled so that they blocked the road and tyre bursters were laid to slow down German troop movements. Hit and run tactics reduced their numbers. Breaking the lock gates near Bray-sur-Seine, reduced water levels in the canal by twenty inches, causing long delays for the barges carrying vital supplies to the beleaguered German Army.

To reduce such attacks, the Germans set up road blocks and check points so Yvonne's journeys became more difficult. Escott described how,

A wallet full of papers was needed and much time wasted, severely affecting the number of visits, some very urgent, that she could do in a day. The Germans also increased paid informers, making receptions and sabotage even more hazardous. Supplying food and necessaries to growing numbers of Maquis and FFI [French Forces of the Interior] troops also put more strain on a population already hit by shortages, especially in the larger towns. Nor were the German troops so well disciplined as before, becoming more nervous as the Allies neared.[102]

The Germans taking hostages and shooting them in broad daylight added to Yvonne's problems. She had to restrain angry *résistants* from taking revenge as it would only draw heavier reprisals. She had to focus their attention on lightning strikes and then disappearing.

On 25 August, shortly after the Allies landed on the Mediterranean coast and began their push north, the Germans in France surrendered. Although there were attacks on the retreating troops, Yvonne and several liaison officers, had to count the cost of liberation, arrange funds for those who had helped and those who had lost family members. They had to collect left-over equipment which might be useful for the Allies in other areas and then extract reports from leading Resistance members before helping the local population celebrate.[103]

Once the American forces reached her area, she was flown back to England on 16 September 1944. Once she had written up her report, she met up with two other female agents, Odette Wilen, and Anne-Marie Walters. Their night chatting about their experiences caused concern to one of the SOE officers present.

I saw these ladies this morning. They are all staying at the same hotel, and I found them this morning for different reasons in a highly excitable and appeared to me, unsatisfactory, frame of mind.

Mme FUAGE. This agent, I think, has probably performed her duties well. Her present nervous condition is largely due to the fact that she blames the organisation for the arrest of her two friends GUERIN AND STEPHANE. Apparentntntly uniformed party was dropped into the Foret de Fontainebleau, which was already being used for two other receptions organised by GUERIN. The result was a thorough search of the woods in which GUERIN AND STEPHANE were caught. I am not anxious to go into details, but I think it is only right to notify the slightly unsatisfactory frame of mind in which she finds herself at present. [...]

I was very seriously shocked by the attitude of these three ladies, who had spent the night in exchanging confidences in the hotel. For one thing they were talking freely of the arrests of a great number of our agents, the facts of which they had no reason to be informed. I pointed out particularly that in the case of GARDE, we did not wish the news of his arrest to be spread since his wife had been seriously ill and we had been unable to inform her of this bad piece of news.[104]

Her debrief is worth including as it sheds light on the members of the MINISTER network:

1. NANGIS

   Brigadier of the gendarmerie of NANGIS, and the gendarme GEORGES.

   MARCEL BALLAGUET, boulanger de NANGIS in whose house FLORIST lived while she was in NANGIS.

   ALFRED BERTIN did reception committee work and also delivered arms by lorry; he was also responsible for cutting underground telephone cables. He formed a group of commandos who were responsible for railway sabotage and who sabotaged road transport by means of tyre bursters.

   M. l'Abbé Henri (Curé of Nangis) was responsible for reception committee work and also for the hiding of sufficient arms for 15 men in the church tower.

   JACQUES LECLERC

   ROGER NOURIE

   AVOIGNE (Garagiste)

   RAYMOND LEMAUR – electrician who was responsible for recharging all batteries etc. together with his assistant JEAN. LEMAUR and his wife were also responsible for cutting overhead telephone wires.

   GEORGES GAUDET who lives in the Ferme de la BERTRAUCHE. The brothers WENDEHAVENNE, who have supplied horses and animal transport for reception committee work and also looked after containers which were dropped in their fields, until they could be distributed to the various depots.

   DUCHATELET who lives on the route de FONTAINBLEAU at the corner of the road leading to FONCAINS. He built a very excellent arms depot by digging four holes in the ground which were lined with cement.

   FAMILLE DUBOIS lived in the Ferme de la CHAISE. They put their house at the disposal of INNKEEPER and VICTOR [?] his assistant, where INNKEEPER did a good deal of his transmitting, their house also served as an ammunition depot for the LECLERC commando unit. Their son ANDRE DUBOIS was taken prisoner by the Germans following MINISTER's arrest.

   All the above formed part of the reception committee teams in the NANGIS area.

2. DONNEMARIN a MOUTOIS

   Here the whole of the Brigaderie of the gendarmerie worked for MINISTER. FLORIST has not got the names of the gendarmes, but before she left, she asked the Brigadier to prepare a list which

he was unable to finish by the time she had to leave. A report by two of the gendarmes which was brought by FLORIST is attached.
<u>CLEMENT PHILLIPE</u>: he was chief of a commando unit, organised reception committees and did good sabotage.
<u>MARC</u> did reception work.

3. <u>JOUY-le-CHATEL</u>
<u>ROGER LOZE</u> marechal ferrant a Jouy-le-Chaval.
<u>LOUIS GAGNON</u> Lieutenant des Eaux et Forets.
<u>ANDRE LABARRE</u> Cdt. De S/Sectour.
All the above controlled groups of persons whose names are attached and who worked for the FFI in JOUY-le-CHATEL.

4. <u>COUR PALLY</u>
MINISTER contacted the Mayor of this village MARCEL CHATRIOUX with a view to his organizing reception committees in this area; this failed because of arrests.

5. <u>LA GRAND PAROISE</u>
<u>CHARLES NOURIE</u> brother of ROGER NOURIE of NANGIS, had an arms depot on his farm, was responsible for sabotage activities.

6. <u>NEMOURS</u>
Boulanger de NEMOURS where RAOUL stayed the Boulanger carried out several successful acts of sabotage.

7. <u>GASTINS</u>
Mme Vouve RENARD and son – this was FLORIST's safe house. Mme RENARD was very helpful in hiding preserves and comforts [tobacco, chocolate, whisky etc.] for MINISTER's groups.

8. <u>BRAY-sur-SEINE</u>
The Maquis de CRISY-sur-SEINE were situated near here, this maquis was responsible for the sabotaging of the lock gate at BRISY which caused the water in the canal to drop 50 centimetres, thus preventing all barges from passing.[105]

Escott added that because Yvonne was registered under her married name of Fauge, Vera Atkins did not recognise her as one of the SOE. Because she worked for the SOE's F Section, the French did not regard her as highly. However, in her citation for the Croix de Guerre, it was stated that she:

Had worked for us since January 1943 in the Seine et Marne. Left France in November 1943 to do some training in U.K. Returned to France 23 March 1944.

She was sent to act as a courier to the Minister circuit and carried out courier work between Melun and Paris. She engaged in reception committee work, gave sabotage instruction and did intelligence work. She was also responsible for transport of stores from the ground to various depots in the area.

Towards the end of April Minister left for Nangis and in his absence Fauge was a courier between the circuit and the W/T operator and after the arrest of Minister continued to do everything possible to direct groups in the area, she continued to work up to the day when she was over-run by the Allies.[106]

When Gubbins was asked to write a citation for an award for Yvonne, he wrote:

Ensign Fontaine was recruited locally by a British organiser in the Troyes area in the autumn of 1942, and from that date onwards devoted herself to resistance work. She played an important part, by providing contacts, safe houses, etc., in the organisation of a circuit in the Aube department which became one of the most effective groups in northern France. She undertook the dangerous task of acting as a courier, which involved continuous travel with compromising papers, W/T material, etc., and she was actively sought after by the Gestapo.

In November 1943, she came to England for training and was sent back to France in March 1944 as assistant to an organiser in the Seine et Marne. With this group, she helped to organise a number of receptions of stores and again acted as courier. She was also responsible for arranging transport and distribution of the arms and explosives received by air. When her commanding officer was arrested in July 1944 and the circuit penetrated by the Gestapo, she carried on with the remainder of the group although she was in considerable danger.

Ensign Fontaine showed remarkable courage and determination and unswerving devotion to duty. It is recommended that she be appointed a Member of the Order of the British Empire (Civil).[107]

There is no evidence that she was given the Croix de Guerre or the MBE. A subsequent note at the end of 1945 stated that she had been 'Slightly querulous, she used her personal charm somewhat unashamedly to get her places. But she got there and was an efficient and loyal courier and assistant. She had the gift for clandestine work and made great efforts.'[108] However, de Gaulle's government awarded her the Medaille de la Resistance. She married a Frenchman called Dupont and died on 9 May 1996, aged 83.

ALIX d'UNIENVILLE

Aged 25. Parachuted from a Halifax between La Raberie and Beauvais, 4.4 km south-west of Châteauvieux (Loir & Cher), on 31 March 1944. Escaped after capture. Awarded the Member of the British Empire and Croix de Guerre.

The next French woman to be flown into France was Alix d'Unienville. Born on 8 May 1918 to wealthy expatriate parents in Phoenix, Mauritius, she had dual French and British nationality. The family moved to a chateau near Vannes in Brittany in 1926 where she continued her education.

Following the German occupation, in June 1940 the family moved to London. When her brother joined de Gaulle's Free French forces, on 12 April 1941, she joined the Corps Auxiliaire Féminin and got a job in the HQ of the Foreign Affairs Section of the French Secret Service on Duke Street, London. Her work included producing radio broadcasts to be transmitted to France.

She then worked at de Gaulle's headquarters in Carlton Gardens as secretary to Alexandre Parodi, the executive director of the Committee of National Liberation, and Roland Pré, one of de Gaulle's deputies in the northern zone.

From September 1942 she worked at the Interior Ministry's Office on Hill Street as Jean-Louis Crémieux-Brilhac's copywriter. Known in England as Brilhac to protect his family in France, he was the secretary of the Free French propaganda committee and Head of the Clandestine Broadcasting Service of Free France., so Alix's work included producing the propaganda leaflets that the Tempsford Squadrons dropped over occupied France encouraging young men and women to join the Resistance and support de Gaulle.

One summer day in 1943, she was called by the BCRA and ordered to go to a meeting with their British counterparts Lieutenant-Colonel Leonard Dismore, then head of the RF Section. He reported to the Training Section that she was 'selected by the French to work as a secretary for a new Chef de Zone, who is being appointed. She will be required to leave during the January moon. It is requested that SAB [Student Assessment Board] be dispensed with also para-military training – she does not need such training. The French have asked that she should follow a B course and training at STS 51.'[109]

Given the cover name of Alix Michel, she was appointed a Lieutenant in the Women's Auxiliary Air Force and sent with other RF students for espionage training to Clobb Gorse, one of the requisitioned houses at Beaulieu, on 9 January 1944. At the end of her course, Major Wedgwood, her instructor, regarded her as,

> well-educated and has a sound intelligence, plenty of common sense and practical ability. These qualities are, perhaps, not apparant until one knows her well and she is modest, shy and not particularly gifted socially. She is keen and worked hard, displaying plenty of imagination

and initiative. Her character is strong, and she seems a courageous young woman. Although she has obviously been strictly brought up, her independence of thought and action have not been adversely affected. Her personality is pleasant; she has a sense of humour, but she is rather lacking in charm. Probably she would find it difficult to get on well with those of a social class different from her own. This student should be good at the work for which she has been selected. She is discreet and inconspicuous, the last person to be suspected. Codes: Taught Innocent Letter based on Playfair, Double Transposition, letter One-Time Pad. (Conventions fixed all three). Considerable practice required.[110]

Back in London, as she was to have two identities in France, her cover stories and identity papers were prepared. To give one an idea of her importance and an insight into the French organisation in London, in January 1944 copies were sent to the Comite d'Action en France, M. le Major Dismore, M. le Chef du B.C.R.A.L., M. le Chef du Bloc Opérationnel, M. le Chef du 4e Bureau (Capitaine Mamy), M. le Chef du 7e Bureau (Lieutenant Sublet), M. le Chef du 6e Bureau (Capitaine Lecointre), M. le Chef du Bureau du Chiffre, M. le Chef du C.E. (á l'attention du Lt Bonnal), 5e Bureau Transmissions and Archives 5e Bureau [M. le Lt-Col. KESWICK].[111]

In an interview she gave after the war, she reported that on her training course

'Specialist instructors came to teach us how to make false keys, to break locks, break into properties, poison dogs, survive in hostile conditions, in thick forests, and to find our way without a compass. I have often thought that if afterwards I had put these skills to work, my life would have been more amusing and profitable.'

She was also given weapons training, learning to turn quickly and fire a pistol in front of a large mirror, and finally parachute training, where her instructors were concerned that such a slim young woman would not be strong enough to control the chute in strong winds.

Once trained, she had to wait for the right weather and moon to jump into France. There were frequent false starts as flights were cancelled and they would go out on the town to drown their disappointment.

'We frequented the bars,' she recalled. 'We sowed seeds of scandal in the dining rooms of solemn London hotels. Clients were indignant. Who had the right to frolic in war? Irresponsible youth.'

Between 6 and 12 January, she stayed at both Dunham House and Fulshaw Hall. Danielle Reddé was her conducting officer as the bad weather that winter had led her flight to be postponed. Alix's instructor reported,

> This student is not very fit and seemed somewhat apprehensive of the course. She was quite keen and worked hard. However, her performance during the ground training was not very good. She had difficulty controlling her arms when making her egresses and on the trapeze. She made three quite good descents, two from aircraft by day and one by night. On each occasion, she made fairly good exits and landings. THREE DESCENTS. THIRD CLASS.[112]

On 31 March 1944, despite having the flu, she and M. Callau, code named Lace, were given their final briefing at 1 Dorset Square and then driven by their accompanying officers to Tempsford. To assist her personally in the field, she was given 50,000 francs. Her cover story in her personnel file explained the large sum as a legacy.

In the early hours of the following morning, she and Jacques Brunschwig were parachuted from a Halifax to the 'Dentelle' drop zone between La Raberie & Beauvais, 4.4 km south-west of Châteauvieux, 8.1 km south of Saint-Aignan, Loire-et-Cher. The reception committee had heard the message personelle on the BBC, 'Two angels will make lace tonight.'[113]

Accompanying the two agents were several dozen containers and two suitcases, one containing important documents, the other forty million francs for the Resistance. She landed in a tree and spent three-quarters of an hour disentangling herself from the parachute with a knife to reach the ground.

Transferring the two million francs in small denominations that she had brought for Skepper from her jumpsuit and burying any incriminating evidence, she was frightened that barking dogs would attract the attention of the Milice. What happened to Callau was not mentioned but, walking until dawn, she had to ask a young boy the directions to her safe house, something she ought to have learnt before the drop.[114]

On Palm Sunday, 2 April, she caught the train to Paris where she worked as a radio operator for Roland Pré, code named Oronte, arranging parachute drops of money and supplies for RF forces loyal to de Gaulle. Based in a grocer's shop on the Place de Passy, her mission was named ORONTES – Meadow Brown.

In Gubbins' citation for her to be awarded an MBE, it stated that, 'She jumped with great coolness and took up her duties with efficiency. In addition to the work specifically allotted to her, Lieut. d'Unienville re-organised a large part of the wireless network which transmitted from her area to the U.K. The group of women whom she recruited for this purpose developed in fact into the French Corps Auxiliare Féminin.'[115] These women were described as 'an important body of secretarial and transmission experts.'[116]

Chrystel Huq of Alliance Française, London, who interviewed Alix and Pré after the war, reported that he knew that,

>...the Allied Landings would happen soon, and the Délégation's mission was to put in place administrative structures that would be operational when the regime changed (for example the commissaires de la république, the préfets, etc.), not a mean task when they were still operating clandestinely. The challenge was to impose these new men in charge as the legitimate interlocutors of the Allies, in opposition to the AMGOT (Allied Military Government in Occupied Territories) that the Americans were in favour of. ORONTE's boss, Parodi, was in effect the successor to Jean Moulin. Their HQ was above the Luce grocer's shop, Place de Passy. As an organiser of W/T services (for which she recruited a number of women), Alix was specifically in charge of the reception and transmission of cable messages between the UK and resisters around Paris. It entailed a lot of walking around Paris, going from rendez-vous to rendez-vous; a lot of waiting too, a lot of memorising addresses and phone numbers. [...]
>
>Her alias was MYRTIL (from the Molière series of pseudonyms); her cover name changed from Michel (for training purposes) to Aline Davelan, a student from Bordeaux-born on 9 October 1922. She was also given another ID with papers, Aline Renault née Tezenas du Montcel, born on 9 June 1916 in Lyon. Her field name, i.e. how she was known in the Resistance, was Marie-France.[117]

Once back in France, she acknowledged a constant fear of being followed and apprehended by the SD, the Gestapo or the Milice.

On D-Day, she was with a small group including Pierre-Henri Tietgen, a future French Minister, awaiting a rendezvous outside a Bonmarche store in Paris when they were arrested by officers in the Sicherheitsdienst, the Nazis' intelligence service. Bundled into a car, they were taken to Avenue Foch, the SD headquarters, where they found the cyanide pill she had decided not to use. She managed to swallow the Metro ticket on which a contact's address was written when she went to the toilet. After a lengthy interrogation, she was transferred to Fresnes Prison. When her apartment was searched, a large quantity of money was found. She was tortured but only gave false information.

After several unsuccessful attempts to escape and desperate to avoid death, Alix feigned madness which led to her being transferred to Saint Anne's psychiatric hospital. She told Huq that she did a lot of silly things; telling her guards that her food was poisoned and refused to eat for a week. This resulted in her being sent to La Pitié, a place renowned for brutal atrocities. According to Gubbins' citation,

'During this period of captivity she behaved admirably, setting a high example of fortitude and refusing to answer when subjected to brutal interrogation. Lieut. D'UNIENVILLE was most highly regarded by all her colleagues and her work both before and after her mission did much to further good Franco-British relations.

On 15 August, as the Allies approached the capital, the Nazis included her as one of 665 women and 1,650 men put in cattle trucks on the 'death train' destined initially for Buchenwald and then Ravensbrück concentration camps. RAF attacks on the railway meant many bridges were blown up, so it took 36 hours to travel 60km. As the prisoners had to walk over a damaged bridge across the River Marne, she decided against jumping in as the drop was too great. While the prisoners surged round a drinking fountain at Méry-sur-Marne, she noticed the guards were not watching so she slipped into an open door. She recalled only hearing blood pounding in her temples while the guards were rounding up the prisoners outside. Hidden by the family, they arranged for her to be treated by a doctor. A local policeman at Thouvenot-á Saâcy-sur-Marne then looked after her until American troops arrived, who drove her back to Paris in a jeep.

Jean-Michel Rémy, a fellow resister, and friend, described her as 'placid, efficient, punctual, was blessed with such composure that allowed her, almost the only one amongst the deportees on the trains of horror [...] to carry off a miraculous escape.' [118]

When she got back to her apartment, she told Huq that,

It was here that I had heard news of the landings and immediately set off on this long journey in the depths of the night. I crossed the same threshold that I had on my way out two months earlier. Just two months. It seemed to me that between those two doorways, a whole lifetime had gone by. And no doubt it was the case as, from then on, a barrier would separate these two eras: Before and After.[119]

Acknowledging that she was very fortunate, she commented that 'Many of my comrades were arrested; many are dead.' She continued, 'Of others I know nothing, and I never will know anything because I have forgotten their names. Only here and there floats a young face, a gesture, a word, a smile, an anecdote. All the rest have plunged into the shadows.'

As well as being awarded the MBE, the French honoured her with the Croix de Guerre and the Légion d'Honneur. After working for several weekly magazines, including being a war correspondent for American Forces in the Far East, she became one of Air France's first stewardesses. Her book *En Voi, journal d'un hôtesse de l'air* won the Albert Londres literary prize in 1950. She died on 10 November 2015, aged 97.

Following Operation *Torch*, the Allied invasion of North Africa in November 1942, a forward base was established in fashionable villas outside Algiers. Code named MASSINGHAM, it included SOE's AMF Section commanded by Dodds-Parker and the French set up offices known as BCRA Algiers. Air and naval operations were coordinated to infiltrate agents and supplies into Corsica, Sardinia, Italy, Greece, Yugoslavia as well as the southern part of France with far less risk of anti-aircraft gunfire shooting the planes down. Operations increased after the Italian surrender in September 1943 as the Allies then controlled the airspace over Italy.

An agreement was made with Admiral François Darlan, Commander in Chief of the French Navy and deputy leader pf the pro-German Vichy regime, whereby he would control the French Forces in North Africa in exchange for joining the Allies.

As German forces invaded the Unoccupied Zone in retaliation, Colonel Lucien Merlin, Commander in Chief of Land and Air Forces in North Africa, needed more French men to support Allied attacks on Greece, Italy, Corsica and eventually the Mediterranean coast of France. With the agreement of General Jean de Lattre de Tassigny, the head of the First French Army, on 20 November 1942, as part of the military reorganisation in North Africa, the Transmissions Army, part of the Ministry of Post and Telecommunications, was expanded to create the Corps Féminin des Transmissions. This allowed the men to be transferred to more active duty and French women living in their North African colonies to play a more important role in the Armed Forces as wireless telegraphists, telephone exchange operators, teletypists, wireless operators, and analysts.

Although not allowed to vote, they were allowed to work with the military. One hundred and fifty women volunteers, who became known as the 'Merlinettes' in honour of the Corps' founder, took part in the Allied advance on Tunisia and then served as wireless operators and teletypists in Tebessa, Sfax, Sousse, Elba Ksour and Le Kef.

In January 1943, following the assassination of Darlan by a Gaullist agent, his replacement, General Henri Giraud, met General Eisenhower, General de Gaulle and Winston Churchill at Casablanca, a meeting which led to the statement of 'unconditional surrender' – the Axis powers would be fought to their ultimate defeat.

The Merlinettes were to play their role in facilitating the ultimate surrender of Italian and German forces. Many took part in the French Expeditionary Corps' campaign of Italy, landing in Naples and being involved in the battles of Monte Cassino and the Garigliano, Rome and finally reaching Siena where they participated in the parade of 14 July 1944. Many were involved in Operation *Dragoon*, the Allied landing, near Saint-Tropez in Provence, and participated in the 1st Army attacks on Germany troops as far as Sigmaringen Innsbruck on 9 July 1945.

Large posters appeared on the streets of Morocco, Algeria, and Tunisia once the occupying German forces had left in May 1943. One showed two young women, one blonde, one brunette, in military uniform with the caption: 'Girls, get involved, your place in the offices will allow a man to take up arms to reform our army.'

Another showing two attractive women looking like air hostesses read: '*To liberate France, Girls, come to* the Corps Féminin Transmissions.'[120]

The Merlinettes were claimed to have been the first French women soldiers, 'because, until then, women's involvement was forbidden by law in the French army. They were in truth not ancillary civilians but soldiers, very often in the front line of the authentic military.'[121]

Paulette Vuillaume, one of the Merlinettes, commented that, even though these young women were well aware of not being soldiers on the front line, their dedication was exemplary. 'We would carry on our heart the same copper badge, the Gallic rooster stood on his spurs [and] represent a single soldier; the soldier in the French Army...'

By March 1944, the number of young women in the Corps de Féminin des Transmissions in the Land Army was about 2000 with about 400 in the Air Force. Army General de Lattre de Tassigny paid them the following tribute:

Female volunteers of the First Army, whatever their task or obscure exhilaration, showed a smiling dedication, zeal without failure, some magnificent heroism. They can be proud of the part they have taken our victory. Tomorrow under the uniform again or return to their homes, they are intimately faithful to the spirit of the army 'Rhine and Danube.' Thus, they continue to serve France.

The life expectancy for wireless operators in France was very low – an estimated 60 per cent did not return. Fifty Merlinettes were sent to work in France behind the lines of whom five were killed, a 90 per cent success rate. Whether this was due to improved training and equipment is not known. It is possible that, by the time they were infiltrated, the German direction finding teams had been disbanded and were on their way back to Germany.

SUZANNE MERTZISEN

Aged 24. Parachuted from a Halifax near Jouac, 25 km north-west of La Souterraine (Haute-Vienne), on 5 April 1944. Captured and executed at Ravensbrück. Awarded the Medaille de Resistance, the Military Cross and later the Chevalier of the Legion d'Honneur.

Suzanne Mertzisen-Boitte was one of the first French women in Algeria to volunteer to join the Corps Féminin des Transmissions. Born Suzanne Boitte Lesmele on 15 May 1919 in Colombes, a north-western suburb of Paris, she grew up in a house on the corner of rue St Denis and Orme.

Little has come to light about her early life, but, to coincide with the unveiling of a memorial in her honour in her birthplace, various articles appeared on a blog and other websites which tell her wartime story.

In 1938, when she was 19, she married Sergeant Gabriel Mertzisen, a 24-year-old French fighter pilot. Following the birth of their daughter, Danielle, in 1940, they moved to Algeria to escape the German occupation and to be near her parents-in-law. She lived at 20 Rue de Constantine, Algiers, but when her husband went off to fight in Syria, she rarely saw him.

On 18 January 1943, she responded to posters asking for volunteers to join the Corps Feminin des Transmissions. Among the other volunteers were Marie-Louise Cloarec, Eugénie Djendi, Pierrette Louin and Elisabeth Torlet. Whether they had known each other beforehand is not known.

Mireille Hui, one of the Merlinettes who was infiltrated into Italy, wrote about the organisation in her book with the same title. She reported that, after their training at Staouëli, about 15 km west of Algiers, Suzanne volunteered to join the Algiers Deuxième Bureau (the French Intelligence Office) which needed wireless specialists. It was headed by Commander Paul Paillole who later offered the female recruits the opportunity of being sent back to France to operate behind enemy lines. Despite being warned of the extreme dangers involved, Suzanne and some others agreed.

In January 1944, along with Marie-Louise Cloarec, Pierrette Louin and other colleagues in the Central Bureau of Intelligence and Action Algiers (BCRAA), they were sent for further training with the BCRA in London. They undertook two operational training courses at Praewood House in St Albans where SIS and OSS officers provided a comprehensive programme that lasted two months. It included general intelligence about their DZ and area of operation, the topography, identification of enemy insignia on uniform and material, identifying targets for the Allies to bomb, combat sport, shooting, handling of explosives, sabotage, driving cars, trucks and motorcycles, transmissions and security. They also received parachute training.

Having been briefed and prepared for her mission, on the night of 5/6 April 1944, Suzanne was flown out of Tempsford in a Halifax piloted by 161 Squadron Flight Sergeant Bransden on Operation *Wygelia*. Accompanied by BCRAA Marie-Louise Cloarec code named Lesaint, Pierrette Louin alias Pierrette Salina, Philippe Cravat and Pierre X, they parachuted near Jouac, 25 km north-west of La Souterraine and about 50 km north of Limoges, Haute-Vienne.[122]

Exactly what their work entailed is unknown, but website articles suggest Suzanne, using the cover names Suzy Leroy and Lemesle, reached Paris on 10 April with Marie-Louise and Pierrette.

Three days later, after being denounced to the Germans, she and the other two women were arrested. Details of her interrogation, imprisonment in Fresnes and Ravensbrück and her execution on 18 January 1945 are referred to in Pierrette Louin's account.

Suzanne was declared 'Died for France' and in recognition of her work she was awarded the Medaille de la Resistance and the Military Cross. In August 2012, she was posthumously awarded the Chevalier of the Legion d'Honneur. Jean-Georges Jaillot-Combelas, the nephew of Suzanne Combelas, another Merlinette, organised a commemorative plaque at her home in Colombes.

MARIE-LOUISE CLOAREC
Aged 26. Parachuted from a Halifax near Jouac, 25 km north-west of La Souterraine (Haute-Vienne), on 5 April 1944. Captured and executed at Ravensbrück. Awarded the Croix de Guerre with palm and the Medaille de Resistance.

Marie Louise Cloarec was born on 10 May 1917 in Carhaix, Finistère, the daughter of Louis Pierre Cloarec, a merchant, and Jane Josephine Clech. Little is known of her early life except that she trained as a nursery nurse and in May 1940, she and a friend left Brittany, hoping to do something to help her country.

She went to Grenoble, Isère, in the unoccupied zone and found work in a nursery. While there she met a French officer about to be transferred to Algiers. She pretended to be the governess in his family, a cover to allow her to leave the country.[123]

On 11 January 1943, she volunteered for the Corps de Féminin des Transmissions and trained with Eugénie Djendi, Pierrette Louin and Suzanne Mertzisen at Staouëli, near Algiers. All four volunteered to become wireless operators in occupied France.

After being sent to Britain for additional training, Marie Louise, Pierrette and Suzanne were parachuted into France on 6 April 1944. Using the cover names of Leclech and Lesaint, after staying with her cousins, Albert and Falquet, in the Dordogne, they moved to Paris where they stayed initially at Hotel Lefevre, rue Clerc, then with Pierrette's cousin, Fernand Louin, a watchmaker, at 88 Rue Saint Dominique.

Following denouncement, they were arrested by the Gestapo on 27 April and after almost a year in Fresnes Prison, on August 8, 1944, she was sent to Ravensbrück with a convoy of other women including Pierrette and Suzanne, where they met Eugenie Djendi. All four were executed on 18 January 1945.

Declared 'Died for France', she was awarded the Croix de Guerre with palm and the Medaille de la Resistance Française. Her name is engraved on the memorial of Mont Valerian.

PIERRETTE LOUIN
Aged 23. Parachuted from a Halifax near Jouac, 25 km north-west of La Souterraine (Haute-Vienne) on 5 April 1944. Captured and executed at Ravensbrück. Awarded the Croix de Guerre with palm and the Medaille de Resistance.

Pierrette Louin was born in Oran, Algeria, on 1 October 1920. Little has come to light about her early life, but the AASSDN (*Anciens des Services Spéciaux de la Défense*) website has provided much biographical detail.

She was one of the young women who volunteered to join the Merlinettes after the landing of the Anglo-Americans on 8 November 1942 in Morocco and Algeria. After training in Staouëli, near Algiers, she volunteered to undertake a dangerous mission behind enemy lines and was sent to London for the additional training mentioned earlier.

Prepared for her mission with identity papers in the name of Pierrette Salina, on the night of 5/6 April 1944, she parachuted with Marie-Louise Cloarec, Suzanne Mertzisen, Philippe Cravat and Pierre X, near Jouac, 25 km north-west of La Souterraine, about 80 km north of Limoges, Haute-Vienne.[124]

Mireille Hui's research shed light on her and the other women's arrest, imprisonment, and death. Having been denounced to the Germans, she was interned at Fresnes for almost a year and was amongst a convoy of women who, on 8 August 1944, were taken from Pantin Station, first to Neue Bremm transit camp and then to Ravensbrück. There they met Eugénie Djendi and, under Hitler's *Nacht und Nebel* (Night and Fog) order, all four women were executed on 18 January 1945.[125]

The AASSDN website quoted Hui's account of 'the Louin case', made in Paris on 22 February 1945 (Arch. of Algiers), saying that the drop took place between Limoges and Angouleme.

According to Albert and Falquet, Mary-Louise Cloarec's cousins in the Dordogne, the three young women joined the Jouac network. When they reached Paris, they were accommodated first at the hotel Lefevre, rue Clerc, then with her cousin Fernand Louin [...].

Questioned after the war, he reported that, '...I had not seen either parent since seeing Pierrette in 1937 ... On 10 April 1944, Ms. Pierrette Louin arrived around 4 am. She asked me for a private interview and immediately told me she had just parachuted in from London and wanted to stay in my home for two or three days. She returned and brought with her one of her friends, Miss Marie Louise Cloarec ... I kept them in the house until their arrest on April 27, 1944.

They told me they had been parachuted in the company of friends (three girls and two men) ... Suzy turned up at my shop about noon. The same day, I had a visit from a fellow whose name I know. They told me that parachute operation was conducted in the region of Angoulême,... They each had a large suitcase and bags of lesser importance.

During their stay in my house, I was struck by their recklessness ... My cousin had an identity card to my mind which had been made in London and bearing the address of my store on rue Saint Dominique. She also had ration cards in her name. Other papers were also provided with valid identification .... I was getting phone calls asking me for Miss Lesaint, [the pseudonym of M-L. Cloarec].'[126]

According to the testimony of Albert Falquet, who had met the sister M.-L. Cloarec, the latter told him that Pierrette had a fairly large sum of money which she had given to one of her leaders in the Resistance.

Fernand Louin's brother, Marcel also testified (November 10, 1944): 'I was invited by my brother to dinner, and the young girls were at his home ... These people told me they had come from London where they had spent six months during which they had to follow a special training including three parachute jumps. They showed their ID cards to me which were perfectly in order. I cannot remember the name that appeared on it, but I think it was theirs. We noticed that they had Gauloises [French cigarettes] slightly larger than the French kind. I know that during their stay at my brother's that they had done several missions before they left Paris. I saw them a second time in order to make them a business suit using cloth they had brought from England. At the first meal were present: my wife, my brother, my son Paul Louin and a boy that I was hiding who bore the fictitious name of Claude Brown, whose real identity is Adrien Dussol. These girls said they had to change addresses every day or every other day. This is why I was anxious to see them stay at my brother's.'

However, Ms. Madeleine Fillon, who had worked with Fernand Louin an hour a day in early March to late April 1944, said she had not known that he harboured girls. Ms. Saisset (the guardian of the building?), reported that she knew this and had noticed that they led 'a very hectic life and that many young people were coming and going constantly.'

Mary-Louise's cousin, Albert Falquet Cloarec saw Pierrette Louin on 25 April and reported that she 'told me she was responsible for transporting weapons and items and, one day, on Pont de l'Alma, she was arrested in the company of a young man, while they were both carrying very heavy suitcases, and one of the officers asked that the bags are opened, which fortunately did not need to be done. I know she was doing other equally dangerous transportation on the Metro.

She said he had contacted the head of its network she called the Colonel. Since she was crossing the Pont de l'Alma I deduce that the material ought to be stored at Rue Saint Dominique. Miss Anne Cloarec, the sister of Marie-Louise, arrived in Paris on 12 October 1944. She came to know where her sister was and what fate awaited her. Thus, Mr. Louin made me feel clear enough ... I learned that Mr. Louin had a tendency to drink, but his patriotic feelings were well known.'

Fernand Louin said: 'We went out to eat at "Little Panama," rue Amélie ... I fear that there was an informer amongst the regulars at this restaurant ...' It was also believed that young women were denounced by an enemy agent who had infiltrated the network.

Fernand Louin continued: 'On Thursday, April 27, 1944, around noon, a man came in asking for Ms. Pierrette. I called her on the phone. She came down with Marie-Louise. They emerged onto the sidewalk with said individual and returned almost immediately, fuelled by five individuals' revolvers. They handcuffed the two young girls while the first held me back into compliance with his revolver and asked me to pretend nothing had happened. My cousin and his girlfriend were pushed into the back shop, and then they climbed the stairs of the apartment ...

The German policeman asked me to report immediately on the arrival of the third person I knew (so he knew that there were three people) ... All afternoon he repeated to me that I had to report the arrival of the third woman, failing which my wife and children would be deported ...

As by 7 pm Suzy had still not arrived, he told me to close the store and follow him to rue Jean Nicot ... Then about a quarter of an hour later, I saw Suzy (probably caught in a trap set near the store), accompanied by two other individuals.'

Ms. Saisset said: 'These girls did not receive any mail with the exception of a mail on behalf of a young girl who visited very frequently but who did not live there. This dispatch was brought on the day of the arrest and refused by me ... The Gestapo were in the apartment. I saw this girl (Suzy), I wanted to prevent it, but I hesitated.'

Fernand Louin said, 'We all went to Avenue Foch ... After arriving at Avenue Foch, we were taken up to the seventh floor. They made me go into a dressing room where I heard the questioning of Pierrette's identity, called over from London' Fernand Louin would also tell his brother that he was surprised when questioned to see that the Gestapo already knew everything and that young women appeared to have been followed since their parachute drop. Louin and Marcel remembered, 'they claimed that the County was aware of Limoges, and the parachute drop was very well organized.'

Fernand Louin continued: 'The next morning around 9.30, they made me go with Pierrette back to rue Saint Dominique, Pierrette was in the apartment, at my store. I had to get out the ban [telling others not to come] ... That night I closed my store at 7 pm and went up to the apartment where I brought dinner for Pierrette and two goaltenders ... The next morning I was able to reopen the store ... then, about 6.30, one of the guards went down, saying: "Pierrette must leave with her German conductor, you can leave with your wife."'

On Friday morning, following the arrest, at noon, Pierrette Louin was able to show her cousin a paper on which were written these words: 'Heads arrested are considered prisoners of war.' If their Chief had been arrested, this could explain the long wait the girls had at rue Saint Dominique.

The Gestapo found in their rooms two wireless sets and four revolvers. During questioning, after the Liberation, the German Ernst Vogt, the [Abwehr] interpreter in Paris, said that after the interrogation of Eugénie Djendi [arrested on 10 April 1944, 'three other girls in the same department of Algiers were parachuted into France. The examination of these three young girls brought us nothing new. They knew nothing of their future work or the organization in France. No arrest was made following their statements.' These were Pierrette Louin Marie-Louise Cloarec and Suzanne Mertzisen.

Ernst Vogt added: 'One of them, Suzy, and one I forget the name, told me on the day of her arrest or the next day that she was to have an appointment at noon at the Luxembourg Gardens with an officer of the organization of France. I accompanied her there with a friend. We left her to walk for about an hour, and watched from a distance. Nobody came'. (The girl had shown a symbol of prudence?)

Georges Pinchenier (alias Lt Lafitte), was parachuted and arrested with two wireless sets. Jenny Djendi and Marcel Leblond [alias of Marcel Corbusier who parachuted with 'Jenny'] wrote in October 1945 to Pierrette's father: 'Transferred Avenue Foch in Paris, where I stayed until April 27th, the day of the Pierrette and Marie-Louise (Cloarec)'s arrest), I was that day confined to my cell at [3, Place des] États-Unis [the Gestapo interrogation centre] but there was no news of Jenny.

A few days later, as things quickly got known in prison, I became convinced that Marie-Louise and her friend Suzy Mertzisen were above me, but I could not make their presence known, my fault [in not] try to communicate them directly.

Finally, on May 15, my two neighbouring cell mates disappeared and were replaced by Pierrette and Jenny. Pierrette had great morale that day. As I prepared my escape for the next night, she managed, through a hole made in the door, to hand me a subway map and 300 francs, which had not been stolen. She gave me that day all the details you know about her arrest and that of our comrades. Finally, she told me she had no intention of staying in jail, and she was already considering the possibility of escape. I can say that it is partly thanks to her that my escape succeeded. Leblond, very depressed, crushed and black, advised me to abandon my project, and it may well be that without the presence in the cell next to my two good friends, I decided not to carry it out. Throughout the night and the nights were long, they attracted the attention of guards on them by their cries, their jokes and songs. So much so that I could finish my work and I was free at daybreak.'

Pierrette Louin, Marie-Louise Cloarec, and Suzanne Mertzisen were interned at Fresnes before being deported to Ravensbrück, probably in the convoy which left Compiègne August 8, 1944. There they met Eugénie Djendi.

A Ministry of Defence paper said: 'After asking several times to the camp commander, Fritz Suhren, for a transfer to a camp of prisoners of war, the young women are called on January 18, 1945, 16,00 to the camp office. From there, the evidence left room for speculation.

Ms. Postel-Vinay (testimony of September 20, 1949, Arch. Algiers) has personal knowledge of the camp and especially Jenny Djendi and Suzy Mertzisen who had become the best friend of her fellow Czech Milena Seborova. She had managed to get hired in the small column of workers that ran the Hilfskommando II, [auxiliary work group] in the real business of sabotage, where S. Mertzisen enjoyed exceptional living conditions.

'Two months before their disappearance, the four girls had been called to the Schreibstube [main hospital administration office] for questioning their identity. It was the custom before the executions, but not invariably. Moreover, these women believed that this was a favourable response to their request for transfer to a British military prison camp, especially as the German who had received them had been very gracious and expressed concern about Jenny Djendi's health.

On 18 January 1945, they were again summoned to the office. They went there happily, still convinced that they would be transferred to a less painful camp. However, Miléna Seborova was concerned about Suzy Mertzisen. She saw her with her three comrades come out of the office. All four had replaced their shoes with light slippers.' The German Ruth Neudecker, who was always volunteering for executions, accompanied them.

In Ravensbrück (ed. of Braconniere, Neuchâtel), it is written: 'At the same time the road that ran past the Crematorium towards Siemens was barred by the SS. Ms. Postel-Vinay and her comrades then assumed they were hanged because they believed that a gallows had been built sometime in 1944, next to the crematorium...

They searched the huge pile of clothes belonging to the dead and Milena Seborova found the grey coat of Suzy Mertzisen and that of another, which still contained their card in the pocket.'

Rosane (Renée Lascroux), professor of CEG, Pierrette Louin's classmate in high school in Oran, who was deported to Ravensbrück and liberated from Bergen-Belsen (quoted in the Bulletin of Austerlitz Club, reprinted in Bulletin No. AASSDN 184), reported: 'On 18 January 1945, the French sheet [?] into mourning. From the morning roll call, Pierrette and Marie-Louise Cloarec, our small parachutist, Suzy and Jenny and their radio companions (...) were warned by the camp commander that they were strictly forbidden to leave the block until the appointed time - 4:30 p.m.

Few of us knew the news, we could not imagine the drama, it was prudent to be silent for a bit and for ourselves. I spent the day with them. Pierrette and Marie Louise were children. Pierrette, twenty-two years old, received her stripes [military promotion] in Algiers, she liked Africa where she helped to prepare for the American landing. Marie-Louise is a brave Breton twenty-four years old; she went to war, and Suzy, of Metz, is the mother of a six-year-old girl. Jenny loves the risk. (...) Would they be treated as soldiers?

The blow broke, what amazement seized us, the most preventable. In the evening we awaited their return to the barracks, without hope. Marie-Louise had devised a thousand conjectures, still full of illusions;

she took several addresses. Pierrette said no word, she thought. However, they were shot. Night falls, the farm block, few slept there. The next day we started our research. A register listed the next four road numbers, the reference wave and classic [?]: 'transport without destination'. It's strange. Between her teeth, a woman whispered: this is how it shows they were shot.'

Later, our Czech friends manage to find clothes and road numbers returned to the oven. Our investigation continues. At six o'clock they left the bunker, we saw them pass. a column outside saw the road blocked to a certain place, and in the woods near a shed, the SS were agitated. We even heard gunshots. A truck headed for the crematorium, unless it was to the mass grave in the forest...

The testimonials do not overlap; the four young women were shot at 18:30 in a shack near the crematorium or hanged on the gallows of the camp. Milena Seborova, assigned to the laundry room, thought they were hanged: there were no bullet marks or blood on their clothes. It was even echoed by Ms. Lindell, a survivor of the camp, who said (Archives of Algiers, Background paper for May 18, 1949) that Miss Kate Johansen, a Norwegian assigned to the clothing store, had received four French clothes without giving civilian clothes in exchange. 'When Ms. Lindell stated about these cast-offs, there was no sign of bullets and blood. It is said in the statement of a witness, a German whom she did not know the name of who worked in the employee's clothing store, she put her hand on her neck, indicating that these women had been hanged.'

A Hungarian survivor of Auschwitz, Dr. Nyisli, reported that there were also lead bullets of very small calibre, shot in the neck. Their bodies were burned or buried in a mass grave of the forest.

Mireille Hui says they were murdered on orders from Berlin, from the testimony of SS camp commander, Suhren, and his deputy, Schwartzhuber, questioned after their arrest by the Allies.

Very aware of the risks that she was taking, Pierrette Louin had written to London, January 23, 1944, before leaving on a mission, a letter for her family, which read:

'Dear All, Before leaving for the great adventure, I wanted to tell you all myself. This may be a consolation to you because if you read it, it is because I am no more. I know what your sentence will be but the only thing that will not diminish, but make it less bitter, is that my death will not have been useless. It will be a service to France.

It you should not be too sad because that death is the only one I want to have because it is the most beautiful. My age does not matter, what matters is that I'm not going to fight as any unit in a herd who fights because "it is well" because it's an obligation. I volunteered – and that means a lot – it's anything but a word – it means above all the lucidity, choice. This mission which I will come back from, maybe not, I have not suffered as a command. I did not blindly accept it. No. I thought, and I have chosen. This my mind has consented to, and therefore giving my life is no longer a sacrifice. But I love life. I feel within me a strength, a taste of the fight that could earn me my life. But I could not keep momentum, nor have the desire to live, if I don't do what is in my mind. And this thing is no longer the sentimental jingoism of my childhood. This is something that is part of me, it is the love of France. A passion that is not instinctive, but lucid, stripped of ridiculous emotion. I'm not going to fight for words or ideas or people. I will not fight against the words, ideas and other people, but to save a whole that cannot disappear, a form of life, an ideal, it is France. I cannot explain it, but I feel France in me, and that's why I chose to leave, I did not want to be a powerless spectator who merely suffers in words, that I refused to buy my life at the cost of my mind. That's why I got involved. Luckily I was quickly served.

In July, I was one of the two girls to whom the opportunity to serve has been given. The next second I had accepted. So I joined the 2nd Bureau. In September, I arrived in London by air. I completed my education by training in technical clandestine radio. Then I did paratrooper training. After a poor start in November, there were the days of waiting and walking – and again the hope was for a few days.

So, one night, when the moon appears, a plane will take me over France. I'll jump by parachute, and accomplish my mission. I have false papers and illegal radios. My mission will be to transmit to London and Algiers information that agents and myself collect. I know none of the dangers I incur. I know I'm unlikely to get away. The least I risk it is the fortress somewhere in Germany. But does that count since I have fought? If I die, it will be the rule of the game, no regrets, no bitterness because my soul is intact. If I live, I have earned my right to life, and the joy of having been faithful to my ideal.

But I think of you, who stay, and I have much trouble. But I know you will understand and approve of me. We will meet again. I bid you farewell, without sadness. Again, I embrace you with all my love. Pierrette.

Declared 'Died for France', Pierrette Louin received the Croix de Guerre with palm and the Medaille de la Resistance. Field Marshal Montgomery, Commander in Chief of the 21st Army Group, awarded her a Certificate of Service A street in Toulouse has been named after her, and there is a plaque in her honour on the wall of her school.

EUGÉNIE DJENDI

Aged 20. Parachuted from a Halifax near Sully-sur-Loire (Loiret) on 9 April 1944. Captured and executed at Ravensbrück. Awarded the Chevalier of the Legion d'Honneur, Croix de Guerre with palms and Medaille de Resistance.

Eugénie Djendi, mentioned earlier, was another member of the Merlinettes. Born on 8 April 1923 in Bone, a coastal town about 10 km south of Annaba, Algeria, she grew up with her parents, Salah ben Chefrai Djendi Fallah and Antoinette Silvani. Details of her early life have yet to come to light but by 1943 she had moved to 94 Rue Michelet, Algiers. Like Suzanne Mertzisen, Marie-Louise and Pierrette Louin, she volunteered to join the Corps de Féminin des Transmissions and was trained at Staouëli before being sent to Britain.

Unlike the other three women, on 5 January 1944 she joined the SOE's French Section in North Africa but a note in her file, dated 2 February, stated that her services had been dispensed with.[127]

Taken on by the BCRAL, she was given identity papers in the name of Jacqueline Dubreuil and prepared for Mission BERLIN to operate in the Paris region and establish links with Algiers and London. Whether she received additional training was not documented.

On 9 April 1944, Flight Sergeant McGibbon of 161 Squadron flew his Halifax from Tempsford on Operation *Syringa/Libelluie* and parachuted her, George Pinchenier and Marcel Corbusier near Sully sur Loire, Loiret.[128]

Details of Pinchenier have yet to come to light but, according to the AASSDN website, Corbusier was a Belgian who was naturalised French in 1938, spoke Flemish, French, English and German and became Secretary for Indigenous Affairs in Hagora, South Morocco, before being taken to Britain.

All three were arrested the day after their arrival with the two wireless sets and all their equipment. Interrogated at 1a Avenue Foch, she was imprisoned initially at 2 Place des États-Unis, then at Fresnes and Compiègne. On 15 August 1944, she was taken initially to the Neue Bremm camp, and then to Ravensbrück concentration camp.

Yvonne Baseden, one of the fifty women who survived Ravensbrück concentration camp, reported on her return to Britain that, after being captured on 26 June 1944 and imprisoned in Dijon,

...on my way to Germany at Saarbrueck I came into contact with three girl parachutists whom I knew DANIEL [Denise Bloch], VIOLETTE

[Szabó] and LILIAN [Rolfe]. With them also were four French girl parachutists whom I had not met before who had been with the British girls. They had come from Fresnes. All of them were in good health and had suffered no ill-treatment after their arrest. Of the French girls I only really knew one; her name is JENNY SILVANI, who, I believe, lived in Algiers. [This must have been Djendi, whose mother's maiden name was Silvani.] These girls told me that, although they had had no ill treatment in Paris they travelled chained to one another because one of them had attempted to escape on the way. They had also been chained in the hut where they were taken but the chains had been removed before I saw them. They left three days after I arrived with a batch of Frenchwomen on their way somewhere in Germany. [...]

In the meantime, the four French parachutists had remained in the camp and I had then seen quite a lot of JENNY SYLVANI. She told me that one of the others called SUZANNE X had been to see one of the S.S. officers to try and see if she could receive Red Cross parcels and better treatment for he two friends who were ill. I understand she was very well received in the S.S. officer and they said they would see what could be done, she was then recalled a few days later with JENNY SYLVANI and was again very well received and Jenny told me that they seemed to have received orders from Berlin about them on a blue telegram form which was lying in front of the officer but she had no idea what these were. They were told that their demands had been considered and they would hear more about them but they should be available for call. A week later Jenny came to see me saying they had been recalled. This was in January this year and was the last time I saw her. I heard a day later that the four girls had been standing in their striped dresses in front of the S.S. office and guarded by an S.S. guard which was most unusual. This information was second-hand. They were taken away by lorry and I heard later they had been hanged. This was more or less confirmed when their clothes came back.[129]

After five months surviving the horrors of Ravensbrück, she was executed with Suzanne Mertzisen, Pierrette Loin and Marie-Louise Cloarec on 18 January 1945. Corbusier was shot on 5 September 1944 in Weimar. Pinchenier's fate is unknown.[130]

The AASSDN website included the following citations: 'Wireless Operator, part of an espionage network, spent countless hours to carry out the task entrusted to her. Established the radio link with Algiers and London and sent important messages to the command.' 'Young

Frenchwoman animated by the purest spirit of sacrifice and a sublime heroism.'[131]

In recognition of her work she was awarded the Chevalier of the Legion d'Honneur, Croix de Guerre with palms and Medaille de Resistance and her name is engraved on the Mont Valerien memorial.[132]

Hui's research revealed ninety-two wireless operators were infiltrated into France, twelve were injured on landing, thirty-two were captured, and six were executed. How many of them were women was not stated, but there were several other Merlinettes not included in Tillet's list of infiltrations. Evelyne Valve was captured in Vendome and killed by the Germans. Fréderique Bigrel, Mlle Moreau and Mlle Martini managed their missions but there were no other details.

MARCELLE SOMERS
Aged 46. Landed by Hudson near Manziat, 9.5 km north-north-east of Mâcon (Saone & Loire), on 3 May 1944. Awarded the Member of the British Empire medal and Croix de Guerre.

On 3 May 1944, the moon period before D-Day, Flying Officer Harold Ibbott took eight passengers in his Hudson to a field 3 km north-north-west of Manziat, north-northeast of Mâcon and about 100 km west of Geneva. Marcelle Somers, code name *Albanais,* was accompanied by seven other passengers, including Commandant Maurice Barthélémy, code named Barrat; Colonel Paul Hanneton, code named Ligne; Jacques Davout d'Auerstaerdt, code named Ovale; Michel Dequare, code named Symetrie; Doctor Limousin and two saboteurs, Auguste Chevalier, who had two code names, Aiguillon and Lt Bernard, and Charles Mengin, code named Batteuse.[133]

She and her two children were all involved with SOE. According to her family's personnel files, she was born Marcelle Georges on 1 October 1897 in Guarbecques, Pas de Calais. Details of her early life were not included, only that she married Joseph Somers, an Englishman, and lived at 4 Rue de Paris, Lens, Pas de Calais.

In June 1940, with 17-year-old Claud and 16-year-old Josiane, they escaped from St Malo. The family's home was at 22 Roland Gardens in Kensington and it appeared that Marcelle worked for de Gaulle's government-in-exile but in what capacity was not mentioned. Josiane lied about her age and joined the Free French Air Force while Claus joined the RAF. Both children were later recruited by the SOE.

On 30 October 1943, when Marcelle was 46, RF Section informed the Training Section that, 'This lady is handpicked by Col. de Cheveigne to work as a courier in a new organisation he proposes to establish. She will do no paramilitary training at his request, but it is felt that during her three weeks' course at Group B commencing 7.11.43. [...] opportunities can be found for her to do open-air exercises.'[134]

Three weeks later, Marcelle was sent to Boarmans and at the end of November, her instructor reported that,

> She is not highly educated but has good practical intelligence. She is sensible, thorough and has plenty of imagination. She plans an operation with business-like efficiency and gives clear, definite orders. She is quick and resourceful when the unexpected happens. She is very keen and worked hard. At the same time, she is not strong and should not have to do very active work. She has a strong character, is determined, loyal and reliable. She is deeply religious. She has a pleasant, cheerful personality and has the authority to inspire confidence in subordinates. She seems well qualified to act as a courier. Her inconspicuous appearance would be a great asset. She is also used to towns as well as the country.
>
> Codes: Showed little aptitude for code work and had the greatest difficulty remembering the systems taught. She worked hard and did her best but, unfortunately, without success. Even with a great deal more practice it is doubtful whether she should be given any responsibility in codes work.[135]

Further attempts to train her in codes and wireless telegraphy at Fawley Court (STS 41 but later STS 54a) and Thame Park failed as, according to one of her instructors, she could not tell the difference between a dash and a dot. As she was considered too frail for parachute training, she was accommodated first at Gorse Hill (STS 50) and then at Gumley Hall (STS 41), Market Harborough, Leicestershire, to await a Hudson flight.

Her instructor praised her conscientiousness and the help she gave to other students but commented, 'I gather a certain amount of anxiety has been caused in her family through her correspondence taking such a time to get through, her son in the RAF wired her the other day as he had not heard from her for some time. She is leaving here tomorrow 9.3.44 and returning to London for an interview with her Section.'[136]

Prepared for her mission, she was flown out of Tempsford on 3 May. When the Hudson landed and the incoming passengers got out, eight other passengers got in, including Mme Fleury and her baby daughter who celebrated her first birthday in the Royal Patriotic School in Wandsworth. Mme Fleury had only recently been released by the Gestapo after four months' imprisonment for questioning over her husband's clandestine radio operations. A stool pigeon, someone planted to win her confidence in order to make her talk, had been in her cell with her but she did not provide any information.

Code named Albanais and given 50,000 francs, Marcelle's mission was to liaise with Chief A.P.[?] and start with a tour of exploration and research potential DZs for future infiltrations in the B.2 area between Bordeaux and Tours before and after D-Day. In *Flight Most Secret*, Gibb McCall says that she worked with CONE, one of the RF networks, and arranged her daughter's parachute reception two months later. Josiane Somers, referred to later, was parachuted in on D-Day, another of the eleven RF agents sent into France.

The saboteurs who arrived with her would have been engaged in training the Resistance initially to blow up the railway lines the Germans had to use if they were to support their troops in Normandy, then to destroy telegraph lines to interrupt their communications and finally to destroy road bridges, bring down trees and harass the Germans as they made their way north.

Details of Marcelle's time in France have not come to light but must have proved successful as after the war she was awarded the MBE and the Croix de Guerre.

MADELEINE LAVIGNE
Aged 32. Parachuted from a Halifax near Taizé, 10 km north of Cluny (Saône & Loire), on 24 May 1944. Awarded the King's Commendation for Brave Conduct.

The next French woman sent into France was 32-year-old Madeleine Lavigne. Born Madeleine Rejeuny on 6 February 1912 in Lyon where her father worked as a fabric designer, she finished her education and married Marcel Lavigne when she was 19. By the age of 24, she had two children, Guy and Noel. In her personnel file, she described her hobbies as dressmaking, music, boating and tennis and knowing the areas of the Midi, Pyrénées, Haute Savoie, Bordeaux, Toulon and Alsace less well.[137]

When the war started, her husband joined the army but was captured by the Germans and made a prisoner of war. Having to survive without him was difficult, so she sent her sons to live with her mother in another part of the city and worked at the Mairie as a clerk. When her husband was released in November 1943, the relationship did not work, and they divorced, never to see each other again.

Having developed a hatred of the German occupiers and being very patriotic, she wanted to help the French Resistance. How she first got in touch with Robert Boiteux, an SOE agent, dropped in Ance in the south-west Pyrénées on 1 June 1942, was not documented in her file.

He was a hairdresser on Bond Street before the war, a gold digger and a boxing champion.

His mission was to work with George Duboudin, an SOE agent who had been sent in September 1941 to build up the SPRUCE network of contacts in and around Lyon. However, as the wireless operator dropped with Boiteux had landed on the roof of a house near the police station, he was arrested. When Duboudin's wireless operator, Pierre le Chêne, Marie-Thérèse Le Chêne's brother-in-law, was also arrested, Boiteux moved into the countryside to escape detection, hiding in woods, water courses, vineyards, and mountains.

Instead of being a propaganda enterprise, his mission was changed to one of sabotage and building up stockpiles of arms and ammunition. To help in this work, it was essential that he obtained official papers, identity papers, and appropriate official stamps so that his men could pass German and French police checks and controls. Despite the dire consequences of being found out, Madeline agreed to supply him with them.

In time, according to Escott, Boiteux recognised Madeleine's unexceptional appearance, untapped intelligence and her careful following of instructions made her a potential courier. Travelling on various missions for him under the name of Marianne Latour, she helped her organiser, in fact, she even loaned him money when he was in need of cash.[138]

It was working in this capacity that she came to the attention of Henri Borosh, who had been a wireless operator of the 'Vic' escape line in the Burgundy area. His organization was also desperate for large quantities of false papers for the escaped prisoners of war, downed aircrews, and evaders who needed help to get out of France. Having to wait for SOE's forgery section to obtain copies and them produce fake ones often took months. She agreed to help and was given the code name Leveller.

Boiteux received few arms drops and was unable to attract new members to his network without guns and ammunition. Also, the failure of the British to invade had made many men disillusioned with the British. Deciding to wind down his network, he advised his men to lie low and got Déricourt to arrange a Hudson pick-up for him, Madame le Chêne and Victor Gerson.

After they were picked up from a hilltop near Angers on 19 August 1943, Madeleine, code named Isabelle, and Borosh, code named Marius, stayed in Lyon. She allowed him to keep his wireless set and other equipment in her house. If the Germans had found out, it was likely she would have been sent to a concentration camp. As the 'Vic' line had been funded by the SIS, Borosh was keen to create another, funded by the SOE's F Section. Travelling around with him, Madeleine helped locate contacts who could help.

When Gerson returned to France in November, the plan was explained, and it was agreed that Borosh should move north. However, in January 1944, when Madeleine was warned that the police were on the look-out for them, Borosh contacted Déricourt to request a pick-up.

According to Hugh Verity, she was brought to England in a Hudson flown by Squadron Leader Leonard Ratcliff on the night of 4/5 February 1944 from a field 1 km south-east of Soucelles, north-east of Angers. In Ratcliff's memoirs, he told how he had been ordered to bring Déricourt back to England. After reports questioning Déricourt's allegiance had reached Buckmaster, he ordered Jerry Morel to go on the Hudson and bring him back. Déricourt refused as he had not prepared for a trip to England and had to sort out his affairs. Verity identified those who returned with Morel as Madeleine, Borosh, Benoist, Liewer, Bob Maloubier code named Clothaire, Colonel Limousin, 'Le Berbu', the innkeeper at Tiercé, her husband and Madame Gouin, the wife of a French politician. Tillet identified two of them as Colonels Paul Ely and Jean Vallette d'Osia.[139]

She had just escaped in time. According to Escott, the Lyon police were planning to arrest her. Tried in her absence, she was sentenced to hard labour for life, though the sentence would be reviewed annually.

Having been debriefed in London, the SOE considered Madeleine's experiences highly suitable for her to be trained and returned to France. Borosh was keen that she went with him.

She was given a commission in the FANY in February 1944 under her cover name of Marianne Latour, which she kept throughout her SOE training. It was to be a source of confusion for years as it appeared on her citation for an award as well as on her gravestone.

Given the emergency of the situation, SOE decided not to send her to Winterfold for assessment but straight to Scotland for paramilitary training. As the training was all in French, it caused her little difficulty. After a fortnight at Rhubana Lodge (STS 22), her instructor commented that her Morse was 9 wpm for both sending and receiving, that she was keen on physical training and nervous with weapons. 'Considering that this student has received only two weeks training she did very well. Though she is not up the standard for 52 [Thame Park] her Morse is fairly good. She is keen and works hard. With more practice she would be an average operator.'[140] As Borosch proposed to provide her with more tuition in the field, SOE decided not to send her to Thame.

She only managed two descents at Ringway and was awarded third class.

Have been briefed for her mission, Madeleine was taken to Tempsford on 24 May 1944 and Geoff Rothwell of 138 Squadron reported dropping her at Saône-et-Loire, near Reims in the Ardennes. The other passengers were Cpt Joseph Benoit, W. T. Joseph Litallien and Lionel Guy d'Artois.

Major Charles Tice, the Liaison Officer, had told Geoff that Madeleine was going back 'into the field' for the second time. She had been captured on her first trip working for the SILVERSMITH network, and the Gestapo stubbed out lit cigarettes on her face to try to get information out of her. She wore make-up to hide the scars. After a daring escape from her jailers, she was picked up, returned safely to Britain and prepared for her second trip.

However, it appears that this was a description of a different woman. There had been confusion when SOE was told Miss Latour's security at Winterfold had been an issue, but as Madame Latour had not attended the assessment course, it was decided that it must have been another student, probably 22-year-old South African Phyllis Latour who was parachuted from a Carpetbagger Liberator on 1 May 1944.[141]

Madeleine worked as Borosh's courier and trainee wireless operator in the new SILVERSMITH network with identity papers as Marianne Henriette Delormes, code named Isabelle. One section was to work in the Reims and Épernay area, the other in the lower Saône valley. The latter would work alongside the ACOLYTE network, and both were to attack the German troops expected to drive north up the Rhône valley after the American landings on the Mediterranean coast.

One of her first tasks was to locate and rent suitable premises from where she and Borosh could transmit. As she got to know Reims, she met Madame and Monsieur Benazat, who owned a restaurant and several properties. Becoming their regular customer, she eventually won their confidence, and they agreed that she rented their apartments in Épernay and, as a reserve, at Ay.

As soon as Borosh moved to Épernay, her work began in earnest. Over the following few months, during the time of the invasion, she travelled north and south carrying messages, arranging with London for arms drops and passing on instructions to sabotage the communications network. On occasions, she had to rendezvous with *résistants* in other networks, encourage people to join Borosh's group and deliver instructions to a small group in Paris. Escott describes how,

Once the northern landings had taken place, Madeleine had also to be even more careful of security, as the Germans were everywhere and more alert and dangerous than the French authorities in watching for saboteurs or spies. She did her work unquestionably well and was of the greatest possible assistance to Borosh. Inevitably, she was sometimes caught up in engagements with the movement of German troops, and often had to pass through areas under fire, showing great courage and common sense.[142]

When the Germans successfully penetrated her network, she went on the run, staying in one of Henri Déricourt's safe houses not far from the DZ. On 13 August 1944, the Allies and the Free French Forces landed on the Mediterranean coast and started a push north up the Rhône valley, forcing the Germans to retreat. The southern group now joined in the action, destroying the rail and telephone lines, forcing the Germans to use the roads. Hit and run tactics harassed, slowed down and delayed the Germans from getting to Normandy for up to two weeks.

With the liberation of Paris, the feeling of success spread amongst the French population. The Americans reached Reims on 29 August and Lyon a few days later. In September Madeleine continued her courier work, unable to return to Lyon until the court commuted her life sentence to hard labour. She was eventually reunited with her two boys for whom, before she left England, she had written a note at Vera Atkins' suggestion: 'In case of accident, the circumstances of my two children be enquired into, with a view to helping them with a pension if necessary.'[143]

She died of an embolism in Paris on Saturday, 24 February 1945. She was only thirty-three. Buckmaster, the head of F Section, wrote; 'We deeply grieve the untimely death of this Frenchwoman, who deserved so much from her country.' In November 1946, she was awarded the King's Medal for Brave Conduct and the King's Commendation for Brave Conduct. In his citation, he stated that, 'At all times she conducted herself with the greatest gallantry and devotion to duty, and it was mainly due to her energy and tact that one of the two main groups of this circuit was established on a firm basis.'[144]

Another statement, possibly by Borosh, was that she was 'A most courageous and tactful woman, who rendered great service to the cause. She was wise and brave, and, if to English eyes her appearance was rather against her, she did her job unquestionably well and was of the greatest possible assistance to SILVERSMITH. A great-hearted lady for whom I have much respect and liking.'[145]

13

French Women Infiltrated
after D-Day

GINETTE JULLIAN
*Aged 26. Parachuted from a Liberator near Saint-Viatre-les-Tanneries
(Loir & Cher) on 7 June 1944. Cited for an OBE but there is no evidence
that it was awarded.*

Lieutenant Ginette Jullian, code named Janitress and Adèle, was dropped
from a Carpetbagger Liberator in the early hours of the morning on
7 June 1944, the day after D-Day. She and three other SOE agents landed
in a field 6 km north-east of Saint-Viatre-les-Tanneries in the Loir and
Cher department. Her companions were her organiser, Gérard Dedieu,
code named PERMIT, Yvan Galliard, code named Hotelier, and Henri
Fucs, code named Abel.[1]

Born in Montpellier on 8 December 1917, little has come to light about
her early life. Her French parents were divorced, and her mother was
living in Nice. After studying at the Sacré Coeur convent, she claimed to
have married when she was 16, divorced when she was 23 and left from
Toulon for England in June 1940.

It is unknown whether she brought her 4-year-old son with her and
what she did during the early years of the war. It is probable that she was
involved with the French community in London. Her personnel file shows
that between January and March 1943 she was a cadet in the Air Transport
Auxiliary, and there had been a plan for her to join the SOE in April but for
the next eight months she worked for the BCRA and lived at 18 Orchard
Rise, Kingston Hill, Surrey. She admitted being engaged but pointed out that
her fiancé, Philippe de Scitivaux, was in Oflag XXIB, a prisoner of war camp.

On 5 January 1944, with the need for more agents, SOE agreed that she
be assessed. According to Escott, she was the last woman to be recruited

315

by the SOE. Given a commission in the FANY and using the cover name Ginette Marie Jourdain, her instructor at Winterfold deemed her to have failed the course. Her intelligence was rated 6; her Morse was good; her mechanical skills were good but although 'a pleasant, quite stable person', she was 'lacking in self-discipline. Both her performances here and her record suggest that she has no great determination or staying power. Under conditions of stress, she is apt to become either impulsive or scatterbrained. She is not considered suitable for work in the field.'²

Despite these negative comments, she was sent to Rhubana Lodge. Her instructor commented that she was 'A very good student with considerable previous experience in Morse. Reads accurately at 16 wpm and has a good style of sending. Very keen on weapon training but is, as yet, inclined to be somewhat "gun shy" but seems full of determination. Not particularly strong but has plenty of stamina. Keen on silent killing and has a fair working knowledge.'³

From Scotland she was sent to Ringway and towards the end of March her instructor reported that she was 'quite happy on arrival although somewhat apprehensive of the course. During the first day's ground training her performance was not good, but it improved a little on the second. On that actual descent she improved with the course and finished up full of confidence. She made three descents, one from a balloon and one from an aircraft by day and one from aircraft by night.' She was awarded second class and did not receive her wings.⁴

From Manchester she was sent to Thame Park for wireless telegraphy training and her instructor reported after a month that she was 'very interested and enthusiastic about her job. Lived in Algiers where she was married. Often talks about North Africa which she knows well. Her character is mentally stable. She is a quiet type of girl, rather on the shy side but is determined and obstinate. She will often try to get her way by persuasion. She is security minded and realises the importance of being so.'⁵

A subsequent report commented that she was 'Something of a wangler and apt to produce all manner of excuses to get her own way in such matters as extra leave, etc. A debrouillarde [resourceful] type whom I think could be relied upon in the Field. [...] No special leanings towards the opposite sex.'⁶

As D-Day was just over a month away, she was excused the training in clandestine warfare at Beaulieu and dropped on 7 June. Escott claimed her to have been one of the luckiest of the wireless operators as she was sent with the latest model – a Mark III transceiver which weighed less than 9 lb (4 kg) in its suitcase. Her mission was to set up a base at Amiens, assist

Dedieu, code name Jerome, in setting up the Permit network in the Somme area, and, if possible, train local recruits in W/T.

According to Escott, they were the only SOE team that only spoke French, all the others spoke English as well. Dedieu had been a schoolmaster before the war and was among a number of Resistance members arrested and imprisoned at Eysses. When he and twenty other prisoners escaped in January 1944, he and other escapees were escorted over the Pyrénées, arriving in Britain in March 1944.

On their return to France, the situation was highly dangerous. Many SOE networks had been infiltrated by the Gestapo and new ones were needed. Much of northern France was in chaos with Allied and German troops in conflict and people fleeing the combat zones.

When they landed, Ginette's transceiver was confiscated by the reception committee organised by someone called Hutton, code named Antoine. He suggested that such a small suitcase would cause suspicion if she carried it around with her in Paris. However, he allowed her to keep her crystals but this meant she had to find another set if she was to be able to transmit.

Arriving in Paris, they found that all their contacts had moved, leaving no forwarding addresses. They had fled following mass arrests. With no alternative, they hitchhiked to Beaumont, where they acquired bicycles and then went to Beauvais. Their contact there had disappeared as the town had been requisitioned by the Germans. As it was too dangerous to stay there, they took the train for Paris and decided to separate. Dedieu went to Asnières to see if his father-in-law might help him locate leaders of the different Resistance groups around Paris. Whilst he managed to contact them, they had too many political differences to agree to work together.

Ginette went to find Hutton to locate a wireless set and see if he could get her some forged papers. On the way, she discovered that several hundred German troops had attacked his Maquis and he had disappeared. Searching for another organiser who might be able to tell her where he was, she was put in touch with one of de Gaulle's groups. It was suggested that she went to work with a group desperately in need of a wireless operator in the Eure-et-Loir department. Eventually, according to Escott, after much difficulty, she met an American group in the Seine-et-Marne department who let her use their set.[7]

RF Section then gave her a new mission, not in Amiens but in the Eure-et-Loir department, the northern part of the Loir-et-Cher and the Orne department. They were to fill the gaps for Claude de Baissac's SCIENTIST II network. Their new headquarters was a safe house in the cathedral town of Chartres.[8]

Claude and Lise de Baissac had also escaped from France. Claude was recruited, trained as an organiser and parachuted near Caissargues, South of Nimes, with Harry Peleuvé as his wireless operator on 29 July 1942. Lise, referred to later, had also volunteered and was trained to be her elder brother's courier.[9]

At the end of June, Ginette rendezvoused with Dedieu and received a new set. Its reception, Escott said, was very good. 'Any lost skeds were due to the current being cut off when the Germans, trying to track her down, came too near. Indeed, there were some lively alerts'.[10]

As the Allied advance progressed, Ginette was busy transmitting Dedieu's plans and requests for arms and ammunition to London. According to Lt-Col. Boxhall's summary of the PERMIT network in his 1960 chronology of SOE operations in France during the Second World War, she sent sixty-seven messages and received fifty-two. With access to supplies, Dedieu was able to win the support of the military delegate of the French Forces of the Interior and through him sixteen groups of *résistants*. Once she had located suitable drop zones, 450 containers were dropped each month, enabling 2,000 Maquis to attack railways, convoys and other German targets, including blowing up the viaduct at Chérisy, which the RAF had failed to destroy in twenty attempts.[11]

In appreciation of Ginette's contribution, Dedieu commented that 'My radio operator always gave me excellent work even on the most demanding of days. She was very brave and never lost her nerve even when the SS arrived to search the house from which she was transmitting. Also thanks to Septime (the code name of SOE agent Captain Ronald Shearn, dropped on 8 August), all was saved and the search was only superficial.'[12]

The circumstances of Dedieu's arrest on 8 August are unknown but according to the Special Forces Roll of Honour, he escaped again on 21 August. While he was in prison the Allied forces in Normandy were given a boost, when the American and French forces landed on the Mediterranean coast and began their northward push up the Rhône-Saône corridor. Helped by information supplied by Ginette, the RAF was able to bomb German garrisons, which helped the Maquis to liberate Bonneval, Dreux, Châteaudun and Nogent. When the Americans met up with Ginette, they helped the Maquis liberate Chartres on 15 August.

Once out of prison, Dedieu found that the military delegate refused to allow him to attend the funerals of those men killed during the capture of Chartres. He was further annoyed when he was not invited to de Gaulle's official visit to the town. De Gaulle was known to have ordered all SOE agents to leave France.

Following the landing of an SAS team, the American Major Rolf utilized Ginette's wireless skills, and London instructed her to accompany them in the Allied push towards Dijon. When they arrived in September, they divided into two teams of two. The first team located German targets for air strikes and the second team, with a USAAF officer, used the first's information and got Ginette to use an S-phone to speak directly to the radio operator on board an overflying bomber who then directed the bomb-aimer to the targets. Escott described her work as being 'intense and dangerous, as they were all on the front line and occasionally ahead of it.'[13]

The rapid advance of the Allies from Normandy met the advance force of the American and French forces from the south at Dijon on 11 September. She was debriefed before being flown back to England on 27 September against her wishes. She indicated that there was some friction between her, Dedieu and Fl/Lt Bruhl, code name Barnabe, another SOE agent, but she was unwilling to elaborate.

After a few weeks in London, she was flown to Algiers. Buckmaster's citation for her to be awarded an OBE read, 'Exceptionally courageous, very frank, sincere, direct, sees problems from a very material point of view, very down to earth. Without panache, she was decidedly opinionated, and she hated bureaucracy. She has rendered very important services and deserves high distinction.'[14]

There was no other evidence that she was given this award. Hutchinson, writing about the Jedburgh teams dropped into France, commented that, 'Although it was officially decided not to use women, one or two girls with SOE experience managed to arrive among us. They included, notably, Paddy O'Sullivan, fresh from Limoges, and Madame Jullian, a compulsive addict of the drug danger if ever there was one.'[15]

She married her fiancé, Admiral Philippe de Scitivaux du Geische, in August 1945 and died during a scuba diving incident in Tahiti on 4 August 1962.

Laurie Dick, one of the American Carpetbaggers, commented in his memoirs in *Flight Journal*, that,

On one mission, the crew was startled when long blonde hair fell from beneath the agent's helmet. This beautiful French girl, whose parents had been killed by the Gestapo, was making a revenge jump over the Bavarian Alps to determine whether Hitler had a last-ditch stronghold to fight off advancing Allies.

We breathed a sigh of relief after she bailed out at 5,000 feet and we saw this brave young lady's chute open. We never knew what became of her.

Who this woman was remains a mystery. Another anonymous agent, who reportedly was dropped several times into France, was described by Frank Griffiths as being 'nearer 65 than 60. She always took half a bottle of good cognac in order to give her courage for the jump, on one occasion her bicycle being parachuted with her.'[16]

GERMAINE HEIM

Aged 32. Parachuted from a Halifax near Donzy (Nièvre) on the night of 5/6 July 1944. Awarded a Certificate of Commendation.

Germaine Heim (Heem), code named *Danubien*, was another member of the Corps Auxiliaire Féminin in the RF section who was parachuted 5 km west of Donzy to work with the SCOPE and PÉRIMÉTRE networks on the night of 5/6 July 1944.

Little is known about her family background except what was included in her personnel file. Born in Ostheim, northern Bavaria, on 17 May 1913, she sailed from Boulogne and arrived in England on 28 April 1939 and found work as a governess in Husbands Bosworth, Leicestershire. In late 1943, when she was 30, she, Marcelle and Josiane Somers, Danielle Reddé, Yvonne Gittus and Germaine Gruner, were identified as potential couriers for Colonel de Cheveigne of the Free French Section

Not having to attend the assessment or paramilitary training, the group was taken to Boarmans where her instructor commented that,

> She is intelligent, practical, very observant and has plenty of imagination. She has the mentality and virtues of the efficient Girl Guide. She was unusually skilful at practical exercises. Nevertheless, she is rather lacking in cunning and savoir faire in her dealings with other people. She is very keen, worked hard and is physically strong and energetic. She has quite a strong character and is determined. She is still, however, rather immature. There is something of the school girl in her make up. She has a pleasant, cheerful personality. She is a good mixer and would be generally liked. Although she would make a loyal subordinate she is lacking in authority; she seems, however, well suited for work as a courier. She would be inconspicuous and would be clever at dodging controls or passing through them unobserved, especially in the country but would be much less equal to the occasion were she to be detained and interrogated.[17]

Between 12 and 15 December, they were at Ringway. However, the camp doctor declared Germaine as unfit, so she took no part in the course. Her instructor commented that 'she seemed a quiet, resolute type, she should be a good subject for this work.'[18]

After celebrating Christmas and New Year, she spent some time at Gorse Hill on security training. Her instructor commented that 'she showed interest and worked hard in all subjects.' The Commandant supported this by adding that she was a 'quiet but very pleasant personality who took a great interest in her work and was very keen to learn. A far more serious type than the others and should do well in the field.'[19]

From there she was sent back to Ringway, staying at Dunham House. This time she was more successful. At the end of January her instructor commented, 'This student was quiet, but cheerful. She was rather nervous on the ground training and while making her first jump. I believe this nervousness was due primarily to a previous parachute training injury [*sic*] rather than apprehension about making parachute jumps. His [*sic*] descents and landings were quite good. TWO DESCENTS. THIRD CLASS.[20]

From there she went to Gumley Hall (STS 41) where Acting Lieutenant Hodson found out more about her background:

> She worked as a Governess at Pebble Hall, near Husbands Bosworth [Leicestershire], not far from here. [6 km] She goes over to Pebble Hall on the weekends. A quiet, unassuming girl not in the least pretentious. She seems very keen on her work, but she does not strike me as the type of girl one would expect to be doing this kind of work. She seems to be such an honest, demure, kind natured young woman. She, with the rest of the group, has been to Group B STS 51 and STS 50 before coming here. I have learnt nothing more about her past history beyond that she was a Governess. She is not at all a French type, she has fair hair, blue eyes and could certainly pass as English.[21]

The Commandant admitted that he only saw her at meal times but thought that, 'She seems a very nice young woman. Serious minded, rather timid manner. Not at all the type one would expect to see in the field.[22]

After ten days' leave, as she was expected to be able to transmit and receive messages in the field, she was sent to Thame Park. In early April, her instructor reported that she was 'A plain and unassuming type of girl. Is intelligent and well educated. Does not often mix with the others except with one or two of her own countrymen. Is not talkative. She is always very willing to oblige others. Her security is satisfactory, and she is very careful about her conversation outside.'[23]

Following a further two months' training, Captain Barber informed Majors Byrne and Fyffe, her RF Section officers, that they had little more to add except, 'She has behaved well and shown herself to be reliable from the security point of view.'[24]

Having been briefed for her mission as wireless operator for Inter Allied Mission Verveine and supplied with the wherewithal for her trip, on the night of 5/6 July, Wing Commander Burnett of 138 Squadron dropped Germain, code named Perimetre, with André Lemaitre, an RF saboteur, code named Quartier, André Michon, code named Physique and Noel Colli, code named Elevation, about 5 km west of Donzy, in Nièvre. From Tillet's list of infiltrations into France, it appears that she was to support Lt-Col. Fernard and G. Viat who were dropped between Lormes and Fetigny, Nievre on 10 June.

Little has come to light of her work in the field except that she managed to survive being caught until Liberation. In her citation for a Certificate of Commendation, Major-General Gubbins reported that 'Mademoiselle HEIM was dropped into France on 5 July 1944, as wireless operator to a mission sent to the Morvan. The mission was at once involved in intense guerrilla warfare but Mlle HEIM continued to send steady and regular messages through to the UK until the complete liberation of her area. Mlle HEIM's excellent work and calm behaviour in exceedingly hazardous conditions cannot be too highly commended.'[25]

Following liberation, in one of her messages to London, she requested to be supplied with a bike and two 'comfort packages', chocolate, sweets, tobacco and whisky. In 1998 she was awarded the Légion d'Honneur after fifty-four years as an active member of the l'amicale des volontaires féminines de La France Libre.[26]

MARIE-MADELEINE FOURCADE
Aged 34. Landed by Hudson near Egligny, 3.7 km south-east of Donnemarie-Dontilly (Seine & Marne) on 5 July 1944. Awarded the Commander of Legion d'Honneur.

The next woman flown out was Marie-Madeleine Fourcade. Her autobiography, *Noah's Ark*, details how she was born Marie-Madeleine Bridou, the daughter of the executive of a steamship company, in Marseille in 1909. As a young girl, she lived for a time in Shanghai before returning to France to study at the Ecole Normale de Musique. She married Monsieur Fourcade in 1929, but they separated, leaving her with two children.

Until war broke out, she worked for a publishing company in Paris, and when Pétain signed the armistice in June 1940, she went to live in Oloron-Saint Marie in the foothills of the Pyrénées where she joined the Resistance. Working with Georges Loustaunau-Lacau and Louis Faye, they set up the ALLIANCE network which had about 3,000 members from across the political spectrum.

Taking advantage of her contacts in business, politics, and the military, she was able to provide the British with valuable and continuous information about German troop movements, their supplies, and the movement of submarines and ships out of Brest and Lorient. It was sent to England along with their political plans, scale drawings of U-boat bases, the launch sites of 'secret weapons' and anything potentially useful to the Allies.

When her organiser was arrested in May 1941, she took command. The British military authorities were so impressed with the quality of this information that they sent her a radio operator in August. Unfortunately, he was a double agent who betrayed many members of her network to the Gestapo.

She was arrested in Aix-en-Provence in 1942 but managed to escape and got into Spain inside a post bag in the back of a diplomatic car. Fearing German reprisals against her family, she was infiltrated back into France where, once she had her children taken into neutral Switzerland, she restarted her resistance work helping to get downed Allied airmen back to Britain.[27]

In Keith Jeffrey's history of MI6, there was an account of how, in 1942,

...reliable information was received that an agent known as Bla, a former French farm manager, had been captured by the Germans and was now working for them. He was caught in France by agents of Alliance, a network of French spies reporting to SIS.

Bla was taken to an Alliance safe house where he was interrogated by the French agent Marie-Madeleine Fourcade (among others) and confessed to 'having given to the Boches all details known to him about us.' They first tried to kill him 'without him knowing it', by putting lethal drugs in his food, but this failed and merely alerted the unfortunate man to 'the attempt we were making.' When he was killed (he was shot) he faced his fate with what Fourcade reported as 'extraordinary moral courage' and 'astounded us by his calm attitude in facing punishment.'

'The way he died,' she wrote, 'did something to mitigate his past record.' Although in her memoirs Fourcade relates that an 'execution order' was received from London, nothing so explicit survives in the relevant files, and her contemporaneous report asserted that over the weekend when Bla was in Alliance hands no contact was established with London.

A subsequent minute, nevertheless, by the Free French Section in Broadway (SIS headquarters), recorded that because the leading Alliance figures were 'known personally to [Bla], the danger was such that eventually we instructed them to do away with him should the opportunity occur.'

When his widow made inquiries about him towards the end of 1944, she was simply told that the authorities had had no information of his whereabouts 'since 1942.' As one SIS officer minuted, 'if any sleeping dogs should be let lie I think this is one'.[28]

Following more arrests, MI6 thought it was too dangerous for Marie-Madeleine to stay in France so they arranged for her to be brought to Britain. The Germans called her network 'Noah's Ark' as all her agents' cover names were animals. Hers was Hedgehog. On 5 July 1943, Affleck was said to have flown his Hudson to pick her up along with her latest batch of airmen. Whether he did or not is uncertain as Hugh Verity says she was returned in a Lysander from a newly cut cornfield at Bouillancy, near Meaux on the night of 17/18 July by Flight Lieutenant Peter Vaughan-Fowler who was able to add a fleur-de-lys on his cockpit for another successful mission. Once safe in England, the BCRA provided Marie-Madeleine with accommodation in Chelsea from where she continued supervising her network and arranging pick-ups.

Aware of the Allied plans to invade Europe, she browbeat her minders into allowing her to return to France.

Yvonne Fontaine and Pierre Mulsant arranged her landing the day after D-Day. In her memoirs, she said that she was given two hours' notice of her departure and had to pack into the false bottom of a large, soft hold-all the crystals for her wireless set, replacement codes, money and a set of dentures that transformed her into a French housewife. Her clothes were in a light fibre suitcase and in her handbag she carried a forged identity card in the name of Marie Suzanne Imbert and her 'L' pills.

She, Pierre Giraud and Raymond Pezet, her 'husband' for the return visit, were driven out of London. From her description, it is not clear whether she went to The Hasells or Gaynes Hall. Her account of her visit is worth including for the additional light it sheds on the agents' preparations for the trip:

We drew up at dusk before the steps of a country house and were immediately taken to a huge dining room that had been converted into a mess, where waiters in white jackets above their service trousers were bustling about.

'So it's to be tonight?' Teutatès asked Ham, who had come back from the phone box.

'No, it's postponed until tomorrow.' My heart sank. After dinner, I invited Ham to drink a last whisky with me.

'You're frightened about going back, Poz?' he asked.

'Yes, I'm frightened; I'm really in a blue flunk. I'm going to be arrested and yet I've got the feeling I shall get away with it.'

We talked until dawn, going over all the ups and downs we had experienced together... His kindness and his tact were a great comfort.

I woke up very late, certainly not before the afternoon. The huge place felt like a haunted house. One sensed the presence of a lot of people lurking behind the partitions, but... no one ever met anyone else. Kenneth Cohen appeared.

It won't be long now, dear Poz,' he said, greatly moved. 'Mary asked me to give you her best love and we'd like you to have this little memento. It's an heirloom.' He handed me a charming ring with a heart-shaped stone. 'Take it with you. It'll bring you luck,' he said when I protested. 'That's why we're giving it to you. And here's a luminous watch from British Intelligence. It's Swiss and it keeps perfect time...

The airfield presented an extraordinary sight with aircraft lined up wing to wing as far as the eye could see, and in the middle a crowd of agile and athletic-looking RAF men moving about. 'You're not going to tell me that all these are off on secret missions?'

Kenneth Cohen laughed. 'No. They're bombers and will be taking off in waves from dusk to dawn. You're going in just behind them so that the enemy radar won't be able to pick you out. They'll think you're one of the raiders.'

On arriving at the mess I saw my travelling companions sitting apart with Ham and, in another corner, half a dozen men of all ages and ranks. 'Those are the other passengers,' Kenneth said, going over to greet them, 'but I'm not making any introductions. Take no notice.'

'But we shall meet on the plane. Do you really imagine we will cold shoulder one another in these circumstances?'

The sun began to go down, and waves of aircraft headed eastwards, disappearing into the oncoming darkness. An officer asked us to follow him. Another, with a poet's face, came over to us with a pile of little cages, each containing a white pigeon. I received one like the rest.

'You'll slip a message into the ring on its leg as soon as you land,' Kenneth told me.

This seems very strange on the day of the V.I.'

'No, we do it for people who haven't any transmitters. That's not the case with you, but as you're with a lot of other people you're getting one of your own, so that nobody's jealous.'

We were driven to the tarmac, where I could see the burly outline of a Hudson, its paintwork chipped by machine-gun fire. I fell for it at once. I had the honour of being the first up the ladder into the fuselage, where I bumped into all kinds of containers piled up by the entrance, and went sprawling.

Our party came in one by one and crouched down in any available corner, the sergeant making sure that the weight was equally distributed; then our luggage and the pigeon cases were passed to us and the door shut with a loud bang. I stood up to try to catch through the window a last glimpse of Kenneth Cohen's tall figure in naval uniform and Ham's familiar cap. I felt a terrible urge to cry.[29]

When they arrived, there was no sign of a reception committee. The pilot had to abort the mission and return to Tempsford. She got back when the other planes were returning from Germany in the early hours of the morning. With the Liberation of France imminent, many more missions were diverted eastwards. Marie-Madeleine awoke the next afternoon and relieved the tension by playing a piano, but she admitted that her fingers had lost all their agility, and she could not remember her favourite piece.

She said that, after a day's wait, she was eventually landed in a field at Maisons-Rouges, near Nangis in the forest of Fontainebleau. Verity claims she was taken out with seven other passengers on the night of 5/6 July in a Hudson piloted by Affleck. In just under three hours they landed 2.5 km north of Égligny, south-west of Provins. Eight others replaced them for the return journey.[30]

After a hearty meal in a nearby farmhouse, she and Pezet hitched a lift in a peasant's cart with squeaky axles to the station and managed after three days to get to Marseille. Within a fortnight she had arranged a drop of six tons of supplies and four million francs. A few days later she was caught and imprisoned by the Gestapo in Miollis barracks. Aware of what would be in store for her, she managed to escape by removing her clothes so that she could squeeze through the bars of a window in her cell room, her slender body lubricated by the sweat of fear. Picking up her cotton batik dress that she had dropped outside, she managed to find safety with the American troops who had just landed on the Mediterranean coast in August. She later found out that 438 out of an estimated 3,000 members of her network had been executed.[31]

After the war, she was awarded the Commander of Legion d'Honneur and went on to create and become president of the *Association Amicale Alliance*, which cared for about 3,000 Resistance agents and survivors, as well as doing social works and the publishing *Mémorial de l'Alliance*, dedicated to the 429 dead resistance members. In 1968 she published her wartime autobiography, *Noah's Ark*, which became a bestseller. She died on 20 July 1989, aged 80.

JOSIANE SOMERS

Aged 19. Parachuted from a Liberator near Liglet, 15 km south-east Le Blanc (Indre) on 6 July 1944. Awarded a Certificate of Commendation and the Military Cross.

On 6 July 1944, an American Liberator from the Carpetbaggers squadron at Harrington, dropped 19-year-old Josiane Somers and Lt Jean Sibileau 1.7 km south-east of Liglet, a rural community about half way between Poitiers and Châteauroux in Indre.[32]

After fleeing France with her family, her brother Claud joined the RAF, and she, lying about her age, was reported to have joined the Free French Air Force. Another source identified her as a member of the Corps Auxiliaire Féminin in 1942 who worked in de Gaulle's department in London. Colonel de Cheveigné wanted her to join Marcelle, her mother, in his planned organisation as a courier. At only 19, she was one of the SOE's youngest women agents.

At the end of October 1943, the Training Section was sent the identical request as her mother that she did not need paramilitary training but that she be given open-air exercises. Her training did not commence until 4 January 1944 when she was sent to Clobb Gorse. After three weeks learning about clandestine warfare, her instructors produced the following reports showing that there were doubts about her:

> Not highly educated, but has a good practical intelligence, is quick & resourceful. A strong, determined character & and would make a loyal subordinate. Should make a good, inconspicuous courier. Weak at codes. Even with more practice, should not be entrusted with this work for which she has little aptitude.[33]

> She is intelligent, practical, cunning, learns quickly and has a retentive memory. She is, however, very young and immature. She is keen and worked hard, displaying a lively imagination and plenty of initiative. For her age, she has quite a strong character, and she certainly seems to be courageous, but she is rather vain and probably inclined to be self-indulgent. She has a pleasant personality, but is rather lacking in in humour; she is shy and does not mix particularly well with others. Although she should do well in the job for which she had been selected, on account of her immaturity and lack of experience she would require constant and strict supervision by a responsible superior.

> Codes: further practice required.[34]

From Beaulieu she was sent to Ringway and on 5 February her instructor reported that she was 'very fit and carried out the P.T. and training in good style. She showed no signs of nervousness and made two very good descents from aircraft by day.'[35]

SOE had a change of plan. It appeared that someone had identified Josiane as being more useful as a wireless operator than a courier. Sent to Thame Park, at the beginning of March her instructor commented that she was sending at 10 and reading at 14 wpm with a 'very good style'. This was significantly better than her mother. She was considered

fit [...] Very keen and attentive and has used some of her spare time to advantage, has made excellent progress and is in the process of perfecting her sending style which is quite good. She, however, has a dislike for sending the letter 'X' which she finds a little difficult, and is sometimes liable to add an extra dash or dot on some of her figures. Should make a very good operator if she does not spoil her sending style. Has a good knowledge of the 'Q' code but not the method of its use.[36]

After a month of training, which included a 'scheme' at Fawley Court (STS 41), it was reported that, 'she was 'a quiet girl, rather flirtatious with the other 27s [French students] with whom she often goes out. Is mentally stable and reliable. Enjoys male company. Has not got much personal initiative, but will if given strict instructions, carry out the job faithfully. Should, however, easily be led astray. Her security is good, as far as can be judged at present.'[37]

Given the code names Venizien and Vénitien, at some stage before her flight she would have been introduced to Lt Sibileau. He had trained as a saboteur and his mission, referred to earlier, was to train the Resistance in the Loudun area of Charente, to attack the communications the Germans would use after D-Day.

According to Tillet, Josiane's mission changed to being the wireless operator to Claude Gros, code named Adiabatique. Apart from his age, 25, little detail about him has come to light. Another source reported her using the cover-name Valentin and operating in area B2, south-west France, where her team received scores of parachute drops. One included a suitcase radio for her mother, who, it was claimed was unaware her daughter was in France.

Sibileau was killed in action on 30 August 1944. Her brother was trained as a wireless operator and landed by HMS *Kelvin* at Sables d'Olonnes in the Vendee on 27 September 1944 as part of Jedburgh team SIMON.[38]

Both Josiane and her mother survived the war when the Americans overran their area. During her mission, she developed a relationship with Gros and, returning to England on 5 October 1944, they got married.

Not only was Josiane the youngest SOE woman agent, but she was also part of the only mother and daughter team and one of two families to have three SOE members. The other was the Nearne family where two sisters and a brother were infiltrated.

The only other details of her wartime experiences that have come to light were in Gubbins' citation for awarding her a Certificate of Commendation.

Madame GROS was dropped to the CHARENTE area of France in July 1944 to act as a wireless operator to the air operations officer of the region, which was an extremely dangerous one at that period. [There were concerted efforts by the resistance to harass the German Panzer Divisions in their attempts to reach Normandy and, following the Americans landing on the Mediterranean coast in August, their full evacuation to Germany.] She was the first wireless operator to survive for any length of time; in spite of frequent denunciations and the constant necessity of changing her wireless post, she never failed to maintain the necessary liaison with the U.K., thus permitting the laying of air operations to a region which was one of the last to be freed and to which supplies were being sent up to the time of liberation.

Madame GROS was slightly injured in a motor accident at the beginning of September, and her mission came to an end on 20th September when she reported to Paris.[39]

In recognition of her work, she is also reported as being awarded the Military Cross. Nothing has come to light about her post-war life except that she died in June 2010.

EVELYNE CLOPET
Aged 22. Parachuted from a Liberator near Liglet, 15 km south-east Le Blanc (Indre), on 7 July 1944. Executed after capture in Lavardin. Awarded the Sussex Medal.

Twenty-two-year-old Sub-Lt Evelyne Clopet was the second female Sussex Plan agent. Little has come to light about her early life except that she was born in the coastal town of Pornic, south of St Nazaire in 1922 and moved to Casablanca in 1930 where her father worked as a captain in the port.

As both her father and grandfather were involved in the Resistance, she must have worked for them but in what capacity is unknown.

In 1942 she started training in wireless telegraphy, initially in Casablanca and later in Algiers. Responding to a call for volunteers, she was sent to

England in February 1944. Like Jeannette Guyot, she was recruited for Plan SUSSEX and given the alias Chamonet. She was described as very clever at shooting and showed the same fearlessness in all dangerous manoeuvres.

On 3 July 1944, she was flown out of RAF Harrington at 2237 hours with Roger Fosset, code named Girard and Gauthier. Accompanying them were other Sussex team members, Aristide Crocq, Marcel Biscaino and André Noël. The men jumped successfully but, according to Merrill, the American Carpetbagger pilot, she was unlucky. 'Everything out OK. One didn't get to the Joe-hole in time. Made another pass, – lites were out. The pilot returned to base at 0415 hours.'

She was supposed to land in Chateau l'Hermitage in the Sarthe and work with Team Colére, Roger Fosset, and Claud Girard, but they had to wait for her. The second attempt on the 7 July by Ben Mead and his Carpetbagger crew was more successful. He reported, 'Dropped on center light – Body went out on middle light + packages strung along.' She was parachuted with two other Sussex teams 1.8 SW Courcité, 4.5 km south-west of Averton, 5 km south-east of Villaines-la-Juhel, and joined Team Colére.

Exactly what happened after her arrival is uncertain. Using the alias *Claudet*, her mission was to report on German troop movements. According to the plan-sussex website, on 9 August, as she and two other teams were driving a truck towards Vendome, they were stopped by a group of retreating German troops just before Lavardin. They wanted to commandeer their vehicle to help them escape to the north. When asked to show their papers. they handed over their fake documents.

The Germans were suspicious that the truck had been stolen, so she and her team were forced to get out and open their luggage. Their weapons and the wireless set were found and, according to the plan-sussex website, Evelyne urged the others not to fight. They were ordered into the back of the truck and the Germans then drove them to the feldgendarmes in Vendome.

One managed to jump out and escape but the other five were interrogated and tortured until 0130 hours. When the Gestapo and the SS got tired, they drove them out on the road to Paris, stopped at a quarry near the little village of St Ouen in Loir-et-Cher and shot them.

However, research by the families of the others killed on that day suggest that this account may be inaccurate but the true story has yet to come to light.

SUZANNE PAX-COMBELAS

Age unknown. Parachuted from a Liberator near Jasseries de Garnier, 6 km south-east of Pierre-sur-Haute (Loire) on the night of 12/13 July 1944.

On the night of 12/13 July 1944, two more Merlinettes were flown out of Algiers, probably from Maison Blanche airfield. A B24 bomber piloted by Lt Richard Yoder of' USAAF 885 Heavy Bomber Squadron parachuted Suzanne Combelas and Denise Colin, trained wireless operators, on DZ Eliezer, near Jasseries de Garnier, 6 km south-east of Pierre-sur-Haute, 50 km south-south-east of Clermont-Ferrand, Loire.[40]

Jean-Georges Jaillot-Combelas, a specialist in the history of female wireless operators belonging to the North African Transmissions service, researched his aunt's wartime role. No details of her early life have emerged, but he revealed that the two women had been sent by the BCRAL.

Details of their mission have not come to light, but he found that the Guilhot family from Tuiches, members of the SR Kleber réseau, helped them carry out their mission

In recognition of his aunt's contribution to France's liberation, Jaillot-Combelas arranged to have a commemorative plate erected at Croix Saint-André, Beal Pass, Auvergne.

DENISE COLIN

Age unknown. Parachuted from a Liberator near Jasseries de Garnier, 6 km south-east of Pierre-sur-Haute, Loire on the night of 12/13 July 1944. Captured and sent to Ravensbrück but escaped execution.

As yet, no information about Denise Collin has come to light except that she was another of the Merlinettes, trained with Suzanne Combelas and was parachuted from the same Liberator near Jasseries de Garnier, 6 km south-east of Pierre-sur-Haute, Loire on the night of 12/13 July 1944.

Denise was captured near Lyon, injured and sent to Ravensbrück, but escaped execution when the camp was liberated by the Russians.

EUGÉNIE GRUNER

Aaged 34. Landed by Hudson near Boueilh-Boueilho-Lasque, 30 km north of Pau (Pyrénées Atlantiques) on 10 August 1944.

On the night of 10/11 August 1944, Wing Commander Boxer flew a Hudson mission, Operation *Poignard*, to a field near Garlin, 30 km north of Pau in the Pyrénées. 33-year-old Eugénie Gruner disembarked with five other passengers. They included Bureau, the wireless operator for the OSS PROUST mission, BCRA Jean-Pierre Rosselli, the Chief of Centre d'Opérations de Parachutages and d'Atterrissages en zone libre (Centre of Parachuting and Landing Operations in Southern France), saboteur Prosper Yafil, Maurice Revel and Emile Behra, another wireless operator. Four passengers returned, Maury, André, Jean Arthex and Paule Viatel.[41]

Born Eugénie le Berre in the XVII arrondissement of Paris on 10 January 1911, she arrived in Plymouth on 22 June 1940 after sailing from Paimpol. Her surname by then was Gruner and her records show her as having a daughter, Yvette, but there is no information on whether she arrived alone or with her family.

After her debrief, like Jeanne Bohec, she was accommodated at Anerley School. Eugénie joined the Corps de Volontaires Françaises in January 1941.

By the end of October 1943, Eugénie had been recruited by SOE. Like Marcelle and Josiane Somers, Eugénie had been selected by Colonel de Cheveigne to work as a courier and that she did not need paramilitary training.[42]

Everything went as planned and at the end of November, her instructor at Boarmans reported that

> She is quite intelligent, practical and full of imagination. She is resourceful, has a good memory and is quite a good actress. She is a much more capable person than would appear on first acquaintance. She is very keen and works hard. Although she is quite athletic, she is, nevertheless, inclined to tire easily. She has quite a strong character and should prove loyal, reliable and trustworthy. Her personality is pleasant, and her amiability should make her popular everywhere. She is lacking in shyness and would be at home in most societies immediately. She is not a leader but should make a loyal, efficient subordinate. She seems well suited to act as a courier. Codes: Taught Innocent Letter based on Playfair, with Conventions. Double Transposition, A–Z Conventions fixed. Letter One Time Pad with conventions. Envelope Opening. Showed great interest, was industrious and successful at this work. More practice desirable.[43]

Before she went to Ringway just before Christmas, she wrote a letter to her daughter, Yvette, pretending that she was in Paris. She was accompanied by two other French women, Mlles Daniel and Gittus. [Their code names Rectangle, Marocain and Corde were written on pencil on the document.] Their instructor reported that,

These students worked quite well throughout the course. They were extremely nervous during the first day's training, so much so that they could not bring themselves to make the practice jump through the fuselage aperture. It was ascertained that they had been in contact with one of our former students who told them that this course was a most terrifying business. It was found possible to dissipate this idea, and although still very nervous indeed they were able to carry out the ground training on the second day. Their first descent was made from a balloon by day, Mme Gruner would not go at first command, but finally went with a little help from the despatcher. Mlle Daniel closed her eyes, said a prayer, and fell out. Mlle Gittus went out all right. Their second descent was from an aircraft by day, they all went all right the despatcher reported, but he gave each just a little assistance. They received lectures on containers and disposal and on reception committees working. TWO DESCENTS THIRD CLASS.[44]

Immediately after Christmas, she was given her code name, Rectangle, her cover name, Yvette Leroy and a detailed cover story, according to which she was a hairdresser in Versailles. All the necessary identification cards, residence and work permits and coupons were forged so as to be up-to-date for her mission.

After the New Year celebrations, she was sent to Gorse Hill for another course. Her report at the end of January stated that she had reached a high standard in physical training and close combat and had,

quickly gained a good knowledge of all weapons taught. Became a good shot. Group 'B'. Still rather slow in coding and needs more practice. In other subjects she has shown intelligence. Has worked well and made headway. Still needs plenty of practice. An excitable personality who gets easily roused but at the same time shows great determination. Took an interest in the work and would do a good job in the field once she has set her mind on it.[45]

While at Gorse Hill, her instructor, noted that she had developed a friendship with 24-year-old Christian Allegre with whom she went up to London for weekends. Her security was clearly checked as his address was given as 62 West Cromwell Road, Earls Court. He was parachuted into France on 11 April 1944.

As RF section's plans for her included being able to use a wireless set, in spring 1944, she was sent to Fawley Court (STS 41) for preliminary training. By early March her sending was 5 wpm but slightly erratic and her receiving was 7 wpm. Acting Lieutenant Hodson reported that,

> She is a married woman, but I do not know if her husband is in England or not, she has never mentioned him to me. She left France after the collapse but has not mentioned how she got out. On security matters, she seems to be sound as far as I can judge. She has a natural reserve, not exactly suspicious nature but the type of woman who does not discuss her affairs with anyone she meets. I would say she is completely callous and would have no scruples in carrying out her work in the field. She seems a practical and intelligent woman and well able to look after herself.[46]

Towards the end of March, she was sent to Thame Park and, after two months' training, Captain Barber commented that,

> She has behaved well and shown herself to be reliable from the security point of view. [...] A quiet girl, is married and has a daughter. Her character is determined, very loyal to the Allied Cause and intensely patriotic. She is very keen on her job, and her security is satisfactory. Only mixes with '27s' [SOE's reference to French students] with whom she goes out quite often. Her habits are very moderate.[47]

By May, she had made little progress, and her instructor reported that she was sending at 12 wpm and receiving at 14 wpm.

> Mme Gruner has been seven weeks in the Morse Room at STS 52 and her progress has been very slow indeed. She appears to have no aptitude for the work and although she has had individual tuition for the last week the results have been very disappointing. She has worked very hard but she is of nervous temperament with little sense of rhythm. Her morse is jerky and erratic and letters are consistently split. At times it seems as if she is making progress, but she soon drops back again If she is urgently required operationally we shall persevere with her training in the hope that she can be eventually turned out as an operator. She is unlikely ever to make a first class operator, although it is possible she will be adequate if she has sufficient time and patience to go through with the training.
>
> Mme Gruner is discouraged with her failure to make progress and undoubtedly the strain of doing morse daily for seven weeks, with the prospect of an indefinite continuation of the elementary training, has

depressed her. She is willing to go on as long as there is hope but unless the demands for operators is desperate it would seem that it would be better to withdraw her as unsuitable.[48]

As she had not improved by D-Day, her training was cut short. Her instructor felt that she was not making the effort to develop the technical skills needed and recommended that she be returned to London to finish her training in the BCRA Transmissions Section.[49]

On 10 August, Wing-Commander Boxer landed his Hudson near Boueilh-Boueilho-Lasque, 2.5 km south-west of Garlin and 30 km north of Pau, Pyrénées-Atlantiques. Eugénie was accompanied by the Proust/ OSS team mentioned above.[50]

Little is known of her mission except she was in place when the American and French forces arrived. The PROUST mission was to provide French intelligence agents to support the Allied advance. As their troops landed on the Mediterranean coast on 15 August, Eugénie only had a few weeks in the field before the war in her area was over and she was able to celebrate liberation.

YVONNE GITTUS
Aged 20. Trained as a wireless operator but not sent.

According to Yvonne Gittus's personnel file, she was born in London on 5 November 1923 and was living at 26 Friars Walk, Southgate, N.14, when she joined the Forces Françaises Combattantes (FFC) as a 'Volontaire Française' on 22 June 1942.

Details of her early life were not recorded. She was selected by RF Section on 21 October 1943 'to be trained as an agent and sent into the field as soon as possible.' The Training Section was told that, 'This lady has been hand-picked by Col. de Cheveigne to work as a courier in a new organisation he proposes to establish. She will do no paramilitary training at his request, but it is felt that during her three weeks' course at Group B commencing 7 November 1943 for which a request has been made, opportunities can be found for her to do open-air exercises.'[51]

The Security Section had no objection to her going straight to Group B Training. With pay of £1 a day, she began the course in early November. Her instructor at Boarmans reported at the end of the course that,

She is not very intelligent, nor well educated but quite sensible, practical and resourceful. She is very keen and worked hard. In character, she seems rather immature, although she is certainly quite loyal and reliable. Her personality is bright and pleasant and she should be generally liked. Although she has no powers of leadership she should make a loyal subordinate and should be quite well qualified to act as a courier. Codes: Not sufficiently patient or accurate in this work. With more practice; and under supervision, should be more successful in code work.[52]

Sent to Ringway, she did not impress her parachute instructor. Although she worked quite well throughout the course, he reported that,

She was extremely nervous during the first day's training, so much so that she could not bring herself to make the practice jumps through the fuselage aperture. It was ascertained that she had been in contact with one of our former students who told her that this course was a most terrifying business. It was found possible to dissipate this idea, and although still very nervous indeed she was able to carry out the ground training on the second day. Her first descent was made from a balloon by day; she went out all right. The second descent was from an aircraft by day, she went all right the despatcher reported, but he gave her a little assistance. If the circumstances had permitted, she would doubtless have completed the course with good results. TWO DESCENTS. THIRD CLASS.[53]

She was 21 at this time and the Commandant reported that she had,

a far more British character than the others. Her reactions are more that of a British girl her age. Though obviously apprehensive at the thought of jumping, she did all she could not to show her feelings. She seems healthy, neat and tidy, but she might be a little apt to be influenced by other people, probably due to the fact that she is so young.[54]

Following Christmas and New Year celebrations, on 9 January 1944 she was sent to Gorse Hill. Towards the end of the month her instructor remarked that she had 'tried hard and made some headway. Will need more practice before she is ready for the field.' The Commandant commented that she was 'a pleasant and very lively type who with a bit more experience would do well. At the moment she seems rather young to stand the strain, and is also dangerously careless about leaving things about.'[55]

Maybe these concerns changed SOE's mind. Instead of being sent as a courier where security was essential, they decided she should be trained as a wireless operator instead and sent her to Fawley Court (STS 41). By the end of February, her instructor reported that her work with Morse was not good. She had not mastered sending skills but she received coded and en clair messages at two words a minute. Although fairly slow, 'she ponders over certain letters when reading thus losing others. She will be alright when she gets over this difficulty. She is not fully confident yet but is slowly gaining this. I think she will catch up with the others.'[56]

In early March, Acting Lieutenant Hodgson reported that,

> she seems an intelligent young woman and serious about her work. She rather gives the impression of being a flighty young woman, but I think it is superficial. She likes men to make a fuss of her and generally has a good time but I don't feel this affects her security. From that point of view, she seems sound as far as I can judge. I understand she is engaged to a Geoffrey Mortlock, who works on the British Council in London, and she sees him when she goes up to London on the day off.[57]

A few months later, concerns about her attitude and security were raised again. Second Lieutenant Bellamy informed Captain Barber in early May that she had returned for training, 'after six weeks of absence due to illness. She does not impress me as being very sincere or serious about her work and from what I have seen of her she seems more decorative than useful. She is a chatterer, and although I have nothing definite against her, she is not in my mind of the calibre necessary for work in the field.'

A week later he added that she did not strike him as being very intelligent or keen about the training. She never went to the Morse room to practice in her spare time. 'Other officers reported that she seemed emotionally stable and more sophisticated than one of the other students but 'her reliability and motive remain obscure.'

Her sending speed had increased to 9 wpm but was erratic, and her receiving was nine words per minutes with occasional errors. 'Considering that she has had three weeks training prior to this, the result now shown is far below standard and her errors in sending and receiving are consistent. There is no change for the better.'[58]

As a result, Senter, the head of the Security Section, was informed that a request had been made for her disposal,

> as she does not appear to have made the grade. Group B reported that she was neither very intelligent nor well educated, but sensible, practical and resourceful. Her character was said to be immature, but reliable and suitable for courier work. Reports from the other schools, however, were less favourable. She appears to have been a disappointing student, having lost

interest in the work. [...] Having failed to qualify for the role assigned to her it is intended to transfer her to [sedentary work at] the Transmissions Section of the BCRAL. I see no security objection to this proposal.[59]

She was 'sworn out' of the SOE on 20 June – promising not to divulge what she had learned about the British Intelligence Service – and started work on 9 September as a transmissions clerk in the 5th Bureau of the EMFFI (*Etat Major des Forces Française de l'Intérieur*).

How long she worked in this section is unknown, but she married Charles G. Mortlock in Marylebone in 1945 and went on to live in Australia, Malta and Malaysia before returning to England with her daughter, Christine. She died in 2005, aged 82.

It is worth noting that de Cheveigné parachuted into the Lille area as a wireless operator to Fassin in early September 1943 and was reported as doing excellent work. However, he was arrested on 2 April 1944. According to his personnel file, he was deported to Germany on 1 September 1944, released at the end of the war and awarded the King's Medal for Courage.[60]

MARIE-ROSE MIGUET
Aged 24. Brought out of France on the night of 8/9 August 1944 to be trained as an agent but not returned.

In summer 1944, Richard Heslop code named Xavier, who had been landed by Hudson in Ain on 21 September 1943 to organise F Section's MARKSMAN network, arranged for the nine crew members of downed Liberator, Stirling and Whitley planes to be picked up by a Carpetbagger Douglas C47a on the night of 8/9 August. The field was near Izemore, 7 km north-west of Nantua, about 40km west of Geneva. As there was room for one more passenger, he decided to send 25-year-old Marie-Rose Miguet. In his wartime autobiography, *Xavier*, he identified her as

> Loulette Miguet. sister of our valiant transport officer, Jean Miguet. Earlier London has asked me to send a French girl to London, who was intelligent, knew the Maquis and could describe its work; I presumed at lectures. We had selected Loulette as all her family were in the Maquis or Resistance and she had worked as a courier in Ain. She was reluctant to leave France, but I persuaded her that she could be trained in Britain and might be able to parachute back later in the war.[61]

In his book *The Bedford Triangle*, Martin Bowman claimed that there was a young French girl among the passengers who was to be sent on a sabotage training course.[62]

After obtaining a copy of Marie-Rose's death certificate from the Hauteville Mairie, the National Archives opened her personnel file. It states that she was born on 27 February 1919 at Librairie, Hauteville, Ain. Her father had died but her mother, brother and two sisters were still in France. Jean worked for the Maquis and Jeanne and Camille worked in the bookshop in Hauteville.

Her hobbies were bicycling and ski-ing and she was fluent in French and Italian but knew a little English. She claimed to know the department of Ain, Savoie, Loire, Ysere, Lyons, Grenoble, Toulon and Marseilles. Between 1932 and 1939 she studied at the Lycee a Bourg en Bresse and won qualifications in Italian, English and Philosophy. She then embarked on a chemistry course in Grenoble.

On arrival in Britain, she was interrogated and a detailed report of her work and conditions in France was written up:

A. HISTORY

1. Introduction

Having completed her studies in July 1943, source returned to her home in Hauteville (Ain), where she lived with her sisters and her brother JEAN. The former kept a bookshop and the latter a garage. Source then learned that her brother JEAN was engaged in resistance activity, sheltering young men who wished to avoid the relève and forwarding them to the Maquis. Source thinks that her brother started this work early in 1942. She herself suspected that he was doing subversive work of some sort, but it was not until her return home in July 1943 that she learned the actual nature of his activity. The young men whom he received came from all parts of France and spent a night at the bookshop before going on to the Maquis. Source stated that the arrival and departure of these young men did not attract any attention, as numerous customers came both to the bookshop and to JEAN's garage. Source's home also served as a meeting-place for the leaders of the resistance movement in the locality. JEAN, who was an active member of the organisation, was present at the meetings and took part in the operations that were planned. He holds the rank of Lieutenant, having been accredited in London on the recommendation of Cdt. XAVIER. Among the leaders who came to source's home and to whom she was introduced were Cdt. ROMANS, local chief of the Maquis, CHABOT, MANTIN, MONTREAL and the couriers BOB, BEBE and LOUISON. Source gave the following descriptions of these persons: -

CHABOT

36 years old; about 1.75 m in height; brown wavy hair; large forehead; always smiling; fairly squat in build.

MANTIN

Age about 30' height about 1.70 m; very dark; black eyes; thin; bronzed complexion; very nervous.

MARCO

Age about 34; height about 1.75 m; fairly well-built; appearance of great energy.

MONTREAL

Age about 36; height about 1.70 m; fairly thin; black hair; black piercing eyes; pointed nose; looked very energetic.

BOB

Tall young man of about 26; very dark; black eyes. BOB's disappeared a year ago and has not been seen since. It is presumed that he has been arrested. No repercussions have resulted. He used to visit Paris frequently to see his family.

BEBE

Appearance gave rise to his nickname. Small round baby face; fair complexion; blue eyes, age about 32.

LOUISON

Medium height; fair; blue eyes; hair "en brosse"; at that time was liaison agent, now chef de groupe.

B. ACTIVITY

In September 1943 source began to work with the resistance as courier. She made three journeys to Amberieu to collect mail from couriers who arrived from Lyons, including ANNIE and another woman whose name source did not know. Source took the mail to the [redacted] at La Cluse, near Nantes, who passed it on to the "boite aux lettres" at the Café BITOU, La Cluse. The mail was destined for Cdt. ROMANS, but source did not know by whom it was sent and did not seek to know. She only saw the couriers for about an hour, as they returned immediately to Lyons.the café RITOU was, source gathered, used fairly frequently as a safe house and "boite aux lettres". In February 1944 it was raided by the Gestapo, but RITOU managed to escape in time. There were numerous Gestapo agents in the district, who appeared to be well-informed, and all the houses which had sheltered refugees experienced some trouble.

Source gave the following description of ANNIE: -

Tall, 1.68 m; very fair, blue eyes, pretty.

Source thinks that ANNIE was in touch with other organisations and had contact with the I.S. [Intelligence Service – SIS] she was later connected with the "Service Sociale" which was concerned with the families of young men in the maquis and the sending of parcels to people in concentration camps. [Redacted], Paul DEBAT, was a member of the resistance group at Artomare, between Amberieu and Culoz. He was taken by the Germans when they entered the district in February 1944 and was sent first to Compeigne and then to Germany. Source does not know with which actual organisation DEBAT was in contact; she thinks that he was in contact with ROMANS. Source describes Paul RABET as follows: -

Very dark; squat in build; black eyes.

The other woman courier whose name source did not know was described by source as follows: -

Age about 30; small, very dark; fairly stout.

3. Contact with GANTINIER (APOTHEME). October 1943.

Some time in October 1943, source met GANTINIER who came to the bookshop in Hauteville. As source was going to Grenoble in November 1943 to continue her studies at the university there, GANTINIER asked her to work for him in the capacity of "boite aux lettres" in Grenoble and courier between Granoble and the departement of Ain. Source agreed and GANTINIER arranged a rendezvous for a certain day on which a girl would contact source with the password "Do you know MARCEL"? Source duly went to the rendezvous, but the girl did not appear. One morning source subsequently met GANTINIER by chance and he told her that the rendezvous would be for that evening. Again source went to the rendezvous and again the girl did not arrive. Source waited for three days but never made the appointed contact. She did not meet GANINIER again, though she had given him her address in Grenoble and he therefore could have contacted her had he so wished.

GANTINIER did not put her in touch with any other members of resistance organisations in Grenoble. Source supposed that the recent sabotage on the railways was the cause of the non-appearance of the girl. While in Grenoble from November 1943 until June 1944 when she finished her examinations source was not engaged in any subversive activity.

4. Source's brother JEAN evades arrest by the Gestapo, December 1943.

In December 1943 the Gestapo arrived at source's home in Hauteville to arrest her brother JEAN. He and his sisters were at lunch when the Gestapo entered the house by a side door. JEAN immediately got out by a back way, while one of the sisters went to speak to the Gestapo men, who asked her if her brother was there. She replied that he was out and the gestapo went away without searching the premises. JEAN had in the meantime taken refuge with some friends and, during the night, he left to join Cdt. ROMANS in the Maquis.

Source thought that this attempt at arrest might have been due to denunciation by an Italian officer, who, she thought, was attached to the German H.Q. this officer whose name source did not know had been coming to Hauteville for some time and had incurred the suspicions of the resistance workers.

5. <u>Contact with MARTIAL and CHAPUIS</u>. December 1943.

While at home for the Christmas holidays 1943 source met a W/Op MARTIAL who was transmitting from the house of CHAPUIS, who belonged to his organisation. Source does not think that MARTIAL actually worked for ROMANS, but believes that they were in touch with each other. Another member of MARTIAL's group was [redacted] of Tenay (Ain). [Redacted], who was a member of the I.S. brought MARTIAL to Hauteville in the first place and installed him in CHAPUIS' house. Source described [redacted] as follows: -

Height 1.70 m; thin; fair hair; light blue eyes' big nose; seemed very nervous.

[Redacted] went into hiding when the Germans came into the district in February 1944. He was not arrested.

6. <u>Death of MARTIAL</u>. 4 or 5 January 1944.

Early on the morning of the 4 or 5 January 1944, about 20 Germans arrived in lorries at CHAPUIS' house. The surrounded the house and started firing. MARTIAL was either killed or shot himself to avoid capture. He was not transmitting at the time, but his W/T set was in the house together with all his material. This was presumably discovered when the Germans searched the house. Source thinks that MARTIAL was probably located by D/F'ing, or possibly the Italian officer to whom reference has already been made had heard something about him and denounced him to the Germans. The Italian did not actually know MARTIAL, but there were so many Gestapo agents living in Hauteville that he had probably learned about MARTIAL through them. In this connection source stated that, because of the presence of these Gestapo agents, great care had to be exercised in conversation on all occasions, even in the bookshop. The agents were not natives of the place, but people who had been living there for six months, ostensibly for health reasons.

7. <u>Second Attempt to arrest JEAN</u>. 4 or 5 January 1944.

About an hour after the attack on MARTIAL the Germans visited source's home for the second time, looking for JEAN, who, however, was still in hiding. A cousin who was living there at the time was taken, but was later released. He was of age to be called up for the Releve, but had received a postponement. On his release, he joined JEAN in the Maquis. The Germans compelled source's sisters to show photographs of the family in an endeavour to identify JEAN. The sisters pretended, however, that none of the photos was that of JEAN. A few phots were taken away by the Germans.

8. Capture of CHAPUIS.

When the Germans arrived at CHAPUIS' house in January 1944, CHAPUIS himself was away in Lyons. On hearing of the attack he joined Cdt. ROMANS in the Maquis and, in February 1944, while carrying out a Maquis patrol in company with source's brother and other Maquisards, he was captured in a skirmish with the Germans. He was shot two months later. His body was eventually brought to Hauteville as a great concession and his brother-in-law was allowed to see it. It bore no signs of torture or mutilation.

9. Source's continued activity. June 1944.

On completing her course of study at Grenoble in June 1944 source returned home. She went via Lyons, where she spent two days waiting for her luggage. From Lyons she took the train to Amberieu and then proceeded by bicycle to Hauteville, as the line from Amberieu onwards had been sabotaged. The whole district was under Maquis control and there were barriers at Tenay and Hauteville. Source was stopped at a barrier on the way and her papers were examined. Fortunately, a young man recognised her and guaranteed her bona fides, so she was allowed to pass. The majority of people were refused permission to continue on their way, the Maquis controls being extremely strict. After about a week ROMANS came to the bookshop and source agreed to work for him. The following day she was taken by car to the Maquis H.Q. at Solonia (about 30km from Hauteville). Here she met XAVIER, Cdt. GAILLARD, Capt. GERARD and Capt. LOUIS in addition to some couriers, COLETTE, JO and MICHETE. As source had already furnished descriptions of these persons in a previous interrogation, she was not required to repeat them. Immediately on her arrival at Solonia source was asked by ROMANS, with XAVIER's approval, to come to the U.K. for a course of training. She was to leave the next day but the plane did not arrive and, in the meanwhile, she carried out some intelligence work, going to Bourg-en-Bresse to obtain information about the German troops in the locality. It was not specially for security reasons that ROMANS wished source to leave the country, she was more blown than the other members of her family, though people rather suspected her of subversive work. At that time the Germans were rounding up all the Maquis camps in the district and operations were becoming increasingly difficult to arrange. The location of the Maquis camps were too well known.

On her journeys to Bourg and other places source had at her disposal a car which had been requisitioned by the Maquis. Before the Maquis was thoroughly organised, they used to requisition cars rather indiscriminately, under pretext that they belonged to the Milice or the Gestapo.

10 Plot by COBRA.

COBRA, who had been in the Maquis for 11 months and who had during that time given rise to no suspicion as to his loyalty, was executed for treason some time in the beginning of July. He had been a Lieutenant in the Waffen SS and had, according to himself, subsequently escaped. He spoke German very well. The circumstances of his arrest by the Maquis and his execution were as follows: -

On account of his knowledge of German COBRA acted as interpreter during the interrogations of German prisoners taken by the Maquis in the battles after D-Day. ROMANS had demanded that French prisoners taken by the Germans should be returned, or else,, for every French prisoners killed, three German prisoners would be killed. Under these conditions the German prisoner was escorted back to the German lines by COBRA, whose attitude towards the prisoner gave rise to suspicion. He was arrested by the Maquis and eventually executed, as, following investigations, it was discovered that he had planned to betray the H.Q. at Solonia. As a result, the H.Q. was moved to Izernore.

11. Source's exfiltration 6.7.44

Source remained in the Maquis until she was exfiltrated by plane on the 8.7.44. she arrived in the UK the following day.

GENERAL INFORMATION.

1. Conditions in the Maquis

    a) Control

    Source stated that the various regions of the Maquis were now well determined. The entire Department of Ain was under the control of the Maquis, who had erected barriers of considerable strength on all the roads. Within the area the members of the Maquis moved with complete freedom, but strangers who approached were subjected to strict examination.

    b) Food.

    According to source the food situation in the Maquis was recently much improved. At first supplies of wheat were obtained to make bread, but latterly each member of the Maquis received 200 grams of bread per day in addition to eggs and meat. The Dept. of Ain was not rich from the point of view of vegetable produce, but the deficiency was remedied by supplies obtained from the Maquis groups in other regions in which conditions in this respect were more favourable.

c) Clothing.

With regard to clothes, source stated that matters were not satisfactory. Few of the men had uniforms; their clothes were worn out and they were in great need of shoes.

d) Arms.

The Maquis was not equipped with any heavy weapons, merely with small arms such as Stens and carbines.

e) Reception of Material.

Considerable quantities of material were received from the UK. Recently a day operation had been carried out in which 36 planes delivered supplies. During the period of the operation strict controls were enforced by the Maquis and people were forbidden to circulate.

f) Attacks by the Germans.

In February 1944, between 200 and 300 Germans came into the region of Hauteville for the purpose of guarding the railway line between Tenay and Culoz, which they wanted to keep free for transport. Sabotage was carried out by the Maquis, who were attacked from time to time by the Germans. In these attacks the enemy suffered considerable losses. They have now abandoned the line.

g) Medical Service.

Attached to each Maquis group was a doctor and medical orderly. Severely wounded cases were transferred to hospital in Nantua. There were fairly large stocks of medical supplies in the Maquis.

2. Documents.

Source had a carte d'identite, a carte d'etudiant, but no carte d'alimentation. Asked whether she had information about a new ration card, source replied that a new card was due to be issued in August throughout the whole of France. The outside cover was completely new. Source had filled up a form for a new card when she was in Grenoble in May 1944.

3. Controls.

On her journeys to Bourg in June 1944, source was stopped by Miliciens who examined her papers and put several questions to her concerning her identity. At certain points small barricades had been constructed, manned by two or three Miliciens armed with carbines. There was little control by Feld-Gendarmes. Groups of about 30 – 40 Germans were stationed at Amberieu and Tenay – they remained for the most part in their barracks. After the sabotage of the railways, there were German controls on all the lines in the district.

Men were searched for arms and even women were sometimes searched on their arrival at a station.

4. <u>Gestapo and Milice</u>.

Source could not state the location of the Gestapo H.Q. in Grenoble, but said that the Milice Bureau was in the Place Victor Hugo. There were in Grenoble about 500 G.M.P. [German Military Police] including 300 who had been transferred from Toulouse. Those originally stationed in Grenoble wore a blue uniform, black boots and a black beret; those who arrived from Toulouse wore a khaki uniform.

5. <u>German Troop Movements</u>.

Source had observed numerous troop trains moving in the direction of Lyons and also some trains loaded with military material, motors, tanks, etc. going towards the south. It was thought that the Germans intended to mass in the region of Lyons. Source had not noticed the particular type of troops being conveyed.

6. <u>Aerial Concentrations</u>.

There are German aerodromes at Amberieu, but there are only a few planes, and they are not particularly active.

7. <u>German Defences at Grenoble</u>.

There were no fortifications of any kind at Grenoble and no D.C.A. [?] in the region. One of the German barracks in Grenoble was blown up by sabotage (see below).

8. <u>Sabotage in Grenoble</u>.

Source mentioned the following two acts of sabotage which were carried out against the Germans while she was in Grenoble: -

a) At the end of November 1943, a depot of munitions was blown up. It was situated near the town gasometer and after the explosion the Germans gave out that it was the gasometer which had been blown up. Half of the town was destroyed and supplies of gas were interrupted for three days; there was only one hour of gas at midday and one hour in the evening.

b) A German barracks was also destroyed by sabotage. Members of the resistance movement entered by the sewers and killed the sentries. The charges were placed near a depot of munitions which exploded. There were many victims among the German soldiers. As a result, severe restrictions were imposed on the inhabitants of the town; there was a curfew at 5 pm.; traffic was stopped; it was forbidden to form groups in the streets and cafes and cinemas were closed.

9. <u>German attitude towards the students</u>.

Orders were issued by the Germans that no demonstration was to take place on 11 November in commemoration of the Armistice.

Students had planned, however, to form a procession and hold a demonstration at the War memorial and this was carried out in spite of the orders issued. The procession crossed the town, singing the Marseillaise, and arrived at the Place Verdun. Police were stationed throughout the town and there were cordons of G.M.R. finally, 100 Germans arrived at the Place Verdun and charged into the crowd. Some students were wounded and many were taken prisoner, the women being released later and the men being sent to concentration camps. This affair produced a feeling of hostility to the students among the inhabitants of the town.

On one occasion a considerable number of students, including source, was in the street during the interval between the examinations. The funeral of a milicien was passing at the time and it consisted mainly of cars containing armed Miliciens and Francists. A student who was smoking was ordered by a Francist to put out his cigarette. Another student, who had not heard this command, started to smoke in his turn. Immediately all the students were rounded up.

10. Bombing at Grenoble.
Source was in Grenoble when the marshalling yards were bombed. The raid, which was carried out in broad daylight, was not particularly successful, a many of the bombs did not fall directly on the target. There were civilian victims in the nearby village of Bussarate.

11. D-Day.
There was little activity in Grenoble on D-Day on the part of the Germans, as the majority of them had been sent to places in the vicinity for fear of attacks by the Resistance Movement. The news of the Allied landing was received with enthusiasm by the inhabitants, as people were beginning to be wearied by the intensive bombing. If this bombing had not been the prelude to the landing, a feeling of hostility would have arisen.

12. Vichy Government.
Source had heard of no changes among the personnel of the Vichy Government.[63]

As with other reports, the intelligence would have been forwarded to the relevant sections. After her interrogation, she would have been interviewed by SOE. Given the cover-name Marie Marnier, she was sent for training at Roughwood Park (STS 42) in Chalfont St Giles, Buckinghamshire. Her instructor's first impression was that she was 'shy and a little nervous. Not a very highly educated person but probably quite reliable. Fairly good security minded.'

After a fortnight, her instructor reported that she was being trained as a courier. She took part in the security scheme and showed a fair understanding of the principles.

> This student worked very hard while here and showed great enthusiasm and keenness in all that she did. She is very good with her hands and can handle weapons and explosives effectively, but she has not great confidence in her own mental power, although in actual fact she appears to be very intelligent. She has picked up a certain amount of English during her time here and was always a delightful person to deal with in the Mess and in her work.[64]

Before being demobbed, she had to sign the Official Secrets Act three days before Paris was liberated. Consequently, there was no need for Marie-Rose to receive the sabotage or other training.

In recognition of her three months' work in France between September and November 1943 and four months between June and September employed by SOE, Heslop managed to persuade the Finance Section to pay her 25,000 francs (£125). The amount was based on the £350 per annum SOE paid full-time female agents, minus pay and advances she had already received. A note recommending the payment acknowledged that it was firstly 'for her work for the Resistance for a considerable time prior to being officially recruited by our people' and secondly for 'Her gallant conduct in guiding British airmen through the German lines to Grenoble.'[65]

CÉCILE PICHARD
Aged 29. Parachuted from a Liberator near Rivière les Fosses (Haute Marne) on 11 August 1944. Cited for an OBE.

Pierre Tillet's research shows that on 11 August 1944, the first sister-brother team was dropped in France. Cécile Pichard was flown on USAAF Woods' BOB 224 Carpetbagger mission from RAF Harrington and parachuted 2 km south-west of Rivière les Fosses, about 45 km north of Dijon in the Haute Marne. With identity papers in the name of Jacqueline Pradier and the code name Altesse, she was accompanied by her brother, Michel Pichard, code named Pic and Generatrice, and Maurice Rosenbach, code name Sevillan, as their wireless operator.

Born in Nesle-Hodeng, Seine-Maritime, on 5 April 1915, she attended the community school in Dieppe in 1921; the High School at Le Havre in 1927 and 'Pigier' Technical College in 1931 where she studied business. She looked after her mother who died of stomach cancer in 1933 and moved to Paris where she lived with an aunt.

Her father, who had been a company director in Le Havre, was conscripted into the army and was killed in action in November 1939. Her only brother, Michel, three years younger than her, spent 1938 at the Office Technique d'Assurance, Paris, and was planning to study Law but was also called up and served as a gunner in the Fontainebleau artillery before being garrisoned in Morocco.

When war broke out, she worked as a stenographer, a shorthand typist, in the fire service section of Assurances Generales, an insurance company. In May 1942, she accepted a job as a secretary in the same firm and was living at 24 Rue Monceau in Paris.

Michel came to England from North Africa in August 1941 and joined the Free French at Camberley. Selected by the BCRA to be sent back to France, he received security and coding training from SOE for Operation *Bel* and, on 6 January 1943, a trawler dropped him on one of the islands south of Concarneau, Finistère. Code named Gauss, his mission was to make enquiries along the coast of German installations and fortifications with a view to their destruction by sabotage or bombing. He had been given 25,000 francs to finance his mission and 10,000 francs for the Confrérie de Notre Dame, a Catholic anti-Nazi network, operating in the occupied zone.[66]

Cécile met him by chance one day in the street in Paris. According to Michel, it was in January 1943, and by June she was working as his secretary and courier in the Paris area and living at 3 Square de Dordogne in the 17th arrondissement. Given the nature of her work, she obtained identity papers in the names of Cécile and Jacqueline Pradier, Annie Cordier and Josette Crusset. She later admitted that,

> Her work consisted of dealing with courrier (she did all the coding with the aid of another secretary), coping with landing grounds, new arrivals and finances. She worked extremely hard and had to get up at 0630 every morning in order to get through the work, staying at her office until late at night.[67]

During her work, she probably met Louis Jourdron, Michel's wireless operator, and Claude Bouchinet-Serreulles, code name Sophie, another RF/BCRA agent who had been infiltrated in June 1943 to work with Jean Moulin, de Gaulle's emissary to the French Resistance. It is possible that she also met Wing Commander Forest Yeo-Thomas, a French-speaking British agent, code named Shelley.

Before the war, Yeo-Thomas worked for Molyneux, a successful fashion-house in Paris, but escaped to England, where he joined the RAF and worked as an interpreter for the Free French forces. In 1942, he joined SOE to work initially in F Section on military planning and later as a liaison officer with BCRA, the Free French intelligence agency. Having undergone all the necessary training, on 25 February 1943, he was parachuted northwest of Gisors with Andre Dewavrin, code named Colonel Passy, to meet with Pierre Brossolette and organise Resistance networks to obstruct the German occupation plans in northern France.

Returning to England by Lysander on 14 April, he was debriefed and prepared for a second mission and on 17 September was parachuted north of Angouleme with Brossolette and André Déglise-Favre on mission Marie-Claire to identify and organise dropping grounds and landing strips. This may well have brought him into contact with Cécile.

Visiting various Resistance groups and dispensing cash raised their morale but the Gestapo, aware of his work but unable to arrest him, dubbed him the 'White Rabbit'. He admitted dining with prolific and infamous Nazis, such as Klaus Barbie, known as the 'Butcher of Lyon', to gather vital information, but with the Gestapo capturing other agents, he needed to get back to England.

Cécile provided details of what the situation in Paris was like before she left.

ARREST OF SOPHIE'S SECRETARIES
SOPHIE's office in PARIS was raided by the Gestapo in September, and several of his secretaries and all his documents were taken. SOPHIE himself is now in hiding, and his place has been taken by BERNARD @ SOLDAT. Source did not know SOPHIE and her information is, therefore, second-hand; she thinks it possible that one of his secretaries has talked. BEL had never been to SOPHIE's office and did not even know where it was.

SOURCE IS FOLLOWED
Source is positive that she herself was followed on one occasion. She came out of a café with three friends, and a man in plain clothes appeared to be waiting for them and began to follow them. Source and her friends noticed this and went down the nearest Metro where they split up, shaking the man off. This was about eight days after the SOPHIE affair. She believes the Germans may know the district in which she lives, but not the exact address, and thinks other members of the organisation were also followed on the same day, and the man who followed her may have picked her up at a previous rendez-vous. As a result of this incident, however, she took the precaution of changing her Identity papers. BEL was never troubled in this way, although he would be easy to identify, having three fingers missing on one hand. To hide this, he generally wears a glove with the missing fingers stuffed to look normal, or keeps his hand in his pocket. The Gestapo in the NIEVRE area may have his description through

NAPO, sub-Chief of the organisation in that area, or his mistress, but Source is sure that the PARIS Gestapo have not got a description of him.

ARREST OF AMPERE AND ETIENNE

Jacques GUERIN @ AMPERE was arrested in September in the YONNE, together with another Agent, ETIENNE, whom Source has never met and whose name she does not know. She thinks however that ETIENNE probably talked. A little while later she heard that he had visited other members of the organisation and told them that he had escaped; that while in prison he had been sent with a message to the two sentries on guard, that they were absent from their posts, and that he had just walked out. There is some doubt however whether he was not freed by the Gestapo in return for information.

The only description of ETIENNE that source has heard is: fairly young, short stature, fair hair.

DOCUMENTS

Source always used her real Identity Card, although she was provided with various false cards from the town hall by friends, for use in her work. She had a ration book and feuille semestrielle [half-yearly account sheet] (valid six months). She never had a Certificat de Domicile as her address was entered on her Identity Card. If one moves, one must go to the Commissariat in the new district and have the new address entered on one's Identity Card. She kept up her worker's contributions (she had formerly worked in an insurance office) as part of her cover.

With the possibility of more arrests if the prisoners talked, plans were made for a Lysander operation to bring back Bouchinet-Serreulles, Yeo-Thomas and Michel. Verity recalled in his autobiography being told by Michel Pichard that,

Yeo-Thomas was to be picked up with Claude Bouchinet-Serreulles ('Sophie') and myself. I got to Arras around the 11th [November] with my secretary Bel-A (actually my sister Cécile, whom we call Jacqueline, now Jacqueline de Marcilly as she kept that Christian name) in case there would be room for her; she had worked with me since January and was 'blown'.

On November 12th or 13th, I rushed back to Paris after hearing that eight BOA (Bureau d'Opérations Aériennes) agents had been arrested at Café Dupont, Versailles ... the situation was quite alarming, and I decided to stay.

Serreulles, disregarding London's instructions, did not show up; so, this left two 'seats' available, and Yeo-Thomas flew back with Mademoiselle Virolle (his agent de liaison) and Mademoiselle Pichard.[68]

In Bruce Marshall's *White* Rabbit, he narrates how Yeo-Thomas returned from France in a Lysander, somewhat overburdened and windswept. Along with fourteen packages and suitcases, he had two young rank and file female members of the Resistance sitting one on each knee. He was not able to reach the cockpit cover that had inadvertently been left open, and neither were the women.[69]

Verity described the flight in detail naming the date as 15/16 November 1943, the pilot as Flight Officer McCairns, the field as being 1 km north-west of Canettemont, west of Arras and that the three of them were brought to the field in an undertakers' hearse as part of a funeral procession! The women's names, Mme M. Guyot ('Mlle Virolle') and Mlle Pichard, were added in the appendix. The Conscript Heroes website reported them returning with invaluable information on the establishment of VI rockets and coastal defences of the Atlantic Wall.

Slightly deviating from Cécile's account is a story one Tempsford pilot told me of how the SOE learned that the safe house of a 19-year-old dark-haired wireless-operator in Paris was in a residential area being searched by the Germans. Her minders knew they were closing in and arranged for a plane to be sent from Tempsford to 'lift her out'. The security was so tight around Paris that the only way the Resistance could get her out was to organise a funeral for her. She was put in a coffin and sent in a hearse to the pick-up point. On the way out of the city, the hearse was stopped by German guards who demanded the driver open the rear door. A machine gun was pointed at the coffin but, before it was riddled with bullets, the driver got in between the guard and the coffin pleading with the soldier, 'Don't shoot! Don't shoot! She's my mother.' It worked. The hearse took her to a remote landing area where she was picked up by a Lysander and flown back to Britain. She was dropped at Tangmere and the pilot flew on to Tempsford. When the pilot next called in at the SOE office at 505 Edgware Road in London, he learned that her hair had turned white as a result of her trauma.

Arriving with identity papers in the name of Jacqueline Pradier, Cécile, like all other women refugees arriving in Britain during the war, would have been interrogated at Nightingale Lane to check whether she might have been a German agent and to obtain up-to-date intelligence of the social, economic and political situation in France. Given her work with the Resistance, especially knowing some of those arrested, she was vetted by the Security Section in their offices at Bayswater. They reported her to be 'a most intelligent and enthusiastic young Frenchwoman. Best woman agent seen at Bayswater.'

Back in France, Michel rebuilt his network and, as he was in charge of about 500 DZs, he was appointed one of the principal air operations officers for northern France and later head of General de Gaulle's Air Liaison, the person responsible for coordinating flights from Tempsford and Harrington into north-eastern France.[70] He was only 25.

The report on Cécile's interrogation shed light on conditions in France at that time:

BRIEF HISTORY

Cecile Eugenie PICHARD @ JACQUELINE @ Cecile PRADIER @ Annie CORDIER @ Josette CRUSSET is the sister of our Agent BEL @ MARTIN @ GAUSS (real name Michel Pichard) and has been working as courier/secretary to him since April of this year, when he returned to France after training in this country. [rest included above]

CONTROLS AND TRAVEL

Source never travelled long distance for the organisation: she lived in PARIS, and her work was there. She definitely thinks that it is safe for a woman than a man to travel about in France nowadays.

Controls on the Metro are sometimes carried out by the French Police. There are still two classes on the Metro; the Germans always travel first [class], and everyone else travels second to avoid the. The first class tickets are orange and cost 3.80 francs. They can be used twice – outward journey and return – or two similar journeys on different days. The double use is only paper economy. Second class tickets are yellow and cost 2.60 francs (also a 'double' ticket). All tickets can be purchased in books of five.

There are very few buses. There are a few velo-taxis, however, but these are very expensive. For instance, a velo-taxi from the Place de Madeleine to the rue du Bac (a very short distance) costs 200 francs. Fares are calculated in the driver's head; there is no set tariff. It is usual however to enquire how much the journey will cost before starting. Mostly tandem bicycles are used, and up to four passengers can be taken.

Long distance trains, especially from the South and the West are frequently several hours late. This is because of sabotage of the lines.

BLACK MARKET

Source very seldom eats in the black market. For one thing, she cannot afford it, and for another, it is not normal to see young people with so much money to spend that they can afford black market meals regularly. Source used to work late at her office and get what she could to eat in the restaurants in the district where she lived. Her ration card was not sufficient to feed her, but she was given extra ration tickets. Good wine may still be had, by paying high prices. One is allowed three bottles of wine per head per month at fixed prices, i.e.one a week, and one wineless week a month.

She stresses that Agents should avoid black market restaurants.

AGENTS' CLOTHING

Asked her opinion about the clothing of Agents coming into the Field, Source said that many of the men wore blue suits with stripes, such as are never seen in France. Plain navy blue is all right, but these suits are a lighter shade, and brand the Agents as foreigners at once. Also Agents seem to arrive from this country with standard wrist watches, and generally on a tan leather strap. A metal bracelet should be substituted for the strap. Agents' shoes are often a red shade of leather, which is obviously not French. Suitcases are also much too standard, both as to size and fabric. Agents arriving together cannot identify their own without opening them.

MATERIAL RECEIVED AND NEEDED

Source has also helped in the reception of arms. The teams say that we send too much explosive, and not enough guns, but Source is not in a position to judge this. On one occasion a parachute containing explosives failed to open; the container hurtled to the ground and exploded. Fortunately, the terrain was isolated and apparently no one heard the explosion.

Source believes that more grounds are found and more teams recruited than the British can use. Her own organisation had some 300 landing grounds (they recently gave away 80 to another organisation) and about 2,500 men recruited for reception work etc. source states that the French expected D-day and allied landings in September and October this year. When nothing happened, except the arrest of a number of patriots, they were naturally very disappointed, and the Germans made good propaganda out of it. Resistance has now been going on for four years in France, and all serious efforts to keep it clandestine have ceased by now.

Warm winter clothing, especially woollens and boots similar to Army boots are needed for the teams and anyone whose work takes him out of doors at night. Presents of chocolate would be very much appreciated, also a few wrist watches. These are now extremely expensive and in short supply. They are needed for rendezvous, reception work, etc. For some of the receptions, the organisation had no transport; the material was removed afterwards in trucks running on black market petrol.

B.B.C. MESSAGES

Source has asked that the broadcast of operational messages on the B.B.C. at 1330 should be reinstated. The next broadcasts are at 1930 and 2200, and this is too late for reception teams who are waiting for operational messages as they often have to travel some distances to the landing grounds. The German jamming is only directed against these messages as most people in France now know that these are in reality operational messages in code. These messages should not be right at the beginning of the broadcast, as with heavy jamming it is difficult to tune in, and the first messages would be lost. The woman announcer speaks more clearly than the man. It is true that she makes mistakes and saves all her corrections to the end of the broadcast. One man reads quickly, but another gabbles so fast that Source (who is a stenographer) cannot get all the messages down and is left behind. She does not think denunciations are much good, as they tend to divide the French against themselves. She thinks that someone should be sent to France to deal with traitors without publicity. All France listens to DE GAULLE. The GIRAUDISTS are viewed with suspicion, as they are thought to be pro-VICHY.

CRITICISM OF CODE

Cables received from this country are often undecipherable, and when Source has requested repeats, they have not been sent. Source was given a silk handkerchief with the code printed on it; the figures are so small that the 3, 5 and 8 are indistinguishable. Also the material frays very badly; Source hemmed it round with a needle and cotton to try and stop the fraying, she did not understand that she is supposed to cut off [and burn] each key after use for security reasons. She has been working with this system since August. She hides it carefully at night, but not in her flat.

GENERAL

It is easy to find flats in the industrial district of PARIS as people are anxious to evacuate these, rents are not much higher than pre-war, but pre-war comforts, such as central heating and hot water are things of the past. Source says she gets one hot bath a month. Gas and electricity are also heavily rationed; for the first offence one is fined, for the next, the supply is cut off.

The Americans are extremely unpopular in France, because of their indiscriminate bombing and also because the French feel that by their inexperience they are a brake upon English preparations for landing in Europe, Source says that Americans have never managed to hit a military objective yet.

The W/T operators of the organisation work with an assistant to keep watch for them. There are now several working, and so far they have had no trouble with D/F cars as they all operate from the country where it is more difficult to D/F them than in a ton. Source does not know where they live; she had contact with them through a cut-out.

In the first days of the German occupation of France, German news-reels in cinemas were greeted with cat-calls. Because of stringent measures, this stopped. Now they have started again. Source puts the number of Gestapo in PARIS now at 3,600, including both German and French, many women informers and agents provocateurs. The Gestapo have an office in the rue de Bac, and have also taken over a hotel near the Bon Marche. The Gestapo offices have thick barbed wire barriers in front of the ground floor windows, to prevent bombs being thrown in. German troops in PARIS are either well over 40 or else extremely young – many still in their teens. There are very few hotels left in PARIS, as so many have ben requisition for the Germans.

Source believes a decree is imminent by which one may not travel more than 100km. away from the town in which one's Identity Card is issued. The regulation is not yet in force, but may come into force at any time.

For security reasons and owing to false alarms, Source's office has already been changed 15 times; each time they have to invent a different cover. On one occasion they were a sports club, and had to go out of PARIS frequently to inspect their football pitch (the landing grounds). Another time, they were students, a signal of a half-drawn curtain at a certain window indicates danger.

After the German occupation, the franc was stabilised at 20 to the Reichmark. Source has seen notes of RM I, 5 and 20 circulated in France, but now everyone is refusing them, fearing to have them left on their hands after the German defeat.[71]

No details have emerged as to what she did over the following five months before BCRA decided to send her back with Michel on another mission. Unlike the other agents, 29-year-old Cécile was not sent on the assessment course, the paramilitary training course or the clandestine warfare course.

At this stage of the war, the primary need was parachute training. Dismore sent a request to Brigadier Mockler-Ferryman, 'The French have requested that this student be given one week's parachute training. She is the sister of our agent GAUSS, has worked in the field, and is destined to return to the field as a liaison agent. Under these circumstances, it is requested that permission be given to excuse her from SAB and security training.'[72]

Permission granted, she was given the rank of Lieutenant in the Corps Auxiliaire Féminin and, keeping the cover name of Jacqueline Pradier, at the end of May was sent to Ringway. She stayed at Fulshaw Hall and on 2 June, her instructor reported her to have been, 'An excellent student who showed plenty of courage and enthusiasm and in some cases met the standard of her fellow [male] students. She showed no signs of nervousness and her training and jumping was above average on the course. THREE DESCENTS. SECOND CLASS.'[73]

In the weeks before and immediately following D-Day, three-man teams of uniformed American, British, French or sometimes Canadian agents, known as Jedburgh teams, were dropped to liaise with the French Resistance groups and coordinate sabotage and small-scale military attacks on the Germans.

At the beginning of July, with de Gaulle's approval, General Marie-Pierre Koenig, who had command of the Free French in Normandy, created a tripartite command, under the control of Supreme Headquarters of the Allied Expeditionary Force (SHAEF). Colonel Henri Zeigler, a French Air Force officer, code name Colonel Vernon, was appointed chief of staff. On 7 July, he informed the First Bureau, Dismore, Lt-Col. Dudley Carleton-Smith, SOE's joint commander of the Jedburgh programme, and Commandant Lejeune, head of RF's Planning Section that from July 7th until about the end of the August moon, Lt Pradier would be working with Section *Jedburgh*. She had replaced Captain Lieutenant Verneuill, one of the Maquis regional commanders, who had been given other duties.[74]

Her task was to contact Captain de Schonen, the French officer in Jedburgh team DANIEL, and help with the development of teams and briefing French officers before their departure.[75]

To ensure she was confident with her parachute jumping, at the end of July she was sent back to Fulshaw Hall. Her instructor commented that she 'was apt and showed no apprehension. Made one descent (3rd) and considering the short time she was here and the disability to her right hand, she did remarkably well. Her ground training was excellent.'[76]

Her personnel file included her cover story which was created for her to be as close to the truth as possible with one major exception. To avoid mentioning Michel, she was told to say she was an only child.

Thomas Ensminger, the late historian for the Carpetbaggers, told me that she, Michel and Rosenbach were flown out of RAF Harrington with Wood's Carpetbagger crew as part of an Inter-Allied Mission team known as ANIS on operation BOB 242.

They landed near Rivière-les-Fosses, Haute-Marne, but very little has come to light of her mission except that it was to organise dropping operations in the Altesse region alongside the A31 between Dijon and Nancy. This was one of the main routes the Germans were expected to take whilst retreating north following the American and French invasion on the Mediterranean coast.

In recognition of Michel's contribution to the war effort, the French made him a Companion of the Liberation. Gubbins described him as

> A courageous, ingenious and very honest man who is a good friend of Great Britain. He organised the reception of 200 parachute operations, and successful reception of 29 agents. In April 1944 numerous arrests took place in Lt. Col. PICHARD's area, and he was compelled to reorganise his réseaux and reception committees. To facilitate the smooth running of his work, Lt. Col. PICHARD was obliged on several occasions to report to his headquarters in PARIS, passing successfully through stringent controls at great personal risk. He was known to the Gestapo and on several occasions only managed to elude pursuers by running.
>
> A prominent British officer was arrested in Paris in February 1944. Lt. Col. PICHARD was able to obtain by bribery an amelioration of the conditions under which this officer was kept. All three contacts were made under conditions of great personal danger and during the negotiations his secretary was arrested.
>
> Lt. Col. PICHARD returned to this country on the eve of D-Day and was again dropped to the field on the night France 11/12 August 1944 to prepare the way for a party of S.A.S. going to N.E. France. Remarkable exhibition of courage sustained over a long period.
>
> It is recommended that for great courage over a very long period and for his leadership and organising ability, this officer should be appointed an Officer (Hon) of the Order of the British Empire (Mil. Div.)[77]

Cécile married after the war and was known as Cécile de Marcilly but, like some of the other French women, she received no recognition from the British, American or the French governments.

ELISABETH TORLET
Aged 29. Parachuted from a Liberator and landed 35 km from their DZ in a field north-east of Sourans, 18 km south-west of Montbéliard (Doubs) on 30 August 1944. Captured on 5 September and executed the following day.

As part of the National Competition of the Resistance and Deportation: 'Resister in Nazi camps', and the Rendezvous History of Blois topic, 'Women in History', students at the Resistance Club at Geneviève de Gaulle Anthonioz college in Bordes shed light on Lt Elisabeth Torlet, another French woman infiltrated into France.

Born on 5 February 1915 at Les Bordes, Loiret, about 50 km east of Orléans, she was one of five children. Her father was Comptroller General of Social Security and mayor of Bordes and served in the military. She studied at Orléans and St Omer and was teaching privately when war broke out. After the armistice was signed, she went to the Free Zone and worked in a social insurance office. In 1942, as her elder sister Madeleine was having problems with her pregnancy, Elisabeth and her sister, Genevieve, took her to Morocco.

On 16 February 1943, Elisabeth and Genevieve responded to the call and, accompanied by Suzanne Combelas and dozens of other women aged between 17 and 30, they reported to Cazes Camp, Casablanca. Here they underwent a medical examination, strenuous physical fitness training and Morse testing before being assigned to a training camp at Rabat. Merlin was reputed to have told them that they could expect days without charm and comfort and that hard work would be their only distraction.

Some were sent to Hydra, a tented camp for the women's corps of wireless transmissions in Algiers. Later, some went to the Armand Falliéres school in Tunis, and were provided with intensive training in Morse, wireless transmission, and reception under the command of Captain Delorme, Chaplain General of all North African Troops. His message to all recruits was, 'Forget your womanhood; you have become soldiers.'

Apart from Eugenie Djendi, none of the Merlinettes have SOE personnel files in the National Archives, probably because their files were kept at Massingham, SOE's code name for its base in Algiers, and they were destroyed after the war.

In August 1943, they were transferred to Algiers and during Elisabeth's wireless training, she demonstrated exceptional qualities that resulted in her being appointed to learn the difficult and delicate operating of illegal transceivers positions. Promoted to Sergeant on 15 September 1943, at the request of the French intelligence services, she was among the thirty volunteers for dangerous missions that responded. Immediately they were assigned to the Directorate General of Special Services in the 805th Communications Company in Algiers.

What happened to Genevieve is unknown, but when the OSS, the American Military Intelligence Service, asked for volunteers, Elisabeth responded. Her guts and dedication were noted. Having completed her parachute training, she volunteered to join an intelligence research mission in enemy occupied territory on Mission JORXEY, a support mission to the FFI in the region of l'Isle-sur-le-Doubs. The maquis delorris website suggested that XEY was a wireless call signal; the J was Jacolin and OR were from TORLET.

Commissioned by the special services of the 1st French Army in Algiers, the SRO (Information Operations Service), the mission was a 'simple' intelligence mission: providing for the advance of Allied troops along the Rhone and Saône valleys. It was to launch teams that would inform the special services of the movements of German units, their lines of retreat and defence, their nature, their staff, their cars, their equipment, etc in an area of Eastern France which would become a strategic sector.

The team consisted of a chief and liaison officer or wireless operator. Lieutenant André Jacolin (named Captain for this mission) and Elisabeth Torlet (named Lieutenant for this mission) were chosen. Jacolin's task was to collect information, Torlet's to inform Algiers round the clock about the military situation in the area. At the last moment, a third agent was attached to the team: Marie-Antoinette Verbeschlag from Alsace, whose interpreting talents were thought to be useful.

They were to be dropped by a Flying Fortress [the American B24 Liberator used by the USAAF 855th Bomb Squadron], the only aircraft able to reach the drop zone and return – it was the extreme limit of its capabilities. Jacolin provided a detailed report of his mission which was also made available (in French) on the maquisdelorris website.

The mission was postponed for various reasons – poor weather, aircraft not available – but finally on 30 August, the B24 Liberator flew out of Algiers. Jacolin mentioned the airfield as Maison Carrée, about 14 km west of Algiers, renamed post-liberation as El Harrach. However, the 885 Bomber Command website claims the USAAF used Maison Blanche airfield, about 15 km south-east of Algiers, renamed Algiers International Airport – Houari Boumediene Dar El Beida. Jacolin, wireless operator Sergeant Elisabeth Torlet code named RXEY3 and Verbeschlag were dropped with team Carolles, Captain J. M. Bressand, Lt Picot and an unknown BCRAA Section R wireless operator. They landed 35 km from their DZ in a field northeast of Sourans, 18 km south-west of Montbéliard, Doubs.[78]

Background information about Marie-Antoinette Verbeschlag has yet to come to light. Elisabeth was collected by the Bertenans family and accommodated in a safe house in Rochet Sourans. Operation *Dragoon*, the landing of American and French troops on the Mediterranean coast on 15 August, had resulted in the expected German retreat to the north. Consequently, there was intense activity in the Doubs valley on the A36 route to Mulhouse.

She was captured by the Germans on 5 September 1944 near l'Isle-sur-le-Doubs and shot the following day. The students commented that she demonstrated a great spirit of sacrifice resisting all interrogations of Gestapo, 'preferring to die rather than betray her comrades' mission.'

In recognition of the students' successful research, Jacolin's testimony is included as it sheds light on their operation and the circumstances of Elisabeth's capture.

Wednesday, August 30

Finally, Wednesday, August 30, the two teams go again to the airfield of Maison Carrée [*sic*]. Aircraft and parachutists were at work. The missions were always accompanied to the airfield by the Lieutenant Tergoul for security reasons and trusting friendships that had developed between him and the beginners during their time of preparation. But on that date he had gone with the Commander Simoneau and Lieutenant Pax (which I will discuss in Part 3 of this report) to Italy with the French Expeditionary Corps General in June. Also we were assigned to a Flying Officer. He did not belong, I believe, to SR, but was sent by his department to introduce us to the American crew and ensure our departure. However, on 25 May 1990 at the AGM of ASSDN held in Paris at the Cercle des Officiers, I was having lunch next to Mr. J. M. Bressand, Chief of the Carolles mission. He then told me the following fact. The lieutenant would have been in the aviation 'service' of the German SR. Knowing our home base in the Doubs, he would have released our departure [time and drop zone details] to the enemy. They had then mounted a 'welcoming committee'. J.M. Bressand told me that he had received this information from Commander Robert DGHS when he had gone to Paris in 1944. It showed him that this officer was the cause of the failure and capture of several airdrops and landings by submarines. Several missions ended tragically, and those transported by submarines were arrested. Intrigued by this information, I sought to have confirmation. Unfortunately, Commander Robert was dead at that time. Colonel Simoneau and Tergoul were consulted, but they told me they had never heard of it. Commander Paillote assured me that at that time his office had destroyed all the enemy's transmitters in North Africa. Knowing the difficult relationship between Paillote and Bressand, I remained perplexed ... I believe Commander Paillote more willingly but a big question mark hangs over this issue.

6:30 p.m.

Boarding and take-off was at 18:30. We just had time to admire the north of Algiers and the Mediterranean, the coast of Provence, and then we headed North through the Alps to avoid flack [anti-aircraft guns] along the Rhone Valley. Clouds over the Alps. We perceive, however, some gaps in the snowy peaks. We experienced a storm with lightning force. From the 'lookout' at the back of the airplane, the show was magical.

11:30 p.m.

We continued on to Burgundy. Then the plane slowed down, lost some height and at 23:30 the red warning light came on telling us to prepare for the drop. We put on the harness and checked there was a good and solid attachment to the junction box. The accompanying officer removed the panel that closes the hatch. Three of the team Carolles were released when the green light came on. It was then expected that after a three-minute fly around the second team would be released with all the containers in view of the first parachutes spread on the ground. My team then sat around the manhole, legs dangling, our hands on the ledge to launch us through the centre of the hole when the signal came to fall straight. The rope was attached above our heads. We saw the green light that gave us the famous 'go' signal. My two teammates then jumped first and I, as the cowardly crew, jumped followed by the baggage.

The sky was an intense blue. We were to be parachuted at the altitude of about 400 m. In fact, we dropped from much higher. No matter because jumping through a hatch in the floor seems much easier than through the door of the driving Dakota. We always risked our parachutes' suspension lines getting caught on the tail. The chute opened, slamming the straps over the shoulders.

To be let go at that height was a drawback, however. Anyway this prolonged our descent and our sway in a silent sky! The light of the moon was dazzling; one could read a newspaper! The view of the hills, forests, valleys and meadows was spectacular, one was struck by the clarity and beauty of the landscape. Arriving from North Africa, where, in summer, everything is dried out, I was dazzled by green meadows and woods. But the ground was getting closer, or rather by the well-known parachutists' feeling it seemed so to us. I stuck my knees together and bent slightly to achieve the rolled ball stage. I landed without difficulty in the middle of a meadow. We had to act quickly: crush the parachute to the ground because it tends to remain inflated under the effect of the breeze and the beautiful white silk is not visible in the blue sky, that task on the green grass. I disposed of my tack. However, I promised myself to embrace my landing ground of France. I did it! ... But without dwelling on it. An emotional moment.

I looked at the blue and red artificial silk petals of our two teams' baggage down in the same meadow. I did not see my two teammates, much less the men of the first mission. I rushed to both containers and three bales of baggage. There was a container missing. I folded the parachutes and carried four items of luggage round the edge of the meadow to hide them in the bushes. I needed to find my teammates. I went looking for them, through barbed wire, meadows, and slopes. The view did not extend far as the area was very hilly. Suddenly I saw above the hills cumulonimbus clouds arrive, usually the warning of a storm. On the blue sky, they approached like galloping horses. Within minutes the sky darkened, the wind picked up, the moon disappeared behind the clouds, visibility was almost zero, then rain fell violently.

Thursday, August 31

I continued my descent through hedges and enclosed fields. It was curious to return clandestinely to this country to participate in its reconquest. The officer accustomed to 'work' in battle dress in constant contact with his troops became a single civilian who must slip incognito in an unknown and often hostile universe. I finally reached a small road. Should I go down? Should I go back? There was no indication. So any decision had to be the effect of chance. Where were the Germans? Was there anyone out there in this sector? I went back and found a milestone. Throwing my jacket over my head and wireless set I turned on my flashlight. I read it and the names were totally unknown to me.

The Americans were wrong and we had been released 35km from the point provided in the woods of Miémont NE Sourans. (Michelin map N ° 66 000 1/200th 6 ° 40/47 ° 25). I must say the plane must have thought to return to Algiers without using their gasoline reserve, all research being for them, without interest! All bases were the same for them. We were far from the conscience of English airmen. I walked in the rain to the D118 when I heard footsteps approaching. Were they civilians, Germans, my teammates? I laid down in the ditch. The night was so dark that the marchers had to pass a few meters from me for I recognised their silhouette. It was my teammates! I called them, and they told me they landed in the valley below the road: Jacqueline in a meadow and Elisabeth ... in a tree. Given the dark undergrowth, Elisabeth hardly realised how high she was hooked. She undid her harness and jumped to the ground landing fortunately without damage! After about twenty minutes she met Jacqueline, and both went up the valley where they found the road. That night luck was with us.

5:00

At 5:00 all three of us reached the hamlet of Rochet (intersection of D 35 and D 118) below the village of Sourans. Two houses, one on the right, one to the left of the road. The more comfortable the more modest. A success that? I decided on the left, the more modest. It was still raining; the day had not yet started. We were soaked and miserable! We knocked. The owner, a labourer in the area, Mr. Charles Bertenand, opened the door. We had to introduce ourselves: 'We got lost, we are wanted by the Germans...' He was a bit wary, and I understood! His wife arrived. Seeing us in this sorry state, she took pity on and allowed us to enter.

Sitting all three around their table she revived her stove to dry us. The conversation continued and playing all out we tell them that we arrived from Algiers and had just been parachuted. It took us to show them our chocolate! our American cigarettes ... to convince them. Soon reassured, they were proud to tell us that they had two young children and a son in the Resistance. So they agreed to welcome us and we were pleased we were sent to them because, face it, these are Swiss Germans which they distrust! After a little rest we were pressed to go search at daybreak, for our luggage and parachutes.

The road mender accompanies us with a cart. We found them easily and also found the container lost in the night. We recovered the parachute Elisabeth left hanging in the tree. I think, as a precaution, we had to burn the parachutes. But Madame Bertenand opposed this because the silk was so rare. Quickly, she cut them for making dresses for her last two children: little twins 7 or 8 years old! Still no news of the other team. So I went with the labourer to search in the area and neighbouring villages. But in vain.

At 18:00 we saw a young FFI who had been sent by Carolles to find us. We then learned that the first team had been parachuted 8 or 10km away as the crow flies, some 20km by road from our home base. The tour made by the aircraft between the two jumps, however, had lasted only 3 or 4 minutes! We, unfortunately, could not let Algiers know of our safe arrival as the whole area was without electricity.

Friday, 1 September

Carolles The search team had just one container and a package.

Saturday, September 2

Jacqueline and I, with the right pass ['ausweiss'], left on foot for the Peugeot factories to buy bicycles. The plant was completely stopped. I still needed some bikes. We bought three and returned to Rochet.

Sunday, September 3

RAS [?] except that there was still no electricity (and I am thirty years old that day). I cycled around. This allowed me to observe some movements of German vehicles, especially the passage (or arrival) of three officers and their driver in a jeep coming down on l'Isle the Doubs. One of the officers was an Air Force General. Indeed, we knew after the carnage suffered by their aviation that they had become superfluous, many Luftwaffe officers had been transferred to the Army. This general, had he come to take command of the group stationed in Isle sur le Doubs? Was it only inspection in its sector?

Monday, 4 September

Finally, the power came back on. Once we had installed a large antenna in the attic, in the framework, we tried to send our first message to the

Central, Algiers. It did not respond to our call. Elisabeth just sent them a message.

I learned that our three ID cards were no longer valid because they were dated more than a year ago and had not been extended. The mayor of Sourans we guessed in Algiers had finally been able to obtain the power boards [?] for the third quarter of 1944. The town hall [Mairie] gave us them. I was able to find detailed maps of the area. Fortunately, the poor map shift schedule [?] shed some light on our position. Realizing that in our isolated location we could also do great work, I considered moving our location. Belfort seemed to me to be a more favourable zone. Jacqueline also had friends in Belfort. She would be safe, provided with some baggage, her bike and money. She went there to prepare our accommodation. I asked her to cycle back to us at this cottage if possible before Thursday, September 7th. Neither in this first part of the mission nor in the second stage did I see her again. It was only several months later, in the liberated area, that I was able to meet her. She told me that she did not hole up with her friends for long as Belfort was captured. It had indeed become quite difficult to move. The front had stabilized and therefore the fighting had become continuous.

That same day, led by the sister of a resistance leader, I went on foot to Fort Montecheroux Lomont, according to my mission order, to organize a mailbox with Switzerland. I met the head of the security service of the FFI group of Fort Lomont. He refused to give me any help. Was it prudence? Was it because of the rivalry among many French resistants against the agents came from outside: England or North Africa?

Tuesday, September 5
8:00
I returned to Rochet at 8:00 to learn that the FFI circulated in the surrounding woods. We sensed there was tension everywhere.
6:00 p.m.
FFI attack Isle sur le Doubs, located 6km to the north, on the left bank of the river. Cécile, the daughter of the labourer, Bertenand, who had two brothers and her fiancé in the resistance, bicycled to the village of Blussans to try to get their news.
6:15 p.m.
Sensing that we were in the action area, I decided to also go to get some information. The road mender and Elisabeth followed me. We took our bikes to Blussans, headed westwards, crossed a small wood which led to fields and crops. We met some people in the village. After the field was the main road (N83) lined with trees on which we saw FFI trucks, buses and VL (light vehicles). Then we met some FFI guarding three German

prisoners. Only I continued to move forward and met the Lieutenant Commander of the section that occupied this area. I offered to give him the few weapons that had been parachuted in our luggage. Indeed, knowing the allied advance, taking Besançon and especially seeing the miserable armaments of these young resistants: revolvers furnished with inlaid pearl handles! and other disparate and obsolete weapons, especially realizing that some did not even possess any weapons.

I thought my material could be more useful to them than to me given the nature of my mission. I wondered how this group of FFI had the temerity to attack the front position of the Isle sur le Doubs, where the Germans had regrouped in order, with weapons, armoured cars, ammunition. They could neither surprise nor attack given the weakness of their means! It was true that all these young people who lived for months in certain inaction at Fort Lomont dreamed to do battle with the enemy before the army that had landed in Provence overtook them. They were all in a hurry as radios announced their rapid approach, the Allies had Lyon and the sixth American Corps and French Second Corps of General de Lattre de Tassigny were progressing towards Besançon and Dijon. I announced to the Lieutenant that in an hour I would give him our armaments.

We all returned to Rochet, and I stated that only the labourer and I would go gown again to Blussans. The girls protested, arguing that all these young people, after a very cold night in the open, had not had lunch and would likely receive no meal tonight. They wanted to bring their supplies. Making these arguments, I accepted their promise that they would return soon. Indeed, I thought that after a little hanging around I could monitor the situation. The girls, therefore, charged to their door to get luggage, cans, bread, etc ... while I unearthed the arms. All four of us then went down to Blussans.

While Charles and I were asking Bertenand about leaving our bikes in a barn, the girls were pursuing the path in the woods, hand pushing their bikes and, therefore, preceded us by a few tens of meters. At that moment, a Citroen arrived driven by a Lieutenant FFI. Seeing me armed, he asked me which group I belonged to. I recognised this officer as I had seen him during my visit to Fort Lomont. In a few words I explained my situation. He left his car, ordered me to keep it and headed off on the forest path. He joined the girls so they would lead him through the wood. They had just stopped, surprised by seeing in front of them a dozen Germans in single file. Immediately they laid down their bikes and fell into the thicket. The Lieutenant fired a loaded gun then withdrew leaving the girls. Returning to his car hurriedly, he said that the two girls were taken and took me up to the labourer and two young men including a policeman who accompanied him in his car. By farm tracks he joined the D31 where we met a small group of FFI carrying a man wounded in the stomach. We helped the injured into the car. The Lieutenant gave me the order to stay with this group and lead us on to Glainans. As for the labourer, he sent him home. This group of twenty men had no officer or NCO. They were totally clueless. A young one rushed over to me and shouted to his comrades 'Here's someone from the PC, we have to follow him.' Demoralised and exhausted, I thought it was useless to disabuse him. Among them were three German prisoners. Some were embarrassed by this hasty retreat and wanted to shoot them. I opposed this and interpolated them in our single file. During this walk we picked up some lost clusters, even twenty men among whom was a group leader.

Arriving at Glainans, we waited for orders. But the village was located on the high road Clerval Pont de Roide. The majority held that little safe area in case the Germans would push them against the attack. We continued on the road beyond the Ferrian Pass to Vellerot. It was nearly midnight. After receiving some supplies, the inhabitants, all men, lay down exhausted in barns while the young people in this village were mobilised to monitor the access roads.

Wednesday, September 6

2:00

An FFI medic came through the village. I met a young man who was slightly injured and three German prisoners. Then a motorcycle courier took us to Glainans by daybreak.

4:00

I woke the whole group. A lively discussion ensued between them, and we all decided to take further rest. But I managed to convince a score to follow me when a violent storm started. They then gave up. I borrowed a bike and went to Glainans where I was aware there was an FFI captain. From there I walked speedily to Rochet, where I found the family of the road mender including their daughter Cécile, but not Elisabeth. Cecilia told me that she had escaped the Germans by rolling and hiding in the brambles. She was also torn and swollen with a thousand abrasions. But she saw the Germans take Elisabeth.

8:30

Accompanied by the road mender, I descended immediately to Blussans. From there we took the same forest path as before.

8:45

Arriving at the end of the wood at the entrance of the meadows we could see about 800 or 1000 meters away some Germans stopped at an armoured car on the main N83 road. There was an abandoned FFI truck nearby. I think Elisabeth had been taken to the Feldkommandantur in Isle sur le Doubs so I went down by bike with the road mender. A few civilians were roaming the streets. We arrived at the town hall. We saw the mayor and a few people safe. They all said they had seen no girl in the hands of the Germans. Leaving the town hall, Bertenand Charles met one of his sons, Robert, 15, who worked in a nearby farm. Given the events, his employer sent him back to his parents.

12:00

We went on to Blussans and, when entering the village, a peasant rushed over to me and wondered if I was not looking for a girl. A young villager had visited meadows – and in the woods at a place called the 'Red Land,' he saw a girl who had just been killed. Frightened, he turned around. All three of us hurried to the specified location.

We found Elisabeth a hundred meters beyond the edge of the wood lying on the track across meadows. She had been killed by a bullet placed below the left eye. It was not damaged. She wore no traces of violence, her eyes; her face reflected a great calm. A little blood still flowed from her mouth. Death must have been instantaneous.

Her papers, ID card, batteries and the French electric torch she was carrying had been removed. Her watch had stopped at 9:15. Under the gaze of the Germans right now, the FFI set fire to trucks. The road worker, his son and I rushed to bring news back to the village. There we loaded her on a cart lent by a farmer and we left for Rochet. We arrived at 13:30. The pain of all these good people was moving. We settled her on a bed in a room of the ground floor of the Bertenand house. In turn I'm sure it had been replaced. The Bertenand lay a tricolor flag on the bed on which they had pinned an FFI. Badge. The priest of Lanthenans and Sourans came in his robes. The latter undertook to prepare the pit and find carriers for the ceremony of the funeral the following day. The brother of the road mender, who was a carpenter, fashioned a coffin.

Thursday, September 7

The mayor of Lanthenans, Mr. Billaud, the priest Reverend Father Meyer, and Bertenand had organized the ceremony.

9:30

In the rain, a peasant cart carried the coffin draped in the tricolor to Lanthenans approximately 1km. We all followed the convoy. But I could not help thinking of the risks we ran for the whole population. This tricolor convoy, after the incidents of the last days, would certainly have attracted the attention of the Germans if, unfortunately, they had driven along that road at that time.

10:00

The church was draped in mourning as was the custom at that time. Four girls returned the casket to the church. The requiem mass was sung by the choir of the parish. The whole village was present. Then it was finished and the coffin put into the grave in the cemetery surrounding the church. The villagers then dispersed. While the priest went to the sacristy to remove his vestments, I followed him to thank him.

I confess that this moment alone with him I could not restrain my emotion, seeing all the tragic moments that I had to live. What was my responsibility in this tragedy? Was it fate? It was not for me, I think, not weakness but I had to relax my nerves a bit.

12:00

What steps were to be taken? What risks were there? I had total confidence in Elisabeth, and I was sure she was not revealed to the Germans who had certainly not failed to try to obtain information, especially since they had been made very nervous by this attack of the FFI and the advance of the Allied armies. If they could have known it was coming in a straight line from North Africa ... it was certainly not 'merely' a summary execution but they could have transferred her to the Gestapo. In agreement with the road mender I decided to stay, especially since it was difficult to improvise another home and luggage. I admired once again their courage and dedication while they were fully aware of the huge risks they were running.

2:00 p.m.

Much business: radio, miscellaneous luggage, money, etc. were in the house and surrounding bushes. I grouped them all to camouflage them in the nearby wood.

6:00 p.m.

These precautions were not in vain because a German Infantry Company arrived to stay in Sourans. But, given the situation up on Rochet, they took up a position with FM, machine guns, reconnaissance cars and armoured cars.

Friday, September 8

9:00 a.m.

This Infantry Company was relieved by gunners who arrived with three vehicles of 77 and a chariot M IV. [?]

6:00 p.m.

In turn, the gunners were found by an Infantry Company of the Air. Traffic on the road from Isle sur le Doubs to Hyemondans was quite active.

Saturday, September 9

The Company continued its installation and landscape shooting positions. I go to Lanthenans to entrust Elisabeth's wallet and ring to the priest.

Sunday, September 10

During these three nights we all slept in the basement of Berthenand in case the Allies would attack this position.

9:00

Great restlessness in the German infantry as they hastily buried mines. They left their quarters, taking their weapons and their bikes. We heard in the distance the sound of tanks. We knew how the arrival of armoured infantry was traumatic for those who felt powerless against steel.

10:00

A French reconnaissance squadron arrived ... and the infantry soon followed. At its head was a captain I had known a lot on the Mareth Line in 1939/1940, Captain Monge (if my memory is not failing) 4th RTT. I recognized him immediately, but he hesitated a moment, surprised to find myself in this place and plainclothes! I explained how quickly the Germans fled. They had not had time to regroup and prepare a defensive position. Why didn't the French continue towards the Isle sur le Doubs? Then he explained that not only had they received the order to occupy Lanthenans, Hyemondans and Sourans and wait for new orders, but mostly they were forced to halt their advance because their ammunition was subject to quotas and gasoline supplies had not arrived. Their progress was much faster than hoped. In short, the 3rd / 4th RTT settled in this area.

The night was quiet.

Monday, September 11:

At daybreak, I joined Captain Monge, who was accompanied by his orderly, a Tunisian sharpshooter. We looked for some signs of enemy presence. Unfortunately, we learned quickly that the Germans were not far behind hedges and copses which were on either side of the road to Isle sur le Doubs. A first warning shot hit us. My upper thigh was torn by an explosive bullet. A strong German attack fired on us.

11.00

The attack against the Germans continued.

I take my business: radio, etc. ... to the wood, so I could dig up a suitcase which had my money in which was hidden 200 meters north of the Bertenand house between the lines.

19.00

At nightfall, assisted by Robert, son of the labourer, I withdrew this case.

Tuesday, September 12

At my request, the 4th RTT could prevent my presence SRO [?]. A car picked me up to take me to Besançon where I met the PC Commander Simoneau on rue Chifflet.

In conclusion, it must be recognized that the circumstances did not allow me to fulfil my mission of information gathering during this first period of my return to France ... but that week was mainly marked by the tragic death of Elizabeth Torlet.

Just days after Elizabeth Torlet's execution, two Signals officers investigated her death. According to the maquisdelorris website, on September 16 1944, they made a very brief and incomplete report based solely on the testimony of Charles and Cécilia Bertenand, the family that housed the Jorxey Mission officers for two weeks. Their report confirmed Captain Jacolin's account and a Google and my translation reads:

<u>Investigation into the death of Miss Elizabeth Torlet of Jorxey Mission</u>

The undersigned Bertenand Charles and his daughter Cecilia residing both in Rochet by Isle sur le Doubs. Lt Beyrard before us and S / Lt Mereau, declare the following:

On the night of Wednesday 30 to Thursday, August 31, at 2:30 am we were awakened by blows struck at the door of our house.

My wife got up, opened the door and found herself in the presence of 3 young people including 2 young girls. They declared to my wife that they were lost and asked her the way to Pierre Fontaine les Varans. Seeing that they were soaked by the rain, my wife invited them to return. It was only during the conversation that we had that I learned that we had to look after three French parachutists. I immediately offered hospitality to these young people and I took all necessary measures so that no indiscretion was committed and therefore to maintain the maximum security. I myself helped these people in fulfilling their mission. They also installed their transmitter in my apartment and Melle Elisabeth started transmitting.

On the following Monday, September 4, according to the statements of Mr. André, Head of Mission, Ms. Jacqueline had to make a mission to Belfort. She left the same day. Since leaving, we had no sign of life of this girl and we do not know if she arrived.

On Monday, September 5, from 1500 hours my daughter Cécile went onto the ridge at the location 'Coteaux' to see if it was possible to get off at L'Isle sur le Doubs and seek supplies.

Arriving at the place, my daughter noticed fighting between FFI and the Germans. There was a control on the road, and while I was accompanied by Elisabeth, I met my daughter who made me aware of events. Together we decided to make contact with the FFI.

Having learned that they lacked food and ammunition, we proposed to re-arm them, especially as everything was hidden at our farm. My daughter and I provided ammunition, weapons and supplies from the Jorxey team; Elisabeth also provided them with food and myself and Mr. André; we headed towards the FFI group. Along the way, Mr. André and I separated, the two girls to join the FFI group by another way. My daughter and Elisabeth, accompanied by an FFI officer, after about 500 meters, suddenly found themselves in the presence of a group of about 50 Germans. The officer gave the order to retreat and to disperse into the woods. After a few metres back, a strong shock to the leg (probably caused by an unexploded German grenade) caused my daughter to lose consciousness.

When she came to, she found herself lying in a bush surrounded by Germans who fortunately had not seen or heard her, but she thought that Elizabeth had probably been taken prisoner.

At night, she came out of her shelter to join us. Concerned about the fate of Melle Elisabeth as we had not had any news, we began looking for her the next morning. At Blussans, we learned that a young girl had been found murdered by Germans at a place called 'Red Earth' in this county. On the scene, we actually found Elizabeth's body and found that her death had been caused by a bullet to her head under her left eye. It had happened about two hours before the time of our discovery at nine; her watch was also stopped at 9hI5. She was stripped of all her papers. We brought her body home and notified the mayor of Lanthenans through the priest. As communications were prohibited, we could not call the doctor who lives in L'Isle-sur-le-Doubs. With Mr. André, we took care of the burial at which a very large number attended. She rests in the cemetery of Lanthenans (Doubs). September 16, 1944, Charles Bertenand, Cécile Bertenand, signed: Lt Peyrard, S/Lt Mereau.

The citation for the award of Croix de Guerre with palm read,

Young girl animated with an ardent faith in the destiny of the country. Volunteer for a fact-finding mission area occupied by the enemy. Was imposed on all the first day by her guts and dedication. Taken by the Germans September 5, 1944, near the Isle sur le Doubs, has shown a wonderful spirit of sacrifice resisting all interrogations of Gestapo. A rather die than betray his comrades mission.

MARGUERITE GIANELLO

Aged 21. Parachuted from a Liberator between Haillainville and Fauconcourt, 10 km north of Rambervillers (Vosges), on 1 September 1944.

The next Corps Auxiliaire Féminin agent was 21-year-old Marguerite Gianello. Little is known of her early life. According to her personnel file, she was born on 19 May 1923 in Viersay, Aisne, and in 1944 was working as a manicurist and living at 40 Rue des Vergus, Suresnes, a western suburb of Paris.

Before coming to Britain, she had worked as 24-year-old Richard Bloc's assistant and liaison officer. As Bloc's personnel file is closed until 2021 or until a copy of a death certificate or obituary is provided, exactly what her work entailed is unknown. Bloc's role was Adjutant of Bloc d'Opérations Aériennes en zone occupée (BOA).

According to Tillet, Bloc had been infiltrated near Saint-Aignan, Loir et Cher, on 5 April 1944 with BCRA Pierre Sonneville, Claude Sendral and saboteur Roland Leroux.

According to the ordredelaliberation website, Sonneville had been appointed military delegate of the Paris region to coordinate the action of the Resistance movements and to convince them to accept instructions from London, especially concerning the decentralisation of the Military Action Committee (COMAC) created by the National Council of the Resistance (CNR). His mission was to make contact with military delegates of the two areas, with the National Military Representative, Jacques Chaban-Delmas and members of COMAC.

He met great difficulties in his task of unifying the military command of the Paris region due to lack of resources and disagreements between the General Delegation and the FFI command on the one hand, and the CNR and COMAC on the other. Despite the arrests, Sonneville, with Bloc as his adjutant, managed to organise the operations of the Paris region in accordance with the directives of General Koenig, commander of the FFI.

Why Bloc arranged for a 21-year-old manicurist to return to England with him is unknown.

According to Tillet, she was exfiltrated from a landing ground named Torticolis 2 km east of Couture-sur-Loir, 27 km west of Vendôme, in a double Lysander pick up on 4 August 1944. Five passengers got out including Louis Gay and Pierre Vigorie. Accompanying her on the flight to Britain were Robert Bloc, Paule-Denise Corre, Anne-Marie Chatenay and John Oliphan, a US Pilot. What role the other two women played is also unknown.[79]

According to her personnel file, she landed at Tempsford on 7 August and, after debriefing, was recruited by SOE to be provided parachute training to be returned to France with Bloc. Once her security vetting had been passed, she went to Ringway and her instructor commented,

> This student was very nervous when she arrived. She was an indifferent performer on ground training and had great difficulty with the apparatus which involved height. After her first descent, she improved considerably and took more interest in the training. She is definitely unsuited for parachuting because of her great fear of dropping. THREE DESCENTS: THIRD CLASS.
>
> Remarks: She was obviously very worried about herself after her first day's training and her relief after the first descent was most noticeable. She seemed to settle down here and except for the period of apprehension, enjoyed her stay.[80]

Given the code name Lancel, she was attached to the PÉRITOINE mission and on the night of 1/2 September 1944 she was flown in a Liberator with Bloc, who had been appointed the Chef Adjutant of BOA in Région C, north-eastern France. They parachuted between Haillainville and Fauconcourt, 10 km north of Rambervillers in the Vosges Mountains.[81]

What became of her remains a mystery.

AIMÉE CORGE
Aged 22. Parachuted from a Liberator near Gerbamont, 60 km north-west of Mulhouse (Vosges) on 11 September 1944.

Little is known about Aimée Corge, the penultimate French woman to be infiltrated into France before the end of the war. She has an SOE personnel file in the National Archives, but as it is closed until 100 years after her death, a copy of her death certificate or obituary is needed to release it into the public domain. The Mairie in Tunis, where she was born on 14 March 1922, will only release her death certificate to a family member.[82]

On 11 September 1944, one of the Carpetbagger's Liberators dropped Aimée, alias Mlle Raymonde Germain, a wireless operator from Corps Auxiliaire Féminin, code named Helene. She landed on DZ Coupole, near Gerbamont, about 60 km north-west of Mulhouse in the Vosges Mountains.

Accompanying her were team PAVOT, Lt-Col. G. L. Prendergast, Cpt Maurice Casset, FFI wireless operator R. Florent, and BCRA saboteur Joseph Wagner.[83]

The landing was just over three weeks after the American and French forces landed on the Mediterranean coast to begin their northward push up the Rhone-Saone corridor. Aimée's job could have been to provide communication with London, arrange further drops of supplies to the Resistance and provide ground intelligence for air strikes.

According to Foot, the team arrived too late to do any useful clandestine work. It parachuted into American-occupied territory in the Vosges Mountains so Aimée would have been able to join in the liberation celebrations.[84]

MICHELE DE DUCLA
Aged 22. Parachuted near Rochefort on the Charente-Maritime Atlantic coast in November 1944. Awarded the US Bronze Cross.

The last recorded French woman infiltrated into France was 22-year-old Michele de Ducla. Born Claude Michele Suzanne Wattebled de Ducla in Pessac, about 40 km east of Bordeaux on 13 February 1922, little is known of her early life. According to her personnel file and her obituary in *The Independent*, she had a boisterous personality which in September 1938 led her mother to send her to be educated under the nuns' strict discipline at the Convent of the Assumption in Kensington Square, London.

She was later reported to have been a teacher with a Cambridge University degree, but a search of the alumni database provided no records for de Ducla. She may have used an English surname. She reported her hobby as Scouting, knowing Landes and the Basque country well, and to have founded two English companies of Wolf Packs before becoming head of the French Girl Guides in London. Princess Elizabeth, the future Queen, belonged to the same Guide unit.[85]

In August 1942, when she was 20, she started work for BCRA in London, but in what capacity is unknown. Towards the end of the war, it was agreed that she should be trained as a wireless operator by the SOE. Her fluency in English and French was thought to be useful for liaising between the American Forces in France and BCRA in London in their attempts to push the Germans out of France.

On 21 April 1944, three weeks before D-Day, she was sent to Winterfold for SOE's standard assessment with the cover-name of Michele Duchet. Her report rated her as B with 8 for intelligence, Average for Morse, Good for Mechanical and Average for instructions.

This student is eminently sensible and used to looking after herself. She is discreet and optimistic, observant and quick. She is pleasant and adaptable and has excellent emotional stability. Although cheerful and dynamic she is of a serious turn of mind and has a high sense of duty. Her good intelligence and general ability convey a feeling of confidence in her. In practical tests, she showed a great degree of curiosity delving into the evidence for procedures and problems. She was self-contained and kept her group on her toes. Although vivacious she was not emotional. But although she was listened to by the men of her group and often her ideas were useful she does not have the aggressiveness nor the forcefulness necessary for distinct leadership. She is well suited to become a W/T operator. Her morse aptitude is a very good average but is not outstanding.[86]

Having passed MI5's security checks, she was sent to Gumley Hall (STS 41) for paramilitary training, where her conducting officer reported that she was,

Very cheery, an excellent mixer and very popular with the male students. A woman of great character and high principles. Her motives and loyalty are excellent. She is intelligent, well-educated and reliable. Altogether she has created a very good first impression.[87]

Towards the end of her course, Second Lieutenant Bellamy reported to Captain Barber, probably a BCRA officer, that she,

Continues to give an excellent impression. By her good sense and happy disposition, she has become extremely popular with the students and the staff. She is very devout and apparently contemplated becoming a nun. She has proved very keen on her work (W/T) and is experiencing little difficulty with it. She is full of pluck, does all the physical training and Assault Course she can, is full of energy and determination. She has obviously set herself an ideal and is out to attain it.[88]

Acting Second Lieutenant Duveen reported to Major Fyffe, her RF Section officer, that he only ever saw her at meal times but that 'She seems a very responsible young woman and is taking her W/T very seriously. Although she mixes well, I feel a life of isolation would not in any way upset her.'[89]

A subsequent note, a week later, stated that 'This student is high-spirited and at times her behaviour is almost childish. This, however, is only a very natural reaction from her work and does not alter the fact that she is very keen and hardworking and that her mentality is mature if less sophisticated than that of OB 53. [An anonymous student].'[90]

After Gumley Hall, she spent a couple of days at the Assumption Convent, Aldenham Park, Bridgenorth, Shropshire. At the outbreak of the war, it was used for fifty-five evacuee convent girls plus their attendant nuns.

She was then taken to Thame Park and on 25 June 1944, her instructor commented that,

> This student has settled down well and has proved to be a very entertaining and sociable person. She has certain boyish traits and always a lot of company around her. She is popular with all the students, and she has a straightforward and truthful character and is always willing to help others. She is very religious (R.C.) and attends Church services whenever possible. She possesses a typical Latin character, enjoys friendly arguments and often gets very excited. Her security is satisfactory, and she understands the need for it.[91]

In the middle of July, while the Allies were fighting in Northern France, she was still studying. Her report stated that,

> This student has an excitable character. She is always very full of life and delights in heated arguments. At first, she went down very well with the students, but they are now becoming rather bored with her continuous teasing which has become rather monotonous. She has, however, a very trustworthy and straightforward character. Her habits are very moderate, she hardly ever goes out and does not drink. Her security is satisfactory, and she understands its importance.[92]

A further report in early August suggested that she had changed little: 'She is still as gay and boyish as ever on the surface, but takes her work very seriously, and fully understands its importance.'[93]

During her training, she met Arthur Breen, an RAF officer destined to be parachuted into France as a wireless officer with one of the Jedburgh teams. She fell in love, and recalled him wearing the same blue silk shirt he wore when he escaped from France.

Having completed her training, on 20 August, the day Paris was liberated, she was sent to Ringway. Her instructor at Dunham House commented that she,

> Did exceptionally well on ground training. She tried very hard all the time and her high spirits did much to relieve the apprehension which they all felt. Although not of ideal physical build for parachuting being thin and bony, her lightness renders her a good object for parachuting. THREE DESCENTS. SECOND CLASS.[94]

From Manchester, after a week's break, on 3 September she was taken for clandestine warfare training to Beaulieu, where she stayed at Saltmarsh (STS 32b). As Breen had been dropped into Tarn by Liberator on 28 August, she was clearly upset, evidenced by her instructor report.

> She is intelligent, well informed, has an aptitude for learning but does not think in an orderly, progressive manner. She appeared to be unable to concentrate her thoughts on any single subject for more than two minutes. She is, however, quick-witted, learns easily and will always argue the point rather than accept anything for which the reason is not apparent. She has quite a strong character, has a will of her own and likes her own way. She is sincere in her religion, which is her guiding principle in everything, but it tends to make her a little narrow-minded. She worked hard and learnt a lot but if used would require strict supervision and strong discipline.[95]

Back in London, she signed the Official Secrets Act and briefed for her mission. On the list of next of kin, she included Mother Margaret Mary at the Assumption Convent.

According to her personnel file in Service Historique de Défense archive in Vincennes, she was registered with the FFI from 1 March 1944 until 30 September 1944 and 'pas parachute'.[96] However, according to her obituary in *The Independent*, she was flown out in November 1944:

> Not even a hail of machine-gun fire from the pocket of German resistance around La Rochelle as the Allies advanced could shake her. Michele de Ducla was a member of General de Gaulle's Free French Forces and had been dropped by parachute in Rochefort on the Charente-Maritime Atlantic coast. It would be her job to liaise between US army units and French resistance networks. She did it from the November after D-Day until the German surrender.
>
> 'She showed the greatest contempt for danger, repeatedly fulfilling her duties under fire during operations against the enemy pockets along the Atlantic coast', a commendation declares. 'A first-class team player, she was noted particularly for her initiative, drive and high spirits.' She had served as Bureau Chief and carried a pass in the name of de Gaulle's provisional government, allowing her authority even when in civilian clothes and licensing her to carry a revolver.
>
> The commendation adds that the establishment of links between the US secret services and the French intelligence service owed much to her good judgement and perfect English.[97]

In recognition of the help she gave the Americans, they awarded her the Bronze Star. When she was eventually reunited with her family who had moved to Biarritz, she learned that her father had been killed in the fighting in 1940.

By chance, when she was walking in the Opera district of Paris after the Victory in Japan celebrations, she spotted Breen. During his work as a wireless operator, he 'had dodged from house to house to avoid detection, and even worked undercover as a cook for the Gestapo, whose conversations he reported to the Allies. He then volunteered to fight the Japanese in Burma. After enduring harrowing conditions, he returned to France weighing less than six stone.'[98]

They married in Biarritz in 1948 at the time of the Berlin airlift, but her decision to renounce her French citizenship scandalised General de Gaulle, the Mayor of Biarritz (Guy Petit, the future French politician), and her family. She and Breen were still reservists in Britain's armed forces, and, should they be called on again, they were both willing to help.

They were to see more action together, in the unrest that accompanied the end of France's colonial empire in Indochina. Breen joined Assurances Generales de France and was made its man in Saigon, acting also as honorary consul for several countries, including Britain.

The couple entertained with bridge parties; she used big American cars and would attend appointments with Japanese political or commercial delegations on her own when Breen, still deeply affected by his war experiences, could not face meeting them. They stayed for 14 years, through the French defeat at Dien Bien Phu in 1954, until they quit in 1962, having three times narrowly escaped being killed.

Once their dogs were poisoned, allowing intruders to creep on to their balcony: they kept Groenedael Belgian shepherds, and at least one is remembered to have died. Grabbing the revolvers, they each kept under their pillows, the couple fired through the windows.

Another time only the need to nurse their son, who was unwell, kept them from a party at a plantation outside the city at which the Viet Cong blew up and killed all 40 guests except for one nanny and her two small charges, who had hidden in a cellar. After a grenade was thrown at their car, they decided to return to Europe for the children's sake.

They lived in Milan, Paris, and finally Dallington, East Sussex. Breen died in 1986. Their eldest son, Michael, died of an aneurysm in 2004. De Ducla revealed her 'silent killing' skills to her grandchildren after a burglary that took place when she was in her late 70s. She told them her special forces tutors had advised getting behind the victim, encircling his neck, and stabbing under the ribs. This she had never actually been obliged to do, even in war; but she told police she was quite unconcerned about the burglar, as had she noticed him she could have swiftly finished him off.[99]

Michele died on 14 February 2015, the day after her 93rd birthday, leaving one daughter and two sons.

Conclusion

There was comic relief for the men responsible for infiltrating the women. One of the Carpetbagger crew members returned from a mission and reported to his Commandant, Colonel Robert Fish, about a French woman agent they were carrying.

> She was slow getting to the Joe-hole because of the heavy gear she was wearing and was not allowed to jump as the reception light went out before she was ready. She sulked on the way back until nature put her under pressure. She was directed to the 'relief tube' in the airplane's rear section. The dispatcher gallantly turned his back while the girl struggled with her zipped-up man's flying suit, in an effort to use the tube that was, unfortunately, designed for the male's anatomy. Finally, the girl burst into laughter, and when the dispatcher turned around, she demonstrated to him in rapid-fire French and gestures that her personal 'operation' had not been completely successful. She was considerably dampened below the waist (but not in spirits).[1]

Laurie Dick, another Carpetbagger, commented in his memoirs in *Flight Journal*, that,

> On one mission, the crew was startled when long blonde hair fell from beneath the agent's helmet. This beautiful French girl, whose parents had been killed by the Gestapo, was making a revenge jump over the Bavarian Alps to determine whether Hitler had a last-ditch stronghold to fight off advancing Allies.

We breathed a sigh of relief after she bailed out at 5,000 feet and we saw this brave young lady's chute open. We never knew what became of her.[2]

Who this woman was remains a mystery. Another anonymous agent, who appeared to have been dropped several times, was described by Frank Griffiths as being 'nearer 65 than 60. She always took half a bottle of good cognac in order to give her courage for the jump, on one occasion her bicycle being parachuted with her.'[3]

One female agent interviewed by Pattinson detailed some of her experiences in Normandy and asked to remain anonymous. Not long after D-Day when the American army was advancing towards Paris, she and her organiser drove back and forth across the lines. Her mission was to provide the Americans with intelligence about the changing position of the German military. She admitted that she survived by trying to be nice with the enemy.

> You just react to the moment and think. I'll get by alright with a nice smile. I just sort of smiled and waved to them. All the time. Women could get by with a smile and do things that men couldn't and no matter what you had hidden in your handbag or your bicycle bag, if you had a nice smile, you know, just give them a little wink. It just happened constantly, all the time. So I got away with it. It becomes sort of second nature ... You did that [flirted] automatically. Absolutely. That was just par for the course. Just sort of went into the role automatically, just quite naturally.[4]

At one point the car she was travelling in was ambushed and fired on, but the driver sped off, and she was uninjured. On another occasion when she was stopped, she was worried the papers hidden in her girdle would be found:

> I heard this marching behind me, and I turned around, and there were these two guys, so I just smiled at them and went on my way, and they followed me in, and they raped me. One held me down. My first instinct was to put up a fight, and then I thought no, I can't. I've got these papers. If I put up a fight, they're going to overpower me and then they'll probably strip me, and we'd be in a worse mess than we are already in. I've just got to let them do it and get on with it. ... Anyway, it was quite an experience! But they didn't get my papers! [laughs].[5]

Pattinson made perceptive comments about the recent interest in female agents. She argued that they transgressed the conventional codes of behaviour and notions of women's 'appropriate' role in the war. They did not stay at home and look after the children, waiting patiently for their husband's return. They went out and did something about it themselves.

> This interest in war women is heightened when it becomes common knowledge that young women, trained in unarmed combat and silent killing techniques, were infiltrated behind enemy lines to wage war against the might of the Nazi war machine… In a total war, anything goes and it is this which is of infinite interest to the public… They were highly motivated, often driven by the desire for revenge and hatred of the Germans, were alert to the dangers they faced, were determined to proceed with their missions, despite the obstacles that were put in their way and accomplished their work with varying degrees of success.[6]

In Simon Mawer's article in the *Paris Review* on the Women of SOE, he commented that,

> They showed that not only could women work like men, they could fight like men, too. A diverse group, they had in common a love of France and the courage to work alone, twenty-four hours a day, seven days a week under the constant threat of the most terrifying secret police of all. The only faith they held in common was a belief in freedom from tyranny. It's a pretty inspiring record.[7]

Any French woman who got involved with the Resistance, either infiltrated or recruited in the field, did so for a variety of reasons. As well as patriotism and hatred of the Germans, perhaps some of her friends were involved. Maybe there was a boyfriend or someone she wanted to impress. Some wanted to escape a failed relationship or a divorce. There was also revenge for having had friends or family arrested, imprisoned, deported or executed. Some did so because they saw what the Germans were doing to the Jews.

Working with the Resistance was a much more exciting existence than working in a shop, office, factory and a lot more active.

Using revolvers, silent pistols, Bren guns, Sten guns and hand grenades for the first time must have given the women unexpected power, something unconscionable before the war. Using home-made explosives and those dropped by the Allies to blow up bridges, tunnels, buildings, trucks, trains, and planes must have been exhilarating, especially knowing how badly it affected the enemy.

Those women sent in from the UK had been specially trained in silent killing so they would undoubtedly have had moral dilemmas to face. There are very few records of the French women ever having to utilise these skills.

Their work built up a camaraderie that lasted their lifetime, and a significant number had relationships, some permanent, with fellow Resistance members. One British woman agent became pregnant in the field but there's no evidence any French women did.

There was also the kudos, to be known as someone who was helping to liberate their country as well as the opportunity to travel to parts of France they would probably never otherwise have visited.

Women sent in by SOE had between £300 and £350 a year paid into their British bank accounts. They were sent with large amounts of forged French francs which paid not only their travelling and accommodation expenses but also meals in black market restaurants. The SOE and SIS provided not just money, but clothes, food, tobacco, chocolate and whisky as well as weapons and ammunition. Some agents were given gold to bribe prison guards to facilitate escapes.

While their religion was identified in their personnel file, rarely mentioned was their religious conviction. But certainly for some, their faith kept them going in the direst of circumstances.

According to Vera Atkins, the women's motivation was their loathing of Nazi ideology, a love of freedom and a desire to make an individual contribution to the liberation of France. They were messengers of hope to the Resistance. In a post-war interview she said:

> I've always found personally that being a woman has great advantages if you know how to play the thing right, and I believe that all the girls, the women who went out, had the same feeling. They were not as suspect as men, they had very subtle minds when it came to talking their way out of situations, they had many more cover stories to deliver than most men and the performed extremely well. Also, they're very conscientious – I'm not saying men are not. They were wonderful radio operators and very cool and courageous.[8]

She described most of the women sent to France by F Section as being mostly in their early twenties, telephonists, shop assistants and clerks. Most had lived in simple, modest accommodation. Some spoke imperfect French and, after only a few weeks of training, 'were sent to pit themselves against German counter-espionage services manned by men of the utmost shrewdness, highly-trained, with many years of experience in that field.' The men in London who controlled them, she described as 'amateurs'.[9]

Elizabeth Nicholas's research led her to be quite critical of the SOE. There are historians on both sides of the Channel, who have suggested that the British Government sacrificed the lives of many of its British and French agents and subagents as part of a grand deception scheme. Its details are outlined in Kramer's work *Flames in the Field*. There are many in Holland and Belgium with the same opinion. They argue that, as part of Churchill's agreement with Stalin, a plan was created to distract Hitler from the Eastern Front by pretending an Allied invasion in Pas de Calais was planned for the summer or autumn of 1943. The increased supply of agents, arms, and ammunition to the Resistance and intensified sabotage activity in the North of France was part of the scheme. Thousands of German troops were sent to counteract the suspected invasion and the Gestapo, Sicherheitsdienst and Abwehr responded by stepping up their counter-Resistance activity and arresting many hundreds of agents and Resistance members.

Of the thirty-six French women mentioned above, one was infiltrated by train, one by motor gunboat, two by felucca, two by a Whitley bomber, three by a Hudson, four by Lysander, ten by a Liberator and twelve by a Halifax. All but ten survived. Of the twelve who were arrested, one escaped from prison; one survived concentration camp, but the others were executed.

Trained in the art of ungentlemanly and clandestine warfare, the women were sent into France where they worked with the Resistance; collected and sent vital intelligence to the Allies; carried plastic explosives and sabotage equipment, wireless sets and parts, weapons, ammunition and messages; liaised between organisers and resistance leaders; helped identify bombing targets for RAF and USAAF planes; found remote fields for landing planes or collecting parachuted supplies; organised and took part in reception committees; found safe houses for other agents and participated in the sabotage of rail, road and telecommunication networks.

In his 2016 talk to the Society of the Study of French History, historian Robert Gildea stressed the important recognition of women's resistance and the wave of texts which have demonstrated how often women served as 'hinges in the resistance.'[10]

In recognition of their contribution to the liberation of France, the British, French and American governments honoured these thirty-six women with forty-nine awards including eleven Croix de Guerre, four with palms, nine Medaille de la Resistance, five Companion de Legion d'Honneur, four King's Commendation for Brave Conduct, four Member of the British Empire Medals, three Chevallier de Legion d'Honneur, two Order of the British Empire Medals, two Certificates of Commendation, two Sussex Medals, one Commander of Legion d'Honneur, King's Medal of Commendation, one Medaille de République Française, one Military Cross, one Mentioned in Despatches, one US Distinguished Service Cross, one US Bronze Star and one George Cross.

On 6 May 1991, a memorial ceremony was held at Valençay on the fiftieth anniversary of the landing of the first French agent in France. It was unveiled by André Méric, the Secretary of State for Veteran Affairs, in the presence of Elizabeth, the Queen Mother. It was designed by Elizabeth Lucas and entitled 'Spirit of Partnership'.

> Two columns – one black for night, one white for the shining spirit of resistance – enclosing the Moon at the top which represents the conditions under which the SOE and the Resistance operated and agents/ logistics dropped, landed or picked up. At the base of the monument, floodlights are laid out in the L-shaped pattern used to signal the landing path for Lysander and Hudson pilots who landed their aircraft by moonlight on the fields of France.[11]

Pearl Cornioley, one of the women agents sent into France and who survived the war, helped raise funds to erect the memorial. It commemorates thirteen very brave women who were involved one way or another with RAF Tempsford who lost their lives while working to liberate France. One hundred and nineteen men from the SOE are also listed. The French women commemorated are FANY officers Denise Bloch, Andrée Borrel and Madeline Damerment.

As the vast majority of the other women agents had no memorial at all, in January 2013, Tazi Hussain, a resident of Tempsford, persuaded the Parish Council to adopt a proposal to erect a white marble monument. On it were engraved all the names of the known women agents sent into occupied Europe from Tempsford, Tangmere and Harrington airfields as well as those sent by boat from British ports. The French women mentioned in this account are honoured on it. The Tempsford Memorial Trust was established and, after pressure from some male historians, the acknowledgement was added to the men of 138 and 161 Squadrons who flew most of them out.

On 6 June 2011, Baroness Crawley started a debate in the House of Lords in an attempt to persuade the British government to commemorate the SOE women sent into France.

> The women concerned were recruited to serve in occupied France. They acted variously as couriers, wireless operators, and saboteurs. They found places for planes to land, bringing more agents and supplies.

They established safe houses and worked with resistance movements to disrupt the occupation and clear the path for the Allied advance.

Those women did these things, given wartime pressures, after a very brief period of training. Apparentntly, they had each been told when recruited that there was only a 50 per cent chance of personal survival – yet, to their eternal credit, off they went. Some had been born in France, some in Britain, a couple in Ireland and some still further afield. Some were Jewish, some convent-educated, one Muslim. Some were already mothers, some just out of their teens; some shop assistants, some journalists, some wives; some were rather poor. In France, they often had to travel hundreds of miles by bike and train, protected only by forged papers, and as they went about their frequently exhausting work they were in constant danger of arrest by the Gestapo. Some were even exposed to betrayal by double agents and turncoats.

The story of what happened to some of those women is often unreadable and, in 21st-century Britain, is perhaps too easily under-remembered. A number were captured in France, horribly brutalised and sent to camps in Germany. There, the torment was often sustained over weeks and months on starvation diets; the women crammed in unsanitary and overcrowded huts with disease rampant. Four of them were killed in Natzweiler by being injected-scarcely credible as it is – with disinfectant. A number, once worked and beaten to a standstill, were shot and hanged at Dachau and Ravensbrück.[12]

Many speeches followed honouring the women involved, not just those sent into France. It was public donations, however, that have helped commemorate them.

There are numerous plaques in France commemorating the French and others who lost their lives in the fight for liberation. In 2012, coinciding with the French government awarding the Legion d'Honneur to surviving Resistance members, Jean-Georges Jaillot-Combelas, the nephew of Suzanne Combelas, organised plaques to commemorate Suzanne at Colombes and for Elisabeth Torlet in Lanthenans.

Shrabani Basu, who wrote a biography of Noor Inayat Khan, one of the women agents executed at Dachau, set up a memorial trust. On 5 November 2012, a bust of Noor was unveiled in Gordon Square, London, by Her Royal Highness Princess Anne.

On 3 December 2013, the Tempsford Memorial was unveiled by His Royal Highness, Prince Charles. The Tempsford Memorial website includes more details of this important international monument.

On 8 February 2015, Her Royal Highness Princess Anne unveiled a plaque at 101 Nightingale Lane, now a Jewish Women's care home, to commemorate Denise Bloch, Andrée Borrel, Madeleine Damerment and other women interrogated there on arrival in Britain during the Second World War.

In November 2016, thanks to the work of Martyn Cox, the founder of the educational charity Secret WW2 Network, four blue plaques were unveiled in Brighton, one commemorating Jacqueline Nearne, an F Section agent.

The contribution made by some of these brave French women to the liberation of their country has been acknowledged in books and websites listed in the bibliography. In addition. my publications, *The Women of RAF Tempsford, Churchill's Agents, Return to Belgium, Return to Holland, Agent Rose: The True Spy Story of Eileen Nearne, Britain's Forgotten Wartime Heroine,* and *Designer: The true spy story of Jacqueline Nearne, a courier sent on a top secret mission to France during World War Two,* tell the stories of other women agents.

This book on the French women agents completes the series and helps keep their memories alive for their families, friends, and those interested in the human side of war. There must have been others, but until documentary evidence is brought to light, their stories remain untold.

Notes

Chapter 1

1 Mackenzie, William, *The Secret History of SOE: The Special Operations Executive 1940–1945*, St Ermin's Press, 2000, p.5.
2 Ibid, p.5.
3 Keene, Tom and Atkin, Michael, *Cloak of Enemies: The Birth of Churchill's SOE and the 'Cockleshell Heroes*, The History Press, 2012; Atkin, Matthew, *Fighting Nazi Occupation: British Resistance 1939–1945*, Pen & Sword, 2015; pp.39–40.

Chapter 2

1 Hutchinson, James, *That Drug Danger,* Standard Press, Montrose, 1977, p.82; Seaman, op.cit. p.48.
2 Seaman, p.53.
3 Hutchinson, op.cit. p.82.
4 Ibid.
5 Ibid.

Chapter 3

1 Quoted in Seaman, Mark, *Bravest of the Brave: The True Story of Wing Commander Yeo-Thomas – SOE Secret Agent, code name 'The White Rabbit'*, Michael O'Mare Books Ltd, (1997), p.32.
2 Sweet-Escott, op.cit; Lynan, Robert, (2014), *The Jail Busters: The Secret Story of MI6, the French Resistance and Operation Jericho*, Quercus Editions.
3 Jauneau, Elodie, Des femmes dans la France combattante pendant la Deuxième Guerre Mondiale: Le Corps des Volontaires Françaises et le Groupe Rochambeau, (2008); https://genre histoire.revues.org/373.
4 www.charles-de-gaulle.com/the-warrior/free-france/the-free-french-in-great-britain.html.
5 Seaman, op.cit. p.44.

6　De Groot, Gerard J. & Peniston-Bird, C. M. (2000), *A Soldier and a Woman: Sexual Integration in the Military,* Pearson Education, p.141.

7　Extract from the *Journal of Free France,* No. 2b in August 1946; www.france-libre.net/volontaires-francaises/.

8　Bohec, (1999), *La Plastiqueuse à Bicyclette,* Le Félin.

Chapter 4

1　O'Connor, B., *Churchill's School for Saboteurs,* Amberley Publishing, 2013.

2　Persico, J. E. (1979), *Piercing the Reich: The Penetration of Nazi Germany by American Secret Agents during World War II,* The Viking Press, New York.

3　Hutchinson, op.cit. p. 83.

4　Foot, M. R. D. (2004), SOE in France, Frank Cass, London.

5　S. Jepson (1986) [9331] Imperial War Museum SA.

6　Piquet-Wicks, E., *Four in the Shadows,* Jarrold, (1957), p.21.

7　Escott, B. (1991), op.cit.

8　Vigurs, K. (September 2011), 'The women agents of the Special Operations Executive F section – wartime realities and post-war representations', Ph.D. thesis, University of Leeds.

9　Rigden, Denis. (2004), *SOE Syllabus: Lessons in Ungentlemanly Warfare,* Richmond, pp.146–7, 150.

10　Rigden, op.cit. pp. 43–45.

11　TNA HS 8/247, 27 November 1941.

12　O'Connor, Bernard, *Agent Fifi and the Honey-trap Spies,* Amberley Publishing, 2015.

13　Clare Mulley, 'Unsealed documents unravel the secretive careers of Britain's forgotten female spies', the *Telegraph,* 18 September 2014.

14　Binney, op.cit.

15　Escott, B. (1991), op.cit.

16　Ibid.

17　Hutchinson, op.cit., p. 87.

18　Pawley, op.cit.

19　Marks, L. (1998), op.cit.

20　Pawley, S. op.cit.

21　Ryder, S. op.cit.

22　Griffiths, F. op.cit.

23　Howarth, P. (1980), *UNDERCOVER, The Men and Women of the Special Operations Executive,* p.33.

24　Quoted in Miller, *Behind the Lines.*

25　Stafford, D. (2000), *Secret Agent: The True Story of the Special Operations Executive,* BBC Worldwide, London.

26　Hutchinson, p.88.

27　Wake-Walker, Edward, (2011), *A House for Spies: SIS Operations into Occupied France from a Sussex Farmhouse,* Robert Hale.

28　Foot, op.cit.

29　Olsen, O. R. (1952), *Two Eggs on My Plate,* Allen & Unwin, London, p.94.

30　Ibid.

31　www.bbc.co.uk/ww2peopleswar/stories/66/a4055366.shtml.

32 *Hunts. Post*, 'Hunts was a Nerve Centre of Allied Espionage...', G. Thomas, (23 December 1954.
33 TNA HS 9/1174/8.

Chapter 5

1 Clark, Freddie, (1999), *Agents by Moonlight*, Tempus, pp.1–26.
2 Clark, Freddie, (1999), *Agents by Moonlight*, Tempus, pp.1–26; O'Connor, B., *RAF Tempsford: Churchill's Most Secret Airfield*, Amberley Publishing, (2010).
3 www.plan-sussex-1944.net; Tillet, P., Tentative of History of in/Exfiltrations into/from France during WWII from 1940 to 1945 (Parachutes, Plane & Sea Landings).
4 O'Connor, Bernard, *Sabotage in France*, www.lulu.com/spotlight/coprolite.
5 Tillet, op.cit.
6 O'Connor, B. *Bletchley Park and the Pigeon Spies*.

Chapter 6.

1 Fraser-Smith (1991), The Secret War of Charles Fraser-Smith, Paternoster Press.
2 Rigden, D. (2004), *SOE Syllabus*, Secret History Files.

Chapter 7.

1 TNA KV3/237.
2 http://forum.axishistory.com/viewtopic.php?t=42375;www.holocaustresearchproject.org/nazioccupation/barbie.html; 'Nazi war criminal Klaus Barbie gets life". *BBC. 3 July 1987*; http://chris-intel-corner.blogspot.co.uk/2012/10/german-counterintelligence-operations.html.
3 Quoted in Binney, Marcus, (2002), *The Women who Lived for Danger*, Hodder & Stoughton, London.

Chapter 8.

1 Jepson, op.cit.
2 Ryder, op.cit.
3 Ibid.
4 Pattinson, J. (2006), 'Playing the daft lassie with them': Gender, Captivity and the Special Operations Executive during the Second World War, *European Review of History*, Vol. 13, No. 2, pp.271-292; Pattinson, J. (2007), *Behind enemy lines—Gender, passing and the Special Operations Executive in the Second World War*, Manchester University Press.
5 Ryder, op.cit.
6 Foot (2004), op.cit.
7 TNA HS9/1458.
8 Escott, B. (1991), *Mission Improbable: A Salute to the RAF Women of SOE in Wartime France*, Sparkford: Patrick Stephens Ltd.
9 Verity, H. (1978), *We Landed by Moonlight*, Ian Allan Ltd, Shepperton.
10 The *Sunday Express*, London, 11 March 1945.

Chapter 9.

1 Crowdy, T. (2008), *SOE Agent: Churchill's Secret Warriors*, Osprey Publishing.
2 Ryder, op.cit.
3 Escott, B. (1991), op.cit.

Chapter 10.

1 TNA HS 9/575/2.
2 Escott, Beryl, *The Heroines of SOE F Section: Britain's Secret Women in France*, The History Press, 2010, p.32.
3 Obituary of Georges Bégué, *Daily Telegraph*, 29 January 1994. p.15.
4 TNA HS9/637/4.
5 TNA HS9/586 Soviet agents in France; Bourgeois, Guillaume, (2015, *Le véritable histoire de l'Orchestre rouge*, Nouveau Monde; O'Sullivan, Donal, 'Dealing with the Devil: Anglo-Soviet Intelligence Cooperation During the Second World War', Studies in Modern European History. The rest of the Pickaxes' story can be found in my book, *Churchill and Stalin's Secret Agents.*).
6 Verity, H. (1978), op.cit.
7 O'Sullivan, D. (2010), *Dealing with the Devil: Anglo-Soviet Intelligence During the Second World War*, Peter Lang Publishing, New York, p.44.
8 TNA HS 4/327.
9 TNA HS 4/342.
10 Ibid.
11 Ibid; KV 2/2827.
12 Ibid.
13 TNA HS 4/342.
14 Ibid.
15 IWM French Resistance, German poster in Album 854.
16 Escott, Beryl, *The Heroines of SOE F Section: Britain's Secret Women in France*, The History Press, 2010, p.39.
17 TNA HS9/1289/7; King, Stella, *'Jacqueline': Pioneer Heroine of the Resistance*, Arms and Armour, 1989.
18 King, S. (1989), Jacqueline: Pioneer Heroine of the Resistance, Arms and Armour.
19 TNA HS9/1289/7.
20 Overton-Fuller, Jean, *The German Penetration of SOE, William Kimber, 1975;* King, op.cit.; Suttill, op.cit. pp.32, 38, 49.
21 Buckmaster, (1946–7), op.cit.
22 Escott, (2010), p.40–41.
23 Ibid, p.41; TNA HS9/1289/7.
24 Suttill, op.cit, p.242.
25 http://en.wikipedia.org/wiki/Yvonne _Rudelatt.
26 Hany-Lefebvre, N. *Six Mois á Fresnes,* Edition Flammarion, 1946.
27 Suttill, op.cit, p.147.
28 Escott, B. (1991), op.cit.
29 Pattinson, op.cit.

30 Foot, M. R. D. (2004), op.cit.
31 Escott (2010), p.43.
32 Buckmaster, (1946–7), op.cit.
33 King, op.cit. p.395.
34 Email communication with Paul McCue, 16 April 2016.
35 Helm, Sarah, (2006), *A Life in Secrets: The Story of Vera Atkins and the Lost Agents of SOE*, Abacus.
36 Judge, Alan, The Intelligence Corps and Special Operations, Chicksands Military Intelligence Museum.
37 TNA HS9/183, 27 April 1942.
38 ['The dirty war on our doorstep', *Sunday Times*, 15 March 2009; TNA HS9/455/5; FO 660/178.
39 TNA HS9/183, 9 May 1942 ['To be put through the cards' was MI6's euphemism for having a full security check to ensure she was not an enemy agent].
40 TNA HS9/183, 21 June 1942.
41 TNA AIR20/8459-60, quoted in Suttill, Francis, *Shadows in the Fog*, The History Press, (2015), p.37.
42 Ibid.
43 Tillet, op.cit.
44 Buckmaster, 1946–7, op.cit.
45 Suttill, Francis, *Shadows in the Fog,* The History Press, (2015), pp.51, 53.
46 TNA HS7/245, November 1942.
47 TNA HS9/183, 24, March 1943.
48 Basu, S. (2006), *Spy Princess, The Life of Noor Inayat Khan*, Sutton Publishing, London.
49 Escott, 2010, p.65.
50 Trenear-Harvey, Glenmore, *Historical Dictionary of Intelligence Failures,* Rowman and Littlefield, New York, 2015.
51 TNA HS6/440, 4 May 1945; In Suttill, op.cit. p.151.
52 Document given to Suttill by Nicholas Laurent, op.cit. p.151.
53 TNA HS9/631/5, 14-20 May 1944; Suttill, op.cit. p.152.
54 Ibid.
55 Suttill, op.cit. p.215.
56 TNA HS9/631/5, 14–20 May 1944; Suttill, op.cit. p.18.
57 Marks, Leo, *Between Silk and Cyanide,* The Free Press, New York, 1998.
58 Archives Nationales, Z 6 NL 17339; Suttill, p.186.
59 Ibid, 15 May 1945.
60 Ibid, 19 January 1945.
61 Kramer, op.cit.
62 Buckmaster, (1946–7), op.cit.
63 Foot, (2004), op.cit.
64 Kramer, op.cit.
65 TNA HS9/183, 15 November 1945.
66 TNA HS9/183, 14 June 1945.
67 TNA HS9/183.
68 Ibid, 24, May 1946.

69 TNA HS9/183; Bourne-Paterson, R., *SOE In France 1941–1945: An Official Account of the Special Operations Executive's French Circuits,* Frontline Books, 2016.

70 Starns, P., *Odette: World War Two's Darling Spy*, The History Press, 2009, pp.13–29; Escott, (2010), p.64.

71 Jepson, S IWMSA. (1986) 9331.

72 Hallowes (Churchill), O. IWMSA 9478/3; 31578/3.

73 HS9/648/4, 28 February 1942.

74 Hallowes (Churchill), IWM O. 9478/3; 31578/3.

75 Tickell, Jerrard, (1949), *Odette: Secret Agent, Prisoner, Survivor*, Chapman and Hall and reprinted 1955, Pan Books. Reprinted 2008 by Headline Review.

76 Hallowes (Churchill), IWM O. 9478/3; 31578/3.

77 Starns, op.cit. p.49.

78 Tillet, op.cit.

79 Jenkins, op.cit. pp.70–71.

80 Jenkins, Ray, (2010), *A Pacifist at War: The Silence of Francis Cammaerts*, Arrow Books, pp.67–8.

81 Churchill, op.cit.

82 Tillet, op.cit.

83 TNA HS9/314-5, 19 February 1942.

84 Jenkins, op.cit. p.67.

85 Starns, op.cit. p.61.

86 Churchill, P. (1954), *Spirit in the Cage*, Hodder & Stoughton.

87 Churchill, op.cit.

88 Tickell, op.cit.

89 Ibid.

90 Ibid.

91 Pattinson, op.cit.

92 Nicholson, M. (1995), *What Did You Do in The War, Mummy?* Chatto & Windus, London.

93 Starns, op.cit. p.10.

94 Szabó, T. (2007), *Young, Brave and Beautiful: The Missions of Special Operations Executive Agent, Lieutenant Violette Szabó, George Cross, Croix de Guerre avec Etoile de Bronze*, Channel Island Publishing.

95 Hallowes (Churchill), O. 9478/3; 31578/3.

96 HS9/648/4, 12 May 1945.

97 TNA HS9/648, 17 May 1945.

98 Ibid, 20 November 1945.

99 Ibid, 20 March 1946.

100 TNA HS9/648/4, 14 September 1945.

101 TNA HS9/648/4, 1 January 1946.

102 Hallowes interview, IWM, 1985.

103 Kremer, L. (1999), *Women's Holocaust Writing: Memory and Imagination*, Nebraska Press.

104 Szabó, T. op.cit.

105 Binney, (2002), op.cit.

106 King's College Library, London: GB99 KCLMA Baynham.

107 Ibid.
108 Ibid.
109 Ibid.
110 Ibid.
111 TNA HS9/304/1, 20 June 1942.
112 Tillet, op.cit. TNA HS9/304/2.
113 Escott, (2010), p.70.
114 Ibid, p.71.
115 TNA HS9/304/1, 12 July 1943.
116 Tillet, op.cit; Escott, op.cit. p.72.
117 Ibid., 21 August 1943.
118 Ibid., 24 August 1943.
119 Ibid., 25 August 1943
120 Ibid., 27 August 1943.
121 Ibid., 2 September 1943.
122 Ibid., 6 September 1943.
123 Ibid., 11 September 1943.
124 Ibid., 18 September 1943.
125 Ibid., 28 September 1943.
126 Ibid., 15 October 1943.
127 Ibid., 29 September 1943.
128 TNA HS9/304/1.
129 Ibid., 15 December 1943.

Chapter 11
1 TNA HS9/10/2.
2 TNA HS9/11/1.
3 TNA HS9/10/2, 3 December 1942.
4 Ibid., 18 December 1942.
5 Ibid.
6 Ibid., 23 December 1942.
7 Tillet, op.cit.
8 TNA HS9/10/2, 18 August 1943.
9 Ibid., 12 September 1943.
10 Ibid., 6 December 1944.
11 Ibid., 12 December 1944.
12 Pawley, Margaret (1999), *In Obedience to Instructions:FANY with the SOE in the Med*, Leo Cooper.
13 TNA HS9/10/2, 27 March 1945.
14 TNA HS9/10/2, 10 January 1946.
15 Riols, Noreen, *The Secret Ministry of Ag. and Fish*, Macmillan, 2013, pp.118–9.
16 Escott, op.cit. p.87.
17 Tillet, op.cit.
18 TNA HS9/421-5; Tillet, op.cit.
19 Marshall, Robert, *All the King's Men*, Collins, 1988.
20 Tillet, op.cit.
21 Verity, Hugh, *We Landed by Moonlight*, Crecy, 1998, p.92; Tillet, op.cit.

22 Verity, H. p.297; Escott, B. op.cit; Nicholas, E. (1958), *Death be not Proud*, Cresset Press, London.
23 Escott, op.cit. p.89.
24 TNA KV2/1131-2.
25 Helm, Sarah, *A Life in Secrets: Vera Atkins and the Lost Agents of SOE*, Abacus, 2006).
26 Tillet, op.cit.
27 Foot, op.cit. p.272.
28 Ibid., 14 April 1944.
29 Tillet, op.cit.
30 Tillet, op.cit.
31 Ibid.
32 Marshall, op.cit; Overton-Fuller, Jean, *Déricourt: The Chequered Spy*, Michael Russell, 1989; Rymills, Frank, *Déricourt: Double, Triple or Quadruple Spy*, Lulu, 2013; Helm, op.cit; http://spartacus-educational.com/SOEdericourt.htm; http://chris-intel-corner.blogspot.co.uk/2012/10/german-counterintelligence-operations.html.
33 Ibid., 14 April 1944.
34 Foot, op.cit. p.273.
35 Ibid., 18 March, 14 April 1944.
36 TNA HS9/140/7.
37 Ibid., 20 April 1944.
38 Ibid., 2 September, 19 December 1944.
39 Ibid., 8 June 1945.
40 Ibid., 21 May 1945.
41 TNA HS9/140/7.

Chapter 12
1 Seaman, op.cit. p.65.
2 Tillet, op.cit.
3 TNA HS9/1176/1, 26 October 1943.
4 TNA HS9/1176/1.
5 TNA HS9/1176/1, 17 November 1943.
6 Ibid., 22 November 1943.
7 Tillet, op.cit.
8 TNA HS9/1176/1, 29 January 1944.
9 Augeard, Michel, Melpomene se parfume á Heliotrope, J. C. Lattes (2012).
10 Tillet, op.cit, Clark, op.cit.
11 The *Miami Herald*, Florida, 5 Aug 1999; www.bassettbranches. org/tng/getperson.php?personID=I27688&tree=1A.
12 www.francaislibres.net/liste/ fiche.php?index=90448, Liz Evans, 1 November 2014.
13 Foot, op.cit, p.418; TNA HS91176/1.
14 The *Miami Herald*, Florida, 5 Aug 1999.
15 Ibid.
16 www.francaislibres.net/liste/fiche.php?index=90448, Patrick Bassett, 3 March 2014.
17 Tillet, op.cit.

18 SHD Vincennes, GR 28 P 4 153-4, my translation.

19 Tillet, op.cit.

20 OSS report related to SUSSEX Pathfinders, Plan-Sussex Collection, Pathfinder, Vol.3, p.183–7.

21 *Daily Telegraph*, 26 April 2016.

22 TNA Operation SUSSEX, Montgomery 173.

23 General Orders: Headquarters, European Theater of Operations, U.S. Army, General Orders No. 85 (May 8, 1945).

24 Foot, SOE in France, p.418.

25 TNA HS9/306/2.

26 Neave, A. op.cit.

27 TNA HS9/392/4, 8 September 1943.

28 Ibid., 14 September 1943.

29 Ibid., 20 September 1943.

30 Ibid., 24 September 1943.

31 Ibid., 25 September 1943.

32 Ibid., 10 December 1943.

33 Ibid., 20 December 1943.

34 Ibid., 11 January 1944.

35 Ibid., 8 January 1944.

36 Clark, op.cit. p.216.

37 Moulin, Lucien, (2010), *Le Resistance de Loire: Marguerite Soulas une Femme d'Exception*, De Bore.

38 TNA HS9/392/4.

39 TNA WO 373/184/101, 15 November 1945.

40 Ibid.

41 Tillet, op.cit; www.storyhouse.org/margie2.html.

42 Adamson, Iain (1966). *The Great Detective; A Life of Deputy Commander Reginald Spooner of Scotland Yard*. London: Frederick Muller Ltd, pp. 287ff.

43 Ibid., 30 June 1942.

44 Ibid., 11 July 1942.

45 Ibid.

46 Ibid., 10 December 1943.

47 Ibid., 3 February 1944.

48 Tillet, op.cit; Foot, (1968), p.342.

49 Kramer, op.cit.

50 Ibid., 25 June 1946.

51 Grehan, John, and Mace, Martin, *Unearthing Churchill's Secret Army: The Official List of SOE Casualties and their Stories*, Pen & Sword, 2012.

52 TNHA HS9/1654, 13 July 1946.

53 Bohec, Jeanne, *La Plastiqueuse à Bicyclette*, Le Felin, 1999.

54 Bohec, op.cit.

55 Bohec, op.cit.

56 TNA HS9/173/2, 8 September 1943.

57 Ibid., 16 September 1943.

58 Ibid., 20 September 1943.

59 Ibid., 19 October 1943.

60 Collins Weitz, M. (1998), *Sisters of the Resistance*, John Wiley.

61 TNA HS9/173/2, 15 November 1943.
62 Ibid.
63 Tillet, op.cit.
64 Ibid., 29 February 1944.
65 Tillet, op.cit.
66 Bohec, op.cit; TNA HS8/145 – SOE Operations C Faure du BCRA à DGSE F Lambert-Saboteurs; www.lesamisdelaresistancedumorbihan .com/styled-9/styled5/page2/page84/index.html.
67 Bohec, op.cit.
68 Bohec,J.op.cit;www.buchenwald-dora.fr/4documentation/rp2/2res/3hist/06/03/02his.htm; http://philippepoisson-hotmail.com.over-blog. com/article--jeanne-bohec-la-plastiqueuse-a-bicyclette—38321016. html.
69 TNA HS9/165/8.
70 TNA HS9/165/8; Tillet, op.cit.
71 Jones, Liane, *A Quiet Courage: Women Agents in the French Resistance,* Transworld Publishers, (1990).
72 Seaman, op.cit. p.63.
73 Tillet, op.cit. www.bbc.co.uk/ history/ ww2peopleswar/stories/13/a2659313. shtml.
74 Buckmaster, op.cit.
75 Tillet, op.cit.
76 TNA HS9165/8, 11 June 1943.
77 TNA HS9165/8, 11 June 1943.
78 TNA HS9/165/8.
79 Tillet, op.cit; Escott, op.cit. p.146.
80 Tillet, op.cit.
81 TNA HS9/165/8.
82 Marshall, *White Rabbit*, Evans Brother, 1952.
83 Szabó, Tania, *Young, Brave and Beautiful: The Missions of Special Operations Executive Agent Lieutenant Violette* Szabó, The History Press, 2015.
84 TNA HS9/165/8, 13 March 1946.
85 Escott, op.cit; Perrin, op.cit.
86 TNA HS9/165/8, 1 April 1946.
87 *TNA HS9/467/6.*
88 Escott, op.cit. p.163.
89 Binney, Marcus, (2005), *Secret War Heroes: Men of the Special Operations Executive*, Hodder & Stoughton, London.
90 Tillet, op.cit.
91 TNA HS9/457/6, Ibid, 6 December 1943.
92 TNA HS9/457/6.
93 Ibid., 16 December 1943.
94 Ibid., 24 December 1943.
95 Ibid., 21 January 1944.
96 Ibid., 22 January 1944.
97 TNA HS 9/457/6.
98 Tillet, op.cit.
99 TNA HS9/457/6.
100 Ibid.

101 Ibid.
102 Escott, op.cit.
103 Ibid.
104 *TNA* HS 9/339/2.
105 Ibid.
106 Ibid., 8 January 1945.
107 *TNA* HS9/457/6, 5 June 1945.
108 Ibid., 7 December 1945.
109 TNA HS9/1498/2, 17 December 1943.
110 TNA HS9/1498/2, 1 February 1944.
111 TNA HS9/1498/2, 31 January 1944.
112 TNA HS9/1948/2, 12 January 1944. A subsequent note added that she had
     been given the lectures on containers, disposal and reception committee.
113 Tillet, op.cit.
114 Ibid.
115 TNA WO373/184/150.
116 TNA HS9/1498/2.
117 www.alliancefrancaise.london/Alix-Marrier-dUnienville.php.
118 Ibid.
119 Ibid.
120 France Horizon No. 498/99 June, July, August 2009.
121 Cassin, Renee, *The New Man*, 19, June 1944.
122 Tillet, op.cit.
123 Mesgouez, Dominique, *Histoire de rues, Carhaix*, Keltia Graphic, 1999.
124 Tillet, op.cit.
125 Hui, Mireille, *Les Merlinettes: pendant la seconde guerre mondiale, période
     de 1942 a 1945*, Lau, 2000.
126 Archives of Algiers, November 7, 1944.
127 TNA HS9/436/3, 6, 28 January, 2 February 1944.
128 Tillet, op.cit.
129 TNA HS 6/567 Mission report – Yvonne Baseden.
130 Tillet,op.cit;www.aassdn.org/araMnbioCl-Cz.html#CORBUSIER;
     www. aassdn.org.
131 Ibid.
132 Ibid.
133 Tillet, op.cit.
134 TNA HS9/1390/3, 30 October 1943.
135 Ibid., 20 November 1943.
136 Ibid., 8 March 1944.
137 Escott, Heroines of SOE, p.198; TNA HS9/895/6.
138 Escott, op.cit. p.199.
139 Verity, op.cit; Tillet, op.cit.
140 TNA HS9/895/6, 22 April 1944.
141 Tillet, op.cit.
142 Escott, op.cit.
143 TNA HS9/895/6.
144 Ibid.
145 Ibid., 15 December 1945.

Chapter 13.
1 Tillet, op.cit.
2 TNA HS9/815/3, 20 February 1944.
3 Ibid., 18 March 1944.
4 Ibid., 24 March 1944.
5 Ibid., 10 April 1944.
6 Ibid. 3 May 1944.
7 TNA HS9/815/3, 24 September 1944.
8 Jacobs, Peter, *Setting France Ablaze: The SOE in France During WWII*, Pen & Sword, 2015.
9 Tillet, op.cit.
10 Escott, op.cit.
11 TNA HS9/815/3, 24 September 1944.
12 Quoted in Escott, op.cit. p.207.
13 Escott, op.cit.
14 TNA HS9/815/3.
15 Hutchinson, p.177.
16 Griffiths, Frank, (1981), *Winged Hours*, William Kimber and Co. Ltd, London.
17 HS 9/688/8, 30 November 1943.
18 Ibid., 19 December 1943.
19 Ibid., 24 January 1944.
20 Ibid., 29 January 1944.
21 Ibid., 8 March 1944.
22 Ibid., 17 March 1944.
23 Ibid., 10 April 1944.
24 Ibid., 19 May 1944.
25 Ibid., 15 October 1945.
26 Foot, M. (2004), *SOE in France*; Tillet, op.cit; www.francaislibres.net/liste/fiche.php?index =73745.
27 Fourcade, M. (1973), *Noah's Ark,* George Allen & Unwin.
28 Jeffrey, K. (2010), *MI6: History of the Secret Intelligence Service 1909–1949,* Penguin Press HC.
29 Ibid.
30 Verity, H. op.cit.
31 Fourcade, M. op.cit.
32 Tillet, op.cit.
33 TNA HS91390/2, 29 December 1943.
34 Ibid., 1 February 1944.
35 Ibid.
36 Ibid.
37 Ibid., 10 April 1944.
38 Tillet, op.cit.
39 Ibid., 24 September 1944; also found in WO 373/184/322.
40 Tillet, op.cit.
41 Tillet, op.cit.
42 TNA HS9/629/2, 30 October 1943.

43 Ibid., 30 November 1943.

44 Ibid., 19 December 1943. In her personal report it was added that, 'If circumstances had permitted, she would doubtless have completed the course with good results.'

45 TNA HS9/629/2, 24 January 1944.

46 Ibid., 8 March 1944.

47 Ibid., 10 April 1944.

48 Ibid., 16 May 1944.

49 Ibid., 8 June 1944.

50 Tillet, op.cit.

51 TNA HS9/587/9, 30 October 1943.

52 Ibid., 30 November 1943.

53 Ibid., 19 December 1943.

54 Ibid., 20 December 1943.

55 Ibid., 24 January 1944.

56 Ibid., 23 February 1944.

57 Ibid., 8 March 1944).

58 Ibid., 4, 12 May 1944.

59 Ibid., 14 June 1944).

60 TNA HS9/306/2; HS7/248 SOE RF Index & App 1-5, M. de Cheveigne – WT Libre).

61 Heslop, Richard, *Xavier: A British Secret Agent with the French Resistance,* Biteback, 2014.

62 Bowman, Martin, *The Bedford Triangle: Undercover Operations from England in the Second World War,* Patrick Stephens Ltd (1989), Sutton Publishing (1996), The History Press (2009).

63 TNA HS9/1301/8.

64 TNA HS9/1031/8, 19 August 1944.

65 Ibid.

66 TNA HS9/1184/9.

67 TNA HS9/1185/4, 30 November 1943.

68 Verity, H. (1978), op.cit.

69 Marshall, B. op.cit.

70 TNA HS9/1184/9.

71 Ibid., 30 November 1943.

72 Ibid., 25 April 1944.

73 Ibid., 2 June 1944.

74 Ibid.

75 Ibid., 7 July 1944; Jones, Benjamin F. (2016), *Eisenhower's Guerrillas: The Jedburghs, the Maquis, and the Liberation of France,* OUP.

76 Ibid., 28 July 1944.

77 TNA HS9/1184/9, 10 September 1945.

78 Tillet, op.cit.

79 Tillet, op.cit.

80 TNA HS9/578/8, 20 August 1944.

81 Tillet, op.cit.

82 TNA HS 9/353/3.

83 Tillet, op.cit.

84 Foot, op.cit. p.371.

85 www.independent.co.uk/news/people/michele-de-ducla-free-french-forces-agent-who-carried-out-vital-work-between-d-day-and-the-german-10239386.html, Sunday 10 May 2015.

86 Ibid., 28 April 1944.

87 Ibid., May 1944.

88 Ibid.

89 Ibid., 18 May 1944.

90 Ibid., 25 May 1944.

91 *TNA HS9/453/4.*

92 Ibid.,15 July 1944.

93 Ibid., 8 August 1944.

94 Ibid., 25 August 1944.

95 Ibid., 18 September 1944.

96 SHD Vincennes GR16P601352.

97 www.independent.co.uk/news/people/michele-de-ducla-free-french-forces-agent-who-carried-out-vital-work-between-d-day-and-the-german-10239386.html.

98 Ibid.

99 Ibid.

Conclusion

1 Fish (1970), *They Flew by Night, Memories of the 801/492nd Bombardment Group.*

2 www.harringtonmuseum.org.uk.

4 Pattinson, J. op.cit.

5 Ibid.

6 Pattinson, op.cit.

7 Simon Mawer, www.theparisreview.org/blog/2012/05/21/special-agents-the-women-of-soe/.

8 Atkins, V. 9551/3; 12302/1; 23237/3; 31590/3; 31592/3; 31586/3 IWM.

9 Nicholas, E. op.cit.

10 Robert Gildea, Robert, 'The French Resistance: Myth, Memory, and Narrative', Senate House, London University, 4 January 2016.

11 www.64-baker-street.org/agents.

12 www.memorialgrove.org.uk/ SOE%20Women.pdf.

Bibliography

WEBSITES
http://en.doew.braintrust.at
www.64-baker-street.org
www.adam-matthew-publications.co.uk/
www.ajex.org.uk
www.bbc.co.uk/ww2peopleswar/stories/
http://camouflage.osu.edu
www.christopherlong.co.uk
www.cometeline.org
www.conscript-heroes.com
www.creativeboom.co.uk
www.dailymail.co.uk
www.deols-tourisme.fr
www.deborahjackson.net
www.destentor.nl
http://entertainment.timesonline.co.uk
www.fondspascaldecroos.org
www.francaislibres.net
www.guardian.co.uk
www.geocities.com
www.hagalil.com
http://harpet.free.fr
http://harringtonmuseum.org.uk
http://herve.larroque.free.fr
http://members.iinet.net.au
http://img.over-blog.com
www.informarn.nl
www.jewishvirtuallibrary.org
www.juppkappius.de
www.nigelperrin.com
www.nytimes.com

www.plan-sussex-1944.net
www.praats.be/zero.htm
www.scrapbookpages.com
www.seanet.com
http://sfloudun.free.fr
www.smithsonianmag.com
http://soe_french.tripod.com
www.spartacus.schoolnet.co.uk
www.specialforcesroh.com
www.telegraph.co.uk
www.thememoryproject.com
www.thompsononename.org.uk
www.timesonline.co.uk
www.usnews.com
www.wartimememories.co.uk
www.wikipedia.org
www.ww2awards.com
www.theaustralian.com.au

BOOKS

Aiti, (2002), *Le Bataillon de Guerrilla de l'Armagnac 158 R.I.*
Aubenas, J. Van Rokeghem, S. & Vercheral-Vervoort, J. (2006), Des Femmes dans l'Histoire de Belgique, depuis 1830, Editions Luc Pire
Aubrac, L. (1993), *Outwitting the Gestapo,* University of Nebraska Press
Basu, S. (2006), *Spy Princess, The Life of Noor Inayat Khan*, Sutton Publishing, London
Binney, M. (2002), *The Women who Lived for Danger*, Hodder & Stoughton, London
Binney, M. (2005), *Secret War Heroes: Men of the Special Operations Executive*, Hodder & Stoughton, London
Body, B. *Taking the Wings of the Morning,* private publication
Braddon, R. (1956), *Nancy Wake*, Cassell
Baynham, N. *'Never Volunteer,' Said My Dad*
Buckmaster, M. (1946–7), *They went by Parachute*, Chamber's Journal
Buckmaster, M. (1952), *Specially Employed*, Batchworth
Body, R. B. (2003), *Taking the Wings of the Morning*, Serendipity, London
Butler, E. (1963), *Amateur Agent*, Harrap, London
Butler, J. (1983), *Churchill's Secret Agent*, Blaketon-Hall
Churchill, P. (1952), *Of Their Own Choice*, Hodder & Stoughton
Churchill, P. (1954), *Duel of Wits*, Hodder & Stoughton
Churchill, P. (1954), *Spirit in the Cage*, Hodder & Stoughton
Clark, F. (1999), *Agents by Moonlight*, Tempus
Collins Weitz, M. (1998), *Sisters of the Resistance*, John Wiley
Cookridge, Edward (1965), *Inside SOE*, Barker
Cookridge, Edward, (1965), *They Came From the* Sky, Heinemann
Crowdy, Terry, (2007), *French Resistance Fighters: France's Secret Army*, Osprey Publishing

Bibliography

Crowdy, Terry, (2008), *SOE Agent: Churchill's Secret Warriors*, Osprey Publishing

De Vomécourt, P. (1959), *An Army of Amateurs*, Doubleday

Escott, B. (1991), *Mission Improbable, A Salute to the RAF Women of SOE in Wartime France*, Sparkford: Patrick Stephens Ltd

Faulks, S. (1999), *Charlotte Gray*, Vintage

Fish, (1990), *They Flew by Night*, Memories of the 801/492nd Bombardment Group as told to Col. Fish

Fitzsimons (2002), *Nancy Wake: The Inspiring Story of One of the War's Greatest Heroines*, Harper Collins, London

Foot, M.R.D. (1999), *SOE: The Special Operations Executive 1940–1946*, Pimlico

Foot, M.R.D. (2001), *SOE in the Low Countries*, St Ermin's Press, London

Foot, M.R.D. (2004), *SOE in France*, Frank Cass, London

Fourcade, M. (1973), *Noah's Ark*, George Allen & Unwin

Fraser-Smith, C. (1991), *The Secret War of Charles Fraser-Smith*, Paternoster Press

Gleeson, J. (1976), *They feared No Evil: The Stories of the Gallant and Courageous Women Agents of Britain's Secret Armies, 1939–1945*, Robert Hale, London

Griffiths, F. (1981), *Winged Hours*, William Kimber & Co. Ltd, London

Heidegger, M. (1962), *Being and Time*, Blackwell, London

Helm, Sarah, (2006), *A Life in Secrets: The Story of Vera Atkins and the Lost Agents of SOE*, Abacus

Heslop, R. (1970), *Xavier*, Hart-Davis, London

Hoffman, A. 'Judith Pearson delivers a talk on Spy Virginia Hall', *The Trinity Tripod*, 4th April 2006

Howarth, P. (1980), *UNDERCOVER: The Men and Women of the Special Operations Executive*, Routledge and Kegan Paul, London

Hudson, S. (2003), *Undercover Operator: An SOE Agent's Experiences in France and the Far East*, Pen & Sword

Hutchinson, James, *That Drug Danger*, Standard Press, Montrose, 1977, p.82

Johns, P. (1979), *Within Two Cloaks*, William Kimber

Jones, L. (1990), *A Quiet Courage*, Bantam Press

King, S. (1989), *'Jacqueline': Pioneer Heroine of the Resistance*, Arms and Armour, London

Kramer, R. (1995), *Flames in the Field*, Michael Joseph

Lynch, D. M. (2007), The Labor Branch of the Office of Strategic Services: An Academic Study from a Public History Perspective, August, University of Indiana, p.33–39

Mackness, R. (1988), *Oradour: Massacre and Aftermath*, Bloomsbury Publishing Plc

Marks, L. (1998), *Between Silk and Cyanide*, The Free Press, New York

Masson, M. (1975), *A Search for Christine Granville*, Hamish Hamilton

McKenzie, W. (2002) *The Secret History of the SOE*, Little, Brown Book Group

Miller, Russell (2002), *Behind the Lines: The Oral History of Special Operations in World War Two*, Jonathon Cape, London

Minney, R.J. (1956), *Carve Her Name with Pride*, Newnes

Neave, A. (1954), *Little Cyclone*, Hodder & Stoughton

Neave, A. (1969), *Saturday at MI9*, Hodder & Stoughton

Nicholas, E. (1958), *Death be not Proud*, Cresset Press, London

Nicholson, M. (1995), *What Did You Do in The War Mummy?* Chatto & Windus, London

O'Sullivan, D. (1997), Dealing with the Devil: The Anglo-Soviet Parachute Agents (Operation 'Pickaxe'), *Journal of Intelligence History*, Vol. 4, Number 2, Winter 2004, pp.33–65

Oliver, D. (2005), *Airborne Espionage: International Special Duties Operations in the World Wars*, The History Press, Stroud

O'Sullivan, D. (2010), *Dealing with the Devil: Anglo Soviet Intelligence during the Second World War*, Peter Lang Publishing, New York

Ottaway, S. (2002), *Violette Szabó*, Pen & Sword

Overton-Fuller, J. (1971), *Noor-un-nisa Inayat Khan (Madeleine)*, East-West Publications Fonds N. V. Rotterdam

Pattinson, J. (2006), 'Playing the daft lassie with them': Gender, Captivity and the Special Operations Executive during the Second World War, *European Review of History*, Vol. 13, No. 2, pp.271–292

Pattinson, J. (2007), *Behind Enemy Lines: Gender, passing and the Special Operations Executive in the Second World War*, Manchester University Press

Pattinson, J. (2008), 'Turning a Pretty Girl into a Killer': Women, Violence and Clandestine Operations during the Second World War, *Gender and Interpersonal Violence*, Palgrave, Macmillan, pp.11–29

Pawley, M. (1999), *Obedience to Instructions: FANY with the SOE in the Mediterranean*, Leo Cooper

Pearson, J. (2005), *Wolves at the Door: The True Story of America's Greatest Female Spy*, The Lyons Press

Persico, J. E. (1979), *Piercing the Reich: The Penetration of Nazi Germany by American Secret Agents during World War II*, The Viking Press, New York

Poirier, J. (1995), *The Giraffe has a Long Neck*, Leo Cooper, London

Rake, D. (1968), *Rake's Progress*, Frewin

Rigden, Denis. (2004), *SOE Syllabus: Lessons in Ungentlemanly Warfare*, Richmond

Rochester, D. (1978), *Full Moon to France*, Robert Hale, London

Rossiter, M. (1985), *Women in the Resistance*, Greenwood Press

Ryder, Sue. (1986), *Child of my Love*, Collins Harvill

Saward, J. (2006), *The Grand Prix Saboteurs: The Grand Prix Drivers who Became British Secret Agents During World War II*, Morienval Press

Szabó, T. (2007), *Young, Brave and Beautiful, The missions of Special Operations Executive Agent, Lieutenant Violette Szabó, George Cross, Croix de Guerre avec Etoile de bronze*, Channel Island Publishing

Tickell, J. (1949), *Odette*, Chapman and Hall, London

Tickell, J. (1956), *Moon Squadrons*, Allan Wingate Ltd, London

Tillet, P. (Body, R., Ensminger, T., Kippax, S., Portier, D., Soulier, D.), (2016), *Tentative of History of In/Exfiltrations into/from France during WWII from 1941 to 1945 (Parachutes, Plane & Sea Landings)*

Valentine, Ian (2006), *Station 43: Audley End House and SOE's Polish Section*, Sutton Publishing

Verity, H. (1978) *We Landed by Moonlight*, Ian Allan Ltd, Shepperton:

Vinen, R. (2006), *The Unfree French: Life under Occupation*, Penguin

Vomécourt, P. (1961), *An Army of Amateurs*, Doubleday, New York

Wake, N. *The White Mouse: The Autobiography of the Woman the Gestapo Called the White Mouse,* Macmillan, Melbourne

Walters, A. (1946), *Moondrop to Gascony*, Macmillan

Walters, A. (2009), *Moondrop to Gascony*, Moho Books, Wiltshire

Ward, I. (1955), *F.A.N.Y. Invicta*, Hutchinson & Co., London

Wake, N. (1985), *Autobiography of the Woman the Gestapo Called the White Mouse*, Macmillan, Melbourne

Willis and Holliss, (1987), *Military Airfields in the British Isles 1939 – 1945*, Enthusiasts Publications

Witherington, P. (1997), *Pauline http://members.aol.com/HLarroque/pauline.htm*

Wynne, J. B. (1961), *No Drums, No Trumpets: The Story of Mary Lindell*, Arthur Baker Ltd

Yarnold, P. (2009), *Wanborough Manor: School for Secret Agents*, Hopfield Publications, Puttenham

NEWSPAPERS

Baltimore Jewish Times, 'Story of an Anti-Nazi Spy', L. Berg (2 June 2006)

Bedfordshire Times and Standard, 'King and Queen Visit RAF Station' (9 November 1943)

Daily Graphic, 'First British Woman GC: Fought Gun Battle Alone with the Gestapo' (18 December 1946)

Daily Telegraph, 'Return of the White Mouse', E. Grice (7 June 1994)

Harrow Times, 'From the typewriter to blazing Sten gun', C. Ramos (20 March 2005)

Hunts. Post, 'Hunts was a Nerve Centre of Allied Espionage...', G. Thomas (23 December 1954)

The Economist, Nancy Wake, saboteur and special agent, died on August 7th, aged 98,' (13 August 2011)

The Guardian, 'Wartime secret agent and survivor of hard labour at Ravensbrück', Foot, M. (Wednesday, 30 October 2010)

The Guardian, 'Nancy Wake obituary' (8 August 2011)

The Independent, 'Revealed: The story of the spy who led the French Resistance' (1 April 2008)

The Independent, 'The 'scatter-brained spy who helped win the war', Terri Judd (29 Friday October 2010)

The Independent, WW2 resistance hero Nancy Wake dies (8 August 2011)

London Gazette, Citation for Violette Szabo's GC (17 December 1946)

The Seattle Times, 'Nancy Wake Famed WWII Agent' (11 August 2011)

The Sun, 'Nancy's Heroes' (23 August 2010)

The Sunday Express, 'WAAF girls parachuted into France', W. Simpson (11 March 1945)

The Sunday Express, 'The Tremendous Things that Happened to a Quiet Little English Secretary: Secret Mission', Y. Baseden (9 March 1952)

The Sunday Times, An MP Paid to Put Paid to Hitler – <u>Before</u> the War (15 December 1946)

The Times, Violette Szabo, Yvonne Cormeau, Kay Gimpel and Nancy Wake's obituaries

The Trinity Tripod Online (4 April 2006) 'Judith Pearson Delivers a Talk on Spy Virginia Hall'
Unnamed, 'Mrs Smith: Train-wrecker, spy and Nazi-killer', S. Rodin (1948) Held at FANY HQ

TV AND FILMS
Now the Story can be Told (1944) RAF Film at Hendon Air Museum
Odette (1950) Wilcox-Neale film directed by Herbert Wilcox
Carve Her Name with Pride (1958) Film directed by Lewis Gilbert
Moonstrike, BBC TV series March (1963)
Wish me Luck, London Weekend Television (1988–9)
Secret Memories, BBC 2 Time Watch (1997) documentary by Jonathon Lewis
Churchill's Secret Army, Channel 4 Television (28 January, 4, 11 February 2000)
Secret Agent: The True Story of Violette Szabó, BBC Midland documentary by Howard Tuck (19 September 2002)
'Histories', Getuigenis van Elaine Madden. *Canvas* (17 April 2004)
Female Agents, Revolver Films (2008)

DOCUMENTS IN THE NATIONAL ARCHIVES
HS 6/112 IMOGEN Mission: Elaine Madden
HS 9/10/2 Françoise/Françine) Agazarian
HS 9/77/1 Lise de Baissac
HS 9/114/2 Yolande Beekman
HS 9/165/8 Denise Bloch
HS 9/183 Andrée Bloch
HS 9/250/2 Muriel Byck
HS 9/298/6 Blanche Charlet
HS 9/339/2 Anne-Marie Walters
HS 9/353/3 Aimée Corge
HS 9/457/6 Yvonne Fontaine
HS 9/578/8 Marguerite Gianello
HS 9/612 Christine Granville
HS 9/633/1 Jeannette Guyot
HS 9/648/4 Odette Sansom
HS 9/836/5 Noor Inayat Khan
HS 9/910/3 Vera Leigh
HS 9/1089/2 Eileen Nearne
HS 9/1089/4 Jacqueline Nearne
HS 9/1185/4 Cécile Pichard (de Marcilly)
HS 9/1301/8 Marie-Rose Miguet
HS 9/1424/7 Odette Wilen
HS 9/1435 Violette Szabó
HS 9/1654 Madeleine Damerment

DOCUMENTS IN SHD VINCENNES
GR16P601352 Wattebled de Ducla

BERNARD O'CONNOR'S PUBLICATIONS RELATED TO RAF TEMPSFORD DURING THE SECOND WORLD WAR

RAF Tempsford: Churchill's MOST SECRET Airfield, Amberley Publishing, (2010)

The Women of RAF Tempsford: Heroines of Wartime Resistance, Amberley Publishing, (2011)

Churchill and Stalin's Secret Agents: Operation Pickaxe at RAF Tempsford, Fonthill Media, (2011)

The Tempsford Academy: Churchill and Roosevelt's Secret Airfield, Fonthill Media, (2012)

Agent Rose: The True Story of Eileen Nearne, Britain's Forgotten Wartime Heroine, Amberley Publishing, (2010)

Churchill's Angels: How Britain's Women Secret Agents Changed the Course of the Second World War, Amberley Publishing, (2012)

The Courier: Reminiscences of a Female Secret Agent in Wartime France, (Historical faction) www.lulu.com (2010)

Sir Frank Nelson, www.lulu.com (2011)

Charles Bovill, www,lulu.com (2011)

Designer: The True Story of Jacqueline Nearne, www.lulu.com, (2011)

Return to Belgium, www.lulu.com (2012)

Return to Holland, www.lulu.com, (2012)

Bedford Spy School, www.lulu.com (2012)

Old Bedfordians' Secret Operations during World War Two, www.lulu.com (2012)

*Henri Dericourt: Triple Agent (*Bunny Rymill's memoirs edited by Bernard O'Connor), www.lulu.com (2012)

Churchill's School for Saboteurs: Brickendonbury, STS 17, Amberley Publishing, (2013)

Nobby Clarke: Churchill's Backroom Boy, www.lulu.com (2013)

Churchill's Most Secret Airfield, Amberley Publishing, (2013)

Sabotage in Norway, www.lulu.com (2013)

Sabotage in Denmark, www.lulu.com (2013)

Sabotage in Belgium, www.lulu.com (2013)

Sabotage in Holland, www.lulu.com (2013)

Sabotage in France, www.lulu.com (2013)

Sabotage in Greece, www.lulu.com (2014)

Blackmail Sabotage, www.lulu.com (2014)

'Mike' Andrews: pilot, manager of Liverpool Airport and secret agent, www.lulu.com (2014)

Agent Fifi and the Wartime Honeytrap Spies, Amberley Publishing, (2015)

Agents Françaises: Frenchwomen infiltrated into France during the Second World War, www.lulu.com (2016)

Visit Bernard O'Connor's website:

www.bernardoconnor.org.uk

Index